TARGET: PEARL HARBOR

TARGET: PEARL HARBOR

MICHAEL SLACKMAN

UNIVERSITY OF HAWAII PRESS

HONOLULU

AND

ARIZONA MEMORIAL MUSEUM ASSOCIATION

© 1990 Arizona Memorial Museum Association

All Rights Reserved

Printed in the United States of America

Paperback edition 1991

92 93 94 95 96 97   5 4 3 2 1

Library of Congress Cataloging-in-Publication Data

Slackman, Michael.

Target—Pearl Harbor / Michael Slackman.

p.   cm.

Includes bibliographical references.

ISBN 0-8248-1123-2 (alk. paper)

1. Pearl Harbor (Hawaii), Attack on, 1941.   I. Title.

D767.92.S57   1990

940.54'26—dc20   90-30063

CIP

ISBN 0-8248-1378-2 (pbk.: alk. paper)

University of Hawaii Press books are printed
on acid-free paper and meet the guidelines
for permanence and durability of the Council
on Library Resources.

CONTENTS

PART VI. AMERICA REACTS

Photographs follow pages 44, 82, and 208

PREFACE

Like a pillar of smoke on the horizon, Pearl Harbor looms as a landmark in the history of one of the twentieth century's most important bilateral relationships. We use that point of reference to triangulate the shifting course of Japanese-American relationships and to illustrate how much—or how little—progress in mutual understanding has occurred since December 7, 1941.

Some invocations of the event are questionable, others absurd, but the power of the image is beyond dispute. For Americans the attack retains the power to evoke memories of shock, humiliation, and blind hatred. For Japanese (at least those of a certain age) Pearl Harbor can recall feelings of pride at the stunning blow delivered against an arrogant power, followed by the dawning realization of the folly of false confidence.

The label "turning point" is often misapplied and certainly overused. There is little argument, though, that the Pearl Harbor attack was a dramatic event which in the space of a few hours plunged the United States into the most destructive war of the twentieth century and changed forever the way most Americans viewed the world around them. It might be argued that even without Pearl Harbor the United States would have become an active combatant in World War II. True, perhaps, but the particular nature of the attack precipitated such a fierce commitment to victory that the conduct of the war and the peace which followed might have been quite different had America been drawn into the war in less dramatic circumstances. Indeed, the far-reaching mobilization of American resources—military, economic, and emotional—set in motion by the Japanese attack remains a force in shaping national policies and attitudes nearly half a century later.

FOCUS AND SOURCES

This study focuses on the central events of Sunday, December 7, 1941. It opens with a brief background survey of prewar contact and rivalry between Japan and the United States. A detailed examination of Japanese–U.S. relations is beyond our scope, but this subject is reviewed to establish the context of the national policy decisions which led to war and to the military deployments prior to the attack.

Although the extensive historiography of the Pearl Harbor attack makes it one of the most thoroughly examined military actions ever fought, this study does break some new ground. First, the attention to U.S. military perceptions of Hawaii's Japanese community makes it clear that the authorities' suspicion and lack of understanding of this group was a major factor in America's unpreparedness. Second, the examination of U.S. Army and Navy efforts to locate and engage the Japanese fleet in the hours after the attack highlights many of the shortcomings of the command structure in Hawaii. Third, the treatment of the post-attack preparations to defend Hawaii from a Japanese invasion evokes a sense of the intense and very real fear that prevailed as the islands braced for siege.

Apart from these thematic treatments, the study incorporates the recollections of many individual actors whose experiences are presented here as part of a full-length study for the first time. This material is taken for the most part from personal interviews and the holdings of oral history programs. Particularly interesting are the stories of George Nakamoto, the civilian tug captain, and Malcolm Reeves, the *Northampton* scout plane pilot.

For American scholars, journalists, and the general public the Pearl Harbor attack has sparked controversy and accusations of incompetence and worse. Any study of the topic demands some examination of the factors which led to U.S. forces being taken by surprise, and it is impossible to ignore the attitudes, assumptions, and judgments in both Hawaii and Washington which resulted in disaster. In the wake of the attack and for years afterward the U.S. commanders in Hawaii were pilloried for their supposed negligence. By the same token their supporters have attacked the actions and motives of officers and officials at the Washington command echelon. This study reviews mistakes made at both ends of the chain of command, but I find no credible evidence to support charges of flagrant dereliction of duty or a conspiracy to "set up" U.S. forces in Hawaii and withhold warning of an impending attack on Pearl Harbor.

This study relies as much as possible on contemporary documents and firsthand personal accounts of the Pearl Harbor attack. In some instances the stress of battle, the torrential rush of events, and (in the case of oral history interviews conducted many years later) the passage of time have combined to produce sources marred by factual errors. Taken as a whole, however, they are largely in agreement and present a remarkably detailed and accurate picture of the Pearl Harbor attack from the American perspective.

The same, unfortunately, is not true of Japanese sources. Many Japanese military documents were destroyed during World War II or when Japan capitulated. Many, if not most, of the Japanese participants in the attack were killed at Midway or in subsequent battles. As a result, this study relies heavily on published sources for the Japanese version of events. Some of the principals survived the war and have written about their experiences. The Japanese Self-Defense Agency's War History Research Section has undertaken a multivolume (more than 100 volumes to date) history of World War II utilizing surviving documents and drawing on the memories of participants. The volume on the Pearl Harbor attack, *Hawai Sakusen,* is an indispensable source. Dr. Gordon Prange's *At Dawn We Slept* is also valuable. Prange spent decades studying the Pearl Harbor attack, and in the course of his studies befriended and interviewed dozens of important Japanese and American participants.

FACT AND FOLKLORE

A body of folklore has developed around the Pearl Harbor attack as stories and "facts" are passed from source to source with little critical examination. This study addresses some of that folklore in an attempt to separate fact from fiction. First and most important is the role of Hawaii's Japanese-Americans. Soon after the attack, wartime rumor and many official reports had it that an enormous pool of fifth columnists had provided vital aid to the attackers. Yet official investigations completed shortly after the war revealed that espionage had been limited to the staff of the Japanese consulate. The Niihau incident with its unusual attendant circumstances was the only instance of actual aid to the enemy. The canard of disloyalty has been thoroughly discredited by scholars and investigators who have examined Hawaii's Japanese community, but it is a persistent myth. A reading of transcripts of oral history interviews with Pearl Harbor survivors, for example, reveals several instances of perfectly sincere belief in swarms of Japanese-American spies and saboteurs. Questions and comments of visitors to the USS *Arizona* Memorial at Pearl Harbor also indicate a widespread belief that Hawaii's Japanese were instrumental in the success of the attack.

Moreover, for years stories have circulated to the effect that divers were killed in salvage operations aboard the *Arizona* wreckage. The most common version holds that explosive gases trapped inside the hull were ignited by a cutting torch. Yet a close examination of contemporary records—particularly the Pearl Harbor Naval Shipyard war diary—fails to confirm these accounts. The diving operations at Pearl Harbor were indeed hazardous and there were indeed casualties, but none apparently occurred on the *Arizona* operations.

The explosion which sank *Arizona* has been the subject of conflicting accounts, as well. Some, including eyewitness reports, say that it was ignited by a bomb which went down her funnel. Subsequent reports suggest that the uptake armor gratings were intact when inspected later by salvage divers, making it impossible for a bomb to have traveled down the battleship's funnel, but the evidence is inconclusive. It has been established, however, that regardless of whether a bomb went down the stack, the fatal damage was caused by the explosion of her forward ammunition magazines, not the ship's boilers. The question of whether a bomb went down the funnel remains unanswerable in light of our present knowledge of the *Arizona* wreckage.

ACKNOWLEDGMENTS

This book would have been impossible without the assistance and encouragement of others. I am grateful for the funding provided by the *Arizona* Memorial Museum Association, the cooperating association of the USS *Arizona* Memorial. The National Park Service staff of the USS *Arizona* Memorial, especially former Superintendent Gary Cummins, former Chief Ranger John Martini, and Dan Martinez, contributed many valuable suggestions. NPS Chief Historian Edwin Bearss and Western Regional Historian Gordon Chappell furnished guidance and encouragement. The divers of the Submerged Cultural Resources Unit made the observations used to document *Arizona*'s present condition. Captain Thomas Kimmel, USN (ret.), was kind enough to provide me with personal papers of his father, Admiral Husband E. Kimmel. Professor Franklin Odo of the University of Hawaii Ethnic Studies Program and Professor Gary Okihiro of the

University of Santa Clara gave me important insights into the history of Hawaii's Japanese community.

I owe a special debt to the many participants in and witnesses to the Pearl Harbor attack who took the time to recount their experiences. These interviews often occurred during their vacations to Hawaii, and recalling the events of December 7, 1941, was a stressful interruption for many. I wish particularly to acknowledge five Pearl Harbor veterans who also provided me with documentary material: Heijiro Abe (*Soryu* pilot); Captain Nathan Asher, USN (ret.) *(Blue);* Captain James Daniels, USN (ret.) (*Enterprise* pilot); Robert Hudson *(Oglala);* and the late Rear Admiral Malcom Reeves, USN (ret.) (*Northampton* pilot).

In conducting documentary research the staffs of many archival agencies rendered important assistance. At the Naval Historical Center's Operational Archives, Dr. Dean Allard and his staff were patient, helpful, and knowledgeable. In the National Archives, John Taylor of the Modern Military Headquarters Branch, Kathleen O'Connor of the Pacific-Sierra Region, and Frederick Pernell of the Modern Military Field Branch provided invaluable assistance. The same holds true for the staffs of the Office of Air Force History, the U.S. Army's Center of Military History, the Marine Corps Historical Center, the Defense Audiovisual Agency, the Smithsonian Institution, the Hawaii State Archives, and the Hawaii War Records Depository. Professor Ron Marcello, director of the North Texas State University Oral History Program, made available the hundreds of transcripts of Pearl Harbor survivor interviews he has conducted. Dr. E. Raymond Lewis, Librarian of the House of Representatives, provided valuable guidance. Thanks are due, too, to librarians at the University of Hawaii's Hamilton Library, the Library of Congress, and the Pearl Harbor naval base library. I also wish to thank Mark Smith, who prepared the maps accompanying the text. Other librarians, archivists, scholars, and friends provided help and support throughout the preparation of this work. At the University of Hawaii Press, Bill Hamilton, Jean Brady, Pam Kelley, and Don Yoder were patient and supportive in seeing this book through the publication process. Any errors of fact or interpretation are my own responsibility.

A NOTE ON TERMINOLOGY AND STYLE

Throughout the book the times and dates given (unless otherwise noted) are local. Geographical names are given in their 1941 forms.

The Dutch East Indies later became Indonesia; French Indochina was divided into Vietnam, Laos, and Cambodia; Malaya formed part of what is today Malaysia. Siam and Formosa are known today as Thailand and Taiwan. This study mentions both Japanese-Americans and Japanese nationals. To avoid confusion all names are rendered in the Western style, with given names preceding family names. The term "Japanese" is generally reserved for references to Japanese nationals. Occasionally it is used here as an adjective encompassing Japanese-Americans and Japanese communities in Hawaii or the mainland United States. In such cases it should be clear from the context that the term is being used in an ethnic sense and carries no connotation of citizenship or loyalty. The term "Hawaiian" properly refers to the Polynesians whose ancestors inhabited Hawaii before its first contact with the Western world in 1778. In cases where the word is part of a proper noun or term of long-established usage (Hawaiian Department, Hawaiian waters) it is used here, but in other cases the word Hawaii is used in adjectival form.

Where possible, I have tried to use the full names of all persons mentioned in the narrative of events. In many cases, however, contemporary reports and other documents give only the last names, or in some cases the first initials, of those people. In some instances, first names were available from other sources. In other cases, particularly those of enlisted men and junior officers, they were not. Although it has led to some awkward usage (such as "Boatswain's Mate Smith"), I have elected to use the available information in order to people this account of the Pearl Harbor attack with the real (albeit incompletely named) figures who participated in the event.

Finally, this study describes the condition of the wounded and the handling of dead resulting from the Pearl Harbor attack. These descriptions may be disturbing to some. They are included not out of disrespect for those who suffered or a desire to sensationalize, but in order to portray as completely as possible the events of December 7, 1941. No historical account can include every detail, but to eliminate these descriptions would be to sanitize the narrative. Historians have a special obligation to present the whole truth, and that responsibility surely applies to recording the sufferings of those killed and wounded in battle.

I

SETTING THE STAGE
FOR DISASTER

1

CHALLENGE
AND RESPONSE

History, like nature, abhors a vacuum. Although the Pearl Harbor attack surprised Americans, it arose from a clearly discernible context. The raid climaxed years of political and economic developments which drew Japan and the United States into conflict. By December 1941, in fact, the U.S. government had been waiting in suspense for the Japanese to initiate hostilities.

Relations between the two countries had begun under an ambivalent sign when Commodore Matthew Perry "opened" Japan to the West in 1853. The feudal Tokugawa government had no choice but to join the community of nations or face the consequences which would issue from the guns of Perry's warships. Japan found itself in the midst of the imperialist era as it struggled to establish a modern society in the late nineteenth century. Japanese leaders saw their task as establishing a strong industrialized state or suffering the fate of China, which had fallen under the domination of Europe. They succeeded well enough to join the ranks of the imperialist powers, defeating China in 1895 and Czarist Russia a decade later.

Far from solving Japan's problems, however, these developments did little to alleviate the weaknesses, real and perceived, of Japan's position in the world. True, Japan had acquired an empire of its own, an impressive industrial base, and a modern army and navy. But these achievements could not disguise—in fact they highlighted—Japan's lack of vital raw materials (especially oil) necessary for the maintenance of a technologically advanced military power. Moreover, the racial attitudes of the European powers and the United States precluded full acceptance of Japan as a great power. The crowning insult in the eyes of many Japanese occurred at the Washington Naval Conference of 1922. The 5-5-3 agreement reached there limited Japan's capital ship tonnage to three tons for every five built by Great Britain and the United States. To many Japanese the formula proved that the Western nations would never willingly concede equal status to their country.

These international frustrations combined with the onset of the Great Depression to effect a radical change in Japanese political life. Japan's military officers grew increasingly skeptical of the government's ability to deal with the crisis. Until the late 1920s a system of civilian party government had been emerging in Japan. The depression dealt a blow to that fragile system and the army stepped into the vacuum.

The links between the depression and the rise of military radicalism have been exaggerated, but each factor tended to reinforce the other's corrosive effect on the nascent parliamentary government. Younger officers in particular attempted in the early and mid-1930s to turn Japan onto the path of authoritarianism and ultranationalism. They hoped to establish a military government based on a vaguely defined ideology which blended, in a uniquely Japanese way, chauvinism, corporatism, and Confucian social ethics.

In 1931–1932 Japanese Army officers acting without authority from Tokyo provoked clashes between their own troops and Chinese in Manchuria. The Japanese Kwantung Army prevailed easily and Manchuria was incorporated into the Japanese political system. The Manchurian incident was followed by unsuccessful rightist-led army mutinies in Tokyo in 1932 and 1936. After the suppression of the 1936 revolt, senior army officers reasserted control. Motivated by a desire for order and authority rather than liberal sentiments, they not only curbed their hotheaded subordinates but dominated the terrified civilian politicians as well.

In 1937 conflict erupted again between Japanese and Chinese troops, this time near Beijing's Marco Polo Bridge. It is uncertain whether the clash was inadvertent or an engineered provocation, but it served as a pretext for further Japanese aggression. The military-dominated government in Tokyo elected to respond with a heavy-handed policy that evolved into full-scale war. This second Sino-Japanese war was to be among the bloodiest in history and dragged on inconclusively until Japan's final defeat in 1945.

Events outside Asia drew the isolated conflict between Japan and China into a larger confrontation. The 1939 outbreak of World War II in Europe inaugurated a stunning succession of German victories. The Third Reich quickly defeated Poland, France, and the Low Countries and imposed something closely resembling a state of siege on Great Britain. These events altered Japan's options because Britain, France, and the Netherlands held sway over the principal colonial empires in Southeast Asia. The lands they ruled—the East Indies, Indochina, Malaya, Singapore, and Burma—were rich in the natural resources Japan needed so desperately. Preoccupation of the colonial nations with European events gave Japan an opportunity for easy pickings.

Ambivalence marked U.S. policy toward these developments. President Franklin D. Roosevelt wished to block the expansion of Japan and Germany, but a large segment of the American electorate demurred. Despite fierce isolationist opposition, however, the United States rendered important financial and material aid to the countries at war with Germany and Japan. Hoping to keep America neutral with the threat of a two-ocean war, Germany (and its European partner Italy) and Japan concluded the Axis, or Tripartite, Alliance in September 1940.

In July 1941 the Japanese government made the momentous decision to secure guaranteed access to the natural resources of Southeast Asia, even though that course might well mean war with the United States. It was a decision made in desperation. Senior Japanese officials had little confidence in Japan's ability to defeat the formidable coalition of Western powers but saw few options. Admiral Osami Nagano, chief of the Navy General Staff, expressed the prevailing mood when he told the emperor, "The government has decided that if there were no war, the fate of the nation was sealed. Even if there is war, the country may be ruined. Nevertheless a nation which does not fight in this plight has lost its spirit and is already a doomed nation."[1]

Wasting little time once the decision had been made, the Japanese Army seized southern Indochina. (Northern Indochina had been occupied a year earlier.) American reaction was swift and drastic. President Roosevelt embargoed the shipment of oil to Japan. The colonial government of the Dutch East Indies, dependent on American support, followed suit. It is difficult to overstate the importance of oil in Japan's 1941 policy decisions. Military and naval authorities calculated that Japanese industry and armed forces would grind to a halt within months if the flow were not restored. Japan depended almost entirely on oil imports, and the nation's leadership viewed the embargo as tantamount to an act of war.[2]

Japan and the United States intensified negotiations to settle their differences in the waning months of 1941, but both countries refused to budge from their fundamental positions. Japan demanded a free hand in China and the lifting of the embargo. The United States refused to restore the flow of oil and other restricted materials unless the Japanese reversed their policy in China. With neither side willing to make any meaningful compromise, war seemed a foregone conclusion. On December 2, with a Japanese carrier force already en route to Pearl Harbor, the inner circle of the Japanese government made a final confirmation of its decision to go to war with the United States.

U.S. policymakers had not failed to note the drift of Japanese policy developments. They knew that Japan's leaders increasingly considered war with the United States as inevitable. They responded to the rising tensions in the Pacific by augmenting American military strength and presence in the region. In the Philippines American and Filipino ground forces under the command of General Douglas MacArthur were growing into a formidable army (at least on paper). More important, the arrival of the new and powerful B-17 bomber greatly augmented the air forces under MacArthur's command. The B-17, with its long range and heavy bomb load, gave American forces the capability (in theory at least) of striking directly at important Japanese bases on Formosa. MacArthur was confident that his increased strength would permit him to defeat any Japanese assault, so confident in fact that he said on December 5, 1941, "Nothing would please me better than if they would give me three months and then attack here."[3]

The most powerful American piece on the Pacific chessboard, however, was not the force in the Philippines but the U.S. Pacific Fleet. Normally, the fleet operated from the West Coast and made a training cruise to Hawaii each year. Hawaii, with its vital Pearl Harbor naval base, stood as the principal American bastion in the Pacific. Its geographical location, roughly halfway between the West Coast and forward Japanese bases in the Marshalls, made this strategic center the natural choice for the Pacific Fleet's advance base in any war against Japan.

The Pacific Fleet, commanded by Admiral James O. Richardson, left the West Coast for Hawaii as scheduled on April 2, 1940. Richardson planned to keep the fleet in the Hawaiian area until May 9, when it would return to the mainland. Less than a week before his departure, though, Richardson received a dispatch from Admiral Harold R. ("Betty") Stark, Chief of Naval Operations, altering the fleet's schedule. The change created a bitter disagreement that eventually cost Richardson his job. Stark's message read:

> In view of the possibility of Italy becoming an active belligerent in May, you may receive instructions to remain in Hawaiian waters with the ships of the fleet then in company with you. Changes in scheduled movements individual units prior nine May not contemplated. Utmost secrecy is desired for the present. Acknowledge.[4]

The implications of Stark's message encapsulate American policy and strategic concerns in 1940 and 1941. They also illustrate the global nature of the world crisis with which the Roosevelt administration was attempting to deal. The movement of the Pacific Fleet might seem remote from events in Europe, but U.S. officials perceived a vital interdependence between events in different parts of the world. President Roosevelt and Secretary of State Cordell Hull were convinced that the positioning of the fleet closer to Japan would have a restraining influence on Japanese expansionism. That restraint, they believed, would reduce the chances of war in the Pacific. As a result, Britain and its allies could concentrate their resources on the fight against Germany and American resources would not be diverted from the programs of aid to the Allies. As it became apparent that Washington intended that the fleet remain in Hawaii indefinitely, Richardson made it clear that he could not disagree more strongly. On May 22 he complained to Stark that facilities in Hawaii were inadequate to maintain and provision the ships, crews, and equipment of the Pacific Fleet. Stark replied five days later that these logistical considerations were secondary; basing the fleet in Hawaii was to act as "the deterrent effect your presence may have on the Japs going into the East Indies."[5] Richardson pressed his argument with Secretary of the Navy Frank Knox and with the president himself in a personal meeting in October 1940.

Richardson's principal objections centered on the decreased efficiency of the fleet resulting from Pearl Harbor's inadequate facilities; he noted the danger of the port's exposed position 2,000 miles closer to Japanese bases as an afterthought. When he spoke with Roosevelt he countered FDR's deterrent argument by stating that the military complexion of the Japanese government equipped those leaders with the professional eye to detect the military disadvantages of basing the fleet in Hawaii.[6] Richardson's vehement exceptions to administration policy led to his dismissal shortly after his confrontation with the commander-in-chief.

Ironically, while Richardson expressed greater concern with the logistical disadvantages of basing the Pacific Fleet in Hawaii than with its exposure to Japanese naval power in the Central Pacific, his superiors in Washington worried about the danger of a surprise attack. On November 12, 1940, less than a month after the Richardson–Roosevelt meeting, British torpedo bombers attacked the Italian fleet anchored in the harbor of Taranto. The resulting destruction sent a wave of unease among those in Washington who contemplated the possibility of a similar strike against the Pacific Fleet in Hawaii. On November 22 Stark wrote Richardson suggesting the placement of antitorpedo nets in Pearl Harbor. Richardson responded, "Torpedo nets within the harbor are neither necessary nor practicable."[7]

The problem was soon out of Richardson's hands. He was relieved of command by Admiral Husband E. Kimmel on February 1, 1941. Kimmel had a reputation as a hard-driving officer who demanded results, not excuses, from his subordinates. When confronted with incompetence his temper sometimes got the better of him. Kimmel's "boiling rage" at a botched assignment remained lodged in the mind of at least one senior staffer decades later.[8]

Kimmel was no more enthusiastic than his predecessor about basing the Pacific Fleet at Pearl Harbor, but he was less prone to argue the matter with the president. He applied himself to making the best of a poor situation by readying the fleet to execute American war plans from its base in Hawaii. The Pacific Fleet's plan (WPPac-46) was subsidiary to the overall strategic plan, Rainbow 5, prepared jointly by American and British military staff officers. Rainbow 5 decreed that if the war became a worldwide general conflict involving both the United States and Japan, the defeat of Germany was to take top priority. The strategy in the Pacific was to be essentially defensive. WPPac-46 set the fleet's primary objective as defense of the Malay Barrier (the geographical swath formed by the Isthmus of Kra, Malaya, the Philippines, and the Dutch East Indies). The presence of thousands of miles of Japanese-controlled waters between the Pacific Fleet and the Malay Barrier, plus the prospect of most resources going to the European theater, made it necessary to adopt a strategy of indirection to accomplish that goal.

The Pacific Fleet, then, would not steam into an encounter with the Japanese Navy on unequal terms but would harass the enemy with diversionary tactics in the Central Pacific. The fleet was to divert Japanese strength eastward by (1) capturing and controlling the Caroline and Marshall Islands; (2) disrupting Japanese trade routes and protecting Allied shipping; and (3) defending Guam, Samoa, Hawaii, and the Western Hemisphere. Although the plan called for the assumption of a strategic defensive position, it did not mean a passive role for the Pacific Fleet. The fleet would be committed over a vast area of the world's largest body of water and would take the tactical offensive against Japanese possessions in the Central Pacific. Kimmel's task, especially with the steadily increasing chances of war between the United States and Japan, was to hone his fleet to a sharp edge in expectation of an assault against Japanese forces, while he himself could expect little in the way of reinforcements.

Kimmel's counterpart on the opposite side of the Pacific was Admiral Isoroku Yamamoto, commander-in-chief of Japan's Combined Fleet. Yamamoto had inherited a strategic doctrine which, in many ways, complemented WPPac-46. The Japanese Navy, conceding a quantitative edge to the United States, envisioned engaging the U.S. fleet in a campaign of attrition as it moved into the Western Pacific. As American units moved deeper into waters closer to the Japanese homeland (and suffered a corresponding reduction in operating efficiency), the Japanese Navy would harass them with submarine attacks until the diminished U.S. forces met the main body of Japan's fleet under conditions favorable to a Japanese victory.[9]

The desperate need for the resources of Southeast Asia entailed grave risks for this strategy. A Japanese invasion of those distant and far-flung territories would tie up nearly all of Japan's military potential, leaving the invasion routes, supply lines, and even the homeland itself vulnerable to American attack. Yamamoto's challenge was to devise a plan which would allow Japan to occupy the Western possessions in Southeast Asia while simultaneously ensuring the security of Japan's strategic flank. The move of the U.S. Pacific Fleet to Hawaii rendered the dilemma even more acute. The threat posed by the Pacific Fleet was augmented by the U.S. Asiatic Fleet based in the Philippines and Dutch, British, and Australian naval units in the Far East. The Japanese Navy was more than a match for these local forces, but their very existence required the commitment of a substantial portion of the Combined Fleet's resources to the Southeast Asia operations.[10]

Yamamoto's plan was bold and original. He envisioned an opening blow directly against the U.S. Pacific Fleet timed to coincide with the start of the Japanese offensive against American, British, and Dutch forces in Southeast Asia. By crippling the main component of U.S. power in the Pacific at the outset of the war Japan could neutralize

the threat of a transpacific naval offensive while it seized the vital natural resource areas.

Yamamoto entertained the unrealistic hope that the surprise blow
would demoralize the United States and lead it to accept a peace settlement which would leave Japan the preeminent power in the
Pacific.[11] That Yamamoto so seriously misread the American character is puzzling, since he had spent several years in the United States as
a language student and naval attaché. But if he underestimated the
American capacity to respond to adversity, Yamamoto was under no
illusions regarding the comparative industrial capacities of the two
nations. He realized that the Japanese victory would have to be swift,
for the enormous industrial potential of the United States could
quickly make good its early losses, and American factories and ship-
yards would soon shift the numerical balance to Japan's overwhelming disadvantage. When Japan had entered the alliance with Germany in 1940 Yamamoto told Prime Minister Fumimaro Konoye:

> If it is necessary to fight, in the first six months to a year of war against
> the United States and England I will run wild. I will show you an unin-
> terrupted succession of victories. But I must also tell you that if the war
> be prolonged for two or three years I have no confidence in our ulti-
> mate victory.[12]

In contemplating the prospect of delivering a decisive initial blow,
Yamamoto realized that the U.S. decision to base its fleet in Hawaii
not only increased the menace to Japan but placed it closer to Japanese-controlled waters. The idea of a surprise attack on Pearl Harbor
had circulated among the officers of both navies for years. In the early
1920s General Billy Mitchell, an early advocate of air power, postula-
ted a raid on the anchorage. U.S. fleet exercises in 1932 were predicated on the assumption of a Japanese carrier raid on Pearl Harbor. In
Fleet Problem XIII that year, the carriers *Saratoga* and *Lexington*
under Rear Admiral Harry Yarnell approached Oahu in secret and
successfully executed a mock air attack.

The lessons of Yarnell's success were lost, however, on naval policymakers of the day. Their skepticism was well expressed by Rear Admiral Harris Laning, one of the umpires for the exercise. He discounted
the feat with the remark, "As long as our fleet exists, no enemy is
likely to make such an attack as this was."[13] His attitude reflected the
prevailing belief that carriers were best suited to auxiliary roles, and
their freedom of movement would be sharply restricted by the pres-

ence of a battleship fleet in Hawaiian waters. The Japanese, however, were less complacent. Six years earlier Lieutenant Commander Ryunosuke Kusaka, who was to serve as chief of staff of the Pearl Harbor strike force, had written a paper on an air attack against Pearl Harbor.[14]

As war between the United States and Japan appeared increasingly likely, Yamamoto saw not only that such a bold move had a reasonable chance of success, but that the development of the aircraft carrier in the 1920s and 1930s provided him with the ideal weapon. While less imaginative naval officers remained wedded to the battleship as the core of the fleet, Yamamoto and like-minded colleagues realized that aviation had increased the striking range of battle fleets tenfold. The success of the British carrier raid against the Italian fleet in Taranto helped to confirm Yamamoto's growing conviction that it was indeed possible to cripple the U.S. fleet with a surprise carrier attack on Pearl Harbor.

Within a month of the Taranto attack he had decided that should war with the United States be unavoidable, Japan should open the war without warning with a carrier attack on Pearl Harbor. A great deal of preparatory work now lay before Yamamoto and the Japanese Navy. Yamamoto's tasks included overseeing the preparation of detailed plans, assembling the right combination of personnel, organizing and training fleet units, developing specialized ordnance, and —perhaps most difficult—convincing other senior Japanese Navy officers that his plan was viable.

He first committed himself in written form on January 7, 1941, in a letter to Admiral Koshiro Oikawa, the navy minister. He outlined his conviction that the U.S. fleet must be neutralized by a sudden blow at the outset of any war with the United States and proposed that this task be assigned to his fleet's air units. In his ministerial role, Oikawa served as the link between the navy and the Japanese cabinet. It seems strange that Yamamoto, one of the nation's highest-ranking military officers, would begin by seeking the approval of the cabinet. But perhaps he had a different motive in confiding first to Oikawa. The Navy Ministry controlled personnel assignments, and Yamamoto was anxious to command the operation himself.[15]

About the same time he also discussed the idea in general terms with Rear Admiral Shigeru Fukudome, chief of staff of the Combined Fleet. Yamamoto set in motion the planning process by assigning members of his own staff aboard the Combined Fleet flagship *Nagato* to work up plans for the Pearl Harbor operation, and he concurrently drew on the talents of the navy's most experienced and competent airmen to work separately on the plan.

This two-track planning process illustrates Yamamoto's talent for getting the most out of his subordinates. By having his Combined Fleet staff develop a plan, he ensured that the project would receive the attention of a closely integrated staff team which would overlook none of the details that, if ignored, can ruin a military operation. By drawing on the abilities of the Japanese Navy's best pilots, Yamamoto injected into the planning process the combination of daring and practical experience that the project needed.

The pilot he first chose to examine the proposal was Rear Admiral Takajiro Onishi, chief of staff of the Eleventh (land-based) Air Fleet. Onishi, one of the navy's senior aviators, achieved subsequent renown as chief of Japan's kamikazes. Onishi's first reaction to Yamamoto's idea was negative. Although his own personal temperament and behavior were far from the norm of Japanese naval officers, he thought the plan was too unconventional and risky. He also predicted that a surprise attack on Pearl Harbor would so enrage the American people that they would be satisfied by nothing less than the complete subjugation of Japan. Of all the Japanese admirals who objected to Yamamoto's plan, only Onishi foresaw the psychological reaction it would engender.[16]

Those reservations failed to halt the gathering momentum of Yamamoto's proposal. Onishi undertook the assignment and chose Commander Minoru Genda, an experienced combat pilot, to help him analyze and enlarge on the idea. Genda worked throughout most of February under Onishi's general supervision preparing the principal outline of the Pearl Harbor attack plan. He developed a number of salient points:[17]

1. Surprise, including secrecy at the planning stage, was paramount. Without it the raiders would find the Americans waiting in ambush; the Japanese would inflict little damage, suffer heavy casualties, and lose their precious carriers.

2. The American aircraft carriers should be the priority targets at Pearl Harbor. Without a carrier force the United States could not hope to challenge Japanese naval domination of the Pacific.

3. Destruction of U.S. aircraft on Oahu would be necessary to ensure that Japanese bombers could attack the fleet unhindered by air opposition.

4. All available Japanese carriers should be used for the operation.

The maximum concentration of Japanese naval air power would ensure the greatest damage to the U.S. fleet.

5. All types of bombing should be used in the attack. Torpedo bombing promised the most effective results, but American ships might be protected by torpedo nets, and there were doubts whether the Japanese could develop torpedoes to run in the shallow waters of Pearl Harbor. Horizontal and dive bombers must be included in the attack force in case torpedoes proved impractical.

6. A strong fighter element should be included to escort the bombers and provide air cover for the fleet.

7. Refueling at sea would be necessary. Japanese ships, designed for their traditional strategic role of decisive battle near Japan, lacked the range to make the round trip to Pearl Harbor without refueling.

8. A daylight attack promised best results. Planes could be launched from carriers shortly before sunrise and arrive over Oahu in the early daylight hours.

Onishi presented Yamamoto with the results of this study about March 10. But while the airmen had been at their labors, the Combined Fleet staff had been busy at the same task. Rather than producing a conceptual framework for an attack plan, the fleet staff focused on the specialized problems presented by the Pearl Harbor raid. Captain Kameto Kuroshima, Yamamoto's senior staff officer,[18] supervised the work of a number of staff specialists in logistics, submarine warfare, navigation, and communications. Yamamoto and his staff also toyed with the idea of coordinating the strike with an invasion of Hawaii, an idea they did not abandon until September.[19]

In April the plan began to move beyond the theoretical stage with major organizational and personnel changes. On April 10 the Japanese organized the First Air Fleet, a revolutionary grouping which concentrated the navy's heavy carriers under a single command. The unit consisted of two divisions of two carriers each. The First Carrier Division included the venerable *Akagi* (flagship for the division and the First Air Fleet) and *Kaga,* each displacing about 42,000 tons and capable of 31 and 28 knots respectively. The newer *Soryu* and *Hiryu* formed the Second Carrier Division. These vessels displaced only 30,000 tons each but were 3 knots faster than *Akagi*. In September they were joined by Japan's newest carriers, *Shokaku* and *Zuikaku,* forming the Fifth Carrier Division.

Commanding the First Air Fleet was Vice Admiral Chuichi Nagumo, who would lead the carrier force from triumph to triumph until it met disaster at the battle of Midway scarcely a year after its birth. Nagumo had spent most of his seagoing career aboard battleships and cruisers and, lacking a background in aviation, was not an obvious choice to command the First Air Fleet. He was aided immeasurably (some would say dominated) by the assignment of Genda as the fleet's air staff officer.

The day the First Air Fleet was organized Fukudome bid farewell to the Combined Fleet and reported to the Navy General Staff in Tokyo as head of its First Bureau, the agency which oversaw the development of plans for the fleet. His successor as Combined Fleet chief of staff was Rear Admiral Seichi Ito, an officer who made little contribution to the Pearl Harbor attack. Ito served only until August, when he was appointed navy vice chief of staff and replaced in the Combined Fleet by Rear Admiral Matome Ugaki.

In late April Yamamoto thought that planning and fleet reorganization had advanced sufficiently to send Kuroshima as his emissary to the Navy General Staff to argue for the adoption of the Pearl Harbor attack plan. Kuroshima met with Captain Sadatoshi Tomioka to present his case. The fact that Tomioka's superior was Admiral Fukudome, Yamamoto's former chief of staff, did not ensure a cordial reception for the plan. Tomioka and other officers in the general staff's Operation Section expressed skepticism. According to Fukudome's postwar recollections, they saw too many unacceptable risks:[20]

1. Surprise, the key to the plan's success, would be difficult to achieve. It was all too likely that secrecy might be compromised by foreign intelligence agents, chance meetings with other ships on the high seas, and American reconnaissance.

2. Japan's traditional strategy, predicated on a gradual American advance through the Japanese-controlled Mandates (the Marshall, Mariana, and Caroline islands) followed by a decisive battle near the homeland, was still sound. There was no compelling need to eliminate the U.S. fleet before seizing Southeast Asia.

3. Operational difficulties were formidable. Maintaining radio silence and refueling at sea offered too many chances for the plan to go awry.

4. Diplomatic negotiations aimed at averting war were still in progress. Japanese naval officers were under no illusions about their chances for success in a war against the United States. A surprise attack on Pearl Harbor would dash any remaining hope of peace.

The convention-bound precincts of the Navy General Staff were not the only center of opposition to Yamamoto's plan. His own key subordinates, the officers upon whom he depended for its success, were also less than enthusiastic. Nagumo and his chief of staff, Rear Admiral Ryunosuke Kusaka, learned of the project not from Yamamoto but from Fukudome shortly after the latter left the Combined Fleet. When Kusaka visited Fukudome in Tokyo in April, Fukudome told him what was afoot. Kusaka and Nagumo were aghast. Perhaps their reluctance stemmed partly from pique at not having been taken into Yamamoto's confidence as soon as the First Air Fleet was formed. That Yamamoto would ignore regular command channels testifies to his unconventional manner, but it is unlikely that the tradition-minded Nagumo would have embraced the idea, regardless of who informed him.

Despite their feelings, Nagumo and Kusaka wasted little time in preparing their fleet for the formidable task set for it in Yamamoto's plan. Not only the carriers but the escort and support vessels had to become accustomed to operating and maneuvering as a unit. The intricate choreography of refueling under way loomed as an especially important part of the training program.[21]

Just as crucial to the success of the plan, obviously, was the training of the air crews. Grouped by type of aircraft, the various air units based at different naval air stations in southern Japan began their training in early May. Genda and his superiors placed great hopes in the effectiveness of the Nakajima B_5N_2 Type 97 (Kate) torpedo bombers, which began training in the Kagoshima area in June. The use of torpedo bombers, however, presented important questions. First, the American ships might be protected by torpedo nets. Second, conventional torpedoes, designed for use in the open sea, would plunge into the shallow bottom of Pearl Harbor (with a maximum depth of 50 feet) before beginning their run to target. The Pearl Harbor attack plan required the development of a new torpedo with a depth of run shallow enough for the U.S. fleet's anchorage. Fortunately for the First Air Fleet the navy's ordnance experts had begun work independently in January on this technical problem.

While staff and support personnel occupied themselves with these problems, the fliers worked to perfect the skills needed for the attack. Screaming over populated areas on the fringes of Kagoshima Bay (which had somewhat the same topography as Pearl Harbor), they put on hair-raising exhibitions of flying skill for local residents. Lieutenant Heita Matsumura, squadron commander of *Hiryu's* torpedo planes, practiced torpedo approaches at 100 knots with his flaps and wheels down—a maneuver which could cause his plane to stall and crash with the slightest mishap.[22]

The horizontal bomber pilots had their work cut out for them as well. If the torpedo planes could not participate effectively in the attack, responsibility for sinking the battleships in Pearl Harbor would devolve on the horizontal bomber pilots (who also flew Kates). The major problem with horizontal bombing was the low accuracy rate. Relentless practice raised the rate of hits at high altitude (10,000 to 15,000 feet) from 10 percent to nearly 50 percent. Another obstacle was the lack of armor-piercing bombs heavy enough to penetrate armored battleship decks. Again the Japanese Navy's resourceful ordnance specialists addressed the problem. By fitting 40-centimeter (15.7-inch) 800-kilogram (1,760-pound) armor-piercing battleship projectiles with fins they produced an improvised but effective bomb.[23]

The Mitsubishi A6M2 Type o (Zero, or Zeke) fighter pilots, whose task was to ensure air control, also underwent training with new equipment and techniques.[24] Voice radio, with a range of about 100 miles, would be inadequate for the Pearl Harbor operation. The fighter pilots had to learn to use Morse keys during flight operations. The crews of Aiichi D3A1 Type 99 (Val) dive bombers, newly issued to the fleet, had to become accustomed to the new planes and succeeded in achieving an accuracy rate of 50 to 60 percent.[25] In late August the training program received fresh impetus with the assignment of Commander Mitsuo Fuchida, an experienced and respected horizontal bomber pilot who took overall command of the First Air Fleet's air units.

The intense training of the crews and work of the ordnance specialists were keys to the successful execution of Yamamoto's plan. Despite their impressive performance, however, Yamamoto knew that it would take more than a well-trained fleet to win the support of Japan's admiralty for his proposal. It would require his continuing efforts to convince the Navy General Staff and concessions to those officers still unconvinced of the effectiveness of naval air power.

2

YAMAMOTO'S
MASTER PLAN

Yamamoto, for all his air-mindedness, hesitated to place the entire burden of the Pearl Harbor attack on the First Air Fleet. His reservations may have stemmed from lack of confidence in Nagumo, nervousness about placing all his eggs in one basket, or simply a politic desire to appease the plan's critics. Whatever his reasons, Yamamoto decided to employ a large submarine force in the Hawaii operation to supplement the efforts of his naval air force. On July 29 he consulted with Vice Admiral Mitsumi Shimizu, commander of the Sixth (submarine) Fleet, and ordered him to prepare a large undersea force to participate—albeit as auxiliaries—in the Pearl Harbor operation.[1]

This force of twenty-five fleet submarines and five midget subs would proceed to Hawaii independently of Nagumo's fleet. Its assignment included reconnaissance, interception of American reinforcements sent to Pearl Harbor and ships attempting to sortie from the anchorage, and rescuing downed pilots. The midgets would penetrate the harbor and torpedo any major warships missed by the attacking aircraft.[2]

The midget submarines were perhaps the most unique weapons used in the attack. Each carried a crew of a junior officer and an enlisted man, displaced 46 tons, and measured 78 feet, 10 inches by 6 feet, 6 inches. Despite their diminutive size, they were formidable weapons. After release from a mother ship they had a 100-mile range (at 4 knots) and could achieve bursts of speed up to 24 knots submerged. Their two torpedoes could inflict as much damage as ordnance delivered by more conventional means.[3] According to the plan developed by Shimizu's staff, they would be launched from the mother subs about 10 miles from the mouth of Pearl Harbor, stealthily enter the anchorage before the air attack, lie in wait until its conclusion, and then torpedo whatever targets of opportunity remained.[4]

Theoretically the crews of the midget submarines had a chance to survive their mission and return to their mother ships, but no one—least of all the crews themselves—harbored illusions about the odds against these tiny craft escaping through Pearl Harbor's narrow channel in the aftermath of the attack. The crews were not fanatical volunteers but carefully selected and trained submariners who, because of a combination of prewar Japanese iron military discipline and social pressure, accepted their fate. Ensign Kazuo Sakamaki, the sole survivor of these ten seamen, summed up their predicament succinctly: "None of us was a volunteer. We had all been ordered to our assignment. That none of us objected goes without saying: we knew that punishment would be very severe if we objected; we were supposed to feel highly honored."[5]

The inclusion of submarines in the Hawaii Operation and the progress in training did not suffice to calm the doubts of the Navy General Staff. When Kuroshima visited Tomioka in August, he met with the same objections that had greeted Yamamoto's plan at its inception. It was too risky, too unconventional, and stretched Japan's limited naval resources far too thin.[6] In a bid to make its case the Combined Fleet staff prevailed on the general staff to set aside time for gaming the Pearl Harbor attack at its annual map exercises at the Naval Staff College. From September 12 to 16 the assembled staff officers and fleet commanders rehearsed Japan's strategic plans for opening the war against the Western powers. The final day was devoted exclusively to Pearl Harbor.[7]

The results reassured no one. On the first round the Japanese lost two carriers sunk and two damaged—a loss rate of more than 50 percent. (The Fifth Carrier Division was not yet assigned to Nagumo.) In addition only half the Japanese aircraft returned to their ships. In exchange for these sacrifices the umpires ruled that the First Air Fleet could expect to inflict only minor damage on the Americans. A second round of maneuvers, in which Nagumo incorporated lessons learned from the first, resulted in much heavier losses for the Americans: four battleships and two carriers sunk and one of each badly damaged. Still, Japanese losses were not insignificant: one carrier sunk, one damaged, and 127 planes lost.[8]

The chief difference between the two rounds was the route to

Hawaii. On the first, American patrol planes spotted Nagumo as he approached Pearl Harbor from an easterly direction. On the second approach, from almost due north, Nagumo used an unexpected route which minimized the chances of discovery. Still, Nagumo was loath to accept the northern option because the bad weather would present formidable problems of maneuvering, navigation, and re-fueling. It was only with great difficulty that Genda persuaded Nagumo to give priority to the element of surprise and use the north-ern route.[9]

The skeptics who witnessed the war games knew they were a highly theoretical exercise dealing only with immutable known factors and general probabilities. Missing were the components of blind luck and human fallibility so often decisive in battle. Even in this highly abstract rehearsal the great risks of Yamamoto's plan were glaringly obvious. What if the carrier force were intercepted? What if the Pacific Fleet were not at Pearl Harbor? What if the weather did not behave as predicted? The September war games seem to have actually strengthened the resolve of the naval officers opposed to the Pearl Harbor attack. After their conclusion, Fukudome reported to the Navy General Staff and recommended against the Pearl Harbor oper-ation. Admirals Nagano and Ito agreed with him.[10]

It is not difficult to imagine the atmosphere of tension and frustra-tion which prevailed in the inner circles of the Imperial Japanese Navy. The likelihood of war was increasing daily. Japan would under-take risky and far-flung operations at the outset against the combined forces of the world's two greatest naval powers, Britain and the United States. In the midst of this grave predicament the commander of Japan's naval operating forces obstinately insisted on a gamble that would stretch naval resources even more and, in addition, put at risk the main strength of Japan's carrier fleet.

In late September Nagumo met with Admiral Nishizo Tsukahara, commander of the Eleventh Air Fleet. Also present were Kusaka and Onishi, their respective chiefs of staff. Tsukahara complained that the Pearl Harbor attack would strip his command of too many airmen and planes to fulfill his assigned objective—air support of operations in Southeast Asia. Nagumo, his uneasiness not assuaged by the map maneuvers, needed little convincing to join Tsukahara in presenting a united front of Japan's senior naval air commanders. Their chiefs of staff, Kusaka and Onishi, were moved to agree.[11]

On October 3 Kusaka and Onishi boarded the battleship *Mutsu* (serving as Combined Fleet flagship while *Nagato* underwent repairs) to present their commanders' and their own objections. Yamamoto refused to bend and invoked his authority as commander-in-chief of the Combined Fleet to make it clear that the Pearl Harbor attack would be part of Japanese naval strategy. Pulling rank was all very well, but Yamamoto knew that leaving execution of his plan to fearful and doubting subordinates could doom the project. At the gangway to see Kusaka and Onishi off the flagship Yamamoto put his hand on Kusaka's shoulder and said: "Kusaka—I understand just how you feel. But the Pearl Harbor raid has become an article of faith for me. How about cutting down on the vocal opposition and trying to help me put that article of faith into practice? Where the actual operation is concerned I guarantee I'll do my best to meet any requests you may have."[12]

The personal approach worked well enough on subordinates, but the planners on the Navy General Staff remained unimpressed. They not only continued to oppose the Pearl Harbor plan but attempted to emasculate it in early October by reassigning *Akagi, Hiryu,* and *Soryu* to operations in Southeast Asia, leaving Nagumo with only three carriers. Once again Kuroshima journeyed to Tokyo as Yamamoto's envoy and on October 18 demanded that all six heavy carriers be assigned to the Pearl Harbor operation. Tomioka countered with the by then familiar objections to Yamamoto's plan. This time Kuroshima played his chief's trump card. Yamamoto, he said, would resign if he did not receive full support for his plan.[13]

Nagano and his colleagues may have been sorely tempted to take Yamamoto up on his offer and be rid of the problem once and for all. But that move would have had disastrous consequences. They knew that Yamamoto's personal charisma and undoubted brilliance made him, for all practical purposes, the Japanese Navy's one indispensable man. It would hardly do to have him leave under disputatious circumstances on the eve of war. The fleet and squadron commanders were accustomed to his methods, and coordinated operations depended upon Yamamoto at the helm. Moreover, the blow to morale at all levels might seriously endanger the navy's chances for success in the rapidly approaching conflict.

The general staff had no choice but to relent. Nagano claimed after the war that it was the threat to resign which compelled him to yield.[14] Once Nagano decided to let Yamamoto have his way, opposition to the Pearl Harbor attack collapsed. The exact date of Nagano's decision is a matter of dispute among historians and participants in the deliberations. In late October or early November Nagano bowed to Yamamoto's will and accepted the Combined Fleet commander's demands.[15]

With the major issue settled Yamamoto and his staff devoted their energies to completing preparations for the attack. One of the most striking features of Japanese planning and preparation is how much uncertainty existed on important questions just weeks before the attack took place. Less than six weeks remained before planners settled on December 7 (Hawaii time) as the date of the attack. They chose early December as a compromise between the need to avoid the worst of the winter storms in the North Pacific and the need to give the First Air Fleet as much time as possible to complete its training. From an operational point of view, December 9 was ideal because it would provide a nearly full moon to aid in night operations, but the Japanese knew that the Pacific Fleet's operating schedule put more ships in harbor on weekends than on weekdays. All these considerations pointed to Sunday, December 7, as the best day to attack.[16]

Tactical questions aside, there remained the delicate issue of coordinating the attack with official notice to the U.S. government that Japan was abandoning the search for a peaceful solution to the differences between the two countries. The Japanese did not consider a surprise attack dishonorable. Indeed, they had begun the Russo-Japanese War with a surprise attack on the Russian fleet, a coup applauded by European and American opinion. There was, moreover, the British example of Nelson's surprise attack (sans declaration of war) against the Danish fleet in Copenhagen in 1801.

But some in the Japanese government, especially diplomats, thought that the record required some sort of formal notice. Obviously, the advance warning would have to be minimal or else the advantage of surprise would be lost. A compromise was struck within the government by which its representatives in Washington would formally break off negotiations a scant thirty minutes before the attack began.

Premier Hideki Tojo told American interrogators after the war that the emperor insisted on the half-hour notice and "repeatedly" demanded that the government notify the United States in advance. Tojo's account is open to doubt. Although the emperor was by all accounts unenthusiastic about Japan going to war, it would have been a radical deviation from the norm of Japanese political behavior in 1941 for him to have taken such a strong stand on what was, under the circumstances, a minor issue. It is more likely that Tojo was trying to protect the emperor from American retribution. The situation in

1945, when the monarch's personal intervention was decisive in bringing about Japan's capitulation, was very different. The Japanese military officers who stood in the way of surrender were then—unlike 1941—thoroughly discredited by an obviously lost war.[17]

There still remained an air of improvisation about the preparations of the First Air Fleet. Not until the eve of the fleet's departure was a sufficient number of specially modified shallow-water torpedoes ready. Bomb racks were modified to accept the special 800-kilogram armor-piercing missiles while the carriers were actually under way.

The lack of adequate time for training the latecomers of the Fifth Carrier Division, which was something of a scratch unit (the final batch of pilots did not report aboard until October 10), forced the Japanese to sacrifice the advantages of a dawn attack. The *Shokaku* and *Zuikaku* pilots had no time to train as a unit for night operations, so they would have to wait until dawn to take off from their carriers. The ninety-minute flying time from the launch point meant the attacking aircraft would arrive over Oahu in full daylight.[18]

The First Air Fleet, complete with supporting units, did not assemble until early November, when it conducted a full dress rehearsal at Saeki Bay in Yamamoto's presence. On November 17 the 100 officer pilots (most prewar Japanese naval pilots were enlisted men) of the attack force assembled aboard *Akagi,* where Yamamoto outlined the plan and appealed for their maximum effort.[19]

On November 23 Nagumo outlined the final plan to the First Air Fleet in a set of operations orders. The task force would form around the six aircraft carriers. The light cruiser *Abukuma* served as flagship of the screening unit of nine destroyers. The battleships *Hiei* and *Kirishima* provided insurance against disaster if the force were forced into a surface engagement. Augmenting the battleships' 14-inch guns were the 8-inch guns of the heavy cruisers *Tone* and *Chikuma*. They were responsible for providing scout aircraft to reconnoiter Pearl Harbor in advance of the carrier planes. Three submarines (not to be confused with the separate submarine force under Admiral Shimizu's command) would patrol in the van of the fleet's course. Seven tankers loaded with precious oil to refuel the fleet en route brought up the rear.[20]

Final plans set the fleet rendezvous at Hitokappu Wan on the island of Etorofu in the Kuriles, departure on an eastward course, with refueling at sea as necessary. Aircraft would be launched at a point about 200 miles north of Oahu. There was to be no aerial reconnaissance or cover en route, but scout planes from the heavy cruisers would precede the attack planes and reconnoiter Pearl Harbor and the alternate fleet anchorage at Lahaina Roads. The attack force aircraft would sortie in two waves thirty minutes apart.

All forty torpedo bombers were grouped in the first wave, where the chance of surprise was greatest and the odds for surviving their low and slow approach was greatest. Specific targets were assigned to different attack elements. The first wave of torpedo planes was to hit the carrier berths on Ford Island's northwest side and the battleship moorings on the island's opposite shore. Dive bombers were to attack Wheeler Field (the Army Air Corps fighters base in central Oahu) and the naval air station on Ford Island. The second wave was to attack Kaneohe Naval Air Station, the marine airfield at Ewa, and the army bomber base at Hickam Field. Fighters would establish air control, and the second-wave dive bombers were to strike any carriers left afloat.

Yamamoto's staff did not overlook the need for contingency plans. If the U.S. fleet were anchored outside Pearl Harbor, all Kates in the first wave were to be armed with torpedoes. Torpedoes would be the most effective means of sinking the American ships in deep waters outside the restricted confines of the harbor. If the First Air Fleet encountered serious opposition, the main body of the Combined Fleet would sortie from Japanese home waters and steam eastward to the rescue. If, on the other hand, the task force failed to encounter the U.S. fleet at or near Pearl Harbor, Nagumo was to return to Japan.[21]

With preparations as complete as humanly possible, the Sixth Fleet submarines scheduled to take part in the attack began leaving their Japanese bases in mid-November. The carriers and escorts rendezvoused as scheduled at Etorofu. Before Nagumo's fleet sortied on November 26 the pilots were briefed on the mission and provided with maps of Oahu and Pearl Harbor to study during the long days at sea which lay ahead.[22]

3

"NO CREDENCE
IN THESE RUMORS"

Secrecy and security were uppermost in the minds of the Japanese planners. Without it they faced little hope of success and every likelihood of disaster. They were preoccupied with fears that U.S. intelligence would learn of the plan and alert the Pacific Fleet. Few aspects of the Pearl Harbor attack have been subjected to such close scrutiny, analysis, and misunderstanding as the state of American intelligence prior to the attack. The topic is strewn with pitfalls, but the questions of what information was available, how it was handled, and what conclusions were drawn from it constitute a key chapter in the Pearl Harbor story.

Before World War II military intelligence was among the least sought after assignments in the U.S. armed forces. Officers who spent their careers in intelligence duty could expect little in the way of prestige and advancement. As one prewar officer wrote, the assignment was "an uninviting professional dead end."[1] Hand in hand with low status went disjointed organization and poor coordination. Interagency and interservice articulation left much to be desired, and cooperation depended more on the goodwill of individual officers than on clear guidelines and policy. Goodwill was not always forthcoming, as one navy staff officer found in January 1941. Walter Ansel, a member of navy secretary Frank Knox's staff, was assigned to draft Knox's letter to Secretary of War Henry Stimson concerning Hawaii's antiaircraft defenses. Army staff officers guarded information so jealously that to obtain the data Ansel had to resort to methods more closely resembling espionage than interservice liaison. When the army and navy decided in October 1941 to establish a joint intelligence committee to provide a forum for the exchange of information between the services, bureaucratic squabbling vitiated its effectiveness. Failure to agree on a place for the committee to convene prevented it from meeting until after the Pearl Harbor attack.[2]

Even within the individual services jealousy and bickering prevented intelligence sections from operating at full efficiency. A case in point is the struggle for control over intelligence functions at the highest levels of the navy command structure. In April 1941 Rear Admiral Richmond Kelly Turner, chief of the War Plans Division, wanted to take control of the preparation of estimates from the Office of Naval Intelligence (ONI). Turner, who won the match, was described by another senior officer as a "martinet, very very gifted, but . . . stubborn, self-opinionated [and] conceited."[3] After Turner's victory ONI was confined to forwarding reports and information to the War Plans office, which analyzed, evaluated, and disseminated the information as it saw fit.

The sorry state of U.S. intelligence, when combined with the tight Japanese security measures, reduced almost to nil the chances of American agents or observers learning about the Pearl Harbor attack plan. But the United States had better luck than it deserved, for the American ambassador to Japan, Joseph C. Grew, relayed to Washington a rumor that the Japanese planned to open hostilities with a surprise raid on the Pacific Fleet base in Hawaii. On January 27—less than three weeks after Yamamoto first committed his idea to paper—Grew cabled the State Department that the Peruvian chargé d'affaires had told him that the Japanese "planned, in the event of trouble with the United States, to attempt a surprise mass attack on Pearl Harbor using all of their military facilities."[4] It is unknown to this day whether the source of the rumor was a leak within the Japanese Navy or whether the originator made an inspired guess. The State Department forwarded the warning to both services, but its subsequent fate illustrates the axiom that even the best intelligence is worthless if it is not believed.

The army's Military Intelligence Division flatly refused to credit the story. Brigadier Sherman Miles, assistant chief of staff for intelligence (G-2), told postwar investigators, "It was inconceivable that any sources in the know in Japan would have communicated" the plan to the Peruvian chargé. The navy was slightly more conscientious in that it shared the substance of the dispatch with Kimmel. On February 1 the chief of naval operations passed on the Peruvian warning but played down its reliability:

> The Division of Naval Intelligence places no credence in these rumors.
> Furthermore, based on known data regarding the present disposition
> and employment of Japanese naval and army forces, no move against
> Pearl Harbor appears imminent or planned in the foreseeable future.[5]

Grew's coup thus came to naught, and U.S. intelligence found it
difficult to obtain and evaluate information from other human
sources. American technological wizardry, however, went at least
partway in filling the gap. In the months before the Pearl Harbor
attack U.S. government officials were reading the most secret messages passing between the Japanese Foreign Ministry and Japan's diplomatic outposts. By using a computerlike machine the Americans
could decode messages in Japan's top-secret diplomatic code, the so-
called Purple code.[6] Encrypted messages to and from Japanese diplomats were intercepted, decoded, and read by U.S. officials in an
operation code-named Magic.

Magic was one of the few interservice operations which worked
smoothly. Codebreaking was performed in the Washington offices of
the army's Signal Intelligence Service under Colonel Otis Sadtler and
the navy's Communications Security Section, headed by Commander
Laurence Safford. After translation they were forwarded to Admiral
Turner and his army counterpart, Brigadier General Leonard Gerow.
The two services took turns (on alternate days) distributing the
translated intercepts to civilian officials. The list of Magic recipients
was tightly restricted: the White House; secretaries of state, war, and
the navy; the army chief of staff; the chief of naval operations; and
the heads of each service's war plans and intelligence divisions.[7]

Dissemination was restricted because it was vital that the United
States keep the Magic operation under the tightest security. If the
Japanese learned that the United States had broken their codes, they
would lose no time in changing them. Even worse, they might send
false messages in the compromised code to deceive the Americans as
to their true intentions. Security, however, fell victim to overzealous-
ness. In protecting the Magic secret those in control limited its usefulness. Instead of showing the messages to lower-ranking analysts who
might have been more sensitive to their implications, they circulated
the intercepts for the most part only among those with the power to
make policy decisions. The selection of translators illustrates the exaggerated security consciousness. Although few Americans in 1941 were
proficient in Japanese, Miles was nonetheless reluctant to accept *nisei*
(second-generation Japanese-Americans) as Magic translators.[8]

Despite the precautions, there was at least one Magic leak. In April 1941 Undersecretary of State Sumner Welles shared information derived from the intercepts with the British ambassador. That information was transmitted from the embassy to London in an insecure code, which was easily deciphered by German cryptanalysts. The Germans correctly inferred that the information came from decoded Japanese traffic and relayed a warning to Tokyo. The Japanese Foreign Ministry tightened security but continued to use the Purple code. The ministry did, however, become more circumspect in the information it included in dispatches from Tokyo.[9] The Americans detected the Japanese concern, and when the Japanese continued to use the Purple code, American codebreakers intensified their precautions.

Secrecy inevitably begat ignorance and confusion. One particularly striking instance was Admiral Stark's misapprehension that Kimmel's command at Pearl Harbor was equipped with a machine capable of decoding Purple. Perhaps the greatest confusion arising from the mismanagement of the Magic operation lies in the interpretation of the information in the Purple messages. These were diplomatic, not military, dispatches. They contained no details of military operations, least of all the Pearl Harbor plans. In fact, Yamamoto's plan was so jealously guarded by the navy that Japanese diplomats were unaware of its existence.[10] The U.S. command in the Philippines, unlike the Pacific Fleet, did have a Purple machine at its disposal, but American forces there were no better prepared for a Japanese attack than the Hawaii commands.

If U.S. intelligence analysts and policymakers had no hint that the Japanese were preparing to attack Pearl Harbor (except Grew's dispatch, which was discounted), what conclusions did they draw about Japanese intentions? The tone of the Japanese messages between Washington and Tokyo indicated quite clearly that Japan was preparing to go to war. Especially ominous were the messages setting deadlines for the conclusion of U.S.–Japanese negotiations regarding the withdrawal of Japanese forces from China and the resumption of trade between Japan and the United States. On November 5 Tokyo cabled its Washington embassy:

Because of various circumstances, it is absolutely necessary that all arrangements for the signing of this agreement be completed by the 25th of this month. I realize that this is a difficult order, but under the circumstances it is an unavoidable one.[11]

The Foreign Ministry relented slightly and on November 22 extended the deadline by four days. But the terms in which the extension was couched were hardly reassuring:

> There are reasons beyond your ability to guess why we wanted to settle Japanese-American relations by the 25th, but if within the next three or four days you can finish your conversations with the Americans; if the signing can be completed by the 29th . . . we have decided to wait until that date. This time we mean it, that the deadline absolutely cannot be changed. After that things are automatically going to happen.[12]

These indications from Magic that Japan was preparing for war served only to confirm what was obvious from public statements of the Japanese government. The question was: Where would the Japanese strike? The most obvious target was Southeast Asia. The pattern of Japanese encroachment in the region, its abundance of natural resources, and its function as a bastion of Western military power in the Orient all pointed to an early move against the Dutch East Indies, the Philippines, and the British fortress of Singapore. American planners generally assumed that the first hostile Japanese moves against U.S. forces would occur in the Philippines. The buildup of Japanese forces in southern China, Formosa, and Indochina suggested to other observers that the Japanese would aim their initial blow against the Kra Isthmus, the strategic neck of land joining the Malay Peninsula to the rest of Asia.[13]

As late as December 5 General Miles outlined a bewildering array of Japan's strategic options:

1. Attack the Soviet Union (then fighting for survival against the German invaders).
2. Open an offensive against the Chinese province of Yunan in an effort to cut the Burma Road.
3. Occupy Siam and use that country as a jumping-off point for attacks against British-ruled Burma, Malaya, or both.
4. Attack the Philippines.
5. Seize Hong Kong.
6. Invade the Dutch East Indies.
7. Launch an assault against Singapore.[14]

The plethora of options was staggering, and those in Washington who tried to read the signs conveyed their misapprehensions to the

U.S. commands in Hawaii. Throughout 1941 Stark sent messages to the Pacific Fleet expressing his belief that Japan would move north and attack the Soviet Union. On October 17 he wrote Kimmel: "Personally, I do not believe the Japs are going to sail into us."[15]

Although those reading Magic failed to divine any sign of an attack on Hawaii, the Japanese plainly were girding for hostilities. One sign was the November 19 "Winds" message from Tokyo to its Washington embassy and other diplomatic posts. In that message Tokyo established a system to relay news of an imminent break in relations. The news could be received even if decoding equipment had been destroyed, because it depended on regular shortwave news broadcasts from Japan. If the severing of diplomatic ties was near, the weather report would include one or more code phrases to alert Japanese envoys. The November 19 message setting up the system was encrypted in diplomatic code, but the actual execute messages would be broadcast in clear. If U.S.–Japanese relations were "in danger" of rupture, the code message would be "east wind, rain." If relations with the USSR were strained to the breaking point, the weather prediction was to be "north wind, cloudy." "West wind, clear" meant relations with Great Britain were at the breaking point.[16]

At last the United States had an opportunity to derive from Magic a clear indication of Japanese intentions. An intense round-the-clock radio watch was established in the military radio listening networks. Whether a Winds execute message was broadcast and intercepted is a matter of dispute. Safford maintained that "east wind, rain" was intercepted on December 4 (Washington time). His claim was supported by testimony from one of the radio operators on alert, but to date no records have been produced to support their contention.[17] Equally authoritative testimony from Commander Arthur McCollum, chief of ONI's Far Eastern Section, denies receipt of a Winds execute message.[18] Japanese communications records were destroyed during the war, but Japanese officials interrogated by U.S. occupation authorities stated that the execute message was never transmitted.[19]

Although the subject remains one of the most hotly debated questions surrounding the Pearl Harbor attack, there is simply no available evidence to settle the issue. More to the point is what the Winds message told, or would have told, American listeners. It would have warned that Japan was about to go to war with the United States. That conclusion, given the strained state of U.S.–Japanese relations, should have come as no surprise. In any event, it would not have precluded other strategic options for Japan—Japan did in fact strike simultaneously along an extended front ranging from Malaya to Hawaii. Most important in terms of the controversy over Pearl Harbor, "east wind, rain" would have contained no hint that the Japanese were about to open the war with a surprise attack on the U.S. fleet in Hawaii. Captain Ellis Zacharias, a U.S. naval expert on Japan, pointed out that an interception "would have conveyed no information of importance which the Navy and War Departments did not already possess."[20]

While Washington scrutinized the message traffic between Tokyo and its embassy in the United States, a more significant set of cables was being exchanged between Tokyo and its consulate general in Honolulu. Ensign Takeo Yoshikawa of the Japanese Navy operated in Hawaii as a solo spy under the cover identity of a vice-consul. Yoshikawa was a graduate of the naval academy at Etajima but had been forced into early retirement for medical reasons. He returned to the navy as a limited duty officer specializing in intelligence and in 1940 was placed on Japan's diplomatic roster. In April 1941 he was posted to the Honolulu consulate under the fictitious name of Tadashi Morimasu.[21]

U.S. codebreakers intercepted Yoshikawa's messages, but since the Honolulu consulate seemed far less important than the Japanese embassy in Washington, his dispatches received little attention. Senior U.S. officers were in fact barely aware of the traffic. So low was the priority assigned to consular traffic that U.S. listening stations mailed the intercepts to Washington rather than relaying them by radio.[22]

Yoshikawa's reports evinced a keen Japanese interest in the defenses of Pearl Harbor and the movements of U.S. vessels in and out of the anchorage. Even more significant were his instructions from Tokyo. On September 24 Yoshikawa was directed to use a schematic plot of Pearl Harbor dividing the anchorage into five areas and report which ships were moored in each sector. That dispatch, after its discovery by postwar investigators, came to be known as the bomb plot message. The plotting, or division of the port into zones, was seen in retrospect as a clear indication of Japanese plans. On November 15 Tokyo instructed him to report on naval units in the harbor at least twice a week and to "take extra care to maintain secrecy" in his spying. On November 29 Yoshikawa was ordered to "report even when there are no [ship] movements." A December 2 cable charged him not only to make daily reports on ships present but also to note "whether or not there are any observation balloons above Pearl Harbor or if there are any indications that they will be sent up. Also advice [*sic*] whether . . . the warships are provided with antisubmarine nets."[23]

In postmortems of the attack, those at the Washington echelon pointed out that Japanese agents in other ports received similar instructions. There was nothing, they claimed, to indicate that the interest in Pearl Harbor signified anything more than a wholly understandable interest in the fleet and principal base of a potential enemy. These protests were disingenuous: Japanese message traffic concerning other ports bespoke a far less intense interest than the dispatches to and from Yoshikawa. Kimmel (who in 1941 was unaware of the traffic between Yoshikawa and Tokyo) maintained that had he known of such interest in his fleet and its anchorage he would have treated it as an important clue to Japanese intentions.[24] In his postwar testimony to Congress he was merciless in his indictment of those in Washington who failed to forward Yoshikawa's cable traffic to the Pacific Fleet:

These Japanese instructions and reports pointed to an attack by Japan on the ships in Pearl Harbor. The information sought and obtained, with such painstaking detail, had no other conceivable usefulness from a military viewpoint. . . .

No one had a more direct and immediate interest in the security of the fleet in Pearl Harbor than its commander in chief. No one had a greater right than I to know that Japan had carved up Pearl Harbor into subareas and was seeking and receiving reports as to the precise berthings in that harbor of the ships of the fleet. I had been sent Mr. Grew's report earlier in the year with positive advice from the Navy Department that no credence was to be placed in the rumored Japanese plans for an attack on Pearl Harbor. . . .

Certainly I was entitled to know when information in the Navy Department completely altered the information and advice previously given to me.[25]

Kimmel went on to say that had he known of the bomb plot message he would have redeployed his fleet to ambush the approaching Japanese. That statement throws into sharp relief one of the most vexing questions surrounding the issue of missed and misread clues to Japanese intentions: There still remained the problem of deducing the particulars of the Japanese plans. Without these details American readiness could have been improved only marginally. Where, for example, would Kimmel lay his ambush? To the southwest of Hawaii

—the direction of the nearest Japanese bases and the most logical direction from which to expect an attack? When was he to expect the attack? Kimmel could hardly keep his fleet at sea in combat readiness indefinitely.

Perhaps the most ironic aspect of Kimmel's ignorance in the matter is that he had at hand personnel capable of breaking Yoshikawa's code and reading his messages. The Communications Intelligence Unit at Pearl Harbor could have broken the consular ciphers (encrypted in a lower-grade code than the ambassadorial Purple traffic) but confined its attentions to Japanese naval codes until just before December 7. By then it was too late to decrypt the consular messages in time for the attack. The undeciphered consular messages were forwarded (by mail) to Washington for decryption and translation by the Magic team there.[26] The Magic team, in turn, usually set aside the consular traffic while they worked feverishly on the higher-priority Purple messages. One of the Magic cryptanalysts recalled the working atmosphere:

> The agency was simply too small and too exhausted. . . . Our eyes were red and glazed; exhaustion and dream consciousness had overcome us months before the event. . . . Had these [critics] been among us and seen how buried we were in stacks of messages through the "Purple" machine which had . . . priority, they would not wonder that we failed to process and translate a few messages [in the consular code].[27]

While the Magic team worked itself into "dream consciousness," other specialists within a few minutes' walk of Kimmel's office were searching for specific clues to Yamamoto's intentions. Commander Joseph Rochefort, chief of the Communications Intelligence Unit and one of the navy's preeminent cryptanalysts, concentrated his efforts on the signals exchanged among the units of the Japanese Navy. The Japanese naval code system (JN 25) proved more difficult to break than the Purple code, and in the weeks before Pearl Harbor Rochefort and the Pacific Fleet staff relied on traffic analysis. By this process intelligence experts deduced the origins and addressees of signals by combining the monitoring of coded messages with known information on the location of various units. Traffic analysis involved the painstaking comparison of large volumes of coded messages and yielded only rough "guesstimates" on the activities of the Japanese fleet. It was much like trying to deduce the nature of postal correspondence by examining envelopes.

The Japanese usually changed their call signs every six months, but after a routine change on November 1 they changed again on December 1.[28] Under these frustrating conditions Rochefort's unit, using techniques such as circuit analysis (establishing the command relationship between stations using a given frequency) and identifying the "touch" of individual operators, could read perhaps 10 percent of the traffic volume carried on the communication circuits of the Japanese Navy.[29] It is not surprising, then, that signal intelligence failed to yield the whereabouts of Nagumo's First Air Fleet as it plunged through the North Pacific swells.

The best guess Rochefort could manage at this point was that at least one division of Nagumo's carriers was in the Marshalls. On December 1, ONI mistakenly placed the carriers in Japanese home waters. On the same day the Pacific Fleet intelligence officer, Lieutenant Commander Edwin Layton, presented Kimmel with a report on the Japanese fleet which omitted any guess on the whereabouts of Carrier Divisions One and Two. Kimmel noticed the omission and asked Layton jokingly, "Do you mean to say that they could be rounding Diamond Head and you wouldn't know it?"[30]

The Japanese themselves may have muddied the airwaves with false transmissions. Although Rochefort disputed the assertion, the Japanese stated that operators in Japan continued to broadcast messages on the same circuits used by the First Air Fleet, making it appear that the force remained in home waters even as it was en route to Hawaii. The purpose was to confuse American radio direction finders and traffic analysis and thus contribute to erroneous estimates of the Japanese carriers' location.[31]

Navy intelligence, then, was not so much oblivious to the danger of a sudden outbreak of war as focused on irrelevant and incorrect signals that war would erupt at places other than Pearl Harbor. Intelligence historian Roberta Wohlstetter calls these misleading signals "noise," which she defines as irrelevant or false indications which may lead commanders to incorrect expectations about enemy plans.[32] The bewildering variety of signals and estimates pointing to imminent Japanese moves in China, Southeast Asia, and against the USSR diverted attention from the possibility that Pearl Harbor might be attacked. Although the Japanese attacked Southeast Asia and Pearl Harbor simultaneously, clues to their Southeast Asia plans must be considered noise because they served to divert attention from Hawaii.

4

THE ORANGE RACE

Noise may have misled the command authorities about Japanese strategy, but military officers in Hawaii were haunted by a more sinister vision. They were concerned to the point of obsession with threats of espionage, subversion, and sabotage by Hawaii's Japanese population. The Japanese constituted a large proportion of the islands' people; about two-thirds of them were Hawaii-born and hence American citizens. The remainder were ineligible for American citizenship, because U.S. law forbade the naturalization of Orientals.

That fixation was deeply rooted not only in the prevailing American racial stereotypes of the day but in the history of Hawaii's multiethnic society. Throughout the nineteenth century the nominally independent Hawaiian monarchy fell increasingly under the sway of its white residents, particularly the sugar planters and other businessmen descended from American missionaries. Though numerically insignificant, this class dominated Hawaii's politics, society, and economy from the mid-nineteenth to the mid-twentieth centuries. Its avowed goal was the annexation of Hawaii to the United States, and in 1898 that objective was achieved in the wake of the Spanish-American War.

Hawaii's sugar plantations required a plenitude of cheap labor, and the oligarchy looked to Asia to supply the work force upon which its wealth and power rested. From the 1880s to the early 1900s thousands of workers were imported from Japan. They were brought to Hawaii as contract laborers with little thought to the long-term implications of their presence. But by 1920 those implications began to become apparent. Industriousness and ambition led many Japanese immigrants and their children out of the fields and into middle-class occupations. And an alarming number, particularly of the second generation, had absorbed American ideas of equality and challenged the immutability of Hawaii's social and political order.

The impact of these trends was magnified by the sheer size of the Japanese community in the Territory of Hawaii. By 1940 it numbered 158,000 and accounted for nearly 40 percent of the territory's people. The interwar period was marked by a growing challenge to—and a sharpening response from—the hegemony of the islands' Caucasian elite. The challenge and response (albeit muted by Hawaii's tradition of congenial race relations) were manifested not only in demographics but in political, cultural, and economic terms as well.

Hawaii's white ruling class and the U.S. military officers stationed in the territory mixed freely and perceived a common interest in preserving the status quo. The local elite generally reinforced the outlook of the military officers of the 1920s and 1930s. Although there were notable exceptions, officers tended to reflect contemporary American racial attitudes and most regarded the Japanese in Hawaii as an unassimilable alien presence. American citizenship, length of residence, and overt manifestations of loyalty to the United States counted for little. They were viewed as a group inherently hostile to American interests and values, and a serious threat to the security of Hawaii.

As early as 1917, a navy officer at Pearl Harbor expressed a worry that was to become an important theme in Hawaii's civil–military relations:

> For the defense of Oahu, the present greatest menace to our security is the large proportion of population of foreign birth and sympathies who are very liable to turn against this country. . . .
>   There are fair hopes of making good citizens of all of the white population, but with the Japanese this can probably never be done.[1]

Certainly the size of the Japanese community boded ill for the continued political dominance of the oligarchy. The prospect of a Japanese majority at the polls alarmed Lieutenant Colonel George Brooke, chief of army intelligence in Hawaii in 1921. In a report to his superiors, he worried about the future in terms that reflected the predominant view among his fellow officers:

> It may be said that the majority of Japanese in this election who are able to vote, will vote for the Japanese Emperor or as he would desire them to vote. It should be realized that if present conditions continue

at the end of no great length of time the Japanese will exercise a controlling influence, through the ballot, on the affairs of this territory. It
may be expected their influence will be for the benefit of the Japanese
Empire rather than that of the United States.[2]

Culture, as well as politics, attracted the attention of those fighting
to keep Hawaii's Japanese in a subordinate position. The principal
venue of that effort was an attempt by the territorial government to
impose controls on private Japanese language schools. The language
school system provided instruction to large numbers of Japanese children after public school hours and served as an institutional focal
point for the Japanese community. The territorial government, however, saw the system as an obstacle to the Americanization of Hawaii's
nisei, and the legislature responded by enacting laws to regulate the
schools. This attempt at regulation was in fact a thinly disguised
move to give local authorities the power to abolish the Japanese language school system. The U.S. Supreme Court eventually declared
the legislation unconstitutional, but while the issue was alive it was
debated in terms which left little doubt that Hawaii's political leaders
saw it as a struggle to keep the islands under the American flag. The
military authorities viewed the question from a similar perspective. In
1922 Major W. T. Hoadley of the Pearl Harbor Marine Barracks confided to his superiors that the language schools were really nothing
less than indoctrination centers for the inculcation of loyalty to the
Japanese Empire. He also argued for their abolition as a means of
extirpating Japanese "habits, customs and morals," which he characterized as "vile."[3]

While the language school dispute illuminated white attitudes
toward Hawaii's Japanese, it was the threat of labor unionism on the
plantations that posed the greatest threat to the elite's continued
dominance. Their docility was among the supposed racial characteristics which had commended the Japanese and other Asian nationali-
ties to the planters in the first place. But when they began to organize
for higher wages and better conditions, they threatened not only
profits but the entire system of paternalistic control of Hawaii's economic foundation.

When Japanese plantation workers went on strike in 1920, military
officers in Hawaii entertained no doubts about the merits of the dispute. Army intelligence forged a close working relationship with the
employers' organization, the Hawaii Sugar Planters Association, and
in fact came to depend upon the association's industrial spy system as

a primary source of information about the Japanese community.[4] It should come as no surprise that the military attitude toward labor, especially Japanese labor, in the Territory of Hawaii was decidedly unfriendly. Colonel Brooke brooded about the implications of the strike with the thought that "the Laborers' Association [the Japanese plantation workers' union] constitutes an economic weapon distinctly adverse to Hawaii, as a territory of the United States."[5]

Military concerns about peacetime order and internal security naturally drifted to consideration of the role of the Japanese community in the event of war with Japan. Brooke, for one, was quite sure that the enemy had already attained a lodgement. "If Japan strikes," he wrote, "so far as this Territory is concerned, she is already in our midst."[6] His successors picked up the thread. One declared flatly, "In the event of war with Japan all Japanese, alien and Hawaii-born, of all ranks, should be considered as enemy aliens ab initio."[7] A 1921 navy plan for the defense of Pearl Harbor warned, "There is reason to believe that the Japanese population is well organized and in case of war, part of its mission will be to damage public and military utilities in Honolulu and at Pearl Harbor."[8]

In 1932 the racial animosities of the military garrison in Hawaii boiled over into hysteria. With the explosion of the Massie case, its worst fears about the islands' racially mixed population appeared to be confirmed. A navy officer's wife accused a group of nonwhite civilians of rape. When a local civilian court acquitted the defendants, navy vigilantes kidnapped and murdered one of the men. The vigilantes (including the rape victim's socially prominent mother) were tried and found guilty of the killing. They received lenient sentences, which they evaded with the collusion of the territory's highest civilian and military authorities.[9] These lurid events exposed the tensions and suspicions which marked the relationship between the military establishment and Hawaii's nonwhite majority. Admiral Yates Stirling, commander of the navy's Hawaiian Detachment, called for military rule to replace the limited self-government which Hawaii then enjoyed. He and sympathizers in Congress muttered darkly about the threat to national security posed by irresponsible natives and un-American elements within America's Pacific bastion.

Suspicion and hostility continued to be manifested throughout the 1930s. When Major General Hugh Drum, the Hawaiian Department commander, contemplated the possibility of a Japanese assault on Hawaii in 1935, he raised the specter of a surprise attack conducted or at least aided by the local Japanese:

We can enumerate [the] enemy's possible modes of action as including blockades, air raids, naval raids, air attacks, naval attacks, landings in force, local uprisings and sabotage or any combination of these. We can assume with some certainty that local uprisings will occur on all the islands of the territory and that the first enemy action will be attempted as a surprise.[10]

The Hawaii garrison was not alone in these views. They were shared at the highest levels of the Washington command echelon. President Roosevelt, to cite the most striking contemporary example, ordered Chief of Naval Operations Admiral William Leahy in 1936 to have the navy compile a list of Japanese-Americans who visited Japanese ships calling in Hawaiian ports. Those on the list, said FDR, should be put in "concentration camps" in the event of war.[11]

One member of Drum's staff had an even more radical prescription. Lieutenant Colonel George S. Patton, Jr., to achieve later fame as World War II commander of the Third Army, served as the Hawaiian Department's intelligence chief from 1935 to 1937. In an undated plan entitled "Initial Seizure of Orange [Japanese] Nationals," Patton named 128 prominent members of Hawaii's Japanese community to be taken hostage (his own word) at the outbreak of war.[12] What exactly did Patton mean by the term "hostage"? Since the plan gave no hint of his intentions regarding their ultimate fate, we can only guess. On at least one previous occasion Patton suggested shooting unarmed prisoners. In a prescriptive analysis of the suppression of the 1932 Bonus March, Patton recommended:

If you have captured a dangerous agitator and some misguided judge issues a write [sic] of Habeas Corpus . . . there is always danger that the man might try to escape. If he does see that he at least falls out of ranks before you shoot [him].[13]

Widely read and a prolific writer, Patton was no stranger to the nuances of language; his choice of words suggests strongly that he regarded the prisoners as bargaining chips whose lives would be forfeit at the discretion of U.S. authorities.

The plan did not specify who was to "ransom" the hostages or what conditions would have to be observed to ensure their safety. The hostage list itself, however, may provide some clues to Patton's assumptions and intentions. Ninety-five (roughly two-thirds) of the designated figures were Japanese citizens, which meant they were predominantly older men. (Only one woman appeared on the list.) An analysis of their professions indicates that the great majority were in high-status occupations: business, medicine, religion, education, politics, law, and publishing. Eight were on the staff of the Japanese consulate in Honolulu. The preponderance of older, prominent men indicates that Patton singled out the leadership of Hawaii's Japanese community. It suggests that the plan was intended to immobilize that community in the event of war, since it was unlikely that the Japanese Empire would be swayed in its strategic considerations by the taking of hostages. The plan reveals a streak of ruthlessness in its author, and, more important, it also constitutes another piece in the mosaic of military animosity toward Hawaii's Japanese, U.S. citizens and noncitizens alike.

Drum's successors, perhaps uncomfortable with the extremity of the proposal, relegated Patton's plan to cold storage in 1940. But military commanders in Hawaii continued to fear the worst from the territory's Japanese. The scenario for the 1940 departmental maneuvers presented a theoretical but highly detailed scheme of a fifth-column campaign by local Japanese.[14] It began with reports of Japanese prowlers in the vicinity of vital installations, escalating gradually to minor sabotage and passive resistance in the form of refusal to work. The imaginary campaign moved into an intermediate phase with the appearance of small organized groups of saboteurs, riots and street fights, the disappearance of sampans, and encoded radio communications from ham operators. More sharply focused activities followed: blockage of troop movements, sabotage and street riots on the Honolulu waterfront, and the secret arrival on Oahu of Japanese from other Hawaiian islands. The climax came with major disorders at Pearl Harbor and seizure of the territorial government.

The armed forces in Hawaii considered these possibilities a real threat. The Hawaiian Division devoted a section of its standing orders to a detailed plan earmarking units for various contingencies which might arise from a fifth-column campaign of sabotage or insurrection.[15] General Short confided to the War Department his worries about "the large percentage of aliens and citizens of doubtful loyalty on Oahu." They justified, he said, a special allotment of $240,000— as an initial installment—for the construction and strengthening of walls, fences, and floodlighting around key military facilities.[16]

Short and his subordinates recognized that Hawaii's Japanese were not an undifferentiated mass of hostility. They recognized that some, at least, would respond positively to fair treatment and prove loyal to

the United States if war came with Japan. The Hawaiian Depart-
ment, he reported, was "engaged in a counter-propaganda campaign
whose object is to encourage loyalty of the Japanese population of
Hawaii on promise of fair treatment."[17] He backed the campaign in
July 1941 when he urged the War Department to dissuade the Justice
Department from prosecuting a number of Japanese consular agents
who, because they had failed to register, were in technical violation of
U.S. law.

These agents, contrary to the suspicions of some, were not spies;
most were residents of remote local communities who served as inter-
mediaries between local Japanese and the consulate in Honolulu,
assisting in the registration of births and deaths and processing other
routine paperwork. An intensive FBI investigation of Hawaii's Japanese community in 1940 revealed that the principal duties of the consular agents were simply

> to aid the Japanese [dual citizens] between the ages of twenty and
> twenty-eight in filing their annual petitions for exemption from mili-
> tary service in Japan. . . . These Consular Agents also handle expatria-
> tion matters and communicate with Japanese governmental agencies
> and business houses regarding the business affairs of the Japanese
> laborer who is incapable of attending to these matters himself either
> because of illiteracy or lack of knowledge of procedure. . . . It appears
> that these Consular Agents are paid by the Japanese who utilize their
> services, in much the same manner as a public letter writer or an at-
> torney.[18]

Short pleaded: "Prosecution at this time would unduly alarm entire
population and jeopardize success [of] our current campaign to secure
loyalty [of the] Japanese population."[19]

The "counter-propaganda campaign," although founded on a
more realistic notion of Hawaii's Japanese, formed only a leitmotif in
the army's assessment of the community's loyalties. The navy, too,
shared the darker view. Captain Irving Mayfield, senior intelligence
officer for the Fourteenth Naval District, was convinced that there
were no really trustworthy Japanese in Hawaii; even those who held
U.S. citizenship were suspect in his eyes. Commander Harold Martin,
commanding officer of Kaneohe Naval Air Station, was so concerned
with the threat that he had his men lectured on the subject at the
weekly inspection on Saturday, December 6, 1941.[20]

When they felt it necessary, military officers had no compunctions about dispensing with legal niceties. Roland Smoot, manager of the Pearl Harbor Naval Shipyard before the attack, later recalled that, when it came to hiring practices,

> we did discriminate against the Japanese [-Americans]. It was difficult to do because of the way the Civil Service lists are made up. . . . The Japanese people out there wanted to know how come they were skipped. We just disregarded it. We just kept putting them down [at] the bottom of the list.[21]

It was natural, almost inevitable, that the army assessed the signals gleaned from Magic against the background of this preoccupation. As it became apparent that war was imminent, the War Department alerted the Hawaiian Department to the danger from within. On November 27, 1941, Miles cabled Lieutenant Colonel Kendall Fielder, the Hawaiian Department G-2:

> Japanese negotiations have come to a practical stalemate. Hostilities may ensue. Subversive activity may be expected. Inform commanding general [Lieutenant General Walter C. Short of the Hawaiian Department] and Chief of Staff only.[22]

Short replied the next day that army forces were alerted accordingly against sabotage. The War Department followed with more comprehensive instructions:

> Initiate forthwith all additional measures necessary to provide for protection of your establishments, property, and equipment against sabotage, protection of your personnel against subversive propaganda and protection of all activities against espionage.[23]

While military authorities scrutinized Hawaii's Japanese community for fifth columnists and spies, Takeo Yoshikawa, the lone Japanese Navy spy operating in Hawaii, continued his work from the Honolulu consulate. The consul general, Nagao Kita, cooperated fully and "Morimasu" acquired a reputation among the consulate employees (most of them ignorant of his true function) as something of a privileged character who kept irregular hours, drank freely, and did little work.[24]

Yoshikawa's activities required the use of few helpers, none of whom needed to know the significance or full extent of his activities. The only exceptions to his solitary modus operandi resulted from the need to establish an agent who could continue to function after the outbreak of war and the closing of the consulate. On October 25 Yoshikawa and Kotoshirodo visited Japan's sleeper spy in Hawaii, Bernard Kuehn. Kuehn was supposed to spy for the Japanese after the consulate was closed, but in fact never had the opportunity to perform the espionage duties for which he was greatly overpaid. Why the Japanese risked Yoshikawa's cover to meet with Kuehn is something of a mystery, but the meeting apparently went undetected by American counterintelligence.

Kuehn was a former German Navy officer, secret policeman, and Nazi Party member who immigrated to Hawaii in the 1930s and operated a succession of small businesses on Oahu. Over the years he had received a considerable amount of money from the Japanese government as a retainer. At the October 25 meeting Yoshikawa passed him $14 thousand in cash, a hefty sum for 1941. The Japanese got little value for their money, for Kuehn was something of a bumbler when it came to even the most elementary principles of espionage. He compromised his cover on a number of occasions when he openly visited the Japanese consulate—usually to ask for more money. It is not surprising to find him identified as a suspected "Nazi agent" by ONI as early as 1939.

The most the Japanese ever got from Kuehn was a scheme for a hopelessly complicated signal system (involving lights, classified advertisements, and sailboat markings) to be used to communicate with Japanese submarines off Hawaii once war broke out. The FBI arrested Kuehn immediately after the Pearl Harbor attack, whereupon he told all. He was tried for espionage and sentenced to death, but his sentence was commuted. Ironically, the consulate clerk who identified Kuehn to the martial law authorities described this Nazi superman as "Jewish looking."[25]

Kuehn and Yoshikawa are the only Japanese resident spies in Hawaii who can positively be identified from available documentation. Were there others? Despite reports of ubiquitous Japanese espionage networks, no evidence has surfaced to support allegations such as those made in 1942 by the army's Military Intelligence Division:

> There is no doubt that the Japanese population was very active in assembling . . . information for Japanese Intelligence. Their organization is so disciplined and deeply rooted that it defies detection.[26]

There remains, however, inconclusive evidence pointing to supplementary intelligence gathering on Oahu before the attack. Mrs.

Motokazu Mori, Honolulu stringer for a Tokyo newspaper, conversed by telephone with a journalist in Japan at 2:00 P.M. on December 3. The call was tapped by the FBI, which provided Short's intelligence staffers with a transcript. The text of the conversation was, on the whole, innocuous. But it did contain references to the numbers of uniformed personnel on the streets, aircraft movement patterns, and talk about different kinds of flowers in bloom, which may or may not have referred to ships in port.[27] Although Short and his subordinates were troubled by the conversation, which they considered highly suspicious, they (and subsequent investigators) believed there was insufficient evidence to conclude that the Mori call was part of an intelligence gathering effort.[28] Postwar interviews with Japanese naval intelligence officers indicate that transpacific telephone calls were used at least occasionally to collect information from sources in Hawaii. They say also that one such call was placed the day before the attack to ascertain the general tenor of military alertness in Hawaii.[29] It may well be that Mrs. Mori's conversation was innocent, or that if she did provide intelligence information she did so unknowingly. The evidence is inconclusive.

Regardless of the numbers or quality of its agents in Hawaii, the Japanese Navy considered intelligence for the Pearl Harbor attack too crucial to be left entirely to agents in the field. The importance of the operation demanded that planners from the Navy General Staff travel to Hawaii personally to check the scene. Lieutenant Commander Suguru Suzuki, an airman in the general staff's intelligence section, was dispatched with two other officers in October. They traveled incognito aboard the liner *Taiyo Maru,* one of the last vessels to make the voyage between Japan and the United States before the war. Suzuki assumed the identity of the ship's assistant purser when it sailed from Yokohama on October 22.[30]

The voyage of *Taiyo Maru* was a dry run which followed the First Air Fleet's route across the northern Pacific. Suzuki and his colleagues made frequent readings of the weather and sea conditions. They were constantly on the lookout for U.S. air and sea patrols, paying particularly close attention to signs of American alertness as they approached Oahu. When they docked in Honolulu on November 1 the naval officers remained aboard ship: It would hardly do to have their cover stripped away with plans so well advanced. Suzuki claims to have viewed Pearl Harbor from *Taiyo Maru*'s bridge, but the 6-mile distance between Honolulu Harbor and Pearl Harbor makes it unlikely. He did, however, hand Consul General Kita an extensive questionnaire containing about 100 queries on Pearl Harbor and its defenses. Kita took the questionnaire back to the consulate, where Yoshikawa provided answers in detail. Kita returned to the liner with Yoshikawa's written replies, taking care to conceal the material when he passed the customs officers who screened everyone boarding and leaving the vessel.[31]

The Japanese intelligence effort in Hawaii was characterized by diligence rather than daring, by precision rather than mass organization. Despite the apprehensions of Hawaii's military defenders, there were no efforts to organize the Japanese community into a fifth column for espionage, sabotage, or insurrection. In their mistaken assumptions about the loyalty of Japanese-Americans, U.S. military officers elevated genetic accident to the level of political principle. Their fears stemmed not from the objective circumstances but from the racial attitudes common to white Americans of that era. Those views were reinforced by the colonial elite whose preeminence was threatened by the empowerment of the Japanese community.

Did the obsession with the "Orange race," as Patton termed Hawaii's Japanese, contribute to an inward-looking fixation that diverted attention from the danger of an overseas attack? It is difficult to establish a direct causal relationship between unpreparedness and the obsessive concern with fifth columnists, but Hawaii's military defenders clearly were braced for an attack directed through the agency of the Japanese community.

Institutional expectations can easily become focused on one alternative at the expense of others, and the tendency is particularly pronounced in institutions, such as the military, which seek unambiguous definitions of objectives, obstacles, and means. The supposed threat of Hawaii's Japanese community fit neatly into an imagined pattern which accommodated those institutional proclivities and the racial attitudes of the time and place.

Japanese workers began arriving in the late nineteenth century to provide labor for Hawaii's lucrative sugar industry. They and their children, American citizens by birth, posed a challenge to the continued domination of the territory's Caucasian elite. U.S. military officers viewed Hawaii's Japanese as a fifth column in the midst of America's Pacific bastion. (Hawaii State Archives photo)

Admiral Husband E. Kimmel (center), Commander-in-Chief of the U.S. Pacific Fleet. Kimmel is flanked by his operations officer, Captain Walter Delaney (left), and chief of staff, Captain William "Poco" Smith (right). They study a map of the Atlantic Ocean, symbolizing their dilemma as resources are drained from the Pacific to prepare for war with Germany. (National Park Service photo)

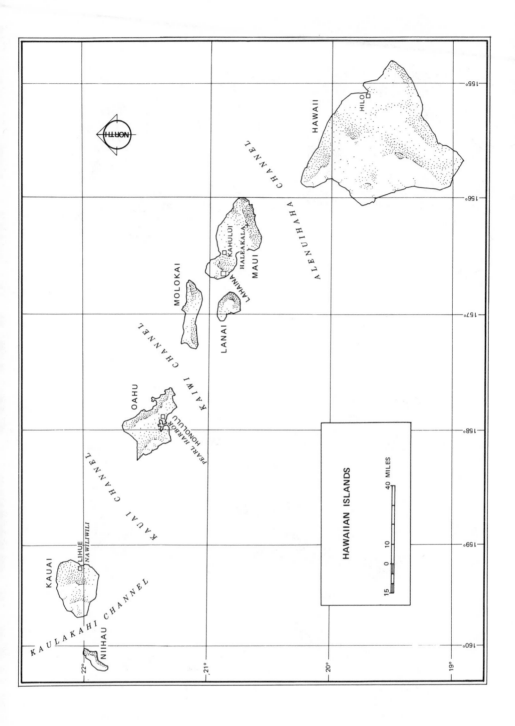

NORTH

KAUAI
NIIHAU
LIHUE
NAWILIWILI
KAULAKAHI CHANNEL
KAUAI CHANNEL

OAHU
PEARL HARBOR
HONOLULU
KAIWI CHANNEL

MOLOKAI
LANAI
LAHAINA
KAHULUI
HALEAKALA
MAUI
KALOHI CHANNEL

ALENUIHAHA CHANNEL

HAWAII
HILO

HAWAIIAN ISLANDS

15   0   10   40 MILES

General George Marshall, U.S. Army chief of staff. Marshall proved no more prescient about Japanese intentions than any other senior U.S. officer, but his organizational skills and leadership were essential to Allied victory in World War II. (U.S. Army photo)

Lieutenant General Walter C. Short, commander of the army's Hawaiian Department. Like Kimmel, he was blamed for U.S. unpreparedness and relieved of command. (National Park Service photo)

Admiral Harold Stark, chief of naval operations. His instructions and advice to Kimmel were often opaque and contradictory. Although Stark was not officially disciplined in connection with Pearl Harbor, he was quietly relieved and transferred to command of U.S. naval forces in the European Theater. (U.S. Naval Historical Center photo)

Rear Admiral Claude Bloch, commandant of the Fourteenth Naval District. The awkward command structure in Hawaii subordinated Bloch to the Pacific Fleet commander at Pearl Harbor while making him the counterpart of the senior army officer in Hawaii. (U.S. Naval Historical Center photo)

Rear Admiral Patrick Bellinger, commander of Patrol Wing Two. His post-attack uncertainty about the location of Japanese carriers exemplified the confusion of the Pacific Fleet command in the scramble to locate and exact a measure of retribution from the First Air Fleet. (U.S. Naval Historical Center photo)

Rear Admiral Richmond Kelly Turner. His two-fisted style made him an effective commander of amphibious forces later in the war, but it rendered him ill-equipped to meet the subtler challenges of intelligence analysis before Pearl Harbor. (U.S. Naval Historical Center photo)

Admiral Osami Nagano, Japanese Navy chief of staff. Like most other Japanese admirals, Nagano was a reluctant convert to the Pearl Harbor attack proposal. Ultimately Yamamoto had to threaten resignation to convince his colleagues to accept the plan. (U.S. Naval Historical Center photo)

Vice Admiral Chuichi Nagumo. The commander of the First Air Fleet led his carriers from victory to victory until he met disaster at Midway. He died during the American invasion of Saipan in 1944, when he chose suicide over surrender. (National Park Service photo)

Rear Admiral Takajiro Onishi. He played a crucial role in the early planning of the Pearl Harbor attack, but unlike other Japanese admirals, he foresaw the fury of America's reaction to the blow. (U.S. Naval Historical Center photo)

Commander Mitsuo Fuchida, one of the Japanese Navy's most able pilots, was selected as air commander for the Pearl Harbor attack. His ability was an important factor in the successful execution of Yamamoto's plan. (Choshobo Company)

Commander Minoru Genda served in the key role of air staff officer for the First Air Fleet. His experience as a pilot and skill as a planner proved invaluable to Nagumo. (Choshobo Company)

Admiral Isoroku Yamamoto. The brilliant and charismatic commander of Japan's Combined Fleet was the architect of Japan's early victories in the Pacific. Nonetheless, he appreciated America's war potential and knew the best Japan could hope for was a negotiated peace. (National Park Service photo)

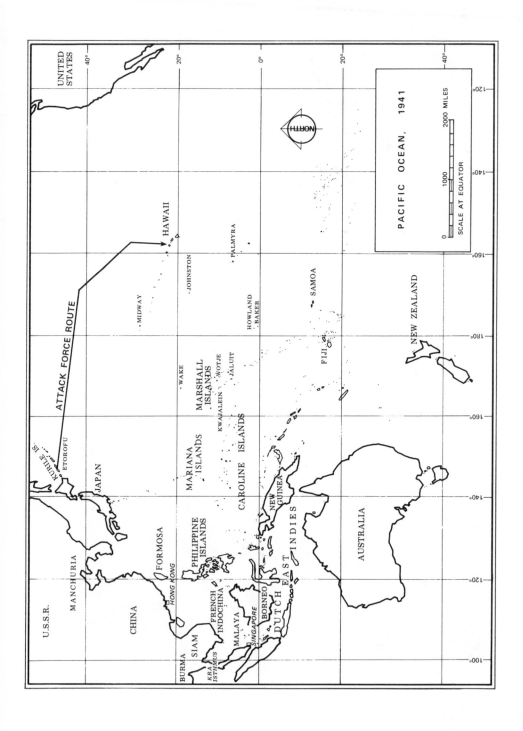

PACIFIC OCEAN, 1941

This photo taken from *Akagi*'s stern shows *Kaga* (left) and *Zuikaku* as the carriers make their way through the heavy seas of the North Pacific. *Kaga*'s central elevator structure is clearly visible. (Choshobo Company)

Ships of the First Air Fleet as they prepare to depart for Hawaii. Note the airman in left foreground dressed for cold weather. This view was taken from *Akagi*'s flight deck, with *Kaga* immediately astern. (U.S. Army Museum of Hawaii photo)

Flight deck and island of *Akagi*, flagship of the First Air Fleet. (U.S. Army Museum of Hawaii photo)

Nagumo's fleet as it assembled at Etorofu in the remote Kurile Islands. From left to right: the battleship *Kirishima*, unidentified tanker, *Kaga*, and the battleship *Hiei*. (Choshobo Company)

The Japanese strike force takes off for Pearl Harbor. The cheering sailors know they are witnessing a historic event. (National Park Service photo)

5

A CLASSIC

MISUNDERSTANDING

n spite of their concern about internal security, army and navy commanders in Hawaii did prepare an interservice plan for joint protection of the islands against external attack.[1] The plan explicitly assigned responsibility to the army for protection of the Hawaiian Islands and their vital military bases against air attack. The army was charged with providing antiaircraft fire and fighter interception to repel air raids. Naval defense forces in Hawaii, under the command of Rear Admiral Claude Bloch, commandant of the Fourteenth Naval District, bore responsibility for conducting long-range air patrols which would spot any hostile forces long before they reached Hawaii. The underlying premise of the plan was that the Pacific Fleet should be free to execute its strategic assignments ranging over the vast expanse of the Pacific without undue concern over security in its principal anchorage.

On paper it was an adequate plan, but those assigned to carry it out were beset with the usual confusion, misunderstandings, and shortages which attend the execution of so many well-laid plans. Colonel Walter Phillips, Hawaiian Department chief of staff, betrayed a fundamental misunderstanding of the army's mission when he told congressional investigators, "We felt secure against a raid, particularly with the Fleet here."[2] He failed to grasp that the army was supposed to provide protection for the fleet while it was anchored in Pearl Harbor, not vice versa. Phillips later admitted, "I never knew what the Navy had [in the way of scout planes]," demonstrating ignorance of a vital element in Hawaii's defense equation.[3] Phillips' position was not some obscure and insignificant slot in the military bureaucracy; as Hawaiian Department chief of staff he coordinated the workings of one of the largest and most important military commands in the prewar army. Even General Short was seduced by the idea of the Pacific Fleet as Hawaii's first line of defense. According to one of his key aides, Short thought that the fleet and the outlying island bases (such as Wake and Midway) constituted a stronger shield than his own forces.[4] It was natural, then, that he would tend to discount the importance of the Hawaiian Department's responsibility for defending the islands from overseas attacks.

Even without the confusion at the command level, it was generally accepted that the physical resources were inadequate to defend Hawaii against serious attack. In a January 1941 assessment, Bloch and Richardson voiced their concern to Stark. The numbers and types of antiaircraft guns in the Hawaiian Department, they wrote, fell far short of the requirements to repel an air attack. The available interceptors were obsolete and too few. Even the 185 P-40s called for in the Hawaiian Air Force's plans (barely half that number were on hand on December 7) would be inadequate.[5] Richardson pleaded with Stark to provide the Fourteenth Naval District with forces "adequate for the protection of naval installations at Pearl Harbor and the Fleet units based thereon." That request tacitly acknowledged the unsatisfactory state of the current defense arrangements. Richardson's plea was to no avail; the limitations which prevented the army from fully equipping the Hawaiian Department applied equally to the navy.

Short and Kimmel got along well personally. They played golf together every other weekend and met at least once a week to discuss common concerns.[6] But personal cordiality could not substitute for institutional articulation. When planning was under way for the construction of a new headquarters building for the Pacific Fleet, the navy's senior construction officer wrote Kimmel suggesting that the building design include a joint command center to facilitate interservice operations. Kimmel, assigning a lower priority to such coordination, replied: "There is considerable doubt as to the practicability or necessity of combining the operating staffs of the Army and Navy in one building."[7] Kimmel justified his position in terms of his fleet's responsibility for waging war on the high seas, not in the restricted area of Hawaiian waters. To establish a joint operating facility, he wrote, "would have at least a psychological tendency to divert Fleet units to defensive tasks."[8]

Kimmel was preoccupied with his offensive mission. He understood his role in U.S. strategy, but he was obsessed beyond the point of prudence with the fleet's assignment to move against the Japanese in the Marshalls. Even after the war he maintained, "I felt, and I believe all the Navy felt, that the real mission of the Pacific Fleet was offensive, and I think that nothing has ever occurred to change that conviction in the minds of any responsible naval officers."[9]

Kimmel's preoccupation with his offensive role was reinforced by Washington. Although he had received worried inquiries about the safety of the fleet in Pearl Harbor, the focus of his correpondence with Admiral Stark was on the broader considerations of Pacific strategy. In a September 23, 1941, letter, for example, the CNO asked Kimmel: "Would it not be possible for your force to 'carefully' get some pictures of the Mandated Islands?"[10]

To the extent that Kimmel pondered the danger of a Japanese attack on his fleet in Hawaiian waters, he never settled definitively on any one direction from which such an attack seemed most likely. The greatest potential for surprise, he realized, lay in an attack from the north, but on some occasions, at least, he believed the greatest danger lay to the southwest, the direction of the nearest Japanese bases.

More important than the anticipated direction of an attack were Kimmel's expectations of what type of an attack the Japanese would mount should they strike Hawaii. Kimmel believed submarines would be the most likely instrument. Under Richardson's tenure as commander-in-chief the fleet had recorded a number of suspected submarine contacts in Hawaiian waters. Kimmel worried about the danger represented by those unproven but highly suspicious contacts and believed "an air attack on Pearl Harbor or anything other than a surprise submarine attack was most improbable."[11]

The perception of the submarine danger illustrates that it was not just interservice coordination and communication that was deficient. Even Kimmel's flag officers sometimes failed inexplicably to circulate information among themselves. Rear Admiral Patrick Bellinger, commander of Patrol Wing Two, was responsible for long-range air reconnaissance from Oahu and played a key role in the joint army/navy defense plan. Despite Kimmel's concern about the danger from Japanese submarines, Bellinger remained ignorant of the suspected submarine contacts prior to the Pearl Harbor attack.[12]

Bellinger may not have known of the submarine contacts, but he and his Army Air Corps counterpart, Major General Frederick Martin, were not oblivious to the possibility of surprise attack. In the spring of 1941 they prepared a plan for joint army/navy air operations for the defense of Oahu. The plan was premised on some very shrewd deductions about likely Japanese courses of action. Martin and Bellinger, looking at Pearl Harbor's vulnerability from their perspective as aviators, stated in their plan that the most likely method of attack was a surprise air raid by planes launched from carriers north of Oahu.[13]

Even nonairmen, including some in Washington, were momentarily discomfited by the possibility of an air raid. After the British raid on the Italian fleet at Taranto, Stark wrote Richardson on November 22, 1940, urging him to look into the possibility of installing anti-torpedo nets around the ships in Pearl Harbor. Richardson replied with misplaced confidence that the harbor was too shallow for torpedo launches. Admiral Bloch dispatched a more detailed reply to Stark:

> Considering . . . the improbability of such an attack under present conditions [and] the unlikelihood of an enemy being able to advance carriers sufficiently near in wartime in the face of active Fleet operations, it is not considered necessary to lay such nets.[14]

Not all senior officers shared Bloch's casual assumption that U.S. forces would enjoy the luxury of a declaration of war before having to worry about Japanese attacks. Colonel Philip Hayes (Colonel Phillips' predecessor as Hawaiian Department chief of staff) warned in the department's standing orders, "It is possible that a declaration of war upon the United States may be preceded by a surprise raid or attack on the Pearl Harbor Naval Base by hostile aircraft, submarines, or surface ships."[15]

Kimmel tended to downgrade the likelihood of an air attack and focused on the danger of a surprise blow by Japanese submarines. He testified: "We considered a massed submarine attack on the ships at sea in the operating areas [south of Oahu] as a probability. . . . We considered an air attack on Pearl Harbor as a remote possibility." Nonetheless, in September he ordered the planes of the fleet air units dispersed as a precaution against air attack.[16]

Perhaps one reason why military commanders in Hawaii seemed to minimize the danger of being caught by a surprise air attack was the new air warning radar system being phased into the islands' defense network. Radar in 1941 was a new invention still not fully emerged from the experimental stage. Although it was slated to be integrated with the interceptor command when fully operational, much work remained to be done before that stage was reached. The army Signal Corps, charged with putting the system on line, was still training operators and trying to establish radar sites throughout Hawaii when war came on December 7, 1941. Temporary mobile sets operated at six locations on Oahu (Fort Shafter, Opana, Kaala, Waianae, Kawailoa, and Koko Head), but transportation setbacks had delayed the arrival of components for permanent installations and the National Park Service objected to the placement of a station on Maui atop Haleakala, one of Hawaii's highest peaks.[17]

Even without these headaches the Air Warning Service (as the radar network was called) labored under serious handicaps. The major problem lay not in the technical difficulties to be expected in making operational any new system, but in the more fundamental lack of interservice and intraservice coordination which typified the U.S. commands in Hawaii. Radar was supposed to function as an adjunct to the interceptor command, but Air Corps involvement throughout 1941 was peripheral and Signal Corps officers found themselves, by default, in effective command. Army/navy cooperation was essential for air defense, but there was no effective liaison between the radar network and the navy. Admiral Bloch admitted he "had no definitive information on or before December 7 as to what the Army [sic] Warning Service was in fact doing."[18]

Another closely scrutinized aspect of the Pearl Harbor attack was the message traffic between Washington and the American commanders in Hawaii from November 27 to December 7. As Japanese preparations for the invasion of Southeast Asia became more obvious and the chances for a diplomatic settlement of Japanese-American differences continued to recede, the War and Navy Departments dispatched a series of signals to Kimmel and Short. Defenders of the two Hawaii commanders maintain that the messages were vague at best, misleading at worst, and withheld information that would have enabled the Pacific Fleet and Hawaiian Department to prepare for the coming attack.

On November 27 Admiral Stark cabled Kimmel:

This dispatch is to be considered a war warning. Negotiations with Japan looking toward stabilization of conditions in the Pacific have ceased and an aggressive move by Japan is expected within the next few days. The number and equipment of Japanese troops and the organization of naval task forces indicates an amphibious expedition against either the Philippines or Kra Peninsula or possibly Borneo. Execute an appropriate defensive deployment preparatory to carrying out the tasks assigned in WPL46. Inform district and army authorities. A similar warning is being sent by the War Department.[19]

Kimmel consulted his staff and senior subordinates regarding the warning. He also conferred with General Short. Kimmel then redeployed his available carrier units in accordance with plans that were already in motion and given additional urgency by the warning. With an enormous geographic area of responsibility the primary focus of his attention continued to be the vast extent of the Pacific. Among those Kimmel consulted about the warning was Vice Admiral William F. Halsey, commander of the Pacific Fleet Aircraft Battle Force and the fleet's senior air officer. He did not, however, consult with Admiral Bellinger, whose responsibility encompassed air reconnaissance of the approaches to Hawaii.[20]

Kimmel was aware, though, of the exposed position of the Hawaiian Islands and responded by strengthening the defenses of American-controlled islands west of Hawaii. On November 28 a task force consisting of *Enterprise* and escorting vessels left Pearl Harbor under Halsey's command. *Enterprise* carried a group of marine fighter planes to reinforce U.S. defenses at Wake, an exposed outpost closer to Tokyo than Pearl Harbor. Because of his consultation with Kimmel, Halsey was aware of the imminence of war. He placed his command, Task Force Eight, on a war footing: The ships observed radio silence and kept their aircraft fully armed.[21] Another carrier task force, organized around *Lexington,* left Pearl Harbor bound for Midway on a similar mission. Kimmel's third carrier, *Saratoga,* was on the West Coast for repairs.

Army correspondence between Washington and Hawaii during this period was more extensive than the navy's, but it left General Short even more in the dark than Kimmel. On November 27 Marshall cabled Short:

Negotiations with Japan appear to be terminated for all practical purposes with only the barest possibilities that the Japanese Government might come back and offer to continue. Japanese future action unpredictable, but hostile action possible at any moment. If hostilities cannot, repeat not, be avoided, the United States desires that Japan commit the first overt act. This policy should not, repeat not, be construed as restricting you to a course of action that might jeopardize your defense. Prior to hostile Japanese action you are directed to undertake such reconnaissance and other measures as you deem necessary, but those measures should be carried out so as not, repeat not, to alarm civil population or disclose intent. Report measures taken.[22]

On the same date General Miles wired the Hawaiian Department G-2: "Japanese negotiations have come to a practical stalemate. Hostilities may ensue. Subversive activities may be expected." The following day General Martin received a dispatch from Major General Henry ("Hap") Arnold, chief of the Army Air Corps. Arnold instructed Martin to guard against internal security threats.[23]

After consulting with his subordinates and with Kimmel, Short had no doubt that Washington considered the most immediate threat to be Hawaii's Japanese. Short put his troops on alert not against an external attack but against the danger of sabotage and other fifth-column activity. His orders included the massing of army aircraft into tight concentrations on the ground, where they would be easier to guard against saboteurs but easy targets for strafing aircraft. On November 28 he informed Washington of these actions in a terse message: "Report Department alerted to prevent sabotage. Liaison with Navy Reurad [regarding your radiogram number] four seven two twenty seventh."[24] Similar messages between the Hawaiian Department and Washington during the next several days confirmed the posture of alert against fifth-column activities.

The apprehension occasioned by the Magic intercepts intensified when, on the night of December 6, President Roosevelt received the initial parts of a fourteen-part Purple transmission. It contained the text of a Japanese note to be presented to Secretary of State Cordell Hull the next day. After reading the intransigent message the president told his adviser and confidant Harry Hopkins, "This means war." By that remark Roosevelt indicated not that the note foretold the time and place of the opening shots, but that the Japanese were giving notice that diplomacy had failed to maintain the peace. Still unanswered was the question of where and at whom the Japanese would strike. Roosevelt's chief worry at the time was that an attack on Dutch or British possessions would put the United States at an enormous strategic disadvantage without automatically triggering an American military response.[25] Clearly he shared the opinion of his military advisers that the first Japanese blow would fall in Southeast Asia.

While FDR and his advisers pondered the approach of war, Magic operators on the morning of December 7 (Washington time) intercepted and decoded a final series of messages from Tokyo to the Japanese ambassadors in Washington. A lengthy message to be delivered to the U.S. government, transmitted in fourteen parts, announced the Japanese government's conclusion that negotiations were futile and that further diplomatic efforts to resolve Japanese-American differences were hopeless. The message, to all intents and purposes, broke relations between the two countries and signified Japan's intention to resort to war to achieve its aims. The message concluded: "The Japanese Government regrets to have to notify hereby the American Government that in view of the attitude of the American Government it cannot but consider that it is impossible to reach an agreement through further negotiations."[26]

That message was followed within a matter of minutes by an instruction from Tokyo to submit the message "at 1:00 P.M. on the 7th, your time [7:30 A.M. Hawaii time]."[27] These intercepts galvanized the Magic staff working that Sunday morning. Officers on duty realized that the situation required an urgent warning be dispatched to the Hawaiian Department and other commands, but neither General Marshall (who was horseback riding) nor any other officer with enough seniority to approve such a dispatch was available that Sunday morning. Aides finally located the chief of staff and told him of the urgent situation. After conferring with Admiral Stark, Marshall dispatched a message to Short shortly before noon (about 6:30 A.M. Hawaii time):

> Japanese are presenting at one pm Eastern Standard Time today what amounts to an ultimatum. . . . Just what significance the hour set may have we do not know but be on the alert accordingly. Inform naval authorities of this communication.[28]

Bad luck and atmospheric conditions conspired at that point to deprive Marshall of the speediest means of transmission to Hawaii. Because the radio army circuit between Washington and Honolulu had faded out that morning, Colonel Edward French, chief of the War Department's Signal Center, relayed the message via Western Union and RCA. It was received by the RCA office in Honolulu at 7:33 A.M. An RCA messenger wasted little time in setting out for Hawaiian Department headquarters at Fort Shafter, but he was caught en route by the Japanese attack. Snarled traffic, general chaos, and roadblocks delayed delivery until 11:45; by then the last Japanese planes were winging back to their carriers.[29]

About 1:30 P.M. on December 7 (8:00 A.M. Hawaii time), Secretary Knox, apprised that Japan was about to break off talks with the United States, was meeting with Stark and Turner. They were interrupted by an officer with a dispatch from Pearl Harbor: "Air Raid on Pearl Harbor. This is not a drill." Knox telephoned the White House. Roosevelt received the news grimly and called Secretary Hull, who waited in his State Department office for Ambassadors Saburo

Kurusu and Kichisaburo Nomura. Hull, like Roosevelt and Knox, knew from the Magic intercepts what the envoys would say. Roosevelt advised him, on the slight chance that the news might not be true, to receive Kurusu and Nomura, listen to what they had to say, and make no intention of the attack.[30]

The envoys brought the note to Hull's office more than an hour late. The secretary pretended to skim the contents. Then, making no mention of the news from Hawaii, he denounced the message in scathing terms. He dismissed Nomura and Kurusu by characterizing the note's attempt to justify Japan's position as "infamous falsehoods and distortions on a scale so huge that I never imagined until today that any Government on this planet was capable of uttering them." The timing of the delivery was later used to portray the Japanese as a treacherous foe who attacked while still engaged in negotiations. Hull himself, however, acknowledged that the late delivery was a result of "ineptitude." Still, it strains credulity to believe that the Japanese thought thirty minutes a meaningful pause between breaking relations and an act of war.[31]

That element of surprise viewed against the background of Magic and the warnings to Hawaii, were guaranteed to generate recriminations about responsibility for American unpreparedness at Pearl Harbor. The warnings illustrate the assumptions, policies, and reasoning of responsible officers and officials in Washington and Hawaii. They form the basis of indictments which have been leveled against Short, Kimmel, Roosevelt, Marshall, Stark, Turner, and others. It is therefore appropriate to make some observations about these messages and the reactions they engendered.

Stark's dispatch to Kimmel was explicitly a "war warning." Did the use of these words place responsibility on Kimmel's shoulders alone for the subsequent disaster? Such an interpretation would be unreasonable in light of the warning's references to Japanese moves under way against the Philippines, the Kra Peninsula, and Borneo. The warning was devoid of cautionary references to his vulnerable position in Pearl Harbor and it had the effect of diverting his attention to a theater of operations thousands of miles distant from Hawaii.

The instruction to "execute an appropriate defensive deployment preparatory to carrying out the tasks assigned in WPL46 [WPPac-46]" also requires a closer look. What Stark meant by this sentence and how Kimmel interpreted the words is far from clear. Of the principal tasks assigned to the fleet by WPL46, the only one for which a Pearl Harbor base was advantageous was the limited offensive against

Japanese bases in the Marshalls. The most reasonable interpretation of the wording would be that Kimmel was instructed to prepare his fleet to attack the Marshalls while simultaneously keeping them in a tactically defensive posture. The problem with Stark's instructions is that they were contradictory: Offensive preparations required concentration of the fleet, and concentration made it vulnerable to attack.

Kimmel's testimony regarding his own interpretation of "appropriate defensive deployment" sheds little light on the subject. It was, he said,

> a strategic matter, not a tactical matter. It was a strategic defensive employment—I mean our understanding was—and that was primarily to make sure that when we deployed the fleet, or put them in any position, that they would not take on an offensive character or anything that the Japanese could consider offensive.[32]

These words only add to the confusion. The original rationale for basing the fleet at Pearl Harbor was to menace the Japanese, so the obvious "strategic defensive" deployment would have been redeployment to the West Coast, and clearly neither Kimmel nor Stark contemplated such a move.

The subject can be argued ad nauseum, but the most important point is that Kimmel's instructions were unclear and he did not insist on clarification. Even if there had been clearer instructions, it is questionable how much better prepared the Pacific Fleet would have been. When Kimmel received the warning he did not consult Admiral Bellinger, the officer in charge of long-range air reconnaissance at Pearl Harbor. When Kimmel conferred with Short after the November 27 warnings, Captain Charles McMorris, Pacific Fleet war plans officer, told them that the chance of a Japanese surprise attack on Hawaii was "none." Even though Kimmel was—in terms of his personal relations with Short—conscientious about army/navy cooperation, he was not aware that the army alert was for sabotage only (despite the fact that the Hawaiian Department had previously given Admiral Bloch copies of its standing alert orders).[33]

The army, too, was beset by confusion and misapprehension. Short's sabotage alert culminated years of obsession with the imagined danger posed by Hawaii's Japanese. Well-conditioned reflex caused the Hawaiian Department to react unquestioningly to Marshall's warning of November 27 by mobilizing against the imagined internal threat. Short correctly interpreted as approval the War

Department's silence when he informed Washington on November 28 that his forces were on sabotage alert.[34] The comfortable circle of unexamined assumptions came a full 360 degrees when Short failed to make sure that Kimmel understood what type of alert he had ordered for the Hawaiian Department.

Underlying the failure to consider a Japanese naval attack on Pearl Harbor as an imminent danger was a consistent and long-standing depreciation of Japan's military capabilities and willingness to take the risks involved in an attack on Pearl Harbor. Admiral Bloch, for one, believed that the limited fuel capacity of Japanese warships would make it impossible for them to approach Hawaii without being detected. General Short thought that, since Japanese forces were obviously preparing to invade Southeast Asia, they would have to commit all their military assets to that theater.[35]

Japanese pilots were considered no match for Americans. They were thought to have genetic tendencies toward myopia and defective inner ear tubes, which affected their sense of balance. Japanese aircraft, too, were scorned. Most Americans, if they thought at all of Japanese planes, thought of flimsy underpowered machines of bamboo and fabric. In fact, the Zero fighter had been introduced into combat in China in 1940 and its successes were widely reported in the Japanese media and by Western observers.[36] Despite these reports, the stereotypes held sway and most Americans who pondered the possibility of war with Japan predicted a quick and easy victory.

Vice Admiral Wilson Brown, commander of the Pacific Fleet Scouting Force, believed that "Japanese fliers were not capable of executing such a mission successfully, and . . . if they did, we should certainly be able to follow their planes back to their carriers and destroy the carriers so that it would be a very expensive experiment."[37] More fundamentally, Brown and his peers assumed that the Japanese would, after considering these risks, come to the same conclusions as Americans. That assumption was a classic case of cross-cultural misunderstanding. An American officer in Yamamoto's position might have been told, "Go ahead and resign; we won't jeopardize our carriers for your pet idea." Japanese culture, however, assigns a higher priority to organizational harmony, and that factor had undoubtedly played a crucial role in the general staff's capitulation to Yamamoto.

General Miles, chief of army intelligence in Washington, expressed the thinking of senior American officers in these words:

We did grant the Japanese the best of good sense. We did very much question whether he would attack Hawaii, because such an attack must result from two separate decisions on the part of the Japanese, one to make war against the United States, which we thought at that time in the long run would be suicidal, as has since transpired, and, two, to attack a very fortress and fleet, risking certain ships that he could not replace, and knowing that the success in that attack must rest very largely on that surprise being successful; in other words, in finding that fortress and fleet unprepared to meet the attack.[38]

Roberta Wohlstetter put it more succinctly:

The Japanese and American estimates of the risks to the Japanese were identical for the large scale war they had planned, as well as for the [Pearl Harbor attack]. What was miscalculated was the ability and the willingness of the Japanese to accept such risks.[39]

With their flawed perceptions and estimates, the principal American actors had set the stage for disaster. The disposition of the Pacific Fleet reflected their assumptions and plans. On the morning of December 7 there were 103 vessels (not counting miscellaneous yard craft) of the Pacific Fleet in Pearl Harbor. This number included eight battleships, two heavy cruisers, six light cruisers, forty-three destroyers, and four submarines. Another 106 of Kimmel's ships were dispersed at other locations in the Pacific ranging from Alaska to the Peruvian coast to the Solomon Islands.

Of the major units absent from Pearl Harbor, the battleship *Colorado* was at Puget Sound; *Saratoga* remained in California; *Lexington* was off Midway delivering planes for the garrison there; and *Enterprise* was about 150 miles west of Oahu steaming homeward toward Pearl Harbor after delivering planes to Wake. Halsey's *Enterprise* Task Force, which included three cruisers and eight destroyers, had actually been scheduled to arrive at Pearl Harbor before the attack began, but heavy weather had slowed the force's progress. *Lexington*'s Task Force Twelve included three cruisers and five destroyers. Task Force Three, consisting of the cruiser *Indianapolis* and five destroyers, was engaged in training near Johnston Island, about 800 miles southwest of Oahu.[40]

Kimmel had gathered nearly half his fleet at Pearl Harbor. He felt forced to do so because of the necessity of concentrating the ships to prepare for wartime operations and because of the logistical difficulties of operating so far from his sources of fuel. He testified: "The thing that tied the fleet to the base more than any other one factor was the question of fuel. I tried to operate more ships at sea and found I could not do it because I was depleting the fuel supply at a time when it was imperative that we bring this fuel supply up."[41] If the disposition of his forces worried Kimmel, he was just as concerned about the readiness of the crews who manned the ships. The 46,000 sailors in the Hawaii area included many reservists recently called to active duty. Many had never heard a gun fired in practice, let alone in anger. In fact, the Pacific Fleet, testified Kimmel, had had no main battery practice for more than a year.[42]

The Pacific Fleet units in Pearl Harbor, however, were not entirely unready. They stood in a state of readiness which required about one-fourth of all antiaircraft guns to be manned at all times. Overnight liberty was restricted to those above the rank of first class petty officer. In general, although Kimmel judged the training of his crews to fall short of the standards which would be required in combat, discipline was good.[43]

The army's Hawaiian Department was in a similar state of unreadiness, only partially ameliorated by a general awareness that hostilities were imminent. The department had a total of 43,000 officers and men (including recently activated National Guard regiments) on the eve of the December 7 attack. The great majority were stationed on Oahu, with the 20,000 troops of the twenty-fourth and twenty-fifth Infantry Divisions at Schofield Barracks comprising nearly half the total. In the critical area of antiaircraft defenses Short commanded eighty to ninety (sources conflict) 3-inch guns (about 70 percent of which were mobile), twenty 37-millimeter guns, and slightly more than a hundred .50-caliber machine guns. Fixed 3-inch batteries at coastal defense installations had ammunition on hand, but it was kept crated to prevent deterioration. Ammunition for the mobile 3-inch batteries (based at Camp Malakole, Schofield Barracks, and Fort Shafter) was stored several miles away in underground shelters at Aliamanu Crater.[44]

The three services had 394 planes in Hawaii when the Japanese struck on December 7.[45] Nearly all were on the ground, unarmed, and with empty fuel tanks. Of the army's 232 aircraft nearly half were obsolete or unsuitable for combat. Bomber strength was concentrated at Hickam Field, adjacent to Pearl Harbor; it consisted of twelve B-17 heavy bombers, twelve A-20 attack bombers, thirty-three obsolete B-18 medium bombers, and a scattering of miscellaneous types. The mainstay of the army's fighter squadrons was ninety-nine P-40s;

thirty-nine obsolete P-36s and fourteen ancient P-26s rounded out the interceptor strength. Most of the fighters were at Wheeler Field in central Oahu, with two squadrons temporarily based at Haleiwa and Bellows Fields.[46]

Navy and Marine Corps air strength totaled 162 aircraft. There were seventy-one reconnaissance patrol planes, divided nearly evenly between Ford Island Naval Air Station and the new air station at Kaneohe Bay on the opposite side of Oahu. Most of the navy's fighters and bombers were at sea with the carrier groups, but Ford Island held twelve F4F fighters and three SBD dive bombers. At the marine airfield at Ewa, west of Pearl Harbor, were twelve F4Fs and thirty-two SBDs. The navy patrol planes, too few to conduct daily long-range flights covering a 360-degree sector around Oahu, had searched south and southwest of the island the day before and lay placidly at anchor and on their airfields as dawn broke on December 7, 1941.[47]

II

THE ATTACK
ON BATTLESHIP ROW

6

THE APPROACH

While U.S. commanders in Hawaii and officials in Washington fretted over Japanese intentions, Admiral Nagumo's First Air Fleet had been under way since November 26. Upon secrecy, more than any other factor, hinged the success of the fleet's mission. To reduce the chance of being spotted at sea, Nagumo sent no planes aloft during the voyage.[1]

At first the seas were relatively calm, considering the season and latitude. After December 4 (Tokyo time) the weather worsened and some of the ships rolled as much as 45 degrees in the heavy swells. Nagumo varied his formation according to weather conditions. Generally a line of four destroyers took the lead, followed by the heavy cruisers *Tone* and *Chikuma*. At the heart of the formation steamed the six carriers in two columns. *Akagi* led the starboard column, followed by *Kaga* and *Shokaku; Soryu, Hiryu,* and *Zuikaku* sailed to port. The tankers and remaining destroyers were scattered throughout the formation. The three submarines, originally to be deployed as advance scouts, stayed at the heart of the fleet (where they would be of little use) because of low visibility conditions. The battleships *Hiei* and *Kirishima* brought up the rear.[2]

The progress of the force was dictated by the maximum speed of its slowest ship, the tanker *Toei Maru* (16 knots). The fleet proceeded at a stately 12 to 14 knots, slowing to 9 knots for the tricky business of refueling at sea. Despite the relatively good weather at the beginning of the voyage, several seamen were swept overboard when securing cables snapped during refueling. The destroyers, having limited fuel capacity, required daily replenishment, while *Soryu* (which returned to Japan with less than 100 tons of oil) and *Hiryu* each carried an additional 700 tons of fuel in barrels stored on deck. Bucket brigades fed the oil to the engines during the final dash to the launch point.

As the fleet approached Hawaii the tankers *Toho Maru, Toei Maru,* and *Nihon Maru,* escorted by the destroyer *Arare,* dropped out of formation on December 4 (Hawaii time) to wait for rendezvous with the main body on its return home.[3]

Important as they were, fuel supply and navigation were not Nagumo's main worry. The all-important question of secrecy was uppermost in his mind. He could do little to prevent an accidental encounter with a stray warship or merchantman, but he could and did impose strict radio discipline on his ships. The removal of vital parts made transmitters inoperative, and the ships communicated with one another by means of signal flags and blinker lights. *Hiei,* which had the best reception, picked up radio messages from Tokyo and relayed them by flag and blinker to the other vessels.[4]

The question of radio silence is important. Revisionist writers have claimed that the First Air Fleet betrayed its progress to American radio interceptors, who conveyed it to the highest U.S. authorities, and those authorities prevented the dispatch of timely warning to Hawaii. Commander Genda insisted in a 1947 interview that radio silence was absolute. One of Nagumo's communications staff officers, Lieutenant Commander Chuichi Yoshioka, also survived the war and maintains that radio silence was in force throughout the voyage to Hawaiian waters. A number of former Japanese naval officers who participated in the attack have told me that no radio signals—not even low-powered "talk between ships"—were transmitted. In the face of such authoritative testimony and the lack of positive proof that the Americans intercepted signals from the First Air Fleet, the preponderance of available evidence indicates that Nagumo was successful in preserving radio silence.[5]

A final and most telling point is the discipline, dedication, and spirit of self-sacrifice which prevailed in the Imperial Japanese Navy. Everyone in Nagumo's force with access to a transmitter was instructed on the subject of radio silence and understood the need for it. It is difficult to believe that any Japanese officer or sailor would have broken radio silence, no matter how dire the necessity, and jeopardized the success of the mission and the fate of the empire.

Radio silence did not, however, prevent the fleet from receiving frequent messages from Tokyo relayed via *Hiei.* Nagumo got daily weather reports and frequent updates from Yoshikawa's intelligence reports (which first passed through the commercial cable, Foreign Ministry, and Navy General Staff). The task force commander received final confirmation on December 2 (Hawaii time) that Japan had abandoned efforts to settle with the United States and that he should proceed as planned. The code phrase "Climb Mount Niitaka" relieved any lingering doubts that Yamamoto's plan would be the opening shot in Japan's desperate strategic gamble.

Three days later, on December 5, the attack force made its sole encounter with another vessel. The Soviet freighter *Uritsky*, bound from Portland to Vladivostok, was too heavily laden to traverse the rough seas on a direct course, which would have skirted the Aleutians, so she followed a more southerly route which intercepted Nagumo's carriers. *Uritsky*'s radio remained silent as she passed under the muzzles of the Japanese guns, and the freighter failed to make the customary plain-language sighting reports once she was out of range.[6] The encounter suggests the intriguing possibility of Soviet foreknowledge of the attack and Japanese-Soviet collusion. Why did *Uritsky* not report the encounter once she was out of range? If she did, why did Moscow fail to inform the United States? The most compelling question arising from the incident is why the Japanese simply did not sink the merchantman. The stakes were so high that the risks attendant on that course would have been justified. These questions by no means prove that the Soviets knew of Japanese plans and had entered into an agreement to keep the secret in exchange for *Uritsky*'s safe passage, but the circumstances are, to say the least, anomalous. Through the Sorge spy ring, Moscow received information on some of the most secret deliberations of the Japanese government. Certainly, the cold calculus of Soviet interests would predispose Stalin to condone any arrangement which would keep the fragile peace between Japan and the Soviet Union.

These mysteries notwithstanding, Nagumo's luck held and the fleet continued undetected toward its objective. On December 4 a message from Tokyo brought the news that six battleships, eleven cruisers, and the aircraft carrier *Lexington* were in Pearl Harbor. Updated reports noted *Lexington*'s departure, and a final signal in the predawn darkness of December 7 brought the most important news of all: There was no activity to suggest that U.S. armed forces in Hawaii were preparing to meet a carrier attack. The Nagumo force received that welcome news when it was well under way in its high-speed approach to Pearl Harbor. On the morning of December 6, some 600 miles almost due north of Oahu, the fleet made a final refueling. The remaining tankers and destroyer *Kanami* then left the carriers. Shortly before noon the carriers and escorts swung south for the final run at 20 knots. This was the most critical period, the point at which discovery by patrolling American planes and ships was most likely. *Akagi* hoisted the famous "Z flag" which had flown during Japan's climactic victory over the Russian fleet in 1905. Also repeated were the words which had inspired Japan's sailors on that day: "The rise and fall of the Empire depends on this battle. Every man will do his duty."[7]

As the fleet sped toward its launch point, crewmen and pilots experienced a wide variety of emotions. Seaman Shigeki Yokota aboard *Kaga* felt "a little frightened." Seaman Masayuki Furukawa on *Shokaku* worried about the possibility of an American counterattack.[8] Enlisted men were not alone in their worries. Officers listened closely to the last-minute results of Yoshikawa's efforts as they came in over the radio. At 7:03 P.M., less than twelve hours from the launch, the Sixth Fleet submarine *I-72* radioed from Lahaina Roads that there were no warships in that anchorage. Some tuned in to radio station KGMB in Honolulu—broadcasting at the army's request past its normal operating hours to guide an incoming flight of bombers from California—listening for any sign of unusual military activity. They were reassured by the normal sounds of music and chatter.[9]

Just before dawn the carriers reached their launch point slightly more than 200 miles north of Pearl Harbor. At 5:30 two Type o reconnaissance seaplanes[10] took off from *Tone* and *Chikuma* to reconnoiter Lahaina Roads and Pearl Harbor respectively. At 5:50 Nagumo turned his ships east into the wind and increased speed to 24 knots. Captain Kiichi Hasegawa, *Akagi*'s skipper, laconically told the assembled pilots: "All right, all the plans are made, let's get going!" Shortly after 6:00 the carriers began to launch the first wave of 51 dive bombers, 40 torpedo bombers, 49 horizontal bombers, and 43 fighters. As these 183 planes winged southward under Fuchida's personal command they left behind two disappointed fighter pilots scheduled to accompany them. One had crashed into the ocean (he was rescued by a destroyer); the other was the victim of engine trouble.[11]

At 6:30 Nagumo launched sixteen additional floatplanes (four each from the battleships and heavy cruisers). They scouted the areas east, south, and west of the task force searching for American ships and aircraft. Discovery at this critical juncture would not only thwart the execution of the attack but would endanger the fleet's carriers.

As the sea became rougher the carriers launched the second wave shortly after 7:00. It included 77 dive bombers, 36 fighters, and 54 horizontal bombers. These 167 planes were followed by a protective cover of fighters which circled over the fleet during the attack. For the sailors of the First Air Fleet the long wait began.[12]

The fighters and bombers of the First Air Fleet were not the only carrier planes winging toward Pearl Harbor that morning. The *Enterprise* task force under Admiral Halsey had completed its delivery of fighter planes to Wake Island and was due in Pearl Harbor at 7:30 A.M. on Sunday. By what turned out to be one of the few strokes of good luck to befall U.S. forces that day, poor weather and refueling difficulties slowed Halsey's progress. Dawn found him still 150 miles west of Pearl Harbor.[13]

At 6:15 Halsey launched eighteen SBD Dauntless dive bombers from Scouting and Bombing Squadrons Six. They were to scout the area between Task Force Eight and Pearl Harbor and land at the naval air station on Ford Island. A two-plane flight led by the *Enterprise* air group commander, Commander Howard L. Young, sped off without delay toward Pearl Harbor. Young carried as a passenger Lieutenant Commander Bromfield Nichol, one of Halsey's aides. Nichol was to report immediately to Kimmel with an account of the delivery to Wake. (Halsey was still observing radio silence.) The rest of the planes assembled in formation and headed toward Pearl Harbor at 6:37 led by Lieutenant Commander Halstead Hopping of Scouting Squadron Six.[14]

At 7:20 Young spotted an unidentified ship headed east in the general direction of Oahu. He investigated and identified her as SS *Pat Doheny*, a Richfield tanker. Ten minutes behind his group commander, Hopping encountered the tanker at 7:30 and noted her position as approximately 50 miles south of Niihau. At 7:40 Young observed the submarine *Thresher*, escorted by the destroyer *Litchfield*, proceeding routinely. By 8:10 Young was abreast of Kaena Point at the northwest tip of Oahu. Anticipating a routine landing at Ford Island, he passed Barbers Point on the island's southwest corner at 8:20.[15]

As planes from *Enterprise* and the Japanese carriers converged on Oahu, two alert Americans spotted the raiders nearly an hour before they reached the island. Privates Joseph Lockard and George Elliott manned the isolated radar station at Opana overlooking the island's north shore. After completing their 4:00 A.M. to 7:00 A.M. duty shift Lockard agreed to give the relatively inexperienced Elliott additional instruction in operating the set while they awaited the truck which would take them to breakfast. No sooner had they begun when a large blip appeared on the screen. Lockard at first thought the set was malfunctioning, but he soon concluded his contact was a large flight 132 miles distant approaching Oahu from the north.[16]

Lockard's and Elliott's alertness availed the sleeping American forces nothing. Sometime between 7:00 and 7:30 Lockard phoned the information center at Fort Shafter. His call was answered by the center's telephone operator, Private Joseph McDonald, who told Lockard that the center had secured and everyone had gone to breakfast. Lockard, however, was concerned by the unusually large size of his radar contact and insisted on speaking with someone—anyone— in authority. After checking the building McDonald located Lieutenant Kermit Tyler.[17]

Tyler, a fighter pilot from the seventy-eighth Pursuit Squadron, was not regularly assigned to the information center but was simply there to spend a few hours for familiarization. Like everyone else connected with the Hawaiian Department's radar operation he was essentially a trainee. As he took Lockard's report he remembered listening to the same all-night KGMB broadcasts which had captured the attention of Nagumo's staff. He reasoned correctly that the broadcast meant an early morning arrival of U.S. planes from the mainland. Tyler concluded mistakenly that the Opana contact was the echo of that flight and told Lockard "not to worry about it." Lockard, uneasy over the size of the contact, was not reassured. He argued with the lieutenant "as far as [I] thought was reasonably safe," but gave up when Tyler refused to become concerned.[18]

The Opana radar sighting was not the only early contact between Japanese and American forces on December 7. In the predawn darkness just a mile and three-quarters south of the Pearl Harbor channel entrance the minesweeper *Condor* conducted routine sweeping operations. Ensign R. C. McCloy, officer of the deck, noticed what looked like a wave. He and Quartermaster Robert C. Uttrich studied the "wave" through binoculars for a few moments and decided they were looking at a periscope—in a restricted area where submerged submarines were automatically presumed to be unfriendly. Seaman Raymond B. Chavez, the helmsman, was not so sure. He could make out the wake about 50 yards away but not the periscope. At 3:57 A.M. *Condor* signaled news of the contact by blinker to the destroyer *Ward* on channel entrance patrol.[19]

Ward's skipper, Lieutenant William Outerbridge, ordered general quarters and began a search of the area. After a fruitless half hour he secured at 4:35. Outerbridge was awakened again at 6:37 by Lieutenant (jg) Oscar W. Goepner, officer of the deck. He reported a strange object following the supply ship *Antares,* which was towing a lighter toward the Pearl Harbor entrance. This time no doubt remained. Outerbridge clearly saw the conning tower and periscope of a small submarine just 50 yards away moving at a respectable 8- to 12-knot clip. At 6:40 Outerbridge gave the order to attack. The first shot from *Ward*'s 4-inch guns went high, but the second struck the intruder at the waterline junction of the hull and conning tower. The submarine heeled over to starbord and sank. *Ward* followed the shots with a depth charge attack, which yielded an oil slick from the 1,200-foot depths a mile south of the channel entrance.[20]

At 7:01 Outerbridge radioed Pearl Harbor: "We have dropped depth charges upon subs operating in defensive sea area." Fearing that his message might be ignored as just another inconclusive submarine contact report, he elaborated in another signal at 7:03: "We have attacked, fired upon, and dropped depth charges upon submarine operating in defensive sea area." The message began making its way up the chain of command to Admiral Kimmel.[21]

The destroyer was not alone in its early morning attack on the submarine. Ensign William Tanner, piloting one of four PBYs from Patrol Squadron Twenty-four on exercises that morning, spotted *Ward* bearing down on the sub. At first he thought it was a friendly submarine in trouble. After briefly weighing the painful alternatives, however, he opted to obey standing orders: Sink all unidentified submerged subs in the restricted area. After dropping depth charges he radioed his report into Patrol Wing Two headquarters on Ford Island. Like *Ward*'s signal, Tanner's message had to pass through many hands before anyone could take decisive action.[22]

7

AN UNOBSTRUCTED RUN

Shortly before 7:30 Kimmel received a call from his headquarters: *Ward* had reported sinking a submarine just outside the channel. While the admiral waited at home for confirmation, Fuchida's first wave used the morning KGMB broadcast as a homing beacon. At 7:35 the *Chikuma* scout plane pilot relayed the disappointing news that Pearl Harbor contained nine battleships, seven cruisers, but no carriers.[1]

Straining to see through the clouds which blanketed the ocean, Fuchida recalls, at 7:40 "a long white line of breaking surf appeared directly beneath my plane. It was the northern shore of Oahu."[2] Then occurred a mischance of war. To deploy his attackers Fuchida had arranged that one shot from his flare pistol would signal that surprise had been achieved and the vulnerable torpedo planes would attack first; two shots meant an alert defense and the dive bombers would make the initial strikes to disrupt the American defenses. Seeing no sign of U.S. planes or antiaircraft fire Fuchida fired one flare, but his squadrons failed to make the proper deployment. He repeated the signal. The torpedo planes saw only the second flare and deployed to open the attack. But the dive bombers had seen both flares and they raced into the lead to strike the first blow.

The bombers jockeyed for position in the confusion, but with the die already cast Fuchida radioed to his planes at 7:49: "*To, To, To*," the signal to attack. Four minutes later he signaled Nagumo: "*Tora, Tora, Tora*," the prearranged code message that the planes had achieved surprise. Incredibly, Fuchida's signal to Nagumo was heard on Admiral Yamamoto's flagship riding at anchor in Japan's Inland Sea.

Despite the mixup with the flares the attack was almost textbook perfect. Dive bombers and strafing fighters attacked U.S. air bases at

Hickam, Wheeler, Kaneohe, Ewa, and Ford Island at almost the same instant that the torpedo planes, divided into two groups, struck the anchorages fringing Ford Island. One group of sixteen torpedo-armed Kates flew straight south across Oahu aiming for the carrier berths on the west side of Ford Island. Another group of twenty-four crossed the southern shoreline, turned east, then inland once more over Hickam Field and the navy yard. They then crossed Pearl Harbor's main channel for an unobstructed run against the ships moored on Battleship Row on the eastern side of Ford Island.

As the attack began at 7:55 unbelieving Americans watched as bombs rained down on Hickam and Ford Island airfields while the low-flying Kates released their torpedoes against the ships. On Ford Island's west side *Utah*, moored in *Enterprise*'s usual place and possibly mistaken for a carrier by an inexperienced Japanese pilot, took two torpedoes. Another struck *Raleigh*, moored in line ahead. Both ships began to list, and the target ship capsized at 8:12 while *Raleigh*'s crew saved the cruiser by heroic damage control efforts.[3]

On the opposite shore of Ford Island torpedoes struck *Nevada, Arizona* (after running under the keel of the adjacent *Vestal*, according to witnesses), *West Virginia, Oklahoma,* and *California. Tennessee,* moored inboard of *West Virginia,* and *Maryland,* inboard of *Oklahoma,* escaped torpedo damage, as did the fleet's flagship *Pennsylvania* in Drydock One. At least one Kate pilot coming in from the west overshot Ford Island, passed over Battleship Row, and unleashed his torpedo at the navy yard docks. It passed beneath the venerable minelayer *Oglala,* moored at the long Ten Ten Dock, and exploded against the light cruiser *Helena* nestled between the dock and *Oglala.* The blast crippled the cruiser but did more damage to the unarmored minelayer, which began to list and capsized.

Aboard each ship the moment fragmented into thousands of individual experiences as each crewman responded to the events around him. Seaman Carl Lee, a mess cook aboard the rapidly listing *Utah,* began to make his way topside. On the way up he passed his locker, which had fallen over and spilled his possessions on the deck. He experienced for an instant a jolting sense of the fragility of life when he saw his mother's picture among the jumble of his belongings. He had no time, however, for philosophical reflection and continued up the ladder. When Lee reached the top he paused before climbing out onto the deck. He saw the heavy timbers which covered the ship's deck (to absorb the impact of practice bombs) being chewed to pieces by machine gun fire from Japanese strafers. Having second thoughts about the wisdom of taking that particular route topside, he retraced his steps down the ladder. On the second deck he passed the mess compartment where he worked and noted that the list had thrown mess tables, dishes, and soapy water into a chaotic mess against the port side of the compartment. Here, he thought, "was one mess I wasn't going to have to clean up."[4]

Others made similar life-or-death choices between the flooding interior compartments and the hazards above. Karl Johnson started down a ladder when the first torpedo hit *Utah;* he wanted to minimize flooding by securing the bilge manhole cover he had been working on. On his way down the second hit knocked him to the deck where he broke sixteen teeth. In the stress of the moment he felt no pain and continued down into the bowels of the ship. While still on the ladder a voice above him asked, "Where are you going?" Johnson looked up, but all he could see was a pair of dungaree legs above him. He told his unknown questioner he was on his way to the bilges, and the voice said, "Don't go down there, you'll get killed!" One look into the inky blackness below was enough to persuade him to start back up. Johnson never learned the identity of the shipmate whom he credits with saving his life with a simple question.[5]

Seaman Robert Johnson (no relation to Karl) was playing cards as he waited below decks for the summons to his coxswain's duties on a ship's launch. When the torpedoes hit, there was a mad scramble for the topside ladders; when the call came to abandon ship, the scramble became chaos. Donald Conley, a veteran sailor, kept his head and restrained Johnson. "Wait," he said, "or you'll get trampled to death." When the press cleared, the two climbed the ladder and emerged on deck.[6]

Conley saved Johnson once again as the youngster started around one of *Utah*'s turrets. A strafer was making a pass over the ship and would have hit Johnson had not Conley tackled him. When they approached *Utah*'s starboard side (the ship was listing heavily to port by then), they were confronted by the exposed hull. Johnson hesitated, saying, "We can't jump, we'll hit the side of the ship!" Conley insisted, so they jumped. Despite a few scrapes from the ship's bottom, the two made it into the water and swam for the safety of Ford Island.

Chief Watertender Peter Tomich stayed below decks, even when he realized *Utah* was capsizing. He remained at his post in the engineering plant to supervise the task of securing the boilers. After the boilers were secured Tomich made sure that all the fireroom crewmen were safely evacuated before attempting to leave. By then it was too late; Tomich was trapped below and perished with the ship.[7]

Another *Utah* sailor, Seaman John Vaessen, was on duty at an electrical switchboard below decks when he felt the first torpedo jar the ship. Knowing nothing of the attack, he assumed that another vessel had collided with *Utah* when his compartment began to flood. Vaessen knew that his switchboard was crucial in supplying lighting current for the ship, so he remained at his post until flooding shorted out the emergency batteries. As he began to make his way out of the compartment the ship rolled over.

Hanging onto hatches and any other fixed handholds within his reach, Vaessen escaped injury as fire extinguishers, steel deck plates, and other pieces of equipment crashed about him. Although he was trapped four decks below, he did not panic: By one of those strokes of luck which transmute inconvenience into good fortune, Vaessen knew the bilges and voids at the bottom of the ship intimately. As an electrician "striker" he had been assigned the dirty and uncomfortable work of stringing lights throughout those spaces for cleaning parties. To compound his luck he had a flashlight and found a wrench which matched the bolts securing the cover to the bilge. Vaessen made his way up to the bottom of the capsized *Utah* and began to hammer on the hull with all his strength.[8]

Aboard the neighboring *Raleigh* Ensign Donald Korn, the officer of the deck, was turning over the watch to his relief. With a launch alongside to take crewmen to divine service it appeared to be a normal Sunday morning when a cloud of planes appeared out of the northwest. Korn assumed it was an air raid drill and called for the antiaircraft batteries to be manned. Seaman Frank Berry pulled the alarm for general quarters when he saw a torpedo splash, but the alarm failed to go off. Captain Robert B. Simons was relaxing in his cabin enjoying a cup of coffee and the morning paper when he felt a dull explosion. Looking out his porthole, he saw water boiling up amidships on the port side.[9]

Korn's quick reaction to the appearance of the Japanese planes, although he thought it was a surprise drill, allowed *Raleigh*'s antiaircraft gunners to put up a systematic barrage within ten minutes. Ensign John Beardall, who had returned from liberty after midnight "not in the best of shape, but not the worst," commanded the port 3-inch battery while Ensign James Werth controlled the starboard.

Ensigns Robert Collins and Jacob Scapa directed the 1.1-inch guns; experienced petty officers handled the .50-caliber machine guns.

Despite the efficient response of the antiaircraft crews, *Raleigh* had already suffered serious damage from the torpedo hit. The missile had struck the bulkhead separating the Number 1 and Number 2 fire-rooms, flooding both areas and causing the ship to list. Damage control parties headed by Ensign Herbert S. Cohn and Carpenter Raymond Telli counterflooded the forward engine room to correct the list, but the situation was still precarious. Captain Simons ordered all unnecessary weight jettisoned. *Raleigh's* two scout planes were lowered into the water by muscle power (internal flooding had knocked out power for the cranes), and they taxied over to Ford Island. The air crews accompanied the planes, realizing that they were more valuable with their aircraft than aboard the battered *Raleigh*.

On the other side of Pearl Harbor a torpedo plane which had overflown *Raleigh* and *Utah* was wreaking havoc at the Ten Ten Dock. There the minelayer *Oglala* was tied up outboard of the light cruiser *Helena*. Seaman Robert Hudson watched from the minelayer as the dive bombers opened up on Ford Island. Then he noticed a Kate coming east across the main channel at 50 feet strafing as it came. As the plane bore down on a moving launch Hudson saw the boats' occupants dive over the side while the craft continued on course without passengers or crew. About 100 yards from the Ten Ten Dock the plane released its torpedo and the pilot had to rise quickly to avoid *Oglala's* superstructure.[10]

Rear Admiral William Furlong, who flew his flag aboard *Oglala*, was pacing the deck waiting for breakfast. He saw bombs fall on Ford Island and the torpedo running for his flagship. As senior officer present afloat he told his signal officer to order all ships in Pearl Harbor to sortie. That order was soon canceled since it would serve no purpose to send out the fleet in the absence of any knowledge of the enemy's whereabouts.[11]

The aborted signal mattered little, for Furlong soon had more immediate concerns. The torpedo passed underneath *Oglala* and exploded against *Helena*, crippling both ships. The blast killed about twenty men instantly below decks on *Helena*. Some died of concussion; others died from flash burns. As on most ships at Pearl Harbor, burn casualties aboard *Helena* were greater than they might have been, because most sailors wore only skivvy shorts and T-shirts in deference to the tropical climate. One of many stunned crewmen, War-

ren Thompson groped about in the darkness (the explosion had
knocked out *Helena's* power) when his passageway was suddenly
illuminated by two or three men coming toward him: Their hair was
ablaze. The sight snapped Thompson to his senses, and he used a
blanket to smother the fires.[12]

Felix Balodis was one of the *Helena* crewmen below decks burned
and dazed by the torpedo blast. With the ship's power knocked out,
Balodis made his way toward his battle station by the light of a flashlight. When he got there he found a shipmate covered with paint. He
had been in the paint locker, the man explained, when the torpedo
hit and the compartment erupted in a shower of color.[13]

While *Helena's* crew struggled to control the chaos below, the
cruiser's antiaircraft guns swung into action in record time. Captain
Robert English claimed in his report that they fired their first rounds
at 8:01. The claim may very well be true, for Signalman Arthur Trimbur, who had a panoramic view from the navy yard signal tower, said
she was the first ship he saw fire.[14]

Despite the fires and flooding below decks, the work of damage
control parties stabilized conditions on *Helena*. It was impossible,
however, to control the flooding on *Oglala*. The old vessel, originally
designed as a coastal steamer, lacked the watertight integrity of a warship. The force of the torpedo explosion had lifted the fireroom floor
plates and ruptured the hull on the port side. The fireroom began to
flood and the minelayer began to list. With the situation moving rapidly out of control, Admiral Furlong and others aboard *Oglala* realized they had to find a way to clear the ship so as not to trap *Helena*
between the Ten Ten Dock and the helpless minelayer.[15]

Flooding in the fireroom eliminated the possibility of moving
Oglala under her own power, but help came from an unexpected
quarter. Two civilian tugs operated by the Standard Dredging Company were working with the dredge *Turbine* in the main channel
between the Ten Ten Dock and Ford Island. George Nakamoto, master of the tug *Balboa,* had just arrived at the dredge to relieve the
other tug, skippered by Sam Keone, when the attack began. Nakamoto saw bombs fall on Ford Island, and the plane which loosed its
torpedo at *Oglala* and *Helena* crossed his bow on its run toward the
Ten Ten Dock.[16]

Furlong summoned the two tugs by "hallooing and motioning"
and by dispatching two officers in a launch to the dredge. In the
midst of the strafing and bombing the tugs attached themselves to

Oglala—Nakamoto at the bow and Keone at the stern. *Oglala's* executive officer, Commander Roland Krause, took charge of the line handling parties, and sailors on the dock shouted directions to the tugs. With the efforts of a cast ranging from the admiral to civilian tugboat deckhands the listing *Oglala* was moved astern, cleared *Helena*, and tied up to the dock.[17]

After months of training and preparation, the attack force aviators were thoroughly prepared for their mission. These pilots head for their planes after a last-minute briefing on the morning of December 7. (U.S. Army Museum of Hawaii photo)

First-wave Zeroes warming up on *Akagi*'s flight deck before takeoff on the morning of the attack. (Choshobo Company)

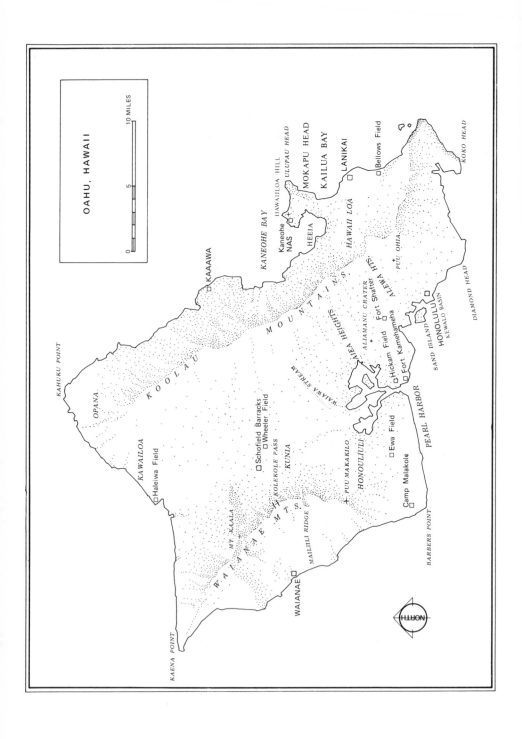

OAHU, HAWAII

0   5   10 MILES

KAHUKU POINT

OPANA

KAWAILOA

Haleiwa Field

KAENA POINT

MT. KAALA

MAILILI RIDGE

WAIANAE

WAIANAE MTS.

KOOLAU MOUNTAINS

KOLEKOLE PASS

Schofield Barracks
Wheeler Field

KUNIA

PUU MAKAKILO

HONOULIULI

Camp Malakole

Ewa Field

BARBERS POINT

KAAAWA

KANEOHE BAY

HAWAIILOA HILL
ULUPAU HEAD

Kaneohe
NAS

HEEIA

MOKAPU HEAD

KAILUA BAY

LANIKAI

Bellows Field

KOKO HEAD

HAWAII LOA

PUU OHIA

ALIAMANU CRATER

AIEA HEIGHTS

WAIAWA STREAM

Fort Shafter
ALEWA HTS.

Fort Kamehameha
Hickam Field
Fort

HONOLULU

SAND ISLAND

KEWALO BASIN

DIAMOND HEAD

PEARL HARBOR

NORTH

Japanese planes preparing to launch. Most Americans in 1941 considered the Japanese incapable of planning and executing a feat as difficult as the Pearl Harbor attack. (National Park Service photo)

A first-wave Kate taking off for the attack. The torpedoes were specially modified for the shallow waters of Pearl Harbor. Most of the damage to the Pacific Fleet resulted from torpedo hits in the opening minutes of the attack. (National Park Service photo)

A Kate from *Zuikaku*'s second wave cruises above Hickam Field as Battleship Row burns in the background. Pearl Harbor's fuel storage tanks stand untouched on the right. (U.S. Army Museum of Hawaii photo)

Japanese dive bombers as seen from a B-17 arriving from California at the height of the attack. Several of the heavy bombers were mistaken for Japanese planes and ran a gauntlet of "friendly" antiaircraft fire. (National Park Service photo)

Forward deck of the target ship *Utah*. The heavy timbers protected the vessel against the impact of practice bombs. When the vessel capsized, the loose timbers rolled off the deck and crushed several men trying to abandon ship. (National Park Service photo)

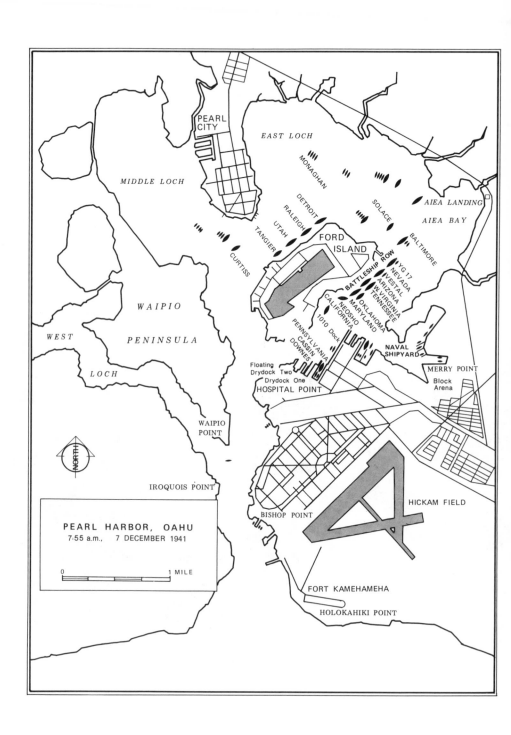

PEARL CITY

EAST LOCH

MIDDLE LOCH

MONAGHAN

SOLACE

AIEA LANDING

AIEA BAY

DETROIT

RALEIGH

UTAH

TANGIER

FORD ISLAND

BALTIMORE

CURTISS

BATTLESHIP ROW

YG 17

NEVADA

VESTAL

ARIZONA

W. VIRGINIA

TENNESSEE

OKLAHOMA

MARYLAND

NEOSHO

CALIFORNIA

1010 Dock

WAIPIO

PENINSULA

WEST

LOCH

PENNSYLVANIA

CASSIN

DOWNES

NAVAL
SHIPYARD

MERRY POINT

Floating
Drydock Two

Drydock One
HOSPITAL POINT

Block
Arena

WAIPIO
POINT

NORTH

IROQUOIS POINT

HICKAM FIELD

PEARL HARBOR, OAHU
7·55 a.m., 7 DECEMBER 1941

BISHOP POINT

0   1 MILE

FORT KAMEHAMEHA

HOLOKAHIKI POINT

Battleship Row from the air during the first minutes of the attack. From left: *Arizona* (inboard) and repair ship *Vestal* (outboard); *West Virginia* (outboard) and *Tennessee* (inboard); *Oklahoma* (outboard) and *Maryland* (inboard). The dark stains next to *West Virginia* and *Oklahoma* are oil slicks spreading from fuel tanks ruptured by torpedoes. (National Park Service photo)

The 1010 Dock, with the damaged cruiser *Helena* on the left. The capsized mine-layer *Oglala*, on the right, was moved clear of *Helena* by George Nakamoto's tug *Balboa*. Smoke in the background rises from the burning *Shaw* and *Nevada*. (National Park Service photo)

A Japanese dive bomber in flight. The attack opened with a miscue when pilots misinterpreted Fuchida's deployment signal. Torpedo and dive bomber pilots both thought they had been ordered to strike first. (National Park Service photo)

Arizona's forward magazines explode minutes after the attack opens. The instant was caught by a doctor with a home movie camera aboard the nearby hospital ship *Solace*. (National Park Service photo)

Arizona's twisted wreckage. The smoke-blackened foremast leans crazily over the water. Few men escaped from the forward areas, but Russell Lott survived because he was blown off his perch on the foremast. (National Park Service photo)

With the capsized *Oklahoma* in the background, sailors scour Pearl Harbor for survivors. Like these men, most sailors wore only skivvy shorts and T-shirts on Sunday morning. The most serious casualties came from burns on exposed skin. (National Park Service photo)

A torpedo hit on *Oklahoma* throws a geyser of water hundreds of feet into the air. Visible in the background to the right are some of Pearl Harbor's fuel storage tanks ignored by the attackers. Had they destroyed the tanks it would have been difficult for the United States to continue using the base as a forward staging area during the Pacific War. (National Park Service photo)

Shaw's magazines explode in a display of pyrotechnic fury. On the right *Nevada* runs for the open sea. (U.S. Naval Historical Center photo)

Fighting fires aboard *West Virginia*. Although resting on the bottom, her deck is still above the surface because of Pearl Harbor's shallow depth. In the background are the masts and funnel of the lightly damaged *Tennessee*, which was sheltered from Japanese torpedoes by *West Virginia*. (National Park Service photo)

When news of the raid reached Task Force Eight at sea, the cruiser *Northampton* dispatched two Seagull scout planes, similar to this one, to search for the Japanese fleet. They miraculously survived an attack by a stray Zero, but the airmen did not break radio silence to notify Admiral Halsey of the encounter. (National Archives photo)

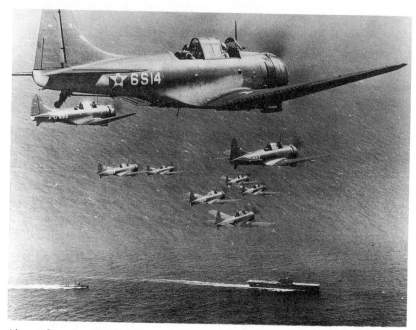

Airmen from Scouting Squadron Six (seen here in October 1941) left *Enterprise* for a routine flight to Oahu and found themselves unexpectedly in the midst of the Japanese attack. (National Archives photo)

Kaneohe NAS sailors struggle to save a burning PBY, but a return visit by Japanese planes destroyed or badly damaged every aircraft on the base. (National Park Service photo)

Repair and cleanup begin at the Ford Island seaplane ramp as warships still blaze in the background. The twin engine PBY seaplane (center) was used for long-range patrols; the single engine floatplanes (right) flew from battleships and cruisers. (National Park Service photo)

A dead American sailor on the shore of Kaneohe Bay. U.S. military casualties were 2,335 killed and 1,143 wounded. (National Park Service photo)

A Japanese view of the destruction at Wheeler Field, Oahu's principal fighter base. Planes were parked wingtip to wingtip to guard against an imaginary sabotage threat. Ironically it made them easier targets for bombing and strafing attacks. (National Park Service photo)

USS *Nevada*. The tug *Hoga* plays a hose on the battleship's fires as she lies grounded at the edge of the Pearl Harbor channel. Had the Japanese sunk *Nevada* in the channel, it would have been blocked for weeks. (National Archives photo)

One of the B-17s arriving from California crash-landed at Bellows Field. This plane, although badly damaged, was repaired and flew again. (National Park Service photo)

Ensign Kazuo Sakamaki's midget submarine beached near Bellows Field. The craft was shipped to the mainland and, after intensive study by naval intelligence, served as a draw for war bond sales rallies. (Choshobo Company)

8

THE TORPEDO ATTACK

While *Helena* and *Oglala* struggled for survival, the principal force of twenty-four torpedo bombers completed their counterclockwise arc over Hickam Field and headed west across the channel toward Battleship Row. A flight of three Kates led by Lieutenant (jg) Junichi Goto dropped to 150 feet on the approach. Goto chose as his target *Oklahoma,* the first battleship he saw. He experienced some momentary confusion, for he could not distinguish between the ship's bow and stern (the battleships were moored facing south, toward the harbor's entrance), but he pressed his attack nonetheless. After dropping his torpedo and clearing *Oklahoma* and the adjacent *Maryland* he looked back and saw that his torpedo had struck home. He experienced a feeling of elation; the hit had consummated months of training and practice.[1]

Other planes, too, zeroed in on *Oklahoma.* The ship took five torpedoes in rapid succession and began a rapid list to port after the first explosion. The senior officer aboard was Commander Jesse Kenworthy, the ship's executive officer. He raced to the conning tower, but was slowed by oil and water thrown onto the deck by the torpedo explosions. While he was still on the boat deck the ship had already listed to port 35 degrees. After a brief discussion with Lieutenant Commander William Hobby, *Oklahoma*'s first lieutenant, the two officers agreed that the vessel could not be saved. They gave the order to abandon ship, telling the crew to leave over the starboard (high) side and climb over the hull and onto the bottom as the battleship rolled over.[2]

Gunners Mate Leon Kolb felt *Oklahoma*'s first torpedo hit as more of a thud or vibration than an explosion. He remembers the entire ship rising and falling about a foot. He wondered what was happening when a message from a loudspeaker dispelled all doubt: "All hands man your battle stations. The enemy is attacking. This is no shit!" Kolb had heard from Asiatic Fleet veterans that the Japanese fleet was "a bunch of junk, and that their airplanes were put together with stove bolts," and that if the United States ever went to war with Japan "we can beat them in one day." He thought first that the Pacific Fleet was under attack from German pocket battleships. The Japanese could never accomplish anything so daring as an attack on America's most heavily defended naval base.[3]

Boatswain Adolph Bothne was preparing to send a party over the side to clean *Oklahoma*'s hull when he heard a mate scream, "Get the guns covered; them Japs are bombing everything in sight!" The ship's massive bulk absorbed the impact of the torpedoes so well that Bothne never felt even one of the hits. He noticed that the antiaircraft guns were silent and quickly learned the reason why. The ready ammunition lockers were locked and no one had a key. Someone either found a key or, in a scene repeated dozens of times that morning, broke the locks off. Access to the ammunition for *Oklahoma*'s port antiaircraft guns made little difference, however. The crews found they had no compressed air to load the guns and, in addition, they were missing vital parts.[4]

The opening of the attack caught Seaman Russell Davenport in a motor launch in the narrow space between *Oklahoma* and her inboard mooring partner, *Maryland,* when he heard the first bombs explode on nearby Ford Island. He quickly climbed up *Oklahoma*'s starboard ladder and ran across the deck in time to see Kates skimming across the channel toward his ship. On his way down the hatch to his battle station in the Turret IV handling room four decks below, Davenport was knocked down by a torpedo explosion. The impact jarred the volume to full on a communally owned phonograph belonging to the turret crew. In an incongruous musical accompaniment to the disaster it played "Let Me Off Uptown." He got to his feet, began to run through a compartment, went down another ladder, and another explosion knocked him off his feet. He picked himself up, sped through the carpenter shop, and was running down another ladder to the handling room when yet another torpedo hit. After reaching his station he joined others in dogging down hatches as the ship began to list badly and the power went off. At that point they received the order of the exec and first lieutenant to abandon ship.

By that time water was pouring through the escape hatch and it was too late for Davenport and the others in his compartment.

Davenport decided to try to make his way up the escape ladder anyway, and that decision saved his life. As he climbed upward the ship
turned completely over and the 14-inch shells in the compartment—
each weighing more than 1,000 pounds—rolled about the handling
room, crushing several of the men left below (now above him). One
man, he remembers, was pinned against a bulkhead, the crushing
weight popping out his tongue and eyes. Davenport made his way
downward through the carpenter shop to a conveyor belt, moving
forward through the conveyor passageway before being driven back
by rising water. In a nightmarish journey, pushing aside the floating
bodies of shipmates as he went, Davenport swam back to his starting
point in Turret IV.

Making their way upward toward the keel Davenport and ten others from his battle station found themselves in the ship's "lucky
bag," the depository for seabags, peacoats, and other personal property. They were trapped in an air pocket with several inches of
armored steel between them and the outside. The only feasible
escape route was below them: five deck levels filled with water, then a
swim across the wide deck (provided they did not get mired in the
muddy harbor bottom). Davenport attempted the escape and made
it to the main deck, where he could feel the teakwood planking, but
he simply could not hold his breath for the additional traverse of the
ship's deck. There was nothing to do but return to the lucky bag.

Wondering whether the compartment would become their tomb,
the men accepted the leadership of Boatswain's Mate First Class
Howard Aldridge. He told the others to remain as quiet as possible to
preserve the limited air and, if possible, sleep. In the hours that
passed, the group's only source of light, a battle lantern, went out.
Hour after hour they waited in pitch darkness, knowing nothing of
the events above them. Water in the compartment came up to their
armpits, and those who fell into exhausted sleep came to a wet awak-
ening. Despite the increasingly foul air, some of the group tried to
find a way out by smashing out adjacent bulkheads with pieces of
metal.

Finally, the eleven men in the compartment felt heat from the cutting torches of rescue teams trying frantically to extract survivors. One
of those trapped inside told the others it was the Japanese—they were
fiendishly torturing those entombed in the hull. Ironically, the rescu-
ers nearly brought doom to those in the lucky bag; the holes they
drilled through the hull allowed the trapped air to escape. The lowered air pressure caused the water to rise, and Davenport swallowed a

large helping of seawater before he finally climbed into the sunshine. It was noon, Monday, December 8. He had been inside *Oklahoma* for twenty-eight hours.[5]

Others in *Oklahoma*'s interior compartments had less harrowing— but still close—escapes. Fireman Chester Kelly just managed to squeeze through a porthole as the ship went over. Others were not so lucky. Many of those in *Oklahoma*'s interior were trapped and drowned when the ship capsized. Some made the deliberate and fatal choice to remain on the battleship as it rolled over to see others safely out of danger. Seaman James Ward and Ensign Francis Flaherty stayed behind holding flashlights in the darkened interior of a gun turret so that others could find their way to safety. Ward and Flaherty were credited with sacrificing their lives to save their shipmates.[6]

Immediately aft of *Oklahoma* lay *West Virginia*. She took a full salvo of seven torpedoes in the opening minutes of the attack. Lieutenant Heita Matsumura commanded a torpedo squadron from *Hiryu* assigned to hit the carriers on the west side of Ford Island. Finding the area empty of his assigned targets, Matsumura led his squadron across the small island, turned counterclockwise, and sought targets of opportunity on Battleship Row. Still worrying about his failure to find an aircraft carrier, he selected *West Virginia* as his secondary target.[7]

Seaman Steven Woznick stood on the deck of the hospital ship *Solace,* moored north and east of Battleship Row, preparing to go ashore for church services. He noticed what may have been Matsumura's squadron come in across the southern end of Ford Island, make a tight turn over the submarine base, and bear down on *West Virginia*. Woznick saw the lead plane drop its torpedo, which exploded against the ship's port side aft. The force of the explosion blew a scout plane off the battleship's after catapult.[8]

Commander Roscoe Hillenkoetter, *West Virginia*'s executive officer, was in his cabin near the stern when he felt the first torpedoes strike. He came up to the main deck and was making his way forward when another torpedo struck and set fire to the planes on top of Turret III. Hillenkoetter noticed the ship beginning to list (he estimated a 20 to 25-degree list within minutes of the first torpedo hit) and used a sound-powered telephone to order counterflooding. So rapid and severe was the damage that he never knew whether his orders were received.[9]

Lieutenant Commander John Harper, the ship's damage control

officer and first lieutenant, had a more precise picture of the ship's condition, but his luck in transmitting counterflooding orders was little better. At his post in central station the inclinometer showed a 15-degree list when he received reports of flooding on the third deck port side. He tried to send word over the public address system to counterflood the starboard voids, but the loss of electrical power made it doubtful whether damage control parties ever received the order.[10]

Fortunately, others reacted independently and began the counterflooding on their own initiative. Technically, Lieutenant Claude Ricketts' duties had nothing to do with damage control; he was senior gunnery officer present and had plenty to keep him busy. Before breaking open the locked fire control tower Ricketts satisfied himself that *West Virginia*'s guns were responding as best they could under the circumstances. Soon Captain Mervyn Bennion, the ship's commanding officer, arrived at the tower. By that time the battleship was listing badly to port. Ricketts asked Bennion, "Captain, shall I go below and counterflood?" When the captain agreed to the suggestion Ricketts lost no time in starting below. On his way he picked up Boatswains Mate First Class Garnett Billingsley.

Moving against the flow of traffic as wounded men were being brought up, Ricketts and Billingsley groped their way across slippery linoleum-covered decks to the first group of counterflooding valves on the starboard side. They found they needed a special crank to turn the valves. Billingsley made his way aft in search of a crank and encountered Shipfitters Murrell Rucker and James Bobick. The three men returned to the waiting Ricketts, and the shipfitters told the lieutenant they had already begun on their own initiative to counterflood the after part of the ship. All four then began working the valves to achieve the same result in the forward voids. Although *West Virginia* had taken too much water to remain afloat, the listing soon stopped and the ship sank on an even keel. The efforts of Ricketts, Billingsley, Bobick, and Rucker probably saved *West Virginia* from capsizing.[11]

Moored at the south end of Battleship Row was the flagship of the Pacific Fleet Battle Force, USS *California*. She too received the concentrated attention of Fuchida's torpedo planes, taking two hits. *California* was even less ready than other ships in the harbor that morning. Her watertight integrity was fatally compromised by nearly a dozen void compartments which were open in preparation for scheduled maintenance work. In addition, another five manholes were

opened to permit inspection of third deck voids for possible fuel
leaks.[12]

One member of the crew had an eerie premonition of the ship's
fate. Warren Harding, a musician in *California*'s band, had played
the previous evening in a competition among the fleet's bands. After
the contest, seeking a solitary refuge on the fantail, he had seen a
meteor shower just before midnight. He remembered a childhood
story from his grandfather: The sight of a shooting star meant someone he knew would soon die. When he saw the meteor shower Harding thought, "My God, how many people do I know that are going
to die soon?"[13]

Harding did not have long to wait. Unlike some of the other ships,
California had a few minutes warning before the torpedo planes
struck. General quarters was sounded at 7:55 with the commence-
ment of dive bombing attacks on Ford Island and strafing of the vessel. Orders were issued to prepare to get the ship under way. Some,
like Seaman Raymond D. Nicholas, were alerted by the noise and
already heading for their stations when the call to general quarters
came over the loudspeakers. Lieutenant Commander Henry E. Bern-
stein, the communication officer, made sure that keys to the ammunition magazines were available before heading for his battle station
in the conning tower. The quick reaction of the officers and men was
of little avail, however, as torpedoes began crashing into *California*'s
port side at 8:00.[14]

Seaman Nicholas was at his post below decks when two torpedoes
exploded just forward of his position. At first he thought the noise
was from casemate guns above him. When someone screamed,
"Nick, come over here!," he thought, "Well, that's probably some
recruit over there that's got scared." Responding to the summons
from the forward compartment, he found two men crumpled over.
When he began moving the casualties he heard a "zing!" as something ricocheted off the bulkhead. When he took another step the
same thing happened again. A close inspection revealed the flying
objects to be rivets popping out of the steel bulkheads which had
been twisted by the force of the torpedo explosions.

The port side torpedo hits caused *California* to list, and for a time
it seemed as though the ship would capsize as *Utah* and *Oklahoma*
had. But, as on *West Virginia,* quick work and unusual initiative prevented *California* from overturning. Gunner Jackson Pharris was in
charge of a repair party below decks when water and fuel oil began to
pour into the ship. With no power and many of his men overcome by

oil fumes, Pharris ordered shipfitters in his party to counterflood and equalize the list. Had he waited for orders from topside Pharris's efforts would have been too late.[15]

Warren Harding, also below decks, manned a telephone at the foreport repair station. A torpedo exploded near him and flooded the surrounding compartments. Although his post still had light and air from the ventilating system, his compartment was isolated and he was trapped four decks below. At 8:10 the power went out. Nicholas, Harding, and the others below were operating on emergency power. Most ventilators were off and the only light came from battery-operated battle lanterns.

Despite these conditions, *California's* crew made a superhuman effort to contain the damage, fight the ship, and perform their duties. When the ship's firefighting equipment could not contain the burning fuel, John Kuzma and other Ford Island firefighters passed hand extinguishers hand-to-hand from shore. Because the Ford Island water main had been broken when *Arizona* sank on the line, the extinguishers were filled from the Ford Island swimming pool.[16]

Machinist's Mate First Class Robert Scott's battle station was a compressor feeding air to *California's* antiaircraft guns. When his compartment flooded and word was passed to evacuate the area, Gunner's Mate Third Class Vernon Jensen called to Scott to join the others who were leaving. Scott refused, saying, "As long as I can give these people air, I'm sticking." His dedication cost him his life and earned him a posthumous Medal of Honor.[17]

Ensign Herbert Jones, Chief Radioman Thomas Reeves, and the ubiquitous Gunner Pharris also won the nation's highest award by organizing and inspiring men to brave the fumes and flooding to move ammunition by hand from the magazines to the guns. The ship's doctor, Commander J. D. Jewell, despite painful burns on his face and arms, continued to attend to the wounded. He was assisted by Mess Attendants Celesteine, Macot, and Wallace.[18]

The torpedo planes scored their greatest successes with hits on *California, Oklahoma,* and *West Virginia,* but they did not ignore other targets on Battleship Row. *Nevada* received one torpedo on the port side at frame 41 (between Turrets I and II). Witnesses reported that another torpedo passed beneath the repair ship *Vestal* and struck *Arizona,* moored between Ford Island and *Vestal,* directly beneath Turret I. Damage to the forward part of *Arizona* was so extensive that any evidence of a torpedo hit was destroyed by subsequent explosions.[19]

The torpedo attacks ended in a matter of minutes. Within that period the attackers had inflicted severe or fatal damage to five battleships, the two light cruisers, and two auxiliaries. That success cost the Japanese five Kate torpedo bombers, but with the heart of the Pacific Fleet battle line crippled, Nagumo's fliers had written finis to the battleship era and ushered in a new age of naval warfare.

9

THE BOMB ATTACK

After the torpedo runs, while dive bombers still pounded airfields, Fuchida led his horizontal bombers in for another blow at the fleet. He kept the group in a holding pattern at 10,000 feet over Barbers Point while the torpedo planes, dive bombers, and fighters performed their tasks. Fuchida brought his Kates, each armed with an 800-kilogram armor-piercing bomb, over Battleship Row shortly after 8:00. The ships' crews below had recovered from the initial shock and delivered antiaircraft fire which made the horizontal bombing run difficult. Fuchida describes the problems of his own approach:

As we closed in, enemy antiaircraft fire began to concentrate on us. Dark gray puffs burst all around. Most of them came from ships' batteries, but land batteries were also active. Suddenly my plane bounced as if struck by a club. When I looked back to see what had happened, the radioman said: "The fuselage is holed and the rudder wire damaged." We were fortunate that the plane was still under control, for it was imperative to fly a steady course as we approached the target. Now it was time for "Ready to release," and I concentrated my attention on the lead plane to note the instant his bomb was dropped. Suddenly a cloud came between the bomb sight and the target, and just as I was thinking that we had already overshot, the lead plane banked slightly and turned right toward Honolulu. We had missed the release point because of the cloud and would have to try again.[1]

Fuchida's target was *Maryland*, which had escaped torpedo damage because she was moored inboard of the luckless *Oklahoma*. *Maryland* suffered comparatively light damage. She was hit twice by bombs. One detonated on an awning rope strung above the forecastle and caused fragmentation and blast damage in the immediate vicinity.

The other penetrated the hull beneath the starboard waterline near the bow, detonated in the hold, and caused moderate flooding.[2]

Twenty-one-year-old Wilford Autry's battle station was in *Maryland*'s "battle bags," a compartment on the quarterdeck where the signal flags were stored. While running across the quarterdeck on his way to the battle bags Autry was drenched by spray from the geyser thrown up by one of the torpedo hits on *West Virginia*. When he reached his station he found the compartment locked and went below to the messhall, where he cleared away tables and helped pass ammunition to the antiaircraft guns. He went above once more to try to reach his battle station, but the door was still locked. By that time sailors were streaming aboard from the neighboring *Oklahoma*. A chief petty officer finally arrived to unlock the battle bags, but the signal gang had little to do but stand by for orders.[3]

Gunner's Mate Third Class Werner Land experienced a similar wait for vital keys. The ammunition magazine for his 5-inch antiaircraft gun was locked and no one could find a chief or an officer with the keys. While the battle raged around them the gun crew debated hotly among themselves whether they should break the lock. The debate was decided in favor of the proposition when they saw *Oklahoma* capsize. "It was humiliating," Land remembers, to see a battleship turned upside down like a child's toy.[4]

Maryland's crew, despite the light damage, had their hands full. The most serious threat came not from her own bomb damage but from the destructive fallout around her. Printer Second Class Merle Newbauer was assigned to man the phones below decks. Frustrated at being so far removed from the action, he responded when a call came from topside for volunteer firefighters. The fires endangering the ship came from the fiercely burning *West Virginia* moored astern. As soon as he got to the weather deck Newbauer was hit in the knee by a bomb fragment or a bullet. One of *Maryland*'s black mess attendants threw him under a turret overhang as strafing planes passed overhead. Feeling fit enough to help, Newbauer joined a group playing a fire hose on a blazing oil slick being pushed by prevailing winds from *West Virginia* toward *Maryland*. He looked at the scene of destruction in the harbor around him and felt as if he had been hit in the solar plexus. Newbauer and those around him, although their own ship was not badly damaged, felt "just dejected at the thought [that] the mightiest fleet that ever had been assembled" was now in shambles.[5] It was not just warships, but military morale as well, which would have to be raised from the bottom of Pearl Harbor.

High above this agonizing scene Lieutenant Heijiro Abe led his *Soryu* squadron toward the mooring where *West Virginia* and *Tennessee* lay berthed. As he peered through his bombsight he saw antiaircraft rounds bursting below him. Praying he would survive at least long enough to release his bomb, he was dismayed to find the target hidden by billowing smoke from *West Virginia*'s fires. Abe resolutely led his planes back and circled around Hickam for a second pass. This time the antiaircraft gunners were getting his range and his plane was buffeted by uncomfortably close bursts. He released his bomb at *West Virginia* and his observer confirmed a hit. So great was Abe's pent-up emotion that he cried in relief. Two bombs hit *West Virginia*. Although they did some damage, both were duds.[6]

Tennessee, moored inboard of *West Virginia*, was comparatively lucky. Her outboard partner protected her from torpedo damage and she was hit, like *Maryland*, by two armor-piercing bombs. A hit on the center gun of Turret II put the gun out of commission. Another bomb penetrated the roof of Turret III but failed to explode with full force. Nonetheless, it killed four men inside the turret. A more serious hazard than the bombs were explosions and fires aboard *Tennessee*'s upwind neighbor, *Arizona*. A massive explosion in *Arizona*'s forward magazine showered *Tennessee*'s quarterdeck with debris. Drifting oil fires on the water forced *Tennessee* to flood some of her ammunition magazines and turn her screws at 5 knots to keep the fire away. Because she was wedged between the mooring quays and the crippled *West Virginia* she could not move, only churn the water with her screws.[7]

Fragments from one of the bombs which hit *Tennessee* (probably the hit on Turret II) sprayed the signal bridge of *West Virginia* and mortally wounded Captain Bennion. Lieutenant Commander T. T. Beattie, the ship's navigator, heard the captain groan. A fragment had torn open his abdomen; Chief Pharmacist's Mate Leslie Leak dressed the wound, but it was apparent that Bennion would require more medical attention. In addition to the task of saving the ship the officers on the bridge also had to find a way to evacuate their captain, despite his protests that he be left on the bridge.[8]

Lieutenant Commander Doir Johnson brought Mess Attendant Doris Miller to the bridge because he thought the husky messman a good choice to carry the captain to safety. At first Bennion was placed on a cot. But it soon became apparent that he would have to be lowered from the bridge and a more solid conveyance had to be found. Captain Bennion was lashed to a wooden ladder and lines attached to

the four corners, but raging fire on the boat deck made it impossible
to lower the improvised stretcher. Smoke and fumes from the conflagration made the signal bridge untenable, and the officers decided to
haul the captain up to the navigation bridge. During this ordeal Captain Bennion suffered intensely but still asked about the progress of
damage control and insisted that those on the bridge abandon him
and save themselves.[9]

While the search was under way for means to move the captain to
safety Miller and Lieutenant (jg) Freddy White teamed up to fight
the ship and control the chaos around them. They manned the two
antiaircraft machine guns forward of the conning tower (despite the
fact that Miller had no machine gun training) and repelled Japanese planes making further attacks. They also rescued men struggling through the flood of seawater and fuel oil on the sinking ship.
Captain Bennion was finally taken off the ladder and carried
up to the navigation bridge, where he died still attended by Chief
Leak.[10]

Conditions below on *West Virginia* produced their share of horrors.
Lieutenant Commander John Harper, the vessel's damage control
officer, directed his repair parties from central station deep in the
bowels of the ship. From his post he had to make choices that con-
demned some men to death so that others—and the ship—might
survive. One particularly agonizing instance is best described in Harper's own words:

> At this time, water commenced to pour down the trunk leading to cen-
> tral station and the watertight door to that trunk was closed and
> dogged. . . .
>   Certain men banged and hammered on the port door from the trunk
> leading to central stating that there was water filling the trunk and
> wanted entrance into central. We asked how much water was in there
> and they stated that it was getting high. In as much as we still had com-
> munication and counter-flooding seemed to be taking effect, I refused
> to allow my men with me to open this door and directed the men out-
> side to try to get through Plot and around to the starboard side in order
> to enter through the starboard door which was not yet leaking water.
> At the same time, I directed repair II to attempt to open the armored
> hatch above the trunk in order to let these men escape. Repair II
> reported back that there was about three feet of water above the hatch
> and they were unable to open it. I believe that these men were lost, as I
> am quite certain that no further personnel entered central through the
> starboard door.[11]

The counter-flooding ordered by Harper distributed the water more or less evenly within the ship. As a result, *West Virginia* maintained her balance and settled upright on the shallow harbor bottom. With her main deck just above the waterline, the battleship's superstructure continued to burn, but her fires were dwarfed by the inferno aboard *Arizona,* anchored directly astern.

10

THE END OF *ARIZONA*

Of all the ships at Pearl Harbor none suffered more than the battleship *Arizona*. Official reports identified eight separate bomb hits in locations ranging from Turret IV to the forecastle deck in the vicinity of Turret I. An even greater blow than the destruction of the vessel was the loss of 1,177 sailors and marines.[1]

Major Alan Shapley, commander of *Arizona*'s marine detachment, was below decks when he heard a loud "bang." He first thought that one of the ship's boats had dropped onto deck and went above to investigate. Not until machine gun bullets splintered the teak planking on the quarterdeck did he realize the battleship was under attack. Someone sounded general quarters and Shapley joined other marines and sailors scrambling up the mainmast to the secondary aft fire control station.[2]

Sergeant John Baker left the marine compartment in the wake of Second Lieutenant Carlton Simonsen. Other men rushing topside jammed the ladderway, and Simonsen had to force his way through the congestion. Still hot on the lieutenant's heels, Baker made his way up the starboard ladder of the mainmast under a hail of shrapnel and machine gun bullets. They had barely reached the first platform when fragments from a bomb explosion on the quarterdeck caught Simonsen in the midsection. The wound, like Captain Bennion's on *West Virginia*, was obviously mortal, and Baker thought he died "almost instantly."[3]

Lying semiconscious in a pool of blood, Lieutenant Simonsen lingered long enough to be discovered by Private James Cory and Corporal Earl Nightengale. The men realized that Simonsen, his skin pale and eyelids fluttering, was dying. Cory and another marine leaned over the officer to see whether they could do anything for him. Too weak to talk, he moved his lips to form the words, "Leave me. Go on." Unable to help Simonsen, they made their way to secondary aft and reported to Major Shapley.[4]

With communications disrupted Shapley and the others in secondary aft could do little but watch from their vantage point high on the mainmast as their ship expired in a hail of bombs and bullets. There was no panic, but an excited babble of conversation in the crowded compartment made it impossible to hear commands. Corporal Nightengale imposed a semblance of order by shouting for silence. Cory tried to open the windows but found them jammed shut by accumulated grime and smoke particles. He need not have worried, for his ship was destroyed moments later (Cory's watch stopped between 8:12 and 8:13) by an enormous blast.

The explosion which sank the ship has occasioned speculation and controversy which persist to this day. The relatively small number of *Arizona* survivors and the thoroughness of her destruction make it difficult to determine the exact cause of the fatal blast. One theory holds that a bomb went down the funnel and the subsequent explosion deep within the ship sank the vessel. Another view, more generally accepted, asserts that a Japanese bomb ignited *Arizona*'s forward magazines and the resulting secondary explosions did the damage.

The available evidence strongly suggests that it was the ignition of the forward magazines which sank the battleship. The enormous damage to the vessel was simply too great to have resulted from a single hit or even multiple bomb hits. Examination of the wreckage revealed that a titanic blast in the forward part of the ship had torn open the sides of the hull and blown armored plating outward to a nearly horizontal position.[5] Further evidence is provided by movie footage taken during the attack.[6] The film clearly shows the fireball of the great explosion coming from the area of the forward magazines. A subsequent jet of black smoke expelled from the funnel was probably caused by the internal blast from the magazines.

Since the destruction of the forward area was so complete and no one from the magazine area survived to tell the tale, it is uncertain exactly what happened. The explosion could have resulted from an armor-piercing bomb detonating within the hull. Or perhaps the hot blast of a lighter bomb exploding on the deck entered the magazines through an unsecured hatch or vent.

The overwhelming evidence supporting the forward magazine explosion as the cause of *Arizona*'s destruction does not, however, mean that a bomb did *not* go down the stack. A number of survivors state that a projectile did, in fact, go down the funnel.[7] John Baker's statement in this regard is particularly convincing. His vantage point in secondary aft put him above the top of the stack, and he was particularly well placed to observe the ship from above. For practical purposes, though, it is immaterial whether a bomb hit the funnel; the effects of such an explosion would have been dwarfed by the results of the forward magazine explosion.

The magazines contained three hundred and eight 14-inch projectiles, thirty-five hundred 5-inch rounds, nearly five thousand cans of powder, and more than one hundred thousand rounds of machine gun and small arms ammunition. Cory remembers the explosion as a soft but mighty "whoosh!" Aviation Machinist's Mate Donald "Turkey" Graham agreed, describing the sound as an "awful 'Swish'." Seaman Artis Teer saw *Arizona* explode from his post on neighboring *Nevada.* "The ship," he said, "seemed to jump at least fifteen or twenty feet upward in the water and sort of break in two." A ball of flame and smoke boiled up to a towering height far above *Arizona's* tripod masts. Survivors of the explosion had different details engraved indelibly in their memories. Chief Gunner's Mate J. A. Doherty saw "the forecastle waving up and down and fire and smoke coming through the deck." When the foremast toppled over, Seaman Russell Lott in the port antiaircraft director thought at first that his director compartment had been dislodged and tumbled free; for a moment he thought he was dead.[8]

Lott was lucky, for the blast killed almost everyone forward of the quarterdeck. The marines in the mainmast stations were protected by the superstructure from the force of the blast, but it was still fierce enough to make Private Cory cringe from the heat. When he recovered he reported to Major Shapley that smoke and flame were curling out of the quarterdeck engine room ventilators. Corporal Nightengale noted that the entire ship forward of the mainmast (two-thirds of *Arizona's* length) was aflame. Clearly it was only a matter of time before the blaze consumed their station, and Shapley feared they would be "cooked to death." Since they could serve no useful purpose by remaining in the director Shapley ordered his men to leave.[9]

Down the mast they went, instinctively obedient at first to the traffic rules which dictated they descend by the port leg of the tripod mast. The railings were hot, and some of the men suffered burns on their hands. On reaching the burning boat deck Nightengale noted that the area was thick with bodies, as burned and wounded men streamed down the break to the quarterdeck. Some fell dead after climbing down the ladder. When he had descended as far as the searchlight platform Cory crossed to the starboard side of the platform to check Lieutenant Simonsen but found no sign of a heartbeat. At that point he decided to ignore the rules and continue climbing down the mast on the starboard leg since it was closest to Ford Island and offered the best chance of escape from the burning ship. Turning his back to the mast (so he would not have to grasp the hot railings), he clambered down to the boat deck, the galley deck, and then onto the quarterdeck. There he found, huddled against the starboard mount for *Arizona*'s yet to be installed 1.1-inch antiaircraft guns, badly burned men "stacked like cordwood." Most were barely alive and scarcely identifiable as human beings.[10]

With the ship all but destroyed, her first lieutenant and damage control officer, Lieutenant Commander Samuel Fuqua, directed rescue efforts from the quarterdeck. The senior officers aboard *Arizona* at the beginning of the attack were Rear Admiral Isaac Kidd, commander of Battleship Division One, and the vessel's commander, Captain Franklin Van Valkenburgh. According to the few surviving witnesses who saw the captain and the admiral, they assumed their stations on the navigation bridge and signal bridge. When the attack began Ensign Douglas Hein went to the signal bridge, where he saw Admiral Kidd. Finding no way to be useful there, Hein joined Captain Van Valkenburgh and the quartermaster on the navigation bridge.

The quartermaster suggested that the captain take cover in the armored conning tower, but Van Valkenburgh refused and was trying to establish telephone communication with other parts of the ship when the magazines exploded. Flame shot through the broken bridge windows, and the three men tried to escape through the port door but were unable to leave by that route. Hein continued in his report, "We staggered to the starboard side and fell on the deck just forward of the wheel. Finally I raised my head and turned it and saw that the port door was open. I got up, ran to it, and ran down the port ladders, passing through flames and smoke." Hein finally escaped halfway down the signal bridge ladder and jumped to the boat deck, which had been bent "way under" by the explosion.[11]

The forward magazine blast wreaked as much death and destruction below decks as it did above. There were no survivors from the crews of the two forward turrets.[12] Those manning Turrets III and IV were protected from the full force of the explosion, but their situation was enviable only by comparison. Boatswain's Mate Second Class

John Anderson was in charge of a party rigging awnings for church services on the stern when the attack began. Anderson, who had had a tour of duty in China, was one of the few who instantly recognized the strange airplanes as Japanese. He and another member of the detail, Coxswain James Forbis, headed for their battle stations in Turret IV.[13]

Their battle stations were at the top level of the turret, but traffic rules required them to descend first to the lower decks and then climb up to their assigned positions. Forbis had almost reached the top when a bomb struck the faceplate of his turret. The force of the explosion threw him down several decks, and smoke in the compartment made it impossible to breathe. He sought refuge in the lower handling room of Turret III. Anderson got no farther than the hatch on the quarterdeck (he had stopped to sound an alarm) when another bomb hit on the stern and blew him down the hatch. After recovering he continued downward, stopping at the magazine to help put powder trays in readiness. Anderson had no sooner reached his station on the gun seat when the same bomb which knocked down Forbis hit his turret and glanced off. It sounded to him like a "terminal explosion" and he and the others inside the turret caught the unmistakable scent of cordite. The turret crew decided their big guns would be of little use in an air attack, so Anderson notified those in the lower levels he was going on deck to help man the antiaircraft guns.

The experience of those in the lower compartments of Turret IV confirmed the wisdom of Anderson's decision. Chief Turret Captain George Campbell, Boatswain's Mate Second Class William Peil, and Gunner's Mate Second Class Earl Pecotte were in the lower reaches of the turret when it seemed as though the ship were being ripped apart by explosions. Darkness, flooding, and choking gas (formed by contact between seawater and batteries) made their position untenable. At Pecotte's suggestion, Campbell ordered everyone to the upper turret. He then sent Pecotte outside to the quarterdeck to check for gas and see if power could be restored. The gunner's mate encountered Fuqua, exposed to machine gun fire, directing the removal of wounded. He asked Fuqua if the ship were being abandoned. When the first lieutenant replied, "Yes," Pecotte reported back to the turret captain. Campbell ordered everyone out, but first he sent Pecotte and Peil below with a flashlight to search for wounded. Finding no one in the lower compartments, they emerged onto the charnel house of the quarterdeck and helped move the more seriously wounded men into the meager shelter provided by the turret overhang.[14]

Turret III was manned by a mixed assortment of men regularly assigned to that turret and refugees, like James Forbis, from neighboring Turret IV. In the lower handling room the effects of smoke and gas were mitigated by compressed air hissing from air lines broken by the force of explosions. Ensign Guy S. Flannigan nearly failed to gain entry to Turret III. He and others trapped in a passage below decks had to pound on a door for several minutes before it was undogged from inside. Bomb explosions had sprung the doors between the after turrets, and it was not long before gas and smoke began to enter Turret III. Noise and confusion reigned at first, but Flannigan and another officer restored order. As the smoke became worse, they ordered the lower room of the turret evacuated. The men left the lower room none too soon, for water had entered the chamber and was 8 inches deep by the time the compartment had been cleared.[15]

Elsewhere in Turret III, the same conditions prevailed. One officer tried to calm the men by giving a running account of the action on the quarterdeck, saying, "There's nothing that we can do." Ensign Jim Miller took his assigned position in the upper booth of Turret III and found at first that he could communicate with central plot by telephone. Gradually, however, gas and smoke made their position untenable just as it had in Turrets III and IV. Forbis and another sailor went to the after steering room in search of gas masks. The masks were there, but locked up securely. The situation became progressively worse, and the men stripped off shirts and stuffed them into embrasures to keep out smoke and gas. A bomb explosion severed Miller's phone link, smoke poured in through the overhead hatch, and he could see nothing but flames outside his turret. Miller left the turret briefly to check the situation on deck. He decided that it would be futile to continue manning the main battery. Miller passed the word to abandon Turret III with little time to spare: Water was already flooding into the lower handling room.[16]

There on the quarterdeck the hellish scene made superhuman demands on the survivors. Lieutenant Commander Fuqua's first priority was to control the fire and prevent it from spreading aft of the mainmast. He directed Ensign Henry D. Davison to call the center engine room to get pressure on the fire mains. Davison went to the officer of the deck's booth to make the call. He was in the booth with a boatswain's mate when a bomb exploded on the starboard side of the quarterdeck near the break. Fire from the explosion trapped them in the booth. They barely escaped by jumping over the side. Davison intended to reboard the ship, but one look at the burning *Arizona*, which had settled down by the bow and was apparently broken in two, convinced him the situation was hopeless. Instead, he climbed into a motor launch and turned his attention to rescuing survivors from the water.[17]

Those manning fire hoses on the quarterdeck experienced the frustration of connecting their hoses and running them out only to find no pressure in the lines. When the bomb struck the top of Turret IV and started a fire, Fuqua ordered "Turkey" Graham, "Put that fire out back aft." Graham in turn directed Aviation Machinist's Mate Milton Hurst, Yeoman Benjamin Bruns, Radioman Glenn Lane, and Aviation Ordnance Mate Edward L. Wentzlaff to rig fire hoses on the quarterdeck. Graham and Bruns seized the hose from its stowage and, with Wentzlaff, took it to the fire plug near Turret IV. Hurst and Lane connected another hose to the plug near Turret III. Fuqua then ordered the water turned on, but neither of the lines had any pressure. He directed Graham to see whether he could raise pressure. Graham tried to call the engine room, but the phones were dead.[18]

With fire creeping aft against the wind, *Arizona*'s crew tried desperate expedients. Fuqua directed men trying to hold back the flames with hand-held CO_2 fire extinguishers. Ensign Jim Miller organized a bucket brigade to fight the smaller fires which had erupted here and there on the quarterdeck. Boatswain's Mate Thomas A. White seized a knife and cut down a burning awning, probably left over from the church service which was never held. These pitiful efforts were obviously inadequate, and Fuqua gave the word to abandon ship. First he ordered Miller and White to go below and check Captain Van Valkenburgh's cabin to make sure he would not be left aboard the burning battleship.[19]

Fuqua recalls ordering *Arizona* abandoned about 9:00, but it was probably earlier. When James Forbis emerged from Turret IV, Fuqua was already ordering men over the side. Forbis was not eager to jump into the water, which was covered with a gelatinous layer of fuel oil. He thought, however, of the after magazines. Steadily heated by uncontrollable fires, they might at any moment explode like the forward magazines. After considering the alternatives he decided to jump. Jump he did, but he was nearly undone by one of *Arizona*'s boat cranes which had toppled into the water and lay just below the surface. He struck his head on the crane and was knocked nearly unconscious. Luckily he was spotted by shipmates in a launch who were pulling survivors from the water. They had trouble hauling him aboard, because he was so slippery from the fuel oil. After they dropped him off on Ford Island he happened to glance at his Waltham pocket watch. Clogged with oil and salt water, it had stopped at 8:50.[20]

Radioman Lane, one of those who tried to fight the blaze with hoses, was blown overboard by an explosion. Knocked unconscious, he woke up on *Nevada* and found himself a member of her crew for the time being. Wasting no time in convalescence, he helped her regular crew serve powder to the 5-inch guns. Edward Wentzlaff and another man swam to a small boat near *Arizona*, cut it loose, and took it to the crew's gangway. They boarded the ship and carried off "wounded, shocked and grotesquely burned shipmates" until the boat was loaded to capacity. Once under way to the hospital ship *Solace* they plucked struggling swimmers out of the water.[21]

Marines from secondary aft, including Private Cory and Corporal Nightengale, made their way to the after mooring quay by means of a gangway which bridged the distance between the ship and the pier. Cory remembers Commander Fuqua directing men over the side "very calmly, no sweat to him" with words like "Over the side, boys! Over the side, boys!" While the marines made use of the gangway, their route had its hazards. The gangway had broken and was turned over on its side, making it nothing more than a precarious two-by-twelve plank spanning the water. In addition, the settling of the ship had put enormous strain on the mooring lines.

Cory weighed the alternative risks and found them unpleasant. If the ship shifted further, Cory would be crushed between the quay and the vessel if he chose to swim. On the other hand, if he used the plank he might well be decapitated by one of the 6-inch mooring cables already under visible strain. Faced with Hobson's choice, he made his way across the plank, and a snapping cable missed his head by inches.[22]

Nightengale, too, made it to the quay. Suddenly he found himself in the water; he was probably blown off by a bomb blast. He began swimming for the pipeline connected to the dredge *Turbine*, but found himself too shocked and fatigued to continue to the pipeline about 50 yards away. He would have drowned had not Major Shapley been swimming nearby. Shapley grasped the corporal by the shirt and told him to hang onto his shoulders. They were approximately 25 feet from the pipeline when Shapley's strength deserted him.

Nightengale loosened his grip on the major and told him to go on alone, but Shapley refused, found an extra reserve of strength, and carried Nightengale to safety.[23]

John Anderson loaded injured men into one of the many small boats hovering around *Arizona*. Some were burned so badly that when he picked them up the skin slid off their arms. Fuqua urged Anderson to get into one of the boats, but the boatswain's mate had compelling business to attend to: His twin brother, Delbert, was missing. He told the first lieutenant, "Listen, my brother's still on this ship. I gotta go back and get him." Fuqua forced him to face reality, saying, "He's gone, they're not gonna make it. And we better get off before everyone else is killed, too." As he left for Ford Island in a boat Anderson looked back at the once mighty warship that had been his home. "Everything was on fire," he remembers, "the ship was on fire, the water was on fire and there was people on the crane . . . and I saw them as we went and they were up in this fire and I thought God amighty, how are they going to make it?"[24]

Once on Ford Island Anderson was still haunted by the vision of the men on the crane. Then he and a shipmate saw an unoccupied whaleboat riding free in the oil-covered water. The same thought occurred to them simultaneously and they swam for the whaleboat, climbed aboard, and maneuvered it through the fire to the crane. They found another boat there already rescuing the trapped men. They took their boat around to *Arizona*'s port side to collect injured men, but found more corpses than survivors. Anderson remembers seeing on the blister top the body of one of the ship's cooks with a knife pushed through him by the force of an explosion. With their load of dead and barely living they made for the Pearl Harbor Naval Hospital. They stopped as they passed the sunken *West Virginia* and asked an officer if they could take any of that ship's wounded, but he declined the offer. The strangest thing, Anderson recalls, is that the officer was dressed in immaculate whites while everyone else was filthy with oil and smoke.

That small boats manned by Anderson and other sailors managed to evacuate *Arizona*'s seriously injured from the blazing wreckage was due in no small measure to the performance of Lieutenant Commander Fuqua, the ship's senior surviving officer. By his own estimate he supervised the placement of about seventy wounded men in launches.[25] Those who saw him on the quarterdeck agree that he set an inspiring example by his coolness in the face of strafing machine gun fire and the uncontrollable blaze.

Fuqua won the Medal of Honor for his actions, but the comments of *Arizona* crewmen testify to his bravery more eloquently than any number of official citations. The authority of his presence was so great that when Earl Pecotte emerged from his turret to leave the ship, Fuqua was the only person he noticed on the quarterdeck. When Fuqua ordered Pecotte over the side the gunner's mate asked him if he, too, were going to swim for shore. The officer replied, "Not until the Japs leave." To "Turkey" Graham, "It seemed like the men painfully burned, shocked and dazed, became inspired and took things in stride, seeing Mr. Fuqua, so unconcerned about the bombing and strafing." One of those inspired by his example was Sergeant John Baker: "His calmness gave me courage and I looked around the deck to see if I could help." To Edward Wentzlaff, he "displayed a courage and bravery second to none. I am proud to say I came under his authority and . . . for the future the confidence of his men is well assured."[26]

Moored outboard of *Arizona,* the repair ship *Vestal* might have escaped unscathed had she not been berthed on Battleship Row on December 7. Her shallow draft allowed the vessel to escape torpedo damage, but horizontal bombers in Fuchida's first wave made two hits, both about 8:05. The first penetrated three decks and exploded in a storage area. The hull was not ruptured by that bomb, but the explosion severed electrical power cables and the ship's fire main and started a fire in the lower hold. The second bomb struck near the stern at frame 110, passed successively through the carpenter shop, shipfitter shop, shipfitters' locker room, and fuel oil tanks, and left a 5-foot hole in the hull near the bilge keel. As flooding from the second hit was compounded by deliberate flooding to protect the forward magazines from the fire ignited by the first bomb, the ship began to settle.[27]

The forward magazine explosion aboard *Arizona* damaged *Vestal* further. It blew a number of men overboard, including her captain, Commander Cassin Young. In the confusion someone gave the order to abandon ship. As men prepared to go over the side Commander Young swam back to *Vestal* and ordered the crew back to their stations. With his ship settling perilously near the burning *Arizona,* Young ordered *Vestal* under way. At first she anchored about 500 yards northeast of her original berth, but as she continued to settle Young ordered her beached in the shoal waters of Aiea Bay. Even if the vessel could not be kept afloat, she would at least settle in shallow water.[28]

Getting *Vestal* under way was a challenge to Young's seamanship. For one thing, she was still moored to *Arizona*. When Chief Campbell emerged from Turret IV an officer (probably Commander Young) on *Vestal* shouted to cast off the mooring lines which bound the two ships together. Campbell looked about for "Turkey" Graham to execute the order, but saw Graham already at work on the lines. Graham and Seaman Bill Garron, braving the machine gun fire from Japanese planes, were using fire axes to chop the lines free. Because *Arizona* was settling, they were too taut to cast off in the normal manner. Someone from *Vestal* called over ungraciously, "Hey, don't cut our mooring lines; we might need them!" Graham kept swinging his ax and retorted, "Get the hell out of here while you can!"[29]

To the sailors on the burning and crippled ships, it appeared as though the attackers could choose their targets at leisure. Where, they wondered, were the interceptors which should have downed the Japanese? The answer lay in the smoking rubble of Oahu's airfields.

THE AIR BATTLES

11

MACHINE GUNS

ON WORKBENCHES

When *Arizona* sank on the freshwater line which supplied the air station on Ford Island, the lack of water hampered firefighting efforts and added to the damage. The dive bombing attack on Ford Island which began simultaneously with the torpedo strikes destroyed many of the thirty-five PBY patrol planes and thirty-one utility aircraft at the air station. Because the fighter and bomber squadrons were with their carriers, there were only four fighters and three dive bombers on Ford Island.[1]

For Aviation Machinist's Mate Third Class Ernest Cochran the first minutes of the attack on Ford Island were marked by the same kind of confusion which beset those aboard vessels in the harbor. Cochran, assigned to a utility squadron with the unromantic duty of target towing, had just been relieved from hangar watch and was in his barracks when he heard the first explosions. A boatswain's mate ordered everyone in the barracks to report to their squadrons, but a marine sentry posted outside the barracks shouted at the sailors crowding out the door, "Where do you think you're going? Everybody back inside!" Common sense prevailed eventually, and Cochran and the others left for their units.[2]

He climbed aboard a truck headed in the general direction of his hangar, but the moving vehicle became the target of Japanese strafers. Cochran jumped off, took shelter in an open trench, and crawled toward his hangar. He took a breather in a junction box, then sprinted across open ground toward his squadron. Once there he was put to work belting machine gun ammunition. His squadron mates had already begun to mount opposition—inadequate though it was —to the attackers. Cochran saw Aviation Machinist's Mate Brigham

Young firing a .30-caliber machine gun from a grounded J2-F biplane. Since their hangar stood near *Utah*'s berth, survivors of that ill-fated ship soon joined them and offered to help.

A senior petty officer, R. E. "Whitey" Flora, took charge of work in the hangar, directing antiaircraft efforts and ordering the removal of planes to less exposed positions. As the men ran low on machine gun ammunition, it became apparent that a party would have to brave the strafing and bombing to cross the exposed area between their hangar and the nearest ammunition supply. When some of the sailors in Cochran's squadron gathered to attempt the dash they were halted by a passing chief petty officer, who ordered them to march in formation to get the ammunition. Flora intervened and told his men to get across the open ground anyway they could. There were limits, after all, to regulations.

Similar improvisation marked the defense of Aviation Machinist's Mate Carl Hatcher's hangar. Hatcher took a portable workbench fitted with casters and used the vise on the bench as a mount for an aircraft machine gun. He was doing his best to shoot down the attacking planes when a bomb dropped nearby. Luckily for Hatcher it was a dud. Still, he thought, it might be a delayed-action bomb. Using another piece of rolling equipment from the hangar, he took an A-frame, hoisted up the bomb, rolled it to the water's edge, and lowered it ever so gently into the harbor.[3]

Nearby stood Hangar 38, occupied by the Kingfisher-Medusa repair unit which serviced the fleet's scout planes. Like other sailors from the repair unit, Merion Croft dashed for the hangar when the bombs began to fall. As he ran he clearly saw the Japanese rear-seat gunner strafing the area. The gunner could barely see over the ammunition cans surrounding him and had to look over the side of his plane to aim his fire. When aircraft and hangars began to burn, Croft helped pull the planes to safety. He was astounded to note that many of the aircraft had 100-pound bombs and 150-pound depth charges in their wing racks. Afraid that the heat would ignite the bombs and depth charges, the sailors carried the explosives and dumped them in the water. When he recalled the experience Croft was amazed he was able to handle the weight.[4]

The Kingfisher-Medusa repair unit suffered no serious casualties. One bomb hit the hangar but failed to explode. Instead, it spewed a yellow sulfuric powder across the hangar causing caustic burns on a few of the men nearby. Like Carl Hatcher, some of the mechanics in Croft's unit mounted aircraft machine guns in vises clamped to portable workbenches. No one shouted orders; people made suggestions in normal tones. Curiosity overcame fear in many cases, and when Japanese planes came in for strafing or bombing runs men forsook shelter and stood up to watch. At one point a Cadillac ambulance sped past Hangar 38 carrying wounded to the sick bay. The driver was trying to make a turn as he crossed the sloping seaplane ramp and lost control. The ambulance overturned, and Croft and others ran out to the ramp without a word among themselves and tilted the vehicle upright. There were no injuries from the accident, and the ambulance continued to the sick bay.

Ford Island served as a refuge and assembly area for surviving crewmen of the sunken ships moored along its shores. Robert Johnson and other *Utah* sailors were gathered together by Lieutenant Hauck, one of the ship's officers. Soaked, shaken, and in some cases wounded, there was little they could do to help in the fight. After ordering the men to take shelter in trenches that had been excavated for utility lines, Hauck went in search of sustenance for his charges. He returned with cigarettes and wine, which he doled out to the *Utah* crewmen as they waited for the attack to pass.[5]

Damage and casualties on Ford Island were surprisingly light, considering the concentrated attention given the air station by the Japanese. The great majority of the 130 casualties treated at the Ford Island dispensary were burned and wounded who swam or were brought ashore from nearby ships. Eleven bombs hit Ford Island—six of them on or near Hangar 6. That hangar was the only one seriously damaged. Even there, the structural steel framing was left intact, allowing the building to be reconstructed. Twenty-six planes, less than half the number on Ford Island, were destroyed. Most of those were in or near Hangar 6. One bomb landed in the dispensary courtyard and buried itself in the ground before it exploded, leaving a hole 7 feet deep and severing electrical, water, and steam service to the building. Fortunately, no one was injured.[6]

The greatest potential disaster for Ford Island came not directly from Japanese bombs but from the tanker *Neosho*. The ship was moored at Ford Island's gasoline dock and, although she had just completed discharging a load of aviation fuel, was still nearly full of high-octane gas. Hoses still joined the ship to Ford Island when the attack began. Ensign Arnold Singleton was directing Chief Machinist's Mate Alfred Hansen and Aviation Machinist's Mate Second Class Albert Thatcher in clearing the gas lines when the first bomb dropped. Working under a hail of shrapnel and machine gun bullets

(Hansen was wounded twice), the three men continued the delicate task of disconnecting the tanker despite the all too obvious danger of immolation. It took them another forty-five minutes, and it was not until 8:42 that *Neosho*'s captain, Commander John Phillips, was able to begin backing the tanker across the channel toward Merry Point. Despite the rain of destruction on battleships moored near *Neosho*, she suffered no damage while on Battleship Row nor on her short journey in reverse.[7]

Even with *Neosho* gone, there still remained the danger from her cargo, much of which had been discharged into Ford Island's aviation fuel storage tanks. Singleton, Hansen, and Thatcher opened the sprinkler valves on the tanks, again risking the danger of fire and explosion. Their work may have averted a much more serious disaster and greater casualties on Ford Island. Singleton was not yet through with his morning's work. He spent the balance of the day supervising the recovery of wounded men struggling ashore, transporting them to the dispensary, and cleaning them of the oil caked on the swimmers. The commanding officer of the Ford Island air station praised Singleton's "bravery and extraordinary devotion to duty" and commended Hansen and Thatcher as well.[8]

Two miles southeast of *Neosho*'s berth lay Hickam Field, which received a heavier pounding than Ford Island. The base housed the headquarters of the Hawaiian Air Force and the Eighteenth Bombardment Wing. The wing's twelve B-17s, thirty-two B-18s, and thirteen A-20s were potentially the most threatening retaliatory force the Americans could launch against Nagumo's carriers. Hickam was, therefore, an important target for the raiders, and the Japanese began their strikes against the bomber base as they launched their torpedoes against the Pacific Fleet. Like the attack on the fleet the raid caught Hickam by surprise. Hangars, planes, and men on the ground quickly fell victim to attacks by fighters, dive bombers, and high-flying horizontal bombers.

Captain Gordon Blake, Hickam's operations officer, was in his office preparing for the arrival of the B-17s from California (the same flight which had caused Lieutenant Tyler to dismiss the Opana radar contact) when the attack began. He first thought to warn the B-17s and raced to the control tower to send a radio message, but he was unable to make the transmission. The next best course, he decided, was to drive out on the field to be there when they landed. Leaving the tower, he found his staff car missing; it had been commandeered as an ambulance to move the rapidly mounting casualties. By one of the incongruities of war Blake found himself riding on the back seat of a motorcycle. His improvised staff car was provided by a member of a Honolulu motorcycle club—dressed in full leather gear—which had turned out its membership to respond in the emergency.[9]

As Captain Blake sped about the base he beheld the appalling spectacle of burning buildings, shattered bodies, and the destruction of more than half the bombers caught defenseless on the ground. Of Hickam's twelve B-17s, all but eight were rendered useless; twenty-two of the thirty-two B-18 medium bombers and eight of the thirteen A-20 light attack bombers met the same fate.[10] Some units were nearly wiped out. The Fiftieth Reconnaissance Squadron had two B-17s and four B-18s; only one B-18 survived the attack. The men of the squadron suffered serious casualties when they were strafed as they fled across open ground to a safer position after a bomb hit their hangar.[11]

Some of the other squadrons were luckier. Quick thinking led the ground crews of the Seventy-second Bomb Squadron to disperse their aircraft as soon as the attack began. As a result of their timely reaction the unit had only one B-18 lightly damaged. In addition, the men of the Seventy-second had the satisfaction of exacting at least some measure of retribution from the Japanese. Master Sergeant Olef Jensen directed the emplacement of machine guns, and one crew under Staff Sergeant R. R. Mitchell was credited with shooting down one plane.[12] Despite the efforts of Jensen and other gunners, the Japanese enjoyed relatively unhindered strafing runs. Lieutenant James Latham of the Eleventh Bomb Group nearly fell victim to one strafer. When the attack began, Latham jumped into his Ford (he had mailed the final payment to the finance company the night before) and set out for his hangar. A low-flying Japanese plane put several bullets into the car, which exploded and turned over. Latham escaped unharmed but his car was a total loss.[13]

Harold Fishencord, a Fifth Bomb Group ground crewman, made it to the hangar line. He taxied a B-18 to the end of the runway where, even if it would not be out of danger, at least it posed no fire hazard to nearby planes. When the B-17s began arriving from California, Fishencord taxied one of the bombers to a revetment and managed to remove the plane's empty bomb bay tank single-handedly. He then climbed into the aircraft and feinted at the Japanese planes by training the unarmed dorsal gun turret. Fishencord's most indelible memory from the day was not his own doings, however, but the screams of an airman who burned to death when he was trapped in the nose compartment of a burning B-18.[14]

On the whole, Hickam's antiaircraft fire was as inadequate as Pearl Harbor's. Lieutenant James Dyson noted that antiaircraft rounds burst consistently short of the horizontal bombers flying at 10,000 feet.[15] It was probably one of those horizontal bombers which inflicted heavy casualties at Hickam's huge new consolidated barracks. The headquarters squadron of the Eleventh Bomb Group reported 245 casualties from among its 350 men, including 16 killed and 50 disabled. One group crowded into a barracks doorway trying to comprehend the events about them when bombs exploded on either side of the door. The Eleventh suffered more casualties when a detail of twenty-one men assembled to receive instructions from their first sergeant; a bomb exploded nearby, killing all but four.[16]

Leon Webster and a small group of men took shelter from bombs and bullets under a building near the post exchange. From there they watched in disbelief as another airman took advantage of the chaos by looting the exchange. The man emerged from the PX loaded with a case of beer and cartons of cigarettes and proceeded across the parade ground. He was caught in the open by a Japanese strafer, and as he fell Webster and his companions watched cigarette packs and beer cans fly in all directions.[17]

First Lieutenant Frederick Cooper, commander of Headquarters Squadron, Seventeenth Air Base Group, saw the bombs strike the barracks and marveled at the flight discipline of the raiders: "The formation was perfect . . . and the timing on the dropping of the bombs was so perfect that I could follow them down in V formation right to the ground, right to impact."[18] Cooper's clerks set up machine guns on the parade ground, but they lacked the water cans necessary for operation. The same cluster of bombs which wreaked havoc on the barracks also struck the parade ground and the baseball diamond. The ballfield was near Hickam's underground gasoline storage, and some speculated that the bombs which fell on the diamond were meant for the gas tanks.[19] There is no evidence, however, to support the view that Japanese intelligence believed the ballfield covered the storage tanks.

Japanese bombs missed the main fuel storage, but they ignited fires aplenty at Hickam. Most of the base's firemen were killed and their equipment destroyed early in the attack. At 8:10 someone from Hickam telephoned Bellows Field, a small airstrip on the other side of the island, and commandeered Bellows' single fire truck. Units of the Honolulu Fire Department's Kalihi and South Beretania Street stations responded to additional calls. When the Kalihi station received the call, the firefighters there were told only to respond to a hangar fire at Hickam; they did not know the field was under attack.[20]

Firefighter Max Itoga's truck approached the gate from Kalihi and was met by a motorcycle escort of MPs. Itoga turned to his companions and joked about the special escort. When firefighters Richard Young and Anthony Lopez, also of Kalihi, arrived at the scene they found the dead driver slumped over the wheel of a Hickam Field fire engine which had been driven only 20 feet before it had been strafed. The other engine had been destroyed in the station.[21]

Honolulu Fire Department Lieutenant Frederick Kealoha assumed command of the civilian firefighters only to find much of his equipment unusable. The water main had been severed by a bomb blast, but Kealoha's men pumped water from the flooded bomb crater to the fires by laying more than a mile of hose from the broken main to the fires. Inside one of the hangars Itoga and Hoseman Harry Pang played a stream of water on one of the burning planes. A strafing attack, followed by a bomb blast, killed Pang and Fire Captain William Macy.

Intermittent Japanese attacks put many of their trucks out of commission, but the resourceful firefighters used brown soap and toilet paper from nearby latrines to plug holes in the radiators. Working under falling bombs and strafing, three Honolulu firefighters were killed at Hickam and five wounded, including Lieutenant Kealoha.

Other civilians also helped fight fires in Hickam's shops, hangars, and flight lines. General Mechanic Helper William Garretson converted a gas tanker to a water truck in record time. The truck was driven to nearby Bishop Point, filled with seawater, and returned just in time to help Kealoha's firefighters save the critically important main shop building. Another mechanic helper, Clifford Oliver, drove a truck into a burning repair building to remove aircraft engines. James Mahr, Robert Awong, Nicolas Lenchanko, Volney McRoberts, and Charles Baker were credited with preventing the fires from spreading to Building 35.[22]

Civilian worker Carl Brown did his unappreciated best to help save an OA4, one of the few undamaged observation planes on the airstrip. When it looked as though the aircraft would be destroyed someone shouted, "For God's sake, save that plane!" Brown, who was neither a pilot nor a mechanic, somehow managed to start the plane and taxi it to a distant part of the runway. Bullets from strafers and antiaircraft machine gun fire pierced the plane's fabric, but Brown zigzagged across the field until he reached a safe spot. After he gratefully abandoned ship, he was confronted by a furious soldier screaming, "Get the hell out of here! Don't you know this is a combat area?"[23]

Under these chaotic conditions the orderly handling of casualties was impossible. Captain Charles Brombach roamed the repair area in a truck looking for men in need of first aid. The Hickam hospital was, in the words of one witness, "covered with wounded and dying, laying on litters and some on mattresses brought to the grounds from the barracks. More wounded were being brought in by every conceivable sort of transportation. Bread wagons, milk wagons, hand carts and anything that was handy."[24]

With regular medical services overwhelmed, makeshift assistance was the order of the day. Private Harold Lenburg, badly wounded by a bomb blast and strafing outside Hangar 11, was carried on a stretcher improvised from window screens. Elsewhere, Ray Dudly and other airmen were pressed into service by a wounded ambulance driver. The driver took them to the parade ground, where they stacked the most badly wounded on top of one another in the back of the ambulance. That many of the wounded were personal friends made the task no easier. James Duncan and Carmen Calderon of the Eleventh Bomb Group also carried the dead and dying to Hickam's small hospital. When the doctor performing triage there saw their blood-soaked clothes, he insisted they undress for an examination. He found that Calderon had been carrying wounded men into the hospital with a broken arm.[25]

The casualties at Hickam Field were the greatest of any army post on December 7. With 158 dead and missing and 336 wounded, Hickam accounted for three-fourths of the army casualties. With more than half the field's bombers out of commission, there remained little chance of immediate retaliation against the Japanese task force (assuming it could be located). Damage to Hickam's ground facilities, although not disastrous, was serious. Among the important buildings which escaped with "light" damage were the new main shop, equipment repair, new steam plant, and the partially completed armament building. Total or near total losses included the engineering administration office, drafting unit, blueprint and specification files, parachute section, and aircraft engine overhaul and assembly section. When General Martin, the Hawaiian Air Force commander, was informed of the damage one witness said, "I never saw a more dejected person."[26]

Adjacent to Hickam Field stood Fort Kamehameha, whose coastal batteries were trained seaward for a big-gun naval attack which never came. Although unimportant as a target, Fort Kamehameha suffered spillover from the attack on the air base. Colonel William McCarthy, commander of the First Battalion, Fifty-fifth Coast Artillery, heard explosions and machine gun fire shortly before 8:00. He ran out of his quarters and saw a Japanese plane streak over the post toward Hickam Field. He alerted his 155-millimeter mobile battery commanders to proceed to their assigned coastal defense positions along Oahu's southwest shoreline. As he reached the battery encamped at nearby Ahua Point, a low-flying Japanese fighter struck a tree, hit another tree, and crashed into a wall. The dead pilot was left lodged in a tree, but the fuselage smashed into the ground and the engine continued tumbling around the corner of the ordnance shop. One coast artilleryman was decapitated by flying wreckage and another killed by the spinning propeller, which cut off his head and all four limbs.[27]

Private Creed Short, the post ambulance driver, was in the motor pool waxing his vehicle. Leaving the wax job unfinished he sped to the dispensary but received no orders from the officers there. He took the initiative and drove to the site of the crash witnessed by Colonel McCarthy to pick up the injured. Captain Frank Ebey, commander of McCarthy's Battery B, quickly organized his men in setting up .30-caliber machine guns on antiaircraft mounts in Fort Kamehameha's tennis courts. He checked his watch when they began firing and noted with satisfaction that it was 8:13—less than twenty minutes after the first bomb fell.

His personal satisfaction notwithstanding, Ebey still had to get his men and guns out to Barbers Point, 10 miles to the west. The problem was not the distance but the route. To reach Barbers Point his battery had to load on a barge, cross the Pearl Harbor channel, and disembark on the other side. They were delayed for a time while the few ships in Pearl Harbor able to get under way sortied at speeds which would have infuriated the harbormaster on any other day. Ebey's barge, handled coolly by Quartermaster Jack Barros and crewed by a mix of soldiers, sailors, and civilians, made six trips across the channel under fire. On one crossing two Japanese fighters singled out the craft and commenced a strafing attack. None of his men were injured, but it seemed to Ebey as though "they were unloading a truckload of high explosive ammunition" on his helpless barge. The battery's .30-caliber machine guns (still on antiaircraft mounts for just such a contingency) fired back, but it was fire from nearby naval vessels, Ebey conceded, that destroyed the planes in midair.[28]

12

AGAINST THE ODDS

Destruction of the bombers at Hickam Field vastly increased the odds for Nagumo's carriers to escape unscathed. But whether the Japanese aircraft could complete their mission depended on forestalling opposition from U.S. interceptors. The Fourteenth Pursuit Wing, headquartered and concentrated at Wheeler Field in central Oahu, was the fighter command responsible for controlling the skies over Hawaii. Commanded by Brigadier General Howard Davidson, the wing included ninety-nine relatively modern P-40s, thirty-nine obsolete P-36s, and an assortment of even older planes. These fighters were unarmed and on a routine alert status, which meant they required four hours preparation before they could be readied for combat.[1] Two of Davidson's pursuit squadrons, the Forty-fourth and the Forty-seventh, were temporarily based at nearby Haleiwa and Bellows Field for gunnery practice.

The first attackers approached Wheeler from slightly north of east at 5,000 feet. (A few strays may have come from the west through Kolekole Pass.) Arranged in a large V formation, they circled counterclockwise and dove toward the hangar line. There the parked pursuit planes sat helpless against the onslaught of bombs, cannon fire, and machine gun bullets. The havoc was so great, in fact, that it disrupted Japanese flight discipline. As Wheeler's official report noted, "After first dive bombing phase enemy planes lost practically all order and all formation. Attack continued with gunfire. During gunfire phase enemy attacked from all directions with complete disregard of collision possibilities."[2]

General Davidson was in his quarters shaving when the Japanese planes screamed down on Wheeler. His first reaction was irritation. He thought the returning *Enterprise* pilots were "flat hatting" the army air base en route to their own airstrips. Davidson made a mental note to write Kimmel and quash the nuisance once and for all. When he heard the first explosions, followed by strafing, Davidson knew that his Sunday morning had been disturbed by something more than a prank. He could do little to save his command from destruction, but he did manage to shepherd to safety his ten-year-old twin daughters, who rushed out of the house to pick up the shiny brass 20-millimeter shells spewed onto the ground by strafing Japanese fighters.[3]

At the other end of Wheeler's rank scale, Private First Class Edmund Russell was on duty at the mess hall. The night before, he had spent a relatively uneventful evening watching the movie *Dive Bomber*. Russell was beginning the day's work by reading the Sunday menu to see how much meat had to be removed from the freezer when he heard the first dive bombers bearing down on the field. His first thought, like Davidson's, was that navy or marine pilots were having a little Sunday morning fun at the army's expense. When he heard the first explosion Russell thought one of the planes had crashed, but when he heard a second and then a third blast he knew it was something out of the ordinary. Russell ran for the nearest cover, a row of eucalyptus trees near Wahiawa School. It was not until the planes began strafing and he saw the rising sun insignia on their wings that he realized the shocking truth—the entertainment of the night before had suddenly been transformed into reality.[4]

The Japanese concentrated their attack on the hangar line, but their bombs found other targets as well. A post exchange warehouse and another storage building were hit. Bombs also struck tents housing sleeping ground crewmen and the Sixth Pursuit Squadron barracks. The explosions blew airmen out of upper-story windows of the barracks. Many of those who survived suffered painful fractures.[5]

Wheeler's disaster planning had been less than brilliant. Antiaircraft defense for the post had been left in the hands of a skeleton crew from the base fire department, which had been given six hours training in the operation of a .50-caliber antiaircraft machine gun. Evidently it had not occurred to anyone that an emergency requiring antiaircraft defense might well place a heavy burden on the fire department too. Nonetheless, the gun was mounted on the firehouse roof. The firefighters decided that, since they had never actually fired the weapon, their services would be more valuable fighting the blazes than in manning the machine gun. Seeing the gun unmanned, a stockade guard and a prisoner took over the weapon.[6]

Others at Wheeler responded as best they could under the circumstances. And the circumstances were grim indeed. The burning planes were igniting nearby aircraft. The entire complement of P-40s belonging to the Seventy-second Pursuit Squadron was destroyed, and exploding ammunition stored in a nearby hangar made rescue efforts particularly dangerous for the men of that unit. Still, Staff Sergeant Charles Fay of the Seventy-second taxied planes clear of the burning hangar area despite two wounds from machine gun fire. Private Donald Plant was killed by strafing fire while removing a wounded man, and others fired small arms at the raiders in a futile attempt at resistance.[7]

Major Kenneth Bergquist, operations officer of the Fourteenth Pursuit Wing, realized there was little he could do at Wheeler. He reasoned that he could be most effective by providing General Davidson with an accurate picture of the overall situation. He commandeered a staff car and driver and headed for the information center at Fort Shafter. Bergquist had barely left Wheeler when he met a string of Japanese planes heading north from Pearl Harbor. They headed toward his staff car, so he ordered his driver to stop and take cover. The driver ran into the brush by the side of the road while Bergquist crouched behind a rear wheel. But the driver, in his haste, had not set the brake securely, and the major had to do a "squat walk" to follow the car as it rolled slowly downhill toward Pearl Harbor. Despite a spray of machine gun bullets from the planes—some of which hit the car—Bergquist's only injury was a cut finger where he had grasped the fender of his rolling vehicle. When the attack ended he was unable to find his driver, and figuring the man had joined another group taking cover in the bushes, Bergquist got in the car and drove to Fort Shafter on his own. Later he learned that the driver had been wounded in the leg. Despite the urgency of his trip to the information center, Bergquist regretted for years afterward that he had inadvertently left the wounded man behind.[8]

Schofield Barracks, the sprawling infantry post next door to Wheeler Field, was also attacked, although damage and casualties were far less severe. One bomb landed in the front yard of Major General Maxwell Murray, commander of the Twenty-fifth Infantry Division. Murray's first response to the attack was to order ammunition issued to his artillery units. Next he ordered machine guns set up on the roofs of the barracks buildings, but he found that his men had already mounted their .30-caliber guns atop the barracks and were firing back.[9]

Elzer Coates, a soldier in the Thirty-fourth Engineer Regiment, had trouble convincing his buddies that Wheeler and Schofield were actually under hostile attack. In fact, several members of the Thirty-fourth climbed to the barracks roof for a grandstand view of the "drill." They were finally convinced by a shower of dirt which dispersed a group of men standing below. The men broke into their armory for machine guns, but found them useless because there was no belted ammunition. While they tried to belt the ammunition a lone Japanese plane flew over their area and bombed and strafed two large tanks which supplied the post with fresh water. The bomb fell between the tanks and exploded harmlessly, but Coates remembers water spurting from the bullet holes in the tanks.[10]

The writer James Jones, then a company clerk in the Twenty-seventh Infantry Regiment, drew on his memories of army life and the December 7 attack when he wrote *From Here to Eternity*. His actual experience that day was more prosaic:

At Schofield Barracks in the infantry quadrangles, those of us who were up were at breakfast. On Sunday morning in those days there was a bonus ration of a half-pint of milk, to go with your eggs or pancakes and syrup, also Sunday specials. Most of us were more concerned with getting and holding onto our half-pints of milk than with listening to the explosions that began rumbling up toward us from Wheeler Field two miles away. "They doing some blasting?" some old-timer said through a mouthful of pancakes. It was not till the first low-flying fighter came skidding, whammering low overhead with his MG's going that we ran outside, still clutching our half-pints of milk to keep them from being stolen, aware with a sudden sense of awe that we were seeing and acting in a genuine moment of history.[11]

Antiaircraft protection for the Schofield area was the responsibility of the Ninety-eighth Coast Artillery Regiment. Ironically, it was not the regiment's 3-inch antiaircraft guns which brought down Japanese planes, but weapons issued to the unit for infantry defense. Lieutenant Stephen Saltzman and Sergeant Lowell Klatt were assigned to communications duties with the regiment. After seeing planes roar through Kolekole Pass they moved their men and equipment to their assigned position at the eastern edge of Wheeler Field. About 8:30 Saltzman heard two Val dive bombers straining to pull out of a dive. He seized a Browning automatic rifle (BAR) from a nearby guard, dropped to his knees, and (after making sure they were not American planes) began firing. Sergeant Klatt followed his example. The two planes continued their dive, and the lead plane began strafing the two men. Then the aircraft passed out of sight behind a building, and Klatt and Saltzman heard a loud explosion. Running around the corner of the building, they found they had downed one of the planes. It is a measure of the confusion which prevailed that they mistakenly identified the plane's wings, engine, and propeller as being American made.[12]

One pursuit squadron normally based at Wheeler, the Forty-seventh, escaped serious damage by virtue of its training schedule. The unit was temporarily posted to Haleiwa Field, about 10 miles north of Wheeler on Oahu's north shore. Haleiwa, unlike the other airfields, was not the object of a concentrated attack. Perhaps the lack of air units permanently stationed there led the Japanese to believe Haleiwa unworthy of their attention. The attackers made one strafing pass about 8:30, but only one plane (a P-36) was damaged and the attack was driven off by rifle and machine gun fire.[13] The Japanese had more important targets elsewhere.

The light damage at Haleiwa permitted pilots of the Forty-seventh to offer most of what little fighter opposition the Japanese faced on December 7. Sunday morning found Second Lieutenants George Welch and Kenneth Taylor at Wheeler Field. A hasty telephone call to Haleiwa alerted ground crews to begin preparing planes for combat. They drove the 10 miles to Haleiwa and discovered the crewmen working feverishly to ready the squadron's pursuit planes. About 8:20 Taylor and Welch were airborne in P-40s. Since their .50-caliber machine guns were inoperable, the planes' only effective armament was four wing-mounted .30-caliber guns in each aircraft.[14]

The two officers winged southward from Haleiwa searching for enemy aircraft. As they passed Wheeler they saw smoke billowing from the destruction below, but the first-wave attackers had already departed from the immediate vicinity. Ground radio control directed Welch and Taylor to the Barbers Point area. There they encountered a group of about a dozen Japanese planes assaulting Ewa Field from an altitude of 1,000 feet. They dove into the formation and began firing. One of Welch's guns jammed, but each man shot down one Val on that first pass. Taylor then downed another dive bomber as it attempted to escape out to sea. Welch's trouble with his jammed machine gun was compounded by a hit from an incendiary bullet just behind his seat. His plane began to smoke and he climbed into a cloud bank to check the damage. The smoke abated and he rejoined

Taylor in the fray. His persistence was rewarded when Welch downed yet another plane over the water. Taylor managed to inflict damage on at least two others.

After the fight at Ewa, Welch and Taylor needed more fuel and ammunition. They landed at Wheeler to replenish and took to the air once again at 9:00. Welch took off without incident, but a second group of Vals arrived at Wheeler just as Taylor was about to leave. Taking off in the face of a strafing attack by the oncoming attackers, Taylor maneuvered too close on the tail of what he thought was the last Japanese in the group. As he fired at his target, however, he himself came under fire from the rear by yet another Val. Wounded by a bullet through his left arm and fragments in his leg, Taylor climbed desperately for survival. His luck held as Welch came to his aid and shot down the attacker. The Val crashed halfway between Wheeler and Haleiwa after his rear gun scored hits on Welch's engine, propeller, and cowling. As the two Americans pursued the retreating Japanese, Welch shot down one more for a tally of four Japanese planes for the day. When Taylor exhausted his ammunition he returned to Wheeler *hors de combat* from his wounds.

Welsh and Taylor were not the only pilots of the Forty-seventh to take advantage of the Japanese inattention to Haleiwa. First Lieutenant Robert Rogers and Second Lieutenants Harry Brown and John Dains also made the drive from Wheeler to Haleiwa. Arriving at the airfield after escaping strafing attacks on the road, the three got airborne individually about 8:50, Dains in a P-40 and the others in P-36s. These P-36s lacked working .50-caliber guns and were armed with only a single .30-caliber weapon apiece. Rogers and Brown found each other near Haleiwa and, after circling warily before establishing identification, found a small group of Japanese planes headed north, probably heading back to their carriers. Brown attacked, scored a possible hit, then overshot his target when the Japanese pilot cut his throttle, dived, and lowered his flaps. Rogers and Brown then proceeded to Kaena Point at Oahu's northwestern tip. Dains engaged at least one Japanese aircraft, returned to Haleiwa with his damaged plane, and took off again. Meanwhile, First Lieutenant John Webster left the small field in a P-36.

Back at Wheeler First Lieutenant Lewis Sanders organized a group of planes and pilots of the Forty-sixth Pursuit Squadron. Sanders, with Lieutenants Othniel Norris, John Thacker, and Philip Rasmussen, obtained four P-36s and readied for takeoff at 8:50. Norris left his plane with the engine running to search for a new parachute, and

Second Lieutenant Gordon Sterling, an inexperienced pilot from the Forty-fifth Pursuit Squadron, seized the opportunity. Sterling climbed into the fighter and joined the rest of the group as it taxied out to the runway. Sanders was directed by fighter control to take his group to Kaneohe and Bellows and provide air cover against Japanese attackers at those bases. Another of the Forty-sixth's pilots, Second Lieutenant Fred Shifflet, commandeered a working P-40 from another squadron, took off from Wheeler, and returned with the plane riddled with holes. About thirty minutes after Sanders' group departed First Lieutenant Malcolm Moore was airborne from Wheeler in another P-36.

While Rogers and Brown patrolled at Kaena Point they were joined by Webster and Moore. (Moore had flown up from Wheeler on his own.) The four found an abundant selection of targets, for the Japanese had designated Kaena Point as the rendezvous point for the return flight to the carriers. Rogers and Webster teamed up to attack two Japanese planes, but Rogers' aircraft was seriously damaged and Webster suffered a leg wound. Both were forced to return to Haleiwa, but not before Brown saved Rogers from a close call. Two planes came after Rogers and he dove into a steep escape. Rogers bluffed one of them off course with a feint and destroyed the other with a burst of fire from less than 50 feet. Moore attacked another plane, but it escaped into the clouds. Brown meanwhile faced more than a dozen Japanese single-handedly, but a head-on approach dispersed their formation and he escaped. He then encountered the plane which had run from Moore. Brown attacked; the carrier pilot headed out to sea trailing smoke, and Brown abandoned the pursuit. Moore, Webster, Brown, and Rogers all landed safely at Haleiwa.

While the other army pilots fought the Japanese along the Ewa–Wheeler–Kaena Point axis, Sanders, Sterling, Rasmussen, and Thacker flew southeast to Kaneohe and Bellows. Flying at 11,000 feet, Sanders spotted Japanese planes about a mile below. He signaled his group to close up for the attack and was shocked to see Sterling had taken Norris's place. He had no choice but to put the inexperienced pilot on his right wing and led the formation into a dive on a group of nine raiders over Kaneohe Bay. Sanders fired on the leader, saw smoke billow from his target, and made a 360-degree turn to clear his tail. He completed the turn in time to see Sterling shoot down a plane. Sterling had no time to savor his victory, for instantly a Zeke was on his tail. The obsolete P-36 never had a chance, and Sterling went down in flames.

Rasmussen, meanwhile, was having troubles of his own. His .50-caliber machine gun malfunctioned and "ran away" in uncontrolled firing when he cocked it. Still, he managed to shoot down a Val. Immediately after his victory, he saw Sterling and his victim both hit the water. Rasmussen continued to watch as Sanders exacted quick revenge by attacking the Japanese fighter from behind. Rasmussen had little time to contemplate the action. Two Zekes made a broadside attack, extensively damaging his plane. He recalls:

> I thought I had been killed. I was sure that the top of my head had been shot off. I could feel a mass up there and felt sure it was my brains, but I was having such a fight to control the plane that it took a minute or two before I could gingerly put a hand to the top of my helmet. All that was there was a pile of plexiglass; no blood, not a scratch.[15]

After downing the plane which had claimed Sterling, Sanders made a circuit of the area and encountered another Zeke head-on. As they closed each pilot began to climb and maneuver to gain a clear shot at the other's tail. Sanders' obsolete P-36 was no match for the more modern and powerful Japanese fighter, so he broke off the engagement before he became yet another casualty. John Thacker's guns jammed on his first pass, but he continued making dry runs at the Japanese. When his plane was hit by 20-millimeter cannon fire he headed home to Wheeler, but he was mistaken for Japanese and driven off by ground fire. Lacking any alternative, Thacker climbed back into the clouds. Rasmussen, barely in control of his plane, soon arrived escorted by Sanders. Rasmussen's plane was in imminent danger of falling victim to the law of gravity, so he had no choice but to attempt a landing in the face of antiaircraft fire from Wheeler's now alert defenders. Miraculously, both he and Sanders made safe landings, followed shortly by Thacker.

Two more interceptor sorties were made on December 7. Dains and Welch left Haleiwa at 9:30 for the third and final flight of the day for each pilot. By this time Dains had traded his battered P-40 for a P-36, while Welch still flew the newer fighter. The Japanese planes were returning to their carriers by then, and neither pilot found any targets. On their return to Wheeler they were fired on by trigger-happy antiaircraft gunners. Welch landed safely, but Dains was killed when he crashed on a nearby golf course. John Dains and Gordon Sterling were the only deaths from among the Wheeler and Haleiwa pilots who took to the air. Collectively, they were credited with ten confirmed kills and an uncertain number of probables.

That total accounted for more than half the Japanese planes downed by the army on December 7. The army's coastal artillery units assigned to antiaircraft defense were for the most part unable to ready their equipment in time to respond to the attack. In many cases these units were assigned battle positions miles away from their quarters, and their ammunition supplies were often stored in distant locations. Typical was the experience of the 251st Coast Artillery Regiment, a California National Guard unit called to active duty and posted at Camp Malakole near Barbers Point.

First Lieutenant Willis Lyman of Battery E was preparing himself for the Sunday morning dedication of Camp Malakole's new chapel when he received a telephone call from the wife of another officer in the regiment. The woman, calling from the Wheeler–Schofield area, was worried. There was a lot of noise and "big black things dropping around the place." Lyman assured her it was nothing to be worried about—just some early morning practice. After hanging up the telephone he stepped out onto his porch and looked in the direction of Pearl Harbor. He saw explosive bursts in the air and at the same time spotted a small group of planes headed for his camp. Lyman reached for his binoculars for a better look. The rising sun insignia on the planes told the story, and he ordered his battery's two .30-caliber machine guns (intended for ground protection, not antiaircraft work) into action.[16]

The post's sergeant of the guard, June Dickens, got his first inkling of the attack when two Japanese planes roared down the camp's main street strafing. Dickens responded with his available armed guards. Two men in a fire tower armed with BARs (posted as antisabotage guards) provided the most effective fire. Machine guns mounted on two trucks on alert for saboteurs gave further help. A marine unit on the beach nearby for aerial gunnery practice got an unexpectedly realistic drill and joined in with their weapons. At least one plane fell into the ocean just off Malakole.[17]

Other Japanese planes in the area encountered the morning *Enterprise* flight which had stumbled into the battle. Some managed to engage the raiders with mutually fatal results. Captain Lester Milz of Battery D reported that a Val and an SBD collided during a dogfight, killing the two Japanese air crewmen and the *Enterprise* airmen, Ensign J. H. L. Vogt, Jr., and Radioman Third Class Pierce Sidney.[18]

It took Battery B nearly an hour to assemble its 75-millimeter guns and move them into position at the West Loch Naval Ammunition Depot. Sergeant Eugene Camp's truck was strafed repeatedly as it moved along the back roads to the battery's assigned location. Camp was surprised that there seemed to be a military policeman stationed at every major intersection along his route. Battery B was luckier than some other antiaircraft units. Since its assignment included the depot's ammunition bunkers, its 75-millimeter shells were already positioned at the firing site. Still, the artillerymen, augmented by some twenty *Oglala* survivors, had no targets by the time they were ready to go into action.[19]

Eight minutes before the bombs fell on Malakole, Hickam, or Wheeler, Kaneohe Naval Air Station suffered the first assault of the day. Kaneohe was home for Patrol Wing One, a PBY unit. The day before the attack, at a Saturday morning inspection, the station's personnel had been lectured on the danger of sabotage. Partly because of the concern with sabotage, most of the planes of Patrol Wing One were parked together on the seaplane ramp; four were moored in the bay about 1,000 yards apart, and four were in Hangar 1. There were thirty-six planes, nearly all of them PBYs, at Kaneohe.[20]

The post commander, Commander Harold Martin, was enjoying a cup of coffee shortly after 7:45 when he noticed about a dozen fighters approaching the base at 800 feet. As they rounded nearby Hawaiiloa Hill and approached the airfield, Martin's young son pointed out the rising sun insignia on the planes. Before he could alert his men the fighters began to strafe the base, setting many of the patrol planes afire with incendiary bullets.

In front of the base administration building the marine guard was assembled for the morning colors ceremony. As the strafing began the corporal in charge of the detail started to run up the colors, but his assistant was resolved to wait until 8:00. The corporal hoisted on the halyard while his helper, a much lighter man, hung on grimly. The determined helper went halfway up the flagstaff before he let go.[21]

The first attack destroyed the patrol planes moored on the bay. At 8:15 a second group of attackers hit Kaneohe. This group of about eighteen planes, mostly dive bombers, inflicted more damage. Sailors and civilian construction workers tried to drag burning planes clear of the ramp area. Some men seized rifles and machine guns and fired back at the Japanese. Chief Petty Officer John Finn took a .50-caliber machine gun from one of the planes on the ground and continued firing even after suffering several painful wounds. Sam Aweau, a quick-witted civilian contractor working on the base, called

Hickam and Bellows and passed on news of the attack on Kaneohe. Aweau, however, was not believed and his presence of mind was of no avail. Construction workers quickly set about repairing severed water and electrical lines. Commander Martin praised Mrs. Spencer, the post's civil service telephone operator, for her "calmness and initiative" throughout the attack.[22]

The base suffered yet a third attack at approximately 9:00 when a squadron of fighters from *Soryu* led by Lieutenant Fusata Iida hit Kaneohe once more. For Lieutenant (jg) Iyozo Fujita, Iida's friend and one of his flight leaders, the Pearl Harbor attack was his first time in combat. The squadron circled the island twice in search of fighter opposition. Finding none they dived on the base from the east across the *pali,* the spectacular line of cliffs behind Kaneohe. Fujita was nervous enough on his first combat mission, and puffs of smoke from antiaircraft bursts did little to calm him. Nervous or not, Fujita and the rest of the squadron did their work thoroughly. This third attack exacted the greatest loss of life at the station when a bomb exploded in a hangar crowded with men drawing ammunition.[23]

The Japanese paid for their persistence when Iida's plane was hit by ground fire and began streaming fuel. Fujita saw the white vapor trailing from the plane. Iida pointed to the remaining planes in the squadron, then northward in the direction of the carriers, then to himself, and finally to the ground. The message was clear to Fujita. The squadron leader was ordering them to return to the task force while he would hold to an agreement previously reached among the pilots themselves: If one of them were unable to return to the carrier he would crash dive into an enemy target rather than bail out. The pilots had even left their parachutes behind on *Soryu* to guarantee the commitment. Iida went down, but missed any targets of importance and crashed into a hillside. Despite the loss of Lieutenant Iida, the Japanese attack on Kaneohe could hardly have been more successful. Every plane on the base was destroyed or badly damaged.[24]

13

A "PRACTICALLY PERFECT" ATTACK

Of all the instances of surprise on December 7, the most inexplicable is that of Bellows Field. Bellows, some 8 miles southeast of Kaneohe, was a small airfield established less than a year before. Most activities were housed in temporary structures, and the personnel slept in tents. The station's only permanently assigned unit was the Eighty-sixth Observation Squadron, but the Forty-fourth Pursuit Squadron was temporarily based at Bellows for gunnery training. Contractor Sam Aweau had phoned the base with news of the attack on Kaneohe, and Hickam Field had called at 8:10 with an urgent request for firefighting equipment (which was dispatched immediately).[1]

It is something of a mystery, then, why the men at Bellows were surprised at 8:30 when a lone Japanese plane (probably a stray from the Kaneohe attack group) made a halfhearted strafing pass over the post. One man suffered a leg wound, but there were no serious casualties or damage. Lieutenant Colonel Leonard Weddington, Bellows' commanding officer, was fetched from his nearby home by his driver, but—incredibly—no one sounded the alarm. Private First Class Raymond McBriarty, an aerial gunner with the Eighty-sixth Observation Squadron, witnessed the attack and saw the Japanese markings on the plane. The event excited an animated discussion among McBriarty and the other men, but they received no instructions from their officers or noncoms.[2]

In the absence of any direction, McBriarty went to church. He could not help wondering about the strafing, though, and had a difficult time keeping his mind on the service. His puzzlement increased when a B-17, one of the flight which had made such an untimely arrival from California, made a forced landing at the small airstrip. The bomber, with three wounded men aboard, went off the runway and plowed into a knoll. Services continued, but the congregation's attention was by now far removed from the divine proceedings.

How much longer force of habit would have held the men in church will never be known, for a group of about nine Japanese planes made a concerted and deadly strafing attack at 9:00. These planes were Lieutenant Iida's squadron, which had just ravaged nearby Kaneohe. They targeted the O-47s, O-49s, and P-40s on the airstrip. They also set fire to a gasoline tanker truck. The air raid signal sounded at last, and the chapel emptied as the men rushed to their units. Some airmen and troops from the 299th Infantry Regiment (a Hawaii National Guard unit activated the year before and bivouacked nearby) fired back ineffectively with '03 Springfield rifles.[3]

Second Lieutenant Phillip Willis of the Eighty-sixth Observation Squadron slept through the first strafing. He had returned to the post just before dawn after a night of vigorous elbow bending at the Hickam officers' club. And why not, he had reasoned. He was going to leave the island Monday as a burial escort for the body of a fellow pilot killed in a training accident. The noise of the second attack roused him from his slumber. Still hung over and wearing his tuxedo trousers and shirt, Willis donned his helmet and flight jacket. To complete the outfit he reached into his footlocker and pulled on a pair of cowboy boots. He remarked, more to himself than anyone else, "Us Texans like to die with our boots on."[4]

When Willis got to the runway he saw Lieutenant Hans Christiansen attempting to climb into the cockpit of his P-40. Christiansen was hampered by his awkward parachute pack, so Willis ran to the plane and pushed the fighter pilot from behind. At that moment one of Iida's pilots found his mark and riddled Christiansen and the P-40 with machine gun fire. Willis was covered with Christiansen's blood but saved from injury by the parachute, which stopped the slugs.

Two other Bellows pursuit pilots got into the air, but without the success enjoyed by their colleagues in the Forty-sixth and Forty-seventh Squadrons. Lieutenant George Whiteman took off from Bellows under fire from two Zekes, but managed to get airborne. Before he reached 1,000 feet he was shot down in flames. Lieutenant Samuel Bishop was lucky enough to escape with his life, but his P-40 was shot down over Kailua Bay before he could engage the Japanese. Despite a leg wound and a badly wrenched back Bishop swam ashore at Lanikai Beach.[5]

Private McBriarty, meanwhile, had gone directly to the armament shack when the air raid signal sounded. He drew the rear-seat machine gun for his O-47 and, followed by another airman carrying ammunition for the gun, mounted the weapon in his squadron commander's plane. He was loading the ammunition for the plane's fixed guns when the strafers returned for another pass. McBriarty dove to the ground, and when the planes passed he climbed into the rear cockpit seat and readied his weapon. When the next flight came by, McBriarty began firing from the grounded plane. He was sure that at least some of the 450 rounds he fired had struck home. McBriarty saw holes appear in the fuselage of one Zeke, although it did not crash, and he fired directly into the engine of another which seemed to be diving right toward him. The second pilot, McBriarty noted,

> pulled awful hard on the stick, not as any regular pilot would do, and I might say he was an awful poor pilot, because the way he was following in on his gunnery line, why, he tried to fire—to follow me straight in, and to correct his fire, why, he gave it too much rudder from one side and then too much rudder on the other side, and he completely missed his target.[6]

Given the disparity between the Japanese and American performances on December 7, McBriarty's criticism seems picayune.

The destruction rained down on Bellows and Kaneohe was repeated at Ewa Field, the Marine Corps air station west of Pearl Harbor. At 7:55 about twenty Japanese fighters streaked around the Waianae Range from the northwest and began strafing the base. Using incendiary, explosive, and armor-piercing rounds from 7.7-millimeter machine guns and 20-millimeter cannons, the Zekes made repeated passes as low as 20 feet. For the first ten or fifteen minutes they concentrated on the tactical aircraft parked on the strip. After these targets were demolished they turned their attention for another five or ten minutes to personnel and aircraft under repair.[7]

During the first strafing attack Lieutenant Colonel Claude Larkin, commander of the installation and Marine Aircraft Group Twenty-one, was wounded. Larkin nevertheless organized the base's meager defenses, which consisted primarily of rifles and .30-caliber machine guns taken from damaged planes. Technical Sergeant William Turnage supervised the setting up of Ewa's improvised antiaircraft defenses. Master Technical Sergeant Emil Peters and Private William Turner operated a machine gun from the rear seat of a damaged plane. Turner was fatally wounded by one of the strafers. The men not only fought fires but they also parked vehicles on the runway to forestall the possibility of a landing by airborne troops.

Others did what they could to aid the wounded. Pharmacist's Mate Second Class Orrin Smith jumped into an ambulance with Private First Class James Mann at the wheel. The two drove out to the burning planes only to be caught by strafers. Mann and Smith crawled beneath the ambulance for shelter. The vehicle proved to be more of a target than a shield, and Smith was wounded in the left calf. (Fifty-two bullet holes were counted in the ambulance.) Returning to the dispensary, Smith had his wound treated and joined the rest of the medical staff in tending to other casualties.[8]

Ewa did not have long to wait for another blow. The second attack came at 8:35, this time from the direction of Pearl Harbor, and included dive bombers. The Vals dropped their bombs on remaining planes and strafed the field with fixed wing guns. The rear gunners threw in parting shots as the bombers pulled up and away. The attack lasted about twenty minutes and completed whatever destruction was neglected by the first group. Again the marines returned fire with rifles, Thompson submachine guns, and anything else at hand. James Mann, who had driven his ambulance to the garage to change its four punctured tires, joined in with his rifle.

In the short lull which followed the second attack, six SBDs from the *Enterprise* air group landed at Ewa at 9:00. The marines expected additional attacks soon. When the navy pilots taxied up to the tent which housed the Group Operations office, Master Sergeant Charles Barker, Jr., climbed onto the wing of the first plane and told the pilot that to remain on the field, even for a quick refueling, would be to court the fate of other planes caught on the ground. He advised them to take off immediately and remain airborne for fifteen minutes. Four *Enterprise* pilots (two SBDs had been wrecked on landing) elected to take their chances with the Japanese aloft rather than the destruction which awaited them if they remained on the ground.[9]

One more group of planes returned to strafe Ewa halfheartedly sometime between 9:00 and 9:30. This attack, by about fifteen planes, was characterized by Larkin as "light and ineffectual." The final attack caught Sergeant Carlo Micheletto trying to extinguish the fires set during the earlier attacks. On the approach of the third group Micheletto seized a rifle and crouched behind a pile of lumber.

While firing at the attackers he was shot through the head and killed instantly. By that time the Japanese had destroyed or put out of commission all forty-seven of the marine aircraft at Ewa. The only flyable planes remaining at the field, ironically, were *Enterprise* planes which had landed late in the attack, refueled, rearmed, and had been ordered held on the ground by Admiral Bellinger.[10]

Most of the other planes in the *Enterprise* morning flight did not escape. Although some managed to land (at least temporarily) at the marine airfield, most had to take their chances in the confusion. Lieutenant Clarence Dickenson was mistaken for an attacker and came under fire from the ground. The Japanese, however, had no trouble recognizing his Dauntless dive bomber and made repeated passes at his plane.[11] Dickenson's rear-seat gunner, Radioman First Class William Miller, managed to shoot down one of the raiders before he fell victim to Japanese gunfire. The plane was crippled by the attacks, and Dickenson had to parachute into the sugarcane fields which covered most of the Ewa plain. The pilot hitchhiked to Ford Island, his original destination.

Other *Enterprise* pilots and aircrewmen were not so fortunate. Some of the aircraft went down on Oahu; some fell into the sea. Eight of the original seventeen planes crashed or disappeared, although some were later repaired. One managed a forced landing on Kauai. Eight of the airmen were dead or missing.[12]

Lieutenant Commander Hopping of Scouting Squadron Six managed to land by making a low approach on Ford Island amid the attack. His first thought was to broadcast a warning to Admiral Halsey and the other *Enterprise* pilots who might be approaching Oahu in blissful ignorance. He tried the radio in the control tower, but it lacked the power to send the message. He climbed back into his own plane and used its radio to broadcast the warning. With little else to do for the moment Hopping occupied himself with professional observations on the techniques employed by his Japanese counterparts. Of the Vals he noted: "Attacks were made in a glide rather than a dive, [and] pull-outs were as low as 400 feet."[13]

Commander Young, leader of the *Enterprise* Air Group, made a similar landing on Ford Island and, like Hopping, had time to make some professional observations. He wrote: "My only criticism of this particular attack [second-wave dive bombers] was that they all came in from the same direction instead of making a divided attack; however the ineffectiveness of our AA fire, lack of air opposition and the manner in which they pressed their attack home in this particular instance combined to make the attack practically perfect."[14]

Like the *Enterprise* pilots, Major Truman Landon's twelve B-17s of the Nineteenth Bomb Group flew into Oahu unaware of the Japanese attack. The heavy bombers approached not in one formation but singly. The long fourteen-hour flight from California required that each plane's course and throttle settings be adjusted individually to minimize fuel consumption. The demands of the great distance on the planes' fuel capacity also dictated that their defensive armament be sacrificed for fuel. Second Lieutenant Irwin Cihak, Landon's bombardier, recalls that he had only a single .50-caliber machine gun aboard, and it was packed in Cosmoline and stored in a crate.[15]

As Landon's plane approached Oahu from the northeast the crew noticed the heavy pall of smoke over the island. Cihak and others aboard the aircraft speculated and wondered: Was it possible that the sugarcane fields were being cleared by burning on a Sunday? Nearing Kaneohe at 5,000 feet the airmen noticed a formation of planes in single file heading their way. Navy fliers, thought Cihak. As his B-17 passed just above the "navy" planes he saw they were marked with the rising sun. Cihak looked down on the formation as the last Japanese pilot in line glanced up at the heavy bomber, and for an instant each glimpsed the face of the enemy.

Landon dove to gain speed as the last Zeke in line pulled out to pursue the B-17. The Japanese pilot fired a few short bursts before returning to his group. He scored no hits, but Cihak had an uncomfortable moment as he saw tracers stream past his plane. Landon flew over Pearl Harbor en route to Hickam (strictly against the rules but quite forgivable under the circumstances). Another plane taxiing on the runway forced him to circle out to sea for a second approach. Landon made it safely this time, touching down about 8:15. Cihak and others in the crew abandoned the aircraft as soon as it stopped rolling and ran for the dubious cover of mangrove trees on the south edge of the runway to avoid the strafing.[16]

Many Americans, including some antiaircraft crews, mistook the planes for Japanese. Even Hickam's Major Brooke Allen—himself a B-17 pilot—failed to recognize Landon's planes as American. Perhaps it was the modified appearance of Landon's new "E" model B-17s; more likely it was the stress of the moment. Allen exclaimed to himself, "Where did the Japs get four-engine bombers?" It was not until he saw one come in for a landing at Hickam that he realized it was a friendly aircraft. The harried bomber pilot made his approach with a Japanese fighter on his tail and antiaircraft bursts exploding around him. To make matters worse, a truck pulled out onto the runway to block his landing. The pilot's perseverance paid off when he landed safely after circling around for another approach.[17]

Miraculously, all of Landon's bombers made it. Two landed at Haleiwa, one at Wheeler, one at Bellows, and seven at Hickam. The twelfth made an expedient landing on the Kahuku golf course. Some came down in forced landings; others were damaged on the ground by strafers. One B-17 was destroyed and three "badly damaged."[18] There were some casualties among the crews from gunfire and the crash landings but, everything considered, they fared far better than might have been expected. The rugged construction of the B-17, which was to figure in its successful career, was undoubtedly a factor in the surprisingly low attrition of Landon's group.

With the massive destruction of American air strength on the ground, the raiders had little to fear from Oahu's interceptor squadrons. The few fighter pilots who did manage to get aloft could not stop the waves of attackers. Not only were the Americans outnumbered and outgunned, many of their adversaries had hundreds of hours of combat flying experience. Accentuating the disparity, the P-40 (not to mention the P-36) was outperformed by the faster and better-armed Zero. Hawaii's air defenders were, in short, overwhelmed by every standard of measurement but courage.

IV

MORE HAVOC
AT PEARL

14

"CAPTAIN, THEY'RE HERE!"

The air attack was a stunning success, but Admiral Shimizu's submarines had contributed little to the Japanese effort. Only one of the midget submarines is known definitely to have penetrated Pearl Harbor. The craft entered the channel lying to the northwest of Ford Island, but her periscope and conning tower were spotted by lookouts on ships in the area. At 8:35 the seaplane tender *Tangier* received a report of a submarine in the channel; within minutes a sailor on *Curtiss*, another seaplane tender, spotted the sub. The destroyer *Monaghan*, skippered by Lieutenant Commander William Burford, noticed *Curtiss*'s flag hoist warning of a submarine in the channel. *Monaghan*, the ready duty destroyer, was preparing to get under way, having received an earlier order to join *Ward* outside the channel entrance and investigate the submarine contact in that area.[1]

To Lieutenant (jg) Hart Kait, *Monaghan*'s gunnery officer, it looked as though the submarine was "bobbing and zig-zagging" near the channel's west bank as it glanced off the channel bed. It is more likely that the submarine was maneuvering desperately to avoid the fire of the ships in the area. The air attack had been under way for more than half an hour, and every deck gun in the harbor was manned by keyed-up crews. Fifty-caliber machine gun bullets churned the water. *Curtiss* opened fire at 700 yards with one of her 5-inch guns; two rounds fell short, and a third seemed to hit the conning tower. *Tangier*'s 3-inch antiaircraft gun got off six rounds. *Monaghan*'s Number 2 gun fired once but missed the sub, hitting and setting fire to a floating derrick moored on the opposite side of the channel.[2]

155

Monaghan was by then under way at 10 knots. Burford ordered flank speed from the engine room and passed the word to ram the sub. The helmsman, Chief Quartermaster D. E. Williamson, assured the captain that he saw the submarine and headed straight for the target about 1,000 yards away. On the destroyer's stern Torpedoman Second Class Andrew F. Parker and Chief Torpedoman Gilbert S. "Al" Hardon worked feverishly to prepare *Monaghan's* depth charges. The submarine fired a single torpedo at the rapidly closing destroyer. To Carpenter's Mate Third Class Glenn J. Bennett aboard *Monaghan* it seemed the missile would strike the protective guard around the ship's screws, but the torpedo porpoised twice and struck the Ford Island shore in a harmless geyser of dirty water. Ensign J. W. Gilpin, *Monaghan's* communication officer, had another worry: As the destroyer converged on her target would other vessels cease fire, or would they continue and destroy both the hunter and her prey?[3]

Fortunately for *Monaghan*, fire control on the seaplane tenders ordered their guns to halt as the destroyer fouled the target. Back on the stern Hardon and Parker set the charges for the shallowest possible depth, 30 feet. Burford's vessel struck the submarine a glancing blow on *Monaghan's* port side as the word was passed to release depth charges. Events were moving too quickly, though, for the normal relaying of orders, and Hardon had already let one charge go before the order was given. He released a second charge in quick succession. The explosions in the shallow channel lifted the destroyer's stern 3 or 4 feet out of the water, and she was lucky not to sustain any damage from the explosions.

The order came to drop a third depth charge just as *Monaghan* ran aground next to the floating derrick. Hardon held his fire, knowing that a blast while the vessel was stationary would destroy the warship. His initiative in releasing the first depth charge and his decision to ignore the order for a third release earned him high praise for his "keen judgement." Luck, too, was with *Monaghan* that morning, for the depth charges were loaded with a low-grade explosive normally reserved for training exercises. A full battle load might have destroyed *Monaghan* as well as the submarine.[4]

Although the submarine was crushed, what else might be lurking under the opaque waters of Pearl Harbor? Burford ordered all engines back full speed to clear his ship, but the destroyer was stuck. On the bow sailors played CO_2 fire extinguishers on the burning derrick as engine room hands strained to deliver full power in reverse.

Someone called out another submarine sighting, and *Monaghan*'s guns opened up on a "periscope" that later turned out to be a black cage buoy.

Monaghan was fouled not on the shoal near the derrick but on one of the structure's anchor cables. Carpenter's Mate Bennett was preparing to go over the side and cut the cable with a fireax. He had already thrown his ax onto the barge and passed a line over when suddenly the destroyer broke free. A final thrust of her engines freed the vessel, but not before giving a civilian yardworker aboard the derrick the fright of his life. A fragment from one of the wild shots at the cage buoy severed a cable on the derrick structure, bringing a clatter of gear down near the man. Bennett saw him throw off his helmet, run off the barge into the shallow water, stagger ashore, and throw himself into the passenger door of his car parked on the beach. He slid over to the driver's side, found himself without his keys, bailed out the driver's door, and fled into the cane fields.[5]

After freeing his ship Burford continued the sortie to his offshore patrol station outside the harbor entrance. The entire action for *Monaghan*, from first sighting of the submarine to clearing the derrick, had taken roughly ten minutes.[6]

Monaghan, unlike most ships that morning, had the advantage of being ready for action. The most helpless were those in drydock. Immobilized and with vital power systems curtailed, they presented the choicest targets of opportunity. Pearl Harbor's largest drydock, Drydock One, held the Pacific Fleet flagship, *Pennsylvania*, and the destroyers *Cassin* and *Downes*. The two destroyers lay side by side at the head of the drydock, with the flagship behind them. Three propeller shafts had been removed from *Pennsylvania* and the hull was covered with scaffolding. *Downes* and *Cassin* were just as unprepared for battle. Neither vessel had belted machine gun ammunition ready, and breechblocks had been removed from their 5-inch guns for modifications. Hatches and passageways were blocked by temporary ventilation ducts. To compound their vulnerability, the bottom of the caisson was far below the surface level; the ships were, in effect, in a "hole" which limited their field of view.[7]

Cassin's skipper, Lieutenant Commander Daniel Shea, learned of the attack when a chief gunner's mate caught him on his way to breakfast and announced, "Captain, they're here, bombing Hickam Field!" *Downes*'s captain and executive officer were ashore; her senior officer, Lieutenant (jg) Jefferson D. Parker, finished checking the ship for fire hazards (navy yard workmen had been working aboard the ship throughout the night) and went to the wardroom for a look at the morning paper. He heard explosions, but thought they were from work in progress in the drydock until the ship's general alarm rang.[8]

On *Pennsylvania* the foremast antiaircraft machine guns were manned and firing back within minutes. Confusion on other guns forced men to break locks on ammunition lockers before they could go into action. Japanese planes soon spotted the battleship and began to strafe the vessel, but without any noticeable effect. Lieutenant Parker set *Downes's* forward repair party to removing the improvised vent trunks so the ship's watertight doors could be sealed. Ammunition crews spurred on by Chief Gunner's Mate Henry Cradoct began the laborious work of belting .50-caliber ammunition. (It took fifteen minutes for the first belt to reach the guns.) Two of *Downes's* resourceful gunner's mates, Michael Odietus and Curtis Schultze, searched for replacement breechblocks for the 5-inch guns. Sailors on *Cassin* turned to the same tasks, but as on *Downes* they were hampered by an interruption of electrical power from the dock.[9]

It took Odietus and Schultze forty-five minutes to secure and install the breechblocks. But with the ship out of the water and perched precariously on blocks, what would happen when the guns were fired? Would the recoil knock her over? No one knew. Lieutenant Parker asked another officer on the dock. He suggested, "Fire a shot and see how you make out." Parker accepted the pragmatic advice and found that a destroyer could indeed fire her 5-inch guns while up on blocks in drydock.[10]

The guns on all three ships in Drydock One, despite their limited field of view, joined the chorus of antiaircraft fire. George Walters, a civilian yard worker, had an unsurpassed view from the cab of a traveling crane 50 feet above the drydock. He moved the crane back and forth over *Pennsylvania* to create an obstacle to low-flying planes. At first, the gunners cursed Walters for interfering with their fire, but they learned to use him as a "director," following his movements to anticipate the approach of planes they could not see. The advantage provided by Walters' unorthodox fire direction was offset by smoke from the battleship's boilers as *Pennsylvania's* engine room gang worked frantically to raise steam.[11]

The Japanese did not press an attack against the drydocked ships during the first-wave attack, but everyone aboard the vessels knew it was just a matter of time. The flagship of the Pacific Fleet, lying helpless in drydock, was just too tempting a target. Two navy yard officers told Commander Shea to prepare for flooding the drydock by closing up exposed openings on the destroyers. Shea immediately set his men to work closing the thirty ports on *Cassin* which had been removed for the installation of heavier hull plating. Aboard *Downes* Chief Machinist's Mate Charlie Johnston drove his men in a race to close the necessary valves. Shortly before 9:00 Captain Charles Cooke of *Pennsylvania* summoned Shea by semaphore to report aboard the flagship. Cooke wanted to make sure the destroyers were ready for flooding.[12]

Cooke's message was interrupted when the anticipated attack began on the ships in drydock. The *Pennsylvania* signalman sending the summons had to dive for the deck halfway through his message— "due," in Shea's words, "to terrific gun fire from enemy and own ship." Only temporarily daunted, the signalman rose to his feet after the first flurry of fire and completed the message. The Japanese planes—horizontal bombers and dive bombers—approached the drydock in several small formations from all directions simultaneously. Parker looked up to see "three shining glints high in the air . . . almost in the sun." The shining glints rapidly became three Vals as they plunged toward their target. As the planes bore in Parker thought at first they would hit *Pennsylvania,* but a bomb hit abreast of *Downes*'s Number 3 gun on the drydock floor between the two destroyers. "The next occurrence," according to Parker, "was a loud explosion . . . followed [by] an instantaneous fire which flamed up above the after decks."[13]

Other hits on all three ships followed in quick succession. Two more bombs hit *Downes* aft. *Cassin* took a bomb on her stern. The clouds of smoke pouring out the hole added to the hellish scene. Two more bombs hit her superstructure. A hit on the drydock near her starboard bow damaged *Pennsylvania*'s hull. Another bomb penetrated the battleship's boat deck and exploded in a 5-inch gun casemate, killing twenty-eight officers and men. Among those killed were Lieutenant Commander J. E. Craig, the ship's first lieutenant, and Lieutenant (jg) Richard Rall, a physician working at his post in the battle dressing station.[14]

With no water pressure, fires on the destroyers raged out of control. Parker ordered gun crews off their weapons to fight the fires, but additional bomb hits fed the flames and made their task hopeless. Parker then ordered the after part of *Downes* evacuated and the after magazines flooded to prevent explosions. Fires aboard *Cassin* were so fierce the Number 3 machine gun erupted in flames. It was soon evident that, regardless of their crews' efforts, the destroyers could not be saved. Reluctantly Parker and Shea gave the orders to abandon ship. Parker attempted to go below to make sure all his men were off, but the flames forced him back. Although obliged to abandon ship, *Downes's* crew showed no diminution of devotion to duty. Chief Johnston saved one man by rolling him over to smother the flames on his burning clothes. Yeoman Second Class Milo Skjerven saved the ship's muster rolls and the transfer and receipt records. Fireman Edward Kwolik at first refused to heed the order to leave and kept a fire hose trained on the after engine room hatch until the men below emerged. Boatswain's Mate Lewis Hite had to chase the last members of the crew off the ship before Lieutenant Parker left. By the time he left the vessel a "solid sheet of flame" covered the quarterdeck.[15]

Damage on *Pennsylvania* was kept under control, but the ship's efforts to repel the attack were hampered by shortages in the antiaircraft gun crews. Henry Danner, a civilian shipyard worker, helped make up for the shortage by joining one of the battleship's gun crews. By 9:15 attacks on the drydock were sporadic and ineffective. One plane spattered the shield of *Pennsylvania's* maintop machine gun nest with bullets, but caused no damage or casualties. *Pennsylvania's* guns returned the fire and scored a hit. The plane went down in flames near the base hospital, nearly hitting the building and adding to the carnage.[16]

When the destroyer crews reached dockside they were greeted by a strafing attack and took cover in a nearby ditch. Parker rallied *Downes's* men. Fires on their own ship were out of control and secondary explosions made it impossible to get near the vessel. Parker sent his crew to man hoses against *Cassin's* inferno. They formed a makeshift firefighting force which included sailors, civilians, and marines. William Blanchard, Norman Delaura, Sau Chan Lee, Jonah Mawae, Nai You Choi, and other yard workers braved the flames.

Marine Sergeant Harold Abbott, in charge of the base fire department, brought his men and equipment to the drydock. The marine firefighters had their problems. Private First Class Omar Hill kept the engine running on his 500-gallon pumper by holding a rag against the circulating water line while someone else went in search of spare parts. Private Marvin Dallman remained working his pumper at the head of the drydock despite clouds of suffocating smoke. Private First Class Don Femmer managed to keep his 750-gallon pumper running only by making emergency repairs on the spot when it broke down.[17]

The shipyard's photographer, Tai Sing Loo, joined the effort. He recorded his experience in stream of consciousness prose:

We put our hoses directed the depth charges keeping an Officer came by said keep up the good work we had our hoses right at it all the time, and I turn around and saw an officer order all men stand back some thing may happen, So I obey his order and ran back sudden really happen the terrific explosion came from the destroyer flew people were hurt and some fell down.[18]

Ponciano Bernardino, a hoseman from Pearl Harbor's submarine base fire station, managed a group of American Legionnaires and other civilian volunteers who arrived at the drydock about 8:30. When the dive bombers began to strafe the area many of his volunteers ran for a nearby lumber pile. He coaxed them back to the hoses by pointing out that a large group of men seeking shelter would present an attractive target, but if they returned to the hoses they would be hidden from strafers by the pall of smoke billowing over the drydock. His logic brought the volunteers back and they remained at their work until the flames were out.[19]

At 9:20 water finally began to enter the drydock caisson. Now burning oil on the surface presented a new hazard. As the water rose the floating blaze threatened to "cook off" *Pennsylvania*'s forward magazines. Although there was no explosion, there were several worried moments as the heat became intense enough to melt the paint on the battleship's starboard bow. Torpedoes and ammunition aboard the destroyers went off like giant firecrackers and metal splinters flew about the drydock area. Lieutenant Parker received a head wound from one of the fragments, but was soon back directing his men. A piece of torpedo tube from *Downes* weighing at least 500 pounds was blasted into the air and landed on *Pennsylvania*'s forecastle. *Cassin* rolled over and smashed against *Downes*, causing still more damage. *Cassin*'s crew was particularly concerned about the ship's depth charges and maintained a constant stream of water on them. It is a tribute to the skill and courage of the drydock's makeshift fire department that the blazes were extinguished by 10:45, less than two hours after the first hits on the three ships.[20]

Some 300 yards west of Drydock One lay the navy yard's Floating Drydock Two. The destroyer *Shaw* and tug *Sotoyomo* were in for repairs and, like the ships in Drydock One, they fell victim to the second-wave attackers. Between 9:00 and 9:30 *Shaw* received three hits. The floating drydock took another five bombs. Uncontrolled fire ignited *Shaw*'s forward ammunition magazine, which exploded in a pyrotechnic fireball hurling debris more than a half mile across the harbor. The ship's bow was severed.[21]

Surprisingly, the drydock remained afloat after the explosion. Yard workers E. L. Bellinger, P. M. Milker, R. A. Christie, F. C. Schilling, M. A. Paulo, and V. E. Teves hurried to the stricken drydock and undertook the hazardous job of disconnecting the live electrical cables leading into the burning destroyer. Other yard workers pitched in to fight the fires. Shop 70 contributed a crew including Lawrence Harnar, Abraham Ignacio, William Broyard, Anthony Cerny, Ralph Tyler, Norman Cabral, John Davis, Lloyd Cantrelle, and Marvin Correa. These men shuttled between Drydock One and the floating drydock trying to fight both fires at the same time. Their best efforts were not enough, however, and it became apparent the fires could not be contained. To prevent the dock from being destroyed by flames it was sunk intentionally by opening the sea valves.[22]

Moored less than a quarter mile southeast of Drydock One were the light cruisers *Honolulu,* commanded by Captain Harold Dodd, and *St. Louis,* skippered by Captain George Rood. Both ships worked frantically to prepare to sortie when the attack began. At 8:10 *Honolulu*'s crew lit the fires under boilers 5 and 6. At 8:20 boilers 1 and 2 were lit. At 8:25 the crew secured electrical and steam power lines from the dock; only the freshwater line remained in place. At 8:28 the fires under *Honolulu*'s boilers 3 and 4 began to burn, and at 9:05 all six boilers were cut into the main steam line.[23]

Honolulu never managed to get under way. At 9:25 a group of dive bombers bore in for an attack. One bomb landed on the adjacent dock 15 feet from the cruiser's hull, penetrated the dock, and exploded underwater. The concussion opened up two of her port oil tanks to the sea. The tops of three other fuel tanks were ruptured, flooding both oil and water into the ammunition storage areas. Oil and water surged into wiring passages, magazine decks bulged from the blast, and the Turret II handling room began to leak. The damage, although not as serious as that suffered by some other ships, was enough to force Captain Dodd to scratch his plans to get under way.[24]

The second-wave dive bombers also found attractive targets in the ships berthed to the northwest of Ford Island. *Raleigh,* still struggling to remain afloat after being torpedoed, fell victim once again to Japanese planes. This time the Vals came in strafing as they dived on the cruiser. Her 1.1-inch guns hit two of the planes. At 9:10 a third plane released a bomb which hit the after deck between a 3-inch and a 1.1-inch antiaircraft gun. It struck a glancing blow on an ammunition locker, penetrated the deck, went through a locker in the carpenter shop, passed through another deck, and crashed through a seaman's bunk. The bomb then penetrated a fuel tank, pierced the hull of the ship on the port quarter below the waterline, and exploded on the harbor bottom.[25]

More dive bombers came at *Raleigh,* but the antiaircraft fire of nearby ships, as well as the cruiser herself, prevented any more hits. Still, the cruiser was in precarious shape. She began to settle ever deeper and developed a bad list to port. Captain Simons ordered all unnecessary topside weight thrown over the side. Airplane cranes, torpedo tubes, torpedoes, booms, ladders, chests, anchors, and chains went into the water. Simons kept a yeoman busy throughout recording the exact location of every object on the bottom—and all, the captain later claimed, were recovered by divers after the attack. *Raleigh's* crew worked all day and throughout the night of December 7 and 8 before the ship was safe from the danger of sinking or capsizing.

Dive bombers from the second wave also attacked *Curtiss,* as if exacting retribution for her part in the sinking of the midget submarine rammed by *Monaghan.* At 9:05 a Val piloted by Lieutenant Mamoru Suzuki attacked the ships northwest of Ford Island and was hit by fire from *Curtiss, Raleigh,* and perhaps other vessels. Suzuki's crippled plane crashed, deliberately according to some observers, into *Curtiss's* Number 1 boat crane on the starboard side. The plane disintegrated, the gas tank exploded, and the tender was in serious danger from the resulting blaze.[26]

At 9:12 another group of dive bombers came at *Curtiss.* One bomb hit the stern mooring buoy, another fell short, a third overshot the mark, but a fourth bomb hit the starboard side of the boat deck. It passed through the carpenter shop, the radio repair shop, and exploded on the main deck in the ship's hangar. It destroyed everything within a 30-foot radius of the blast, compounded the fire started by Suzuki's crash, and killed twenty-one men. Within fifteen minutes the after engine room had to be evacuated because of smoke and broken steam and water lines. Still, *Curtiss's* crew continued to fight. The forward antiaircraft gun crews remained at their stations and at 9:28 reported firing at a group of high-flying planes passing over the ship from bow to stern. In the radio transmitting room the bomb explosion broke the back of Radioman Second Class James Raines and ignited reels of film stored in the adjacent movie projection booth. Despite his injuries and the flames and choking smoke,

Raines helped another radioman remove a man from beneath a fallen transmitter.

Ensign R. G. Kelly was injured by the bomb blast, but he continued directing his midship repair party in fighting fires and repairing damage. Shipfitter First Class Henry C. Dorsett's thorough knowledge of the ship's structure proved invaluable in rescuing injured men and minimizing the damage. Chief Water Tender James H. Mosher, Chief Machinist's Mate Floyd Beach, and Machinist's Mate First Class Stephen F. Safransky braved the smoke and steam to return to the evacuated after engine room. They started the pumps and managed to clear the area of water. On the boat deck Seamen R. R. Bieszoz and J. A. D'Amelio worked under a hail of machine gun fire to control the flames there. The work of *Curtiss*'s crew was rewarded at 9:36, when the fires were brought under control.[27]

On the opposite shore of Ford Island only one of the eight battleships, *Nevada,* succeeded in getting under way during the attack. Despite the torpedo and bomb damage inflicted by the first-wave attackers, the senior officer aboard *Nevada,* Lieutenant Commander Francis Thomas, wanted to get the ship moving. Fires from neighboring *Arizona* were becoming so severe that they threatened his own ship. Thomas took his post managing activities below decks and left the work above decks to Lieutenant Lawrence Ruff. Normally it took hours for a battleship to get under way, but by chance *Nevada* was halfway ready when the attack began. Ensign Joseph Taussig, officer of the deck on the last peacetime watch, had ordered a second boiler lit to relieve the load on the boiler supplying auxiliary power for the ship. The result was that *Nevada* had two hot boilers—the one supplying the power and the one which had just been lit.[28]

Below decks the crew worked urgently to raise steam pressure as quickly as possible. Fireman Dan Wentrcek bent to the task of changing the burner tips on boiler 1. The size of the burner tips determined the size of the flame, and Commander Thomas had ordered the largest be put into service. Wentrcek removed the burners, which were covered with hot oil, juggled them onto a workbench, replaced the tips, and struggled to replace the burners. It was a dangerous job, because concussion from bombs and antiaircraft guns could create a "backblast" forcing air down the stack—throwing a sheet of flame into the face of a man unlucky enough to be standing in front of the burners at the wrong moment. Wentrcek was acutely aware of the possibility as he replaced the burners. He "was moving pretty dadgummed fast" and had barely finished and stood to the side when a blast of flame came through the spot where he had just been working.[29]

Topside the deck gangs labored at the thousand and one tasks necessary to get a great ship under way. Chief Boatswain Edwin Hill, at forty-seven no longer a young man, clambered onto one of the mooring quays, cut loose an ammunition lighter, and cast off *Nevada*'s lines. As the battleship drifted away Hill dove into the harbor and swam to his ship before it could leave him behind. Thomas requested a tug, but none was available. It mattered little, because with Chief Quartermaster Robert Sedberry at the helm the ship moved away so smoothly that Chief Signalman Wilbur Pryor watching from the signal tower reported, "I could see no tugs, apparently they pushed her out from the inboard side."[30]

As was true of so many events on December 7, no one was sure what time *Nevada* got under way—Pryor thought it was 8:55; the ship's action report said 8:40. All agreed, though, that it was shortly before the arrival of the second-wave bombers. Chief Quartermaster Sedberry did a masterful job of maneuvering the ship down the channel past the burning *Arizona*, the sunken *West Virginia*, and the capsized *Oklahoma*. Deftly the quartermaster slipped the battleship between the dredge *Turbine* and the listing *Oglala*—a gap barely 100 yards wide. *Nevada* had the bad luck to be caught in the narrow channel just as the second wave of Japanese bombers appeared over Pearl Harbor. Commander Fuchida, circling high over the harbor, recognized a golden opportunity. If his planes could sink the battlewagon in the channel, his airmen could turn *Nevada* into a cork which would bottle up Pearl Harbor for weeks, perhaps months, to come.[31]

The battleship was abreast of the blazing floating drydock at 9:07 when dive bombers swarmed down on *Nevada*. Ensign Taussig, seriously wounded in the earlier attack, lay immobilized in a stretcher near the starboard antiaircraft director. Communication cables from the director were severed and the guns operated under local control, so there was little Taussig could do in any case. Ensign Thomas Taylor, commanding the port antiaircraft battery, directed his guns under strafing and falling bombs. Wounded, burned, and deafened when a blast ruptured his eardrums, Taylor continued to direct his battery. At one point a pile of ammunition boxes turned red hot from flames; Taylor grabbed a hose and played the stream on the boxes until they were no longer in danger of exploding. Others on the antiaircraft guns, inspired by the examples of Taussig and Taylor, remained at their posts despite the rain of bombs and bullets. *Nevada*'s battle report singled out Boatswain's Mate First Class Adolfo Solar and Seaman William Neundorf, both killed in action, as gunners whose leadership and courage were especially worthy of mention.[32]

During the brief but ferocious attack most of the bombs hit *Nevada*'s forward deck, turning the area into useless wreckage. There were so many holes in the deck, some from bombs penetrating on their way down, others from explosions within the ship, that it was impossible to tell with any certainty how many missiles had struck the vessel. As power failed on ammunition elevators, crewmen carried antiaircraft shells topside by hand. Some gun crews suffered terrible attrition. A bomb exploded in the casemate adjacent to Seaman Artis Teer's 5-inch gun. The blast blew through the steel bulkhead killing two men outright and knocking out Teer and severely wounding him in the back and buttocks. The rest of the crew abandoned the position, and thinking Teer dead, left him behind. He came to feeling no pain, but disoriented and in shock. He saw the gun mount in flames and through the fog of shock remembered there was a round in the chamber. He knew it would explode from the heat, so Teer staggered to the gun, elevated it, trained it out to sea, and fired. That done, he was overcome with exhaustion. He said to himself, "I'll lay down here and die."[33]

He passed out once more and then regained consciousness again. He walked up to the next gun emplacement, where the bomb had exploded, and found two survivors there. One, terribly burned, was walking back and forth screaming in pain. The other walked with him, offering what comfort he could. With dive bombers still raining bombs and bullets on *Nevada,* Teer moved forward to the next gun. He was still in shock "just looking for somebody to talk to." There the crew was uninjured. They wrapped Teer in a blanket and lowered him in a stretcher to a small boat alongside the stricken ship.

Crewmen below decks, too, faced their share of danger. Chief Carpenter's Mate James Curley commanded a repair party in the forward part of the ship which was sealed in a watertight compartment while bombs exploded nearby. He and his men watched helplessly as the armored deck heaved up and down from repeated blasts. Curley was overcome by smoke and passed out. When someone brought him to with artificial respiration he must have wondered whether it might have been better to remain unconscious. Machinist Donald Ross's station was in the forward dynamo room. When the smoke, steam, and heat became too much he drove the other men out of the compartment. He manned the dynamo alone until he passed out. When he was rescued and resuscitated he went back and secured the station. Ross then went to the after dynamo, where he worked until he collapsed again. Once more he was carried out and brought around, and once again he returned to the dynamo until finally he was ordered to abandon the post.[34]

Ensign Charles Merdinger was deep below, five decks down in the plotting room, the communications nerve center of the ship. Because of heavy casualties on the antiaircraft guns, word was passed below to send some of his men above as replacements. Merdinger selected those he felt superfluous. It was "a real Hobson's choice," he remembered. Some of the men sent above were certain they were going to their deaths; some of those left behind thought they were doomed to drowning. Still, no objections were voiced, even though Merdinger knew that "by virtue of experience or age or anything else I certainly wasn't the senior man there." It was at that moment the young ensign "realized the value of the gold braid on the hat."[35]

The fury of the attack soon had *Nevada* listing to starboard and settling by the bow. It was as clear to observers on shore as it was to Fuchida that the ship might well sink in the channel. Accordingly, Commander Thomas ran the ship aground at 9:10 at Hospital Point, just below the floating drydock, in obedience to a signal from the tower. To Seaman Eric Rabe in the signal tower it looked as though her bow almost touched *Shaw*'s stern. Again, Boatswain Hill had a key role to play. The ship was still under attack, but someone had to go forward and release the anchor. Hill moved across the forecastle, began to prepare the anchor, and perished in a series of bomb explosions. Once she was aground the attacks on *Nevada* ceased, but the current swung her stern around into the channel stream. Several tugs, including *Hoga*, *YT 129*, *YT 152*, and *YT 153*, came alongside her port bow and played hoses on the fires. When the fires were under control an hour and a half later the tugs shifted *Nevada* to the opposite shore of the channel and grounded the ship on Waipio Point.[36]

With *Nevada* aground, the Japanese lost the chance to block the Pearl Harbor channel. To the preoccupied crews of the Pacific Fleet, keeping the channel clear meant little at the time, but it was to loom large in the critical months to come. As a staging and supply base Pearl Harbor was vital in the efforts to stem the Japanese advance. Rendering it unusable, even temporarily, might well have allowed Japanese forces to drive the U.S. Navy from the Central Pacific and jeopardize American control of Hawaii.

15

A BATTLESHIP
ADMIRAL'S NOTICE

The drama enacted on the warships was played out on a reduced scale aboard the small auxiliaries and ships' boats in the harbor. Tugs, lighters, gigs, and small craft of every kind rushed across the waters of Pearl Harbor rescuing swimmers, transporting wounded, fighting fires, and assisting ship movements. When the attack opened, Boatswain's Mate First Class James D. Shepard was acting as dispatcher for Pearl Harbor's yard craft. As the first torpedo planes flew over and the rear gunners strafed at random he thought, "surely they wanted to get me and everybody else around here." He searched desperately for cover aboard the old barge that served as the dispatcher's office, but he saw only wood and glass partitions. "I thought," he reported later, "any second would be my last one." He composed himself and dispatched several small craft to where they were needed most—Battleship Row. Within minutes Lieutenant Commander Joseph P. Tomelty, the yard craft repair officer, arrived to take charge. Tomelty continued throughout the attack to direct the small craft around the harbor in response to directions from Commander Harry Hayes in the signal tower.[1]

Most of the yard craft spent the day moving from one place to another, sometimes finding their services needed and sometimes not. The saga of *YT 129* was typical. First she was ordered to Drydock One to stand by to move *Pennsylvania*. When it was plain that it would be some time before the drydock was flooded, Boatswain's Mate First Class Thomas Miechurski, master of *YT 129*, proceeded to Battleship Row to assist *Nevada* as she prepared to sortie. *Nevada* got under way

168

without help, but Miechurski followed the battleship down the channel to the end of Ten Ten Dock. *YT 129* then returned to Battleship Row to help the burning *Arizona*. But smaller boats, like the one manned by John Anderson, were so thick around *Arizona* that *YT 129* could not get close enough to help. Looking about the harbor it seemed once again to Miechurski that *Nevada*, now foundering under a rain of bombs, needed help. *YT 129* made her way to Hospital Point, but while standing by to help the grounded battleship, an officer approached the tug in a motorboat and ordered her to return to the yard craft office.

Sometime after 9:00, *YT 129* got under way once more, this time with a new crew under the command of Chief Boatswain's Mate Daniel C. Fisher. She was ordered to join the firefighting efforts at *Nevada*, so for the third time that morning *YT 129* headed for that vessel. Once again her crew was frustrated: Two tugs were already secured to the port bow, and the water off the starboard bow was too shallow for *YT 129*. Fisher brought the tug as close as he dared to the burning *Shaw* and the floating drydock, but hose pressure was too weak to reach the flames. Orders were relayed by semaphore to proceed once again to help *Pennsylvania* exit from Drydock One. While *YT 129* was lying off the drydock an officer approached and asked Chief Fisher to help the slowly settling *California*. When Fisher told him he was under orders to aid the flagship the officer left in search of assistance elsewhere. No sooner had the officer shoved off, however, when *YT 129* received a message to proceed to *California*. By then the air raid was over, and the chaos had abated somewhat. The itinerant tug chugged over to *California* and spent the next three days there assisting in salvage work.[2]

Many of the undamaged larger ships dispatched their own boats to help during the attack. The repair ship *Rigel* put two of her launches in the water. Launch 1 was manned by a volunteer crew of Ensign Charles Hake, Seamen Keith Miller, Robert Shepherd, and William Blair, and Fireman Eugene Weinbarger. The boat rescued between 50 and 100 swimmers from *West Virginia* at the height of the bombing attack. A fouled screw halted rescue work at a bad moment. Burning oil floating on the surface threatened to engulf the launch, but the crew cleared the screw just in time. Ensign James Biena, Seamen Stanley Dziduch and Robert Rogers, and Fireman Robert Stocker were detailed to take *Rigel*'s Launch 2 on a similar mission, but they never got a chance. As they prepared to get under way from the ship's starboard bow a Japanese bomb passed through the boat and exploded in the water below. The blast splintered the boat's planking and seriously injured Stocker and Rogers.[3]

YT 153 had been ready to pick up a tow from *Antares* near the harbor entrance when the attack began. Boatswain's Mate First Class Ralph L. Holzhaus, the tugmaster, saw two small civilian planes from nearby John Rogers Airport shot down. A Japanese plane spotted the tug and swooped low for a strafing run. As the water churned with bullets a mere 15 feet to starboard, Holzhaus thought "everything was finished for the 153," but the approach of a B-17 offered bigger game and distracted the strafer. The tug reversed course to return to the yard craft office, and *YT 153*'s crew "had a good session of swearing" as they watched the planes work their will on the fleet and nearby installations.

It was then that Boatswain's Mate Second Class Russell Ludwig spotted a submarine periscope heading into the North Channel. Holzhaus did the only thing he could think of: He tried to run the sub down. The periscope disappeared before he could reach the submarine, though, and the tug cruised around slowly, an unlikely warship stalking a still more unlikely prey. *Tangier* and *Monaghan* relieved him of the task when they spotted the sub and opened fire. After negotiating flotsam from the overturned *Utah*, especially the massive timbers used to cushion the target ship's decks from practice bombs, *YT 153* headed for *Nevada*. The tug joined the fire brigade around the stricken battleship and turned her hose on the ship's bridge. She took aboard some of *Nevada*'s wounded and patched them up with the boat's first aid kit. *YT 153* had within the space of a few hours performed as a tug, a fireboat, a submarine hunter, and finally a floating clinic.[4]

Chief Boatswain's Mate William L. Fielder, master of the tug *Nokomis*, was preparing to get his boat under way when he saw the first torpedo planes hit *West Virginia*. At 8:05 he was under way for *Arizona* and arrived at her berth just after the battleship's magazines exploded. *Nokomis* picked several men out of the water and offered to pull *Vestal* clear. The offer was refused, and Fielder was told to stay and fight *Arizona*'s fire. He maneuvered the tug between *Arizona*'s stern and *Nevada*'s bow and pulled three men out of the oil beneath *Arizona*'s starboard quarter. Fielder could still see men among the flames firing antiaircraft guns as Commander Fuqua directed firefighting efforts on the quarterdeck. Fielder was then told that the best he could do was evacuate the wounded and burned survivors. He took some off *Arizona*'s after quay, backed out into the channel, brought a few more wounded aboard, and took a load from a small boat. *Nokomis* proceeded to the Ten Ten Dock, where the evacuees received medical attention and the serious cases were taken in trucks to the nearby naval hospital.[5]

The most unlikely small craft made their unique contributions on December 7. The garbage scow *YG 21* had a temporarily assigned skipper, Chief Quartermaster James J. Reams. When he "saw what appeared to be the sky filled with Japanese planes" Reams started to leave for his permanent duty station at staff headquarters. Commander Tomelty, however, needed experienced masters for his small craft. As soon as Reams stepped onto the dock Tomelty intercepted the quartermaster and ordered him under way to rescue men in the water.

Reams proceeded to the overturned *Oklahoma*, but found there were enough small boats to conduct rescue operations. He returned to the yard craft office for additional orders and was instructed to go next to Merry Point and load firefighting equipment for Ford Island. Merry Point was also the dock for the ferry which ran regularly between the navy yard and Ford Island. The ferry was still at Merry Point when *YG 21* arrived. Jammed with frantic men returning to their stations on Ford Island, the ferry was behind schedule on the morning of December 7. Reams moored at the nearby fleet landing at 9:00, and after fifteen minutes decided it would be better to take the firefighting party (which made the rendezvous) over to Ford Island than to keep waiting for their equipment which might or might not show up at the landing.

Reams let off the firefighting party on Ford Island, but not before commandeering two of its members to round out his shorthanded crew. *YG 21* put out a fire at the gasoline dock recently vacated by *Neosho* and then secured along the port side of *California*. The garbage scow fought *California*'s fires until released. She then proceeded to *West Virginia*'s port side, playing two streams of water on the burning ship. There were no direct attacks on *YG 21*, but her crew had some anxious moments when the hose handlers were threatened by periodic explosions of ready ammunition aboard *West Virginia*.[6]

Chief Boatswain's Mate Leonard M. Jahnsen's *YG 17*, another garbage scow, was alongside *Nevada* taking on the customary load of waste when the first torpedo planes streaked over the navy yard. *YG 17*'s crewmen were ordered aboard the battleship for their own protection. After the first wave of the attack passed they emerged from the armored protection below decks and cast off at 8:42. Returning to the yard craft office for instructions, *YG 17* was ordered to *West Virginia* to fight fires.

The scow tied up alongside *West Virginia* at 9:44, about the time the last Japanese planes began the return flight to their carriers. Chief Jahnsen placed *YG 17* alongside the battleship with her bow completely enveloped at times in smoke and flames and joined other small vessels in playing streams of water on *West Virginia's* fires. Citing Jahnsen and his "gallant crew" for braving the hazards posed by exploding ammunition and burning fuel, Rear Admiral Walter Anderson, who witnessed the scene from aboard *Maryland,* issued a formal commendation. The document must be unique in naval history—garbage scows seldom rate a battleship admiral's notice, much less a commendation.[7]

As antiaircraft ammunition ran low all manner of small boats plied the harbor offering replenishment for the guns. The main source of ammunition was the naval ammunition depot at Pearl Harbor's isolated West Loch. Japanese planes for the most part ignored this important facility. But not entirely. The ammunition ship *Pyro* was tied up at the depot's dock with a load of ammunition when she was nearly hit by a bomb at 9:20. It landed on the dock a scant 12 feet from the ship, penetrated the concrete, and exploded underneath the pier. *Pyro's* crew felt the shock of the blast, but the ship suffered only minor damage.[8]

The bomb was so close that marine Private First Class Ben Cummings, a member of the depot's guard force, was sure the ship had taken a direct hit. Cummings and others at the station knew that the ships in the harbor needed ammunition. With no time to go through channels, he and other marines commandeered a motor launch and as much antiaircraft ammunition as they could load in the small boat. They motored from ship to ship offering their cargo to any and all takers. Sailors aboard the ships were astounded to see a boatload of marines cruising Pearl Harbor, but the improvised delivery system got the ammunition to the fleet.[9]

Although most of the small craft in Pearl Harbor performed auxiliary albeit dangerous and important functions, one group had the satisfaction of shooting back. A squadron of PT boats, still a novelty in 1941, was awaiting transshipment to the Philippines aboard the tanker *Ramapo*. Some of the boats of Torpedo Boat Squadron One were already aboard the tanker, some were in cradles on the dock, and others were still in the water. When Ensign Niles Ball, the squadron duty officer, first saw the planes from his post aboard the barge which served as the unit's temporary headquarters, he could not believe Pearl Harbor was really under attack. Once he recognized the danger, however, Ball passed the order to start the air compressors which provided power to the boats' .50-caliber machine gun turrets.[10]

Norwood McGill's *PT 26* was sitting high and dry on the dock waiting to be hoisted aboard *Ramapo*. The boat's crew was frustrated by her dry gas tanks, because the air compressors supplying power to the turrets ran on gasoline. The crew stood by "just itching to get at it" until they realized they could simply cut the air hoses and one man could turn the turret by hand while another fired the guns. McGill, wearing only undershorts and a World War I "soup dish" helmet which kept falling down into his face, took turns with another sailor alternately firing and turning the turret.[11]

Aboard *PT 23* Gunner's Mate First Class Joy Van Zyll De Jong and Torpedoman First Class George Huffman used the same technique. They hit one torpedo bomber with a steady stream of tracers into the fuselage belly and claimed it as a kill. Below decks in the cramped engine spaces of the small boat Machinist's Mate First Class Clarence Tiller worked frantically to start *PT 23*'s temperamental compressor.[12]

The PT boats on the dock never had a chance to fight back from their natural element. Nor did *Nevada* ever make it to the open sea where her crew hoped to bring her big guns to bear on the Japanese fleet. Some ships, however, did manage to get under way and sortie from the anchorage despite the chaos and suddenness of the attack. Most of the ships which sortied during the raid were destroyers which proceeded individually, usually under the command of junior officers, to the area just outside the harbor entrance. There they took up antisubmarine patrols until organized later in the day into a makeshift task force. Although they went to sea and operated under highly adverse conditions, these destroyer crews and officers were among the unsung American heroes of Pearl Harbor. Due in no small measure to their initiative and efforts only one midget submarine is known definitely to have penetrated the harbor, and the Japanese fleet submarines lurking outside the channel scored no kills on U.S. warships during the attack.

The first warship to leave the anchorage was the destroyer *Helm*, which enjoyed the advantage of already being under way when the attack began. *Helm*'s captain, Lieutenant Commander Chester Carroll, had just brought his ship around Waipio Point and was heading up West Loch for the deperming buoys. When he saw a bomb strike a hangar at the southeast end of Ford Island, Carroll backed his engines and maneuvered the ship in reverse out of West Loch. Within ten minutes he had reached the main channel. At 8:18 he was out of the harbor moving at an emergency speed of 25 knots. On the way out *Helm* spotted a submarine periscope, which disappeared before she could bring her guns to bear. Two minutes later the conning tower surfaced 1,200 yards west of the channel entrance. The sub seemed to be touching the fringing reef at the breaker line. The destroyer fired, but no shots struck home. At that moment *Helm*'s steering gear broke down, and Carroll was unable to press the attack.[13]

The next ship to sortie, *Dale,* was backing into the North Channel as *Monaghan* was closing in on the midget submarine. The torpedo fired at *Monaghan* barely missed *Dale* before exploding on Ford Island. *Dale*'s skipper, Lieutenant Commander Anthony Rorschach, raised her speed to 25 knots and exited the harbor under dive bombing and machine gun attacks, clearing the channel at 9:07. As she took up her antisubmarine patrol duties south of the harbor her crew spotted fishing sampans (most manned by Japanese-Americans) flying white flags and streaming toward Kewalo Basin. The sampan crews were just as surprised as *Dale*'s crewmen. But some of the crew were so enraged by the surprise attack that they cast aside any distinction between the Japanese Navy and the hapless fishermen. "Difficulty was had," Rorschach reported, "in restraining several members of the crew" from opening fire.[14]

Monaghan, done with the midget submarine, left the harbor a scant 1,500 yards behind *Dale.* Just astern of *Monaghan* was the destroyer *Blue. Blue*'s commanding officer and executive officer were ashore Sunday morning, and command of the destroyer devolved on Ensign Nathan Asher, the senior officer aboard. Asher was assisted by three other ensigns who also happened to be on the ship: M. I. Moldafsky, J. P. Wolfe, and R. S. Scott. As ship after ship fell victim to Japanese bombs and torpedoes in the first moments of the attack, Asher was increasingly anxious to get *Blue* out of the crowded harbor. He was handicapped in his preparations to get under way by the absence of the ship's boats, which were overdue in returning with weekend liberty parties. He needed the boats to unhook the cables and chains which linked the destroyer to her mooring buoys. Rather than continue waiting, Asher sent some of the more nimble members of the crew scrambling onto the buoys to try their hand. They had to wait, however. Rear Admiral Milo Draemel, commander of the Battle Force destroyers, radioed an order from his flagship, *Detroit,* for his ships to remain in port until he gave the word to sortie.[15]

The word from Draemel finally came about 8:40. Since they lacked the launches to release the ship properly, the sailors on the buoys simply cut the cables and *Blue* got under way. Asher slowed the destroyer as she passed through the floating debris and desperate swimmers from the overturned *Utah*. When *Blue* was abreast of Hospital Point Asher thought briefly about stopping to pick up some of the men in small boats signaling frantically for a pickup. They wanted to get to sea in a fighting ship, and the sooner the better. Another destroyer rapidly closing from astern changed his mind. As he sped through the channel the young ensign was faced with another problem—the slow minesweeper directly ahead. This was no time for fancy maneuvering, so *Blue* thundered past. She missed the minesweeper, but came close enough to shear her starboard paravane cable.

On any other day the maneuver would have brought forth curses from the minesweeper crew and serious disciplinary action. On this morning the minesweeper sailors lined the rails cheering and waving their hats. By the time *Blue* made the passage through the channel at 9:10 she was making 25 knots. The speed was necessary, because she was under air attack throughout the sortie. As the seemingly endless numbers of Japanese planes swooped about the harbor Asher, in a fit of frustration, hurled a pair of binoculars at the attackers.[16]

Henley was another destroyer caught with her captain and executive officer ashore. With Lieutenant Francis Fleck in command and Chief Quartermaster Melvin C. Nelson at the wheel *Henley* was unshackled from her mooring and under way about 8:30. Passing Hospital Point the ship was subjected to a strafing attack. The destroyer returned the fire and claimed a kill. *Henley* brought another plane under fire inside the channel entrance, and her crew believed it crashed at sea. Once outside the channel she made a "fairly certain" submarine contact. *Henley* dropped depth charges, but without noticeable results. Around noon she reclaimed her commanding officer and executive officer, who had hitched a ride to sea on another destroyer. When the other ship slowed to 5 knots to sweep for submarines *Henley* streamed a life raft on a long piece of manila line. The captain and the exec jumped overboard, climbed into the raft, and were hauled aboard their ship with a minimum of ceremony.[17]

Like many of the destroyers, *Alwyn* left Pearl Harbor under the command of a junior officer. On the morning of December 7 Ensign Stanley Caplan had a grand total of seven months sea duty in his navy career. But, as senior officer aboard, he took command of the ship (with the assistance of Ensign H. C. Anderson, who was even more junior). Lieutenant Commander Robert Rodgers, *Alwyn's* captain, just missed the sortie and gave pursuit in a motor launch. He finally caught up with his ship about 10:00 just outside the harbor entrance. There he found to his frustration that the squadron commander, exhibiting a justifiable fear of submarines, refused to let *Alwyn* slow down to take Rodgers aboard.[18]

Unlike *Alwyn* and the destroyers preceding her, *Phelps* got under way from a "cold iron" watch. Because her boilers 3 and 4 were partially dismantled for cleaning, she was receiving steam, electricity, and water from the tender *Dobbin*. Although the captain and executive officer were ashore, *Phelps* had men with the right combination of skills and initiative. Electrician's Mate First Class Joe Harrison shifted the electrical load from *Dobbin* to *Phelps's* own emergency diesel generators as soon as the first bombs fell. Lieutenant Bruce Trippennsee, the engineering officer, was the senior officer aboard. He set in motion the lighting of boilers 1 and 2 and put Chief Watertenders Bert Ellstrom and Edgar DeWitt to work reassembling the other two. Trippennsee got his ship under way at 9:26 and cleared the outer entrance buoys at 9:50 just as the air raid subsided.[19]

The last destroyer under way before the attack ended was *Bagley*, with Lieutenant Philip Cann the senior officer aboard. *Bagley*, undergoing repairs on her bilge keel, was berthed at the navy yard near *St. Louis* and *Honolulu*. Her crew had to run lubricating oil into one engine room system before she could get under way at 9:40. During the 45-minute preparation *Bagley's* antiaircraft batteries were active and the ship's report claimed an improbable six planes downed. Because of fear that the channel might be blocked by *Nevada*, the destroyer was ordered to sortie via the channel north of Ford Island. After clearing the channel Cann risked stopping to pick up *Blue's* commander and executive officer from a small boat. They hoped to catch up with *Blue* at sea but remained aboard *Bagley* as passengers until the next day.[20]

The only capital ship to leave the harbor during the air raid was *St. Louis*. Repair and maintenance work in progress had two of the cruiser's boilers dismantled, and the ship was receiving power from the dock. Captain George Rood ordered all impediments cut away, and the hasty dismantling of the water line left a 12-inch hole in the side of the ship. Shipfitter Henry E. Bullock turned to and welded up the opening in record time. At 9:31 *St. Louis* was under way on six boilers with steam pressure for 29 knots.[21]

At 10:04 the cruiser was nearly clear of the channel, where a few of the destroyers were waiting to form an antisubmarine screen for *St. Louis*. At that moment *Blue* picked up a submarine on her listening gear, and the operator heard a torpedo being fired at a range of 1,500 yards. Ensign Asher signaled the cruiser. Although she had no time for evasive action, the torpedoes missed and exploded on the reef to the west of the dredged channel. *St. Louis*'s crew spotted a conning tower at the source of the torpedo tracks and opened fire with her 5-inch guns. No hits were observed, and *Blue* moved in to finish the job with depth charges. Asher was satisfied when he saw an oil slick, air bubbles, and debris.[22]

The ships of the Pacific Fleet and installations on Oahu were not the only targets of the raiders. Although the Japanese concentrated their attack on military objectives, a few planes sought targets of opportunity at Honolulu Harbor, the commercial port a few miles to the east.

When the tug *Keosanqua* took over a tow from *Antares*, just outside Pearl Harbor, Japanese planes aimed bombs and gunfire at the two vessels. They completed the transfer undamaged, and *Keosanqua* proceeded to Honolulu with the barge. The planes made more passes at the tug, but again without effect. The Dutch freighter *Jagersfontein* was off Honolulu Harbor and attacked as she stood into the port. The freighter responded quickly with antiaircraft fire (the Dutch had been at war for eighteen months), but there was no damage on either side.[23]

Ashore, the Honolulu Gas Company's storage tanks in the Iwilei waterfront district caught fire from stray shrapnel. Honolulu Fire Department units from the Central and Kakaako stations responded to the alarm. While they fought the blaze four Japanese planes appeared and circled the fire, but they left without attacking.[24]

At nearby Pier 31A Charles Harkins was supervising the transfer of 3,000 cases of dynamite from a cargo ship to trucks. The explosives were to be used for blasting seaplane runways out of coral reefs throughout the Central Pacific. Sunday morning was chosen for the transfer because the light traffic minimized the chance of accidents. Shortly before 9:00 A.M., 500 cases had been unloaded onto the dock and 2,500 remained aboard the ship. Harkins thought that "things were going along nicely," and he looked forward to completing the job by noon.[25]

When billowing smoke from Pearl Harbor signaled the beginning of the attack, Harkins halted the unloading and ordered the dock cleared of the 500 cases already off-loaded from the ship. At first the Coast Guard officer overseeing the work refused to halt the unloading without orders from a superior. When Harkins told him that he would order his men off the dock if the unloading continued, the officer responded with a threat of arrest. Harkins ignored it and called a halt to the unloading.

Then the stevedores refused to transfer the 500 unloaded cases from the dock to the waiting trucks. Enlisting the aid of a marine detachment assigned to guard the shipment, Harkins compelled the dockers to put the dynamite aboard the trucks. Next some of the drivers proved reluctant to take to the highways with the explosive cargo while the attack was still in progress. Again the marines provided the decisive *force majeure,* and the drivers reluctantly drove the trucks out of town and into the canefields near Pearl Harbor. The drive toward the focal point of the attack was hazardous, but Harkins reasoned that if the trucks blew up on the dock, Honolulu's commercial harbor and industrial section would disappear in the blast.

When the docks were cleared Harkins went into his office on the pier about 11:00 A.M. to write his daily report. He had warned his men not to cluster in large groups: If a bomb landed on the dock he wanted as few casualties as possible. Seeing his men gathered in a large group watching planes (probably American) over the harbor, Harkins came outside to remonstrate with them. It was at this moment that a "bomb" (almost certainly an antiaircraft round) exploded nearby.

Harkins and several others were badly injured. Taken to Queen's Hospital in downtown Honolulu, his ordeal continued. The emergency room resembled a slaughterhouse, with bloodstains and corpses covering the floor. After two hours in a small room where two other patients "close enough to touch" died beside him, Harkins was taken to an operating room on an upper floor. The elevator was out of order, so American Legion volunteers operated a makeshift arrangement to hoist him up the outside of the building with a block and tackle. Once in the operating room, a surgeon tried unsuccessfully to remove the shrapnel (without anesthetic). If Harkins had been inclined, he might have reflected on the fact that his determination and judgment had spared the community a serious hazard and the possibility of an even worse disaster.

Harkins's feat, the work of small craft crews, and the sortie of a few warships required courage, coolness, and determination. But these individual efforts, impressive as they were in the face of chaos and danger, could not affect the extent of the Japanese victory. With command organization and communication paralyzed, American successes could be measured only by the standards of rescue, escape, and the mitigation of disaster.

16

TENDING THE WOUNDED

Throughout the attack, and for some time afterward, physicians, nurses, and medical corpsmen worked aboard the ships and at their posts tending to the wounded. Those on undamaged ships cared for the injured from ships which had been disabled. *Rigel's* gangway watch, for example, collared an *Oglala* sailor wandering about the dock in a state of shock and sent him below to the sick bay.[1] Some ships' medical personnel, like *California's* Commander Jesse Jewell and Chief Leslie Leak on *West Virginia,* cared for the wounded at great personal risk. Others became casualties themselves. It was obvious, however, that casualties were so heavy and wounds so serious that the principal burden of caring for the injured would fall on the larger and better equipped medical facilities ashore.

At Pearl Harbor Naval Hospital the doctor on duty, Lieutenant Russell Jensen, had just completed a full night taking care of the usual Saturday night liberty casualties. Nagumo's fliers arrived to shatter the Sunday morning calm as he was suturing a gash on an officer who had cut himself shaving. The hospital staff manned their air raid stations at 8:00 and released patients in the locked wards and hospital brig. Jensen and other doctors were in the process of discharging patients receiving nonessential care when the first casualties began to arrive.[2]

If people at the hospital thought they were immune from danger, they quickly corrected their thinking. No direct attacks were made on any of the medical facilities on December 7, but the flying steel, once on its way, did not distinguish between noncombatants and other targets. Ten minutes into the attack a crippled Japanese aircraft (several ships submitted rival claims for the kill) crashed on the hospital grounds, hitting one of the chief's quarters. Pharmacist's Mate Third

Class Charles Brewer, working in the hospital laboratory, was so close to the impact he could feel the heat from the blazing wreck. Antiaircraft rounds—some with improperly set fuses, some just poorly aimed—began to crash into the area. Seaman Clay Musick, an *Arizona* casualty, wondered about his chances of recovery when a blast blew out one of the hospital's windows and showered him with broken glass. Spectators gawking at the downed plane were ordered under building eaves for protection. Someone quickly put the spectators to work, dispatching them to the warehouse for more mattresses and cots.[3]

Excitement at the hospital was, if possible, soon intensified. At 8:25 Pharmacist's Mate Third Class Edwin Soreside, standing watch on the waterfront, spotted what he thought was a submarine periscope (probably the sub later sunk by *Monaghan*). The news was relayed to the Pearl Harbor duty officer. Soon those on duty at the hospital had more urgent matters at hand. By 9:00 the casualties were arriving in a heavy stream from the damaged ships. Most of the serious casualties were burns from the fires and explosions. Dr. Jensen estimated that perhaps a third of the burn cases, particularly flash burns, were fatal. Many men had been wearing only undershirts and shorts, and the large amount of exposed skin surface resulted in more serious injury than would have otherwise been the case. The hospital's chief medical officer noted that few of the flash burns were deep third-degree burns, but the large proportion of exposed body surface often made the "light" burns fatal. Fuel oil covering the burns of those rescued from the water added to the complications. The flood of casualties was too heavy to permit cleaning off the oil before treatment, so the burns were treated as if the skin were clean. The hospital staff noticed "no difference in the efficacy of treatment."[4]

The hospital admitted as patients 545 battle casualties (350 with extensive body burns) on December 7. By midnight the patient count was 960. Countless others were treated for less serious injuries and returned to duty. Some 313 bodies were brought to the hospital, and the lab basement and nurses' quarters were pressed into duty as temporary morgues. The load taxed the hospital's physicians to the maximum. The navy's Mobile Base Hospital Two (MOB 2) in nearby Aiea contributed two doctors. Lieutenant Commander Herman Gross, a physician-patient recovering from recent surgery, waived his convalescent status and returned to the operating rooms in his more familiar role. Other medical officers from the sunken ships reported to the hospital. Some eight or ten navy wives with nursing training arrived to provide "valuable assistance" to the overworked navy nurses. Supplies, too, could be a problem. The many burn cases exhausted the hospital's supply of intravenous stands, and plasma was in woefully short supply. Navy carpenters improvised stands on the spot, but there was little they could do about the plasma shortage.[5]

At the navy yard dispensary, nearer the boat landings than the hospital, casualties began to arrive in large numbers at 8:20. The officer of the day, Lieutenant (jg) G. S. Hardie, was soon joined by two other medical officers to cope with the flow. He needed the assistance badly, because the dispensary was usually the first stop for casualties arriving from first aid stations set up at Bloch Arena, the receiving station, and the officers' club. Patient outflow, too, had to be supervised. Some of the less severely wounded were transferred to the seventy-five beds made available by the First Marine Defense Battalion. Mobile Base Hospital Two, although still not completed, took another 100. Like their counterparts at the larger and better equipped hospital, they treated a large number of burned men who, in addition, were coated with oil. Unlike their colleagues at the hospital, however, they found that the fuel "greatly complicated" treatment. Flying shrapnel of unknown origin menaced staff and patients alike. While working on the patio Pharmacist's Mate First Class James C. Davis, for example, had a close call when a rotating band from a bomb or shell grazed his leg.[6]

Pearl Harbor's large complement of civilian workers and dependents working and living on the installation responded to the emergency alongside the sailors and marines. Bernard Linberg, a pipefitter from Shop 56, dove into the water to rescue a struggling sailor. Shikumi Yoshida and other crewmen from the dredge *R. W. Atkinson* joined the mixed group fighting fires at Drydock One.[7]

In the Pearl Harbor housing area, Kathy Cooper, wife of Ensign Bud Cooper, was living with her parents, Captain and Mrs. Henry Burns, while her husband was at sea. As the attack continued, she dwelled on her and her husband's chances for survival. As she thought about it, she was seized with the conviction that Bud would survive, she would be killed, and he would marry someone else. "It just made me so mad," she recalled, "but maybe it's nature's way of getting you going and able to cope."[8]

Civilian workers at the navy yard contributed to the medical effort, as they did to firefighting, ship handling, and even antiaircraft work. From Shop 02, On Tai Pang, Robert Puetz, and Chin Hu Pang handled and transported the injured to the dispensary and the hospital.

From Shop 70 came Lawrence Childers, Robert Hecathorn, Leo Clapp, James Bass, Ed Dehning, and Carl Carlson to join in the effort. Other Shop 70 civilians worked feverishly to build more stretchers.[9] In Shop 51 Elmer Perry established an impromptu first aid station. Walter Downing, another Shop 51 employee, painted red crosses on the radiator and sides of his station wagon and brought loads of patients for Perry to treat. William Hoffman commandeered a rowboat and made three trips to Ford Island to bring in the wounded.[10]

Mary Helen Stevens, Pearl Harbor's base librarian, gathered a group of women volunteers. She had some initial difficulty in getting volunteers from the base housing area. Runners went from house to house issuing contradictory instructions: Stay inside . . . no, get out in the street and lie prone. After calming the women in base housing she took them to Bloch Arena, where an emergency first aid station had been established. There they tended to the needs of a steady stream of sailors, some wounded, others searching for dry clothing. The women made coffee by the bucket and sandwiches by the hundreds so that treatment of the wounded could continue without interruption.[11]

Nineteen-year-old Hospitalman Apprentice John Cowden watched the air raid from the vantage point of his station at Mobile Base Hospital Two on Aiea Heights. The panorama seemed to him "just like pushing a button where something exploded." He and the other staff had little time to take in the scene below. Casualties began to come in from the overloaded medical facilities down the hill, and Cowden and his mates were busy rendering whatever aid they could in the incomplete facility. Although designed for a 300-bed capacity, the unit had only about two dozen hospital beds set up. Corpsmen's cots were used for the casualties (mostly burns), and those whose cots had been expropriated spent the next several nights sleeping wherever they could find space to stretch out. Unlike the situation at Pearl Harbor Naval Hospital, the medical supplies on hand were sufficient for the patient load.[12]

The only hospital ship in Pearl Harbor, *Solace,* had her work cut out for her on December 7. Hospitalman James Anderson was waiting on deck for a liberty boat to take him ashore so he could attend services in Honolulu's Episcopal cathedral. When he saw the Japanese planes approach he thought at first he was watching a drill. He abandoned the notion when he saw the nearby *Utah* list to port, stop, then capsize to starboard. The heavy timbers loose on the target ship's deck slid to the port side and piled up like jackstraws. The roll to starboard brought them crashing across the deck, crushing some men and throwing others into the water. Anderson watched horrified for a moment, then he and two shipmates shut by hand a cargo hatch which normally took an electric winch to close.[13]

The officer of the deck, an inexperienced ensign, panicked and froze. He was rescued by Chief Pharmacist's Mate Joseph A. Cunningham, who emerged from below pulling suspenders over his shoulder. The chief sent the officer to the bridge and told him to begin preparing the ship to get under way. Cunningham then phoned the engine room to raise steam in the boilers. The chief had anticipated orders which were soon forthcoming. It was apparent that Solace's isolated position would be hazardous if the Japanese planes made her a target. The unarmed ship shifted position to a spot near a destroyer squadron, where she would at least have the protection of the destroyers' antiaircraft guns. It was a doubtful trade-off, though, because her new position near more worthwhile targets put her in harm's way.[14]

Cunningham soon had other matters to occupy his attention. He organized a stretcher party of ten other pharmacists' mates and put them into the ship's Number 2 motor launch. Pay Clerk John Keefer formed a similar detail which embarked in the Number 1 launch. Both boats proceeded to the burning Arizona. The corpsmen boarded the battleship as her crew was abandoning ship and rescued injured crewmen from the flames. They made several other trips back to Arizona and West Virginia to rescue more men from the battleships, some from mooring quays, and others swimming in the water. Of the many acts of courage performed that morning, those of Solace's boats stand out as exceptionally noteworthy. Once, when an explosion forced some three dozen men to jump overboard from West Virginia, the men on Launch 1 ignored the danger of imminent secondary explosions and remained to rescue other sailors from the burning oil-covered waters. Fireman Second Class Fredrick C. Ley, Jr., the boat's engineer, jumped overboard to rescue one man. The coxswain, Seaman First Class James V. Saccavino, maneuvered the launch directly into the flames for the rescue and had to dive overboard to quench his own burning clothes.[15]

Aboard Solace the medical personnel and ship's crew handled the casualties as they came aboard. They conducted the grim business of triage on deck. In the passageways below, those in pain—primarily burn cases—were given morphine. Nurses marked an "M" on their foreheads with lipstick. Most of the burned men quickly lapsed into shock. James Anderson remembers treating one man for burns who did not suffer so extensively. The patient was *Nevada*'s chief master-at-arms, whose full duty uniform had protected him from explosion flash burns. The blast, however, had ripped off all his clothing except for his webbed duty belt to which was still attached his master-at-arms badge.[16]

Distinctions between ship's crew and medical personnel vanished; everyone did whatever was required. After *Solace* had been moved to the dubious protection of the destroyer nest, Anderson and others were sent on deck to roll plaster of paris bandages. Japanese planes flew so close the sailors could look "straight into the cockpits . . . and see the pilots as they went by us." They had no assurance that the Japanese would respect the large red cross painted on the ship. As if to intensify their fears, a bomb landed in the water close by, and the near miss killed three men on the destroyer tender *Dobbin*. Even if they did pass up *Solace* for the combatant ships, it seemed to Anderson that the Japanese were flying deliberately close to the hospital ship in order to protect themselves against antiaircraft fire.[17]

Patient care continued on *Solace* for some time after the attack. Additional medical personnel, including nurses, were brought in from shore facilities, but still more were needed. The navy requested civilian nurses to help with the load of patients, and several were brought in from Honolulu. Ruth Winne was one of a group of eight ferried out to *Solace* on the morning of December 8. Because she was married, Winne was allowed to go ashore that evening (the unmarried nurses were kept aboard that night); casualties were still being brought aboard *Solace* when she left.[18]

Army casualties were treated ashore, the most serious at Tripler General Hospital, the post medical facility at Fort Shafter.[19] Lieutenant Elizabeth Elmer, one of the nurses on duty, remembers the hospital being so crowded with casualties that amputations were performed on stretchers. After working all day her shoes and stockings were covered with blood from carrying out the severed limbs for disposal. Remarkably, she found she still had an appetite late that day when she was relieved for a short time.

There was danger, too, as well as gore. Shrapnel from misfused antiaircraft shells spattered the building from time to time. Lieutenant Elmer was reminded of the sound made by walnuts rattling to the ground when, as a girl, she climbed the trees to shake the nuts loose. Some of the patients received additional wounds when curiosity led them outside for a look.

Help arrived from an unexpected source late in the day. Military wives and daughters and civilian employees from Fort Shafter showed up at Tripler to assist the nurses, and a contingent of prostitutes arrived wanting to help. These auxiliaries were dispatched to purchase small items like pencils and candy for the patients. They found few shops open for business that day, but they wanted to do *something*. When some of the casualties recognized the prostitutes, Lieutenant Elmer was in a quandary. Should she accept their help or not? She asked her supervisor, who replied, "Well, they [the men] spent enough on them; now it's their turn to spend some money on the boys."[20]

The help of the civilian community proved invaluable. The assistance provided by practitioners such as Dr. Frederick Alsup and nurses Ruth Winne and Ethel Brown was badly needed. Civilian doctors and nurses arrived shortly after the attack began. Ethel Brown, a Honolulu nurse, found a shortage of gloves in surgery. Instead of being discarded, used gloves were "boiled and all put in a basin, and people had to go to the basin and fish out a right and a left of the proper size for themselves." Dr. Alsup, a Honolulu surgeon, was impressed with the stoicism of one of his patients. The man silently endured an operation on his shattered shoulder without anesthetic while a patient on the next table screamed in pain. Alsup's patient complained only about the screaming of the man next to him.[21]

In some ways the civilians were better prepared for the disaster than the armed services. Hawaii's government and community leaders had taken to heart the lessons of the London blitz and were determined not to be caught short if the islands should face a similar emergency. In June 1941 the City and County of Honolulu established the Major Disaster Council to deal with unexpected crises. Most important, the council provided leadership which prompted organizations like the Red Cross to be ready.

The Hawaii Medical Association had sponsored a Sunday morning lecture by Dr. John J. Moorhead, a visiting specialist on wound surgery. Moorhead began his talk with a biblical quotation: "Be ye also ready, for in the hour that ye know not, the Son of Man cometh." Someone threw open the door to the lecture hall and announced that surgeons were needed at Tripler at once. Speaker and audience sped off to substitute the scheduled lecture for urgent practice. The civilian physicians gradually replaced army doctors in the operating rooms as the day progressed. The latter, more familiar with army procedures, attended to the equally important work of selecting patients for surgery, evacuating the wounded, and arranging for X-rays.[22]

Early in the attack the Major Disaster Council put into effect its carefully prepared plan for emergency ambulance service. It ordered litter frames installed in private trucks which had been previously designated emergency ambulances and dispatched the vehicles to military bases. Marine Captain Alexander Holcomb, on his way to Pearl Harbor, noticed the makeshift ambulances "loaded with wounded people, blood running out of the back." The council also dispatched medical supplies to military hospitals, and the Chamber of Commerce blood bank exhausted its supply of 200 bottles of blood plasma.[23]

Queen's Hospital in Honolulu handled the bulk of the civilian casualties. Volunteers flocked to Queen's to assist the staff. Patricia Morgan came from nearby Manoa Valley and was put to work feeding a small girl who had lost an arm. Outlying hospitals on the sugar plantations surrounding Pearl Harbor treated more than 130 navy casualties. Civilian hospitals in Honolulu had their hands full with civilians injured in the attack.[24]

One of the most trying tasks of the medical staff was dealing with hundreds of bodies, many unidentifiable, and parts of bodies. At the Pearl Harbor Naval Hospital Lieutenant (jg) John Shaver, the staff pathologist, was assisted by Ensign Chester Fay in identifying the dead. Lieutenant James Justice, a dental officer, helped them by comparing unidentified corpses with dental charts. Soon there were just too many remains to be housed at the hospital compound, and a temporary morgue was established at Aiea Landing. The hospital commander characterized the work there as "most unpleasant and difficult."[25]

Boatswain's Mate Second Class Nick Kouretas of *Raleigh* was one of those assigned to comb the harbor in small boats after the attack in search of remains. They did not load them into the boats, remembers Kouretas, but "we would lasso a leg, an arm, a head, and maybe tow four or five or six bodies behind us slowly in the launch over to the landing." Corpsmen there "would jump in the water with sheets . . . and scoop up the bodies." When they brought their cargo to Aiea Landing, most sailors left as quickly as they could. Kouretas, however, forced himself to linger. His younger brother, Jim, was among the missing. The bodies were stacked in rows "like cordwood

. . . with a walkway down the center." Kouretas patrolled the walkway but could not look at the faces. He checked hands—Jim had
been an incorrigible nail biter. It was several days before he encountered his brother, who somehow had wound up aboard *Blue* and sortied with the destroyer.[26]

Bodies decomposed quickly in the water and tropical weather.
Charles Brewer was among the medical personnel assigned to take
fingerprints. Sometimes the skin would "just pull off" the fingers.
Nearly forty years later Karl Johnson from *Utah* retained an indelible
memory of a case-hardened marine sergeant stripping the skin from
corpses' fingers and putting it over his own fingers to get readable
fingerprints. The presence of the dead, though, was not the worst
part. There were some who looted the bodies of their comrades. In
fact, the Pearl Harbor Naval Hospital had to post a guard over the
morgue to keep away the ghouls. Even so, Brewer recalls, "somebody
had stripped a lot of our boys, officers and sailors, would take their
rings and watches off and you could tell by the white spots on their
arms that weren't tan."[27]

Robert Johnson and other *Utah* survivors were formed into a burial
detail. After the third day, Johnson recalls, "they brought them out
in a dump truck. They would pull the chain just like it was a load of
dirt and dump them out." In mid-December a call came for volunteers for unspecified duty. Everyone in the burial party joined the
mad scramble to volunteer, because to Johnson and his mates "anything was better than the burying party."[28]

Given the circumstances, the military was remarkably conscientious, although not successful in every case, in its attempts to identify
the bodies. Temporary burials for eighteen Kaneohe casualties took
place with military honors in sand dunes near the air station. Even
Lieutenant Iida, who had fruitlessly crash-dived his plane at a hangar,
was accorded a military burial in a spot near, but separate from, the
American dead. Some 328 navy dead were buried at Honolulu's
Oahu Cemetery; when Oahu Cemetery's navy plot was full, an additional 204 were interred at nearby Red Hill. The army buried its dead
at the Schofield Barracks post cemetery.[29]

V

THE AFTERMATH

17

RETURN FLIGHT

The first-wave Japanese airmen (except Commander Fuchida, who lingered to observe the damage) set down on their carriers at 10:00. Breaking off the attack and leaving the carnage behind, the second-wave pilots began the return flight to their carriers about 9:45. It would have been better to fly an indirect return route to confuse U.S. tracking aircraft, but limited fuel capacity forced the Japanese to return via the direct route. Fuchida circled at the rendezvous spot just off Kaena Point waiting to guide the stragglers back to the safety of Nagumo's fleet.[1]

The return flight was untroubled by U.S. air pursuit, but the journey was not at all anticlimactic for some of the planes. Lieutenant Fujita's engine had been damaged in the dogfight with the P-36, and he flew back to *Soryu* with his oil pressure gauge dropping steadily. Another Zeke in his squadron had been set afire and emitted smoke and flames for much of the return trip. A navigation error by his group's escort nearly cost the Japanese as many losses as U.S. antiaircraft fire and fighter opposition. When they met the bomber which was to guide them back to the fleet, Fujita (with one eye on his compass and the other on his oil pressure gauge) noticed that his course was off by 30 degrees. Fujita altered his course to the correct bearing and waited for the others to follow. At first the group continued to follow the lead of the escort, but gradually they broke off and fell in behind Fujita. Finally the escort joined, too. The group was among the last planes to land, about 1:00 P.M., and it was a close call for many. Some Japanese aircraft were so badly damaged they barely made it back. Fujita's oil pressure gauge read zero, and one of his engine cylinders tumbled onto the deck as his plane caught the arresting hook.[2]

As the planes came in Nagumo broke radio silence briefly and sent a short message to Yamamoto summarizing the successful results. At 1:30 Admiral Nagumo ordered his fleet to begin the return voyage to Japanese home waters. But in the half hour between Fuchida's return and Nagumo's order there occurred a brief, confused debate which altered the course of the Pacific War. Should the fleet return posthaste, or should the carriers remain to inflict still more damage?

For Genda, Fuchida, and most of the other pilots there was no doubt. Genda urged that they stay and seek a decisive battle with the U.S. carriers at sea, the Japanese thought, in the fleet training area south of Oahu. Fuchida agreed at first, but he changed his mind when it was pointed out that the Japanese tankers were waiting for a rendezvous to the north. If Nagumo redirected them to the south they could not meet the First Air Fleet soon enough to replenish the task force's fuel tanks. Fuchida then urged Nagumo to send the planes back to Pearl Harbor and destroy the U.S. fleet's shoreside facilities, which had been left relatively untouched. The difference of opinion on this point between Genda and Fuchida highlights the most serious flaw in the Pearl Harbor attack plan: lack of a contingency provision to exploit an unexpectedly complete success.[3]

The unpreparedness was only one of several considerations which influenced Nagumo. The task force commander was satisfied he had accomplished his assigned objective: The U.S. Pacific Fleet was incapable of interfering with the Japanese invasion of Southeast Asia. Nagumo betrayed his line of reasoning to Fuchida when he interrupted the airman's initial report with the question, "Do you think that the U.S. fleet could not come out from Pearl Harbor within six months?" When Fuchida, despite his misgivings about the question's implications, replied in the affirmative Nagumo broke into a broad smile.[4] For Americans the Pearl Harbor attack was the overwhelmingly decisive blow which plunged the United States into World War II. For the Japanese, however, it was, in strategic terms, a subsidiary operation. Their primary aim was to secure access to the natural resources of Southeast Asia.

There were important tactical and operational considerations as well which influenced Nagumo. Although Japanese aircraft losses were light (twenty-nine planes), the fighter opposition and antiaircraft fire had been vigorous. The first wave, which achieved surprise, lost nine planes; the second wave, which found U.S. forces more alert, lost more than twice that number. The U.S. interceptor command had been almost entirely destroyed, but the Japanese were unsure how many planes had been demolished and feared that a return engagement might be met with swarms of P-40s. All in all, they were not sanguine about the prospect of a follow-up attack on Oahu. Then, too, the Japanese mistakenly believed some fifty heavy U.S. aircraft had survived the raid and might at that very moment be on their way toward the task force bent on revenge.[5]

And what if Nagumo decided to seek out the U.S. carriers? The Japanese did not know their whereabouts, whereas the Americans almost certainly knew the general position of the First Air Fleet—or so the Japanese believed. What if the enemy carriers (not to mention submarines) caught Nagumo's force by surprise? A carrier battle would require rearming the planes just back from Oahu, a process which would temporarily incapacitate the aircraft and bring bombs and torpedoes onto the flight and hangar decks. This risky business would leave the carriers terribly vulnerable, even if only for a short time, and was in fact an important element in the Japanese disaster at Midway six months later. Finally, as if to clinch the argument, the weather turned nasty. The high seas and limited visibility would make continued flight operations not only difficult but dangerous.[6]

For Nagumo to remain was a risky course of action. But there were enormous benefits which might be reaped from accepting these risks. Destruction of U.S. carrier forces and incapacitation of the Pearl Harbor naval base would, for all practical purposes, compel the Pacific Fleet to retire to the West Coast. The six-month cushion sought by the Japanese would be extended considerably and the chances of obtaining American acquiescence to Japanese domination of East Asia increased commensurately. In the final analysis Nagumo's temperament and predisposition were the decisive factors. He was cautious by nature, a conventional naval officer with an uncertain mastery of aerial operations, and acutely aware of his responsibility for the safety of the emperor's entire force of heavy carriers. He had initially opposed the Pearl Harbor operation and even after accepting Yamamoto's plan was by no means confident of success. He felt, in the words of one historian, "like a gambler who has staked his life savings on the turn of a card and won. His only idea was to cash in and go home as quickly as possible."[7]

Still in a state of shock, army and navy forces in Hawaii tried to respond to the attack. It was obvious that the raid had been launched from nearby carriers, and the remaining fleet and air units now turned their attention to locating the Japanese task force—and, if possible, hitting back. Heavy losses in ships and planes made the task more formidable. But an even greater handicap was the disorganization and confusion which prevailed at the command echelon. Indeed, the bumbling search for Nagumo's force illustrates glaringly just how unprepared for war were the U.S. armed forces in 1941. That unpreparedness was manifested not so much in shortages of personnel and weapons as in organizational and psychological inability to respond effectively.

These shortcomings were reflected in the failure to consult the radar network for information on the attackers' outward-bound course. When Lieutenant Tyler was relieved about 8:30 he did not mention the Opana sighting. The radar plot showed clearly that the planes had come from and departed to the north. If Tyler's failure to react to the early morning contact can be explained by his assumption that the planes were American, his failure to report the facts to his relief cannot. Even a nonspecialist such as Tyler should have realized the implications of the Opana report. Even more inexplicable is the failure of the specialists who took over operation of the Fort Shafter information center. They neglected to gather and pass on tracking information from Opana and other stations which could have indicated the outward path of the Japanese aircraft and, by extension, the approximate location of the Japanese task force. An official U.S. Army history explains these shortcomings with the observation that the aircraft warning system was still in an embryonic stage and its personnel, even those in authority, were too inexperienced in the new technology to use it effectively.[8]

Kimmel bitterly characterized the inadequate performance of the army radar network as "incomprehensible," but navy radar made at least one contact which was not exploited. The hills surrounding Pearl Harbor screened the Japanese attack and retreat routes from radar detection by ships in the anchorage, but there were ships at sea with radar. *Enterprise*'s radar, according to the ship's gunnery officer, tracked the Japanese aircraft in their retreat to the northwest. The novelty of the device, however, inhibited exploitation of the contact, and Halsey remained ignorant of Nagumo's whereabouts.[9]

Kimmel, too, lacked accurate information. At 11:05 A.M. Kimmel radioed the warships which had managed to sortie from Pearl Harbor and designated the group as Task Force One under the command of Rear Admiral Milo Draemel. The makeshift task force consisted of the light cruisers *Detroit* (Draemel's flagship), *Phoenix,* and *St. Louis,* rounded out by a dozen destroyers. It was hardly an impressive force, and Kimmel wisely ordered the ships to join Halsey's Task Force Eight.[10]

Before these survivors of the attack could join the *Enterprise* task force they received a signal indicating that a Japanese task force, which included heavy warships, was off Barbers Point. The Task Force One sailors hardly considered their group a match for the Japanese attackers who, they correctly surmised, were vastly superior in numbers and firepower. Nevertheless, they were all that stood between the enemy and what remained of the U.S. Pacific Fleet. There was little choice but to attack and perhaps inflict some damage.

Blue received orders from *St. Louis* to launch a torpedo attack against the force off Barbers Point. Ensign Asher, for the first time that day, was badly frightened. He convened a council of ensigns and chief petty officers to work out a plan. *Blue* would, they decided, make a high-speed run toward the target, fire the eight torpedoes from her port tubes, make a 180-degree turn while laying a smoke-screen, come about, and then fire her starboard torpedoes. As the destroyer maneuvered she would fire a continuous barrage from her 5-inch guns. While *Blue* attacked, *St. Louis* would bombard the target with her 6-inch guns. No one was optimistic about the plan's chances for success, or even about his own chances for survival.

While closing with the "enemy" off Barbers Point *Blue*'s crew confronted a more immediate hazard. In the haste to prepare for battle routine, safety precautions went by the board. One of the torpedoes began running while still in its tube. The explosive warhead fell onto the wildly pitching deck as the destroyer plowed through heavy seas at high speed. Quick work by Chief Torpedoman Charles Shaw saved the ship as he directed his men in heaving the warhead over the side. Shortly after that close call *Blue* learned that the report of Japanese ships off Barbers Point was a false alarm and the attack was called off. The crew, although no one knew what hazards lay ahead, must have felt that *Blue*'s fortunes during the first hours of war warranted fervent prayers of thanksgiving.[11]

There was little chance that Draemel's task force would find the Japanese, but if employed intelligently the remaining aircraft on Oahu might search out the enemy carriers. Contingency planning for long-range search operations called for the navy to assume overall control of army aircraft on Oahu. Coordination between the air arms of the two services was practically nonexistent. Admiral Bellinger later wrote: "I never did know actually what the Army air had available and I never did know what they had actually done." The assertion seems incredible in light of the fact that Bellinger had at least two telephone conversations with General Frederick Martin while the attack was in progress. Bellinger also spoke with General Jacob Rudolph, Martin's bomber commander, during the closing minutes of the attack. Mid-level operational officers found the difficulties of interservice communication more formidable. Commander Charles Coe of Bellinger's staff was unable to establish any contact whatsoever with his army opposite number.[12]

Martin, in turn, complained that the navy failed to assign any search missions to army aircraft until midafternoon, when a flight of the precious few remaining B-17s was dispatched on a wild goose chase to the south. The army, on its own initiative, dispatched a flight of four A-20 attack bombers at 11:27 to join the search for the phantom fleet off Barbers Point. They were joined by two B-17s which lifted off from Hickam at 11:40. These missions were planned and assigned using guesswork rather than reliable information. Major Landon tried but failed to interest anyone in his observation that the Japanese planes seemed to be coming in from the north.[13]

Shortly after noon a solid piece of intelligence became available and, more important, came to the attention of the command level. A chart showing the course of the Japanese carriers was recovered from the plane which crashed at Fort Kamehameha. Captain William Smith believed that the army failed to recognize the value of the chart and that it was not brought to the attention of the navy until late afternoon. Martin, however, testified that he realized its importance immediately. The record tends to support Martin, at least circumstantially, for three A-20s took off at 1:00 for a search to the north and two B-18s were sent in the same direction half an hour later. The air search effort became even more confused later in the day when General Martin was hospitalized with what today would be called a nervous breakdown.[14]

Confusion and uncertainty were the order of the day not only at the air commands, but at Admiral Kimmel's CincPac headquarters as well. According to Captain Charles McMorris, the Pacific Fleet staff believed there were Japanese naval units in the waters south *and* north of Oahu. McMorris thought the chances of intercepting the carriers to the north of the island were slim, but the prospect of making contact with units to the south "looked at least to hold some promise." Apparently the fleet staff officers based that judgment on the fact that there were already a number of U.S. warships to the south. In any event, it was not until 2:35 P.M. that CincPac notified fleet units at sea of its belief that Japanese forces lay in both directions. Throughout the morning and early afternoon it had issued a stream of conflicting messages alternately locating the enemy fleet to the north and south.[15]

At 9:50 CincPac radioed Task Force Eight that two Japanese carriers were reported 30 miles southwest of Barbers Point. Twenty-five minutes later fleet headquarters directed Bellinger's patrol planes to search for Japanese carriers to the north. At 10:18 Kimmel signaled Task Forces Three, Eight, and Twelve that there was "some indication" of a Japanese force northwest of Oahu. At 10:46, less than half an hour later, he flashed word to Halsey of a Japanese carrier south of Barbers Point. The cruiser *Minneapolis,* which had been exercising in the fleet training area south of Oahu, was directed shortly before noon to use her floatplanes to scout the southern area for Japanese vessels. *Minneapolis* herself was mistakenly identified as a Japanese ship. To confuse matters further, when the cruiser spotted no enemy units her message that *no* Japanese ships were in the area was misread to the effect that there were *two* Japanese ships south of Oahu. At 12:08 CincPac broadcast the message that headquarters had no confirmed location of the Japanese carriers, but that four surviving planes of the *Enterprise* morning flight had been dispatched to search to the northeast. The pendulum swung south again at 12:32 with a message to "all ships" that Japanese transports lay off Barbers Point.[16]

Admiral Bellinger's deployment of his few remaining patrol planes mirrored the confusion at CincPac. Three small unarmed floatplanes from the utility wing at Ford Island scouted close to the Oahu shoreline but found nothing. While the attack was in progress Bellinger contacted Commander Knefler McGinnis, commanding officer of Patrol Wing One at Kaneohe. Ascertaining that McGinnis still had two PBYs in commission, he ordered the commander to send them scouting to the northwest. The last stages of the attack, however, destroyed those two planes. Then communications broke down between Kaneohe and Bellinger's Ford Island command post, and McGinnis was on his own. He reasoned—correctly as it turned out—that a search to the northwest should be given the highest priority. Still in the air, searching sectors to the south, were the planes of McGinnis's dawn security patrol, including the one which had joined *Ward*'s 7:00 A.M. attack on the submarine. McGinnis diverted two of his dawn patrol planes from the south to cover the northwest. His instinct was sound, for he sent his planes in the right direction, but they failed to make contact with Nagumo's fleet. Bellinger's confused grasp of the situation is illustrated by his disapproval of McGinnis's initiative and judgment. Bellinger labored under the illusion that McGinnis should have left the dawn patrol uselessly crisscrossing the seas south of Oahu.[17]

Only once did navy officers on Oahu get a solid lead on Nagumo's whereabouts. About 10:30 A.M., when the Japanese briefly broke radio silence to report to Tokyo, the message was intercepted by the navy radio station at Heeia. Navy radio technicians, however, were able to take only a reciprocal bearing on the signal. The reading could be interpreted as originating from a source bearing either 357 degrees (almost due north) or from the opposite direction. The U.S. Navy's run of bad luck on December 7 continued: The signal was interpreted erroneously as originating from south of Oahu.[18]

Captain Smith said the interpretation was made in the wake of the inaccurate reports claiming *Minneapolis* as a Japanese carrier. Kimmel and his staff knew the cruiser was operating to the south and were unsure about the report's accuracy. Smith was considering the problem with Captain McMorris and Captain Walter DeLaney. While they were deliberating, Lieutenant Commander Layton came into the room with word of the intercept. The fleet intelligence officer, according to Smith, "ran over to the plotting board with radio bearings and stated, 'Here they are' and he cut them to southward." At 1:32 Kimmel signaled his task force commanders at sea near Oahu that radio intercepts indicated *Akagi* and "another unit" were south of Oahu.[19]

In the absence of orderly control of the search it was inevitable that friendly vessels would be mistaken for Japanese. Major Brooke Allen nearly mistook *Enterprise* for an enemy carrier and made a pass on her before he realized his error. A similar mistake was made by a pilot from the PBY squadron which had been recalled from Midway to search for Nagumo's carriers off Oahu. South of Pearl Harbor the patrol pilot mistook the cruiser *Portland* and her escorting destroyer, *Porter*, for a Japanese carrier and a light cruiser. The pilot dropped two bombs, which missed both ships, and chased the vessels for 80 miles before they found refuge in foul weather. When asked later how he was sure the ships were Japanese he replied with more imagination than consistency that the "carrier's" deck was painted with a rising sun and, besides, she had the plan of a heavy cruiser painted on her deck for camouflage.[20]

Especially at hazard were the fishing sampans which had the bad luck to be caught off Oahu on December 7. U.S. authorities in the best of times regarded them with intense suspicion as Japanese spies

and naval auxiliaries. Intensive investigation after the attack uncov-
ered no instances of collaboration with the Japanese Navy among the
fishermen. But in the aftermath of the Pearl Harbor attack some
Americans, enraged and frustrated by their inability to hit back at the
attackers, considered them fair game. Sampans working off Barbers
Point were strafed by army A-20s and attacked by a coast guard cutter
when they were "observed" attempting to aid a Japanese submarine.
Several of the fishermen were killed and others wounded.[21]

18

WHAT NEXT?

After receiving word of the attack on Pearl Harbor, Task Force Eight remained in the area southwest of Kauai. Admiral Halsey, eager to close with the Japanese fleet, seethed in frustration. The confusing stream of messages from CincPac, he wrote, "succeeded only in enraging me. It is bad enough to be blindfolded, but it is worse to be led around the compass."[1] In response to dispatches from Pearl Harbor *Enterprise* searched fruitlessly for the Japanese. At 10:20 fifteen scout bombers were dispatched to the area south of Barbers Point. At 1:45 a force of nine scout bombers searched a sector bearing 110 to 200 degrees to a distance of 175 miles from Task Force Eight. This wedge-shaped pattern duplicated the searches being launched from Oahu to the south and southwest of the island.[2]

The 1:45 search produced yet another false lead. One of the bomber pilots reported in error that he had sighted a carrier accompanied by a cruiser about 50 miles south of Pearl Harbor. The pilot radioed, in addition, that he had been attacked by fighters. At 4:42, as dusk neared, Halsey launched six fighters, six dive bombers equipped with smoke generators, and eighteen torpedo planes. The force was led by Lieutenant Eugene Lindsey, commander of the *Enterprise* torpedo squadron. The scout from the early afternoon mission had probably mistaken one or more of the U.S. cruisers and destroyers south of Oahu for Japanese. When the pilot was questioned later about the "Japanese fighters" he described them as twin-engine planes, leading Halsey to conclude he had encountered a group of army bombers.[3]

The late afternoon mission encountered no Japanese, but the airmen faced more than their share of hazards. Nervous antiaircraft gunners on the ships below fired intermittently on the circling combat air patrol from 4:00 to 5:15. The pilots he had dispatched to strike the phantom Japanese fleet would, Halsey realized, have to land in the dark. The fighters, led by Lieutenant (jg) Francis "Fritz" Hebel, returned first. They had become separated from the bombers in the dark, but Hebel managed by skillful navigation to find *Enterprise.* They circled once but did not land. Instead, Halsey ordered the fighters to proceed to Ford Island. The torpedo planes returned shortly afterward and were recovered—still armed—without injuries by the darkened *Enterprise.*[4]

With all the air searches for Nagumo's force it was almost inevitable that there would be at least one positive contact. It was not one of the aircraft dispatched from Oahu, nor was it one of the carrier planes which made the contact. It was two Seagull scout planes from the cruiser *Northampton,* one of *Enterprise*'s escorts. About 11:00 A.M. the three cruisers with Halsey's force each launched two of the slow, lightly armed biplanes to scout 150 miles to the north of Task Force Eight and then return to Oahu. *Northampton*'s planes, piloted by Lieutenant Malcolm Reeves and Ensign Fred Covington, were launched at 11:15 and five minutes later winged away on a course slightly east of north.[5]

When they were about 100 miles north of Kauai at 11:40 a Zeke approached the planes. Reeves led his two-plane section down to 300 feet. The fighter attacked at high speed from the port, but was foiled when the biplanes made an easy turn to port at 80 knots, one-third the speed of the Japanese plane. Reeves' rear-seat gunner, Radioman First Class Robert Baxter, and Covington's gunner, Radioman Second Class John Melton, swung their .30-caliber machine guns around and fired. They drove off the Zeke, which then climbed and made six successive diving attacks. The Zeke had a decided advantage in speed and armament, so Reeves chose to maintain a low altitude and use the biplanes' superior maneuverability to best advantage. Each time the Japanese plane dove on them Reeves led Covington into a diving turn. The tactic offered their gunners a good target as the fighter pulled up or to the side at the end of each dive.

Reeves' plane took fourteen hits and Covington's eleven. Miraculously, none of the Americans were wounded in the uneven fight, and the Zeke, trailing smoke, broke off his attack after twenty minutes. *Northampton*'s commanding officer observed that for the two biplanes to repel the attack "speaks very highly for the skill and presence of mind of the pilots and gunners" of the scout planes. The praise was well deserved, but Admiral Halsey was less pleased. Reeves and Covington, instead of breaking radio silence to report the encounter, continued flying the search pattern. No one knew of the presence of the Japanese carrier plane northwest of Oahu until they landed at Ford Island at 3:27 that afternoon.[6]

The position of the Zeke, probably a stray from the first wave, might have alerted Halsey and Kimmel to the whereabouts of Nagumo's carrier force. When he learned of the contact Halsey made his displeasure known and demanded an explanation from his cruiser commander, Rear Admiral Raymond Spruance, but the Japanese by that time had put many miles between themselves and Hawaiian waters. Even had he received the news in time Halsey would have faced a dilemma more taxing than the frustration which consumed him. He reflected later:

> Suppose that the enemy was located, and suppose that I could intercept him: what then? A surface engagement was out of the question, since I had nothing but cruisers to oppose his heavy ships. In addition, we were perilously low on fuel. . . . On the other hand, my few remaining planes might inflict some damage, and by the next forenoon the *Lexington*'s task force would reach a position from which her air group could support an attack.[7]

Halsey's chances of success notwithstanding, his six *Enterprise* fighters approached Oahu shortly before 9:00 P.M. without making contact with the Japanese. The pilots had trouble identifying the island and thought the fires still burning at Pearl Harbor were canefields being burned off on Kauai. Believing Oahu lay still farther east, they continued until they were well out over the channel dividing Oahu and Molokai. Recognizing their error, the group made a 180-degree turn and flew west along the south shore of Oahu and headed for the Pearl Harbor channel entrance. Hebel made contact with the Ford Island control tower, where Commander Young kept vigil. The tower radio told Hebel's group to make a standard approach to the field. Hebel formed up the group with himself in the lead followed in line by Ensigns Herbert Menges, Gayle Hermann, and David Flynn. Ensign James Daniels and Lieutenant (jg) Eric Allen would bring up the rear. Acting on the instructions to make a normal approach, the first four came in with their wheels down and landing lights lit. Daniels and Allen were to circle above, ready for any emergency, until the others were safely down.[8]

Admiral Bellinger maintained that the approach should have come as no surprise. He claimed his headquarters had received advance word of the incoming flight and that the Navy Yard Defense Center had been requested to alert all antiaircraft batteries of the friendly planes expected that night. It was too much, though, to expect efficient communications in the wake of the morning's disaster. Also, the antiaircraft gunners were far too tense to hold their fire until planes approaching in darkness could be identified. As the fighters approached it seemed as though every gun in the fleet opened fire. Bellinger thought *California's* gunners fired first; to Merion Croft, spending the night in his Ford Island hangar, the first shooting came as "a little tat tat tat" of a machine gun from Ewa. Within seconds the sky was ablaze with gunfire of every type from pistols to 5-inch guns.[9]

The approaching planes were caught in a barrage of fire which brought Herb Menges down in a fiery crash on the Pearl City peninsula. Eric Allen managed to bail out but was fatally wounded as he drifted to earth. Fritz Hebel made for Wheeler but met a similar reception there; he crashed and suffered fatal injuries. Gayle Hermann took a 5-inch round through his engine, but he was so low the projectile had no time to arm. He brought the crippled plane in for a landing at Ford Island. The aircraft was badly damaged but Hermann was intact. Flynn's plane lost power; he parachuted and broke a leg on landing.

Daniels escaped to the west, and when he reached Barbers Point he saw that the antiaircraft fire had died away. He raised Commander Young in the tower and asked for instructions. Young, now uncertain the planes were actually his, asked the pilot for his name. Daniels, unsure whether he was really speaking with another American, turned the question around and demanded to know to whom he was speaking. Young replied he was the *Enterprise* air group commander. Young was godfather to Daniels' daughter, so the ensign told him he was speaking to his goddaughter's father. He then asked Young for his (Daniels') middle name. Young replied correctly and, just to be sure, asked Daniels for his nickname. The game of Twenty Questions ended with both men satisfied they were in fact speaking to a friend.

Young instructed Daniels to come in low, fast, and with his landing lights off. He brought his plane in at more than 150 knots—too fast, theoretically, for his flaps to work. Daniels overshot the Ford Island runway and flashed past the beached *Nevada*. The grounded battleship's gunners turned their fire on him, but he was too low; the streams of tracers converged above him in a cone of fire. On his next approach his flaps somehow worked and he landed with only a single bullet hole in the plane. A marine antiaircraft gunner on the field, though, had not gotten the word. He opened up on Daniels with a .50-caliber machine gun as he taxied the fighter to a halt. It took Gayle Hermann's direct intervention—swatting the gunner on the head—to make him cease firing.

Daniels and Hermann embraced in an emotional reunion on the field. They reported to Commander Young in the tower, and Young found abandoned quarters on Ford Island where the three could spend the night. The commander was acquainted with the quarters' regular occupant and, more important, also knew the whereabouts of his liquor supply. Daniels took a badly needed shot of whiskey before turning in for the night. He spied a telephone and asked Young if he could call his wife, Helen. Young told him not to bother trying—all the civilian lines were down. The longer he looked at the telephone, the more Daniels wanted to speak to his wife. He picked up the receiver and to his surprise was greeted with a dial tone. He called Helen, assured her he was still alive, and turned in for the night. It would hardly have been a restful night in any event, but the house was near the still burning *Arizona*. Ammunition exploded at irregular intervals, and once Daniels was nearly hit by shrapnel smashing into his headboard. For the third and final time that day Ensign Daniels narrowly escaped death from "friendly" fire.[10]

Daniels' experience typified the state of mind prevailing on Oahu. Both the military and the civil population were beset by confusion, fear, and sometimes panic. The raid was a hit and run operation, but it was widely believed to be the opening blow of a Japanese campaign to seize Hawaii. What next? wondered soldiers, sailors, marines, and civilians. Would the Japanese attempt an invasion? And just how loyal were Hawaii's 160,000 Japanese residents?

Whatever the answers to these questions, they involved formidable challenges in feeding, mobilizing, and controlling Hawaii's 400,000 civilians. Joseph Poindexter, the territory's appointed governor, already had wide emergency powers under legislation enacted at General Short's urging earlier that year. Governor Poindexter invoked these powers in a radio broadcast shortly before noon, but Short considered the step insufficient to meet the emergency. Emergency rule still left governance of the territory in civilian hands.

Just after noon Short called on the governor at his offices in Iolani Palace. The general briefed Poindexter on the damage done by the attack, expressed his belief that an invasion and uprisings might be in the offing, and asked for a declaration of martial law. The governor was reluctant to abolish civil rule, but Short was adamant. The elderly Poindexter was no match for Short's determination. In any event, the governor could hardly ignore the extraordinary measures which would be needed if a siege or invasion were in the offing. He telephoned President Roosevelt, who approved of the step.[11]

The short call to the president was made even more difficult by the long distance operator, already under control of military censors, who demanded to know Poindexter's business with Roosevelt before she placed the call and interrupted the conversation several times. Poindexter acceded to Short's request shortly after the talk with Roosevelt. The governor's sweeping proclamation of martial law gave to the Hawaiian Department commanding general all the powers of the civil executive branch. In addition, he suspended the writ of habeas corpus and the functioning of the territory's civil courts.[12]

Few civilians in Hawaii had any real idea of the extent of the damage and casualties. Rumor quickly took the place of facts, as reports of enemy troops ricocheted through the community. Police were besieged with reports of Japanese soldiers who, on investigation, turned out to be innocent strollers. Another story which enjoyed wide currency was that the water supply had been poisoned. The December 8 edition of the *Honolulu Advertiser* amplified the confusion with stories of enemy paratroopers roaming Oahu. The paper even added such convincing details (in a front-page story headlined "Saboteurs Land Here") as the fact that the enemy troops could be identified by red disks on their shoulders.[13]

Kaneohe Naval Air Station received word that the descending paratroopers wore dungarees. Sailors there were ordered to change into whites, which were first dyed brown. The Barbers Point lighthouse keeper was possessed of an exceptionally vivid imagination. He reported a wholly imaginary gun battle (complete with casualty count and burial) between Japanese paratroopers and soldiers of the Fifty-fifth Coast Artillery Regiment.[14] Headquarters tried vainly to keep up with the stories. On Monday night Japanese troops were reported to have landed on the neighboring island of Molokai and captured the small airfield there. Lieutenant Colonel Kendall Fielder, Hawaiian Department intelligence officer, phoned the field and was reassured that the island was still in American hands.[15]

Other rumors were the products of fervent but unfounded wishful thinking. Wild stories circulated to the effect that U.S. forces had successfully repelled the attack and sortied to win a victory at sea.

Mrs. Robert Thompson heard, for example, that the battleship *Idaho* [*sic*] had left the harbor and surprised a formation of Japanese ships drawn up in two columns. *Idaho*'s captain, according to the report, told his crew, "O.K., boys, let 'em have it!"—whereupon the battleship sent the entire Japanese fleet to the bottom.[16]

These rumors were supplemented by a torrent of baseless reports concerning Hawaii's Japanese community. An army photographer at Wheeler Field claimed that the dead pilot of one of the downed Japanese planes wore a class ring from a Honolulu high school. An intelligence report of December 8 helped perpetuate another persistent rumor—that "a wide swath cut in the form of an arrow pointing directly to Pearl Harbor and Hickam Field" was discovered in a nearby cane field. In the excitement no one stopped to reason that Oahu's small size and Pearl Harbor's geographical prominence made such a beacon unnecessary.[17]

Although navy policy kept the civil service lists at Pearl Harbor closed to Japanese-Americans, the various contractors working on the base did employ a number of Japanese workers. Those working on December 7 came under immediate suspicion. Wymo Takaki, a machinist on the dredge *Marshall Harris,* saw a Japanese plane fall into the waters of Middle Loch. When the dredge crew recovered a life jacket from the water, they demanded that Takaki translate the Japanese writing on the vest. Unable to do so to his companions' satisfaction, he was accused of being a spy, assaulted, and put ashore during the attack.[18]

At Drydock One, Shikumi Yoshida and other crewmen from the dredge *R. W. Atkinson* joined the sailors, marines, and shipyard employees in fighting the fires which raged on the *Cassin* and *Downes.* After working there for about an hour, he and others from the dredge reported to Pearl Harbor's main gate to see whether they could help anywhere else. The marine sentry eyed them suspiciously and asked whether they were Japanese. When they replied in the affirmative, the guard confiscated their base passes and dismissed them.[19]

Kimmel blamed fifth columnists for the confusion in his command structure during and just after the attack. He wrote Short that the volume of false reports flooding his communications network suggested that navy telephone lines had been tampered with. To Stark he reported: "The Fifth Column activities added great confusion." Kimmel was probably sincere in his belief, but there was confusion aplenty without the work of saboteurs.[20] Secretary of the Navy Frank

Knox visited Hawaii within days of the attack. On his return to Washington he put an official imprimatur on the stories of disloyalty when he told reporters, "The most effective fifth column work in this war was done in Hawaii, with the exception of Norway."[21]

The intensity of the spy mania is well illustrated by the case of an innocent newspaper advertisement which was misinterpreted as a coded advisory of the attack. On December 3 and 5 a drygoods firm owned by local Japanese advertised a variety of fabrics in stock. Overactive imaginations scrutinizing the ad saw "war clouds" in the advertisement's graphic design. By reading backwards, holding the paper up to a mirror, eliminating prefixes and suffixes, some amateur sleuths managed to fashion a coded message warning of the raid. After an exhaustive investigation, military intelligence concluded that "all the . . . interpretations are forced" and the ad was exactly what it purported to be. Further, investigators found that the company had placed a virtually identical advertisement the year before in anticipation of the Christmas shopping season.[22]

For others it was a case of "damned if you do, damned if you don't." To the commander of the Marine Barracks at the Naval Ammunition Depot the very quiescence of the islands' Japanese was suspicious. In requesting more troops he wrote:

> The failure to initiate any previous sabotage locally indicates . . . a well controlled and organized fifth column on this Island whose control and organization has been so efficient as to prevent any outbreak even by isolated fanatics prior to this time. It is believed that when the enemy judges the time judicious that an unprecedented wave of sabotage will sweep the Island.[23]

The fifth column stories making the rounds were false, but at the time there seemed little reason to doubt that commando raids were imminent or that an invasion fleet lurked just over the horizon. The night of December 7 was punctuated with rifle shots from nervous sentries who saw danger in every shadow. For *Pennsylvania* crewmen toiling through the night working to repair their ship the guards were nearly as dangerous as the Japanese. Albert Fickel remembers: "It was just as dark as inside a cat's stomach and of course they had marines stationed everywhere with their guns ready and you'd better sing out real loud and clear when you moved on that ship because if you showed a light or you just made a wrong move or a wrong noise, you didn't know if you were going to take a bullet or not."[24]

Troops from Schofield Barracks were sent around the island to occupy defensive positions. Elzer Coates's unit, outfitted in World War I dishpan helmets, went first to Kaneohe, where they found their brand-new M-1 rifles still encased in Cosmoline. No sooner had they begun to clean the weapons than they were called back to Schofield. Their blacked-out truck convoy had trouble negotiating the narrow winding coast road going back to the barracks, and one of the trucks ran off the road. Luckily, no one was killed. When they finally arrived at Schofield sleep was out of the question. Random machine gun fire from frightened gunners forced the platoon to lie on the barracks floor; Coates thought, "I'd hate like hell to be shot by one of my own people."

The first sergeant told the men to make sure their bayonets fit the new rifles. Coates found that a wooden protrusion prevented his bayonet from fitting, so with his pocket knife he tried to whittle off the piece. In the dark the knife slipped and he cut his wrist. Now his worries about being hit by a stray bullet were replaced by the fear that he might bleed to death in the dark and everyone would think he had committed suicide rather than face the enemy. Soon the gas attack Klaxon began to blare and Coates was sure he could smell the gas. It seemed there might be no one left to misinterpret his slashed wrist. The alarm passed and the first sergeant came into the barracks again, this time with word that a Japanese unit had been spotted in a nearby ravine. The men were moved out into a nearby field position just before daylight. A light rain began to fall and Elzer Coates greeted his first full day of war huddled miserably beneath the inadequate shelter of a raincoat.[25]

Coates's miserable predicament mirrored the plight of U.S. forces on the night of December 7. Confused and misdirected, they braced for a follow-up attack that never came. Dispatched on wild goose chases and uncertain of who or what lurked in the darkness around them, they had more to fear from their compatriots' panic-stricken shooting than from the retreating Japanese.

Franklin D. Roosevelt addresses Congress on December 8. Few Japanese planners, including Yamamoto, realized how the attack would dissolve isolationist sentiment and unite Americans in a furious resolve to fight Japan to the finish. (National Park Service photo)

Governor Joseph Poindexter. Hawaii's civilian governor acceded to Short's demand for immediate declaration of martial law. Military administration of the islands lasted far beyond the emergency period of suspended habeas corpus, and checked the growth of labor unionism in Hawaii. (Hawaii State Archives photo)

Navy Secretary Frank Knox shared Roosevelt's deep suspicion of Japanese-Americans. His "fifth column" remark after Pearl Harbor perpetuated the canard that their primary loyalty was to Japan and not the United States. (U.S. Naval Historical Center photo)

Drydock One. The destroyer *Downes* leans drunkenly against *Cassin*. Secondary explosion from these ships' torpedoes caused so much damage that their hulls were scrapped and virtually new ships built around the destroyers' old machinery. (National Park Service photo)

West Virginia in drydock. She took seven torpedoes in the starboard side but was refloated and, after extensive repairs, was present in Tokyo Bay for the signing of the Japanese surrender. (National Park Service photo)

Sailors and civilian workers labored frantically for several days to cut through *Oklahoma*'s overturned hull to rescue crewman trapped within. Russell Davenport and his companions waited more than twenty-four hours for rescue. (National Archives photo)

Salvaging *Arizona*'s Turret III. The navy turned over the battleship's 14-inch guns and assemblies from Turrets III and IV for use as coastal artillery batteries. The danger of invasion, however, was long past by the time the first turret was installed and ready to fire. (National Park Service photo)

An Air Corps pickup truck heavily damaged by the attack on Hickam. Moving vehicles were prime targets for Japanese strafers. (National Park Service photo)

Damage to fighters at Wheeler Field was so extensive that the wreckage had to be bulldozed off the runways. These P-40s never flew again, but they may have provided spare parts for other planes less heavily damaged. (National Park Service photo)

Righting *Oklahoma*. This winch and cable arrangement was an ingenious piece of engineering, but although the ship was righted, *Oklahoma* was too badly damaged to be repaired. It sank at sea in 1947 while being towed to a West Coast scrap yard. (National Park Service photo)

The Zero fighter that crashed at Fort Kamehameha. Despite reports from observers who had encountered the plane in China, Americans discounted Japanese ability to design, build, and fly superior aircraft such as this. As a result, U.S. airmen were unprepared for the high-performance Zero and the skill of Japanese pilots. (National Park Service photo)

An iconographic group portrait of the nine midget submariners killed at Pearl Harbor. Conspicuously absent is Ensign Kazuo Sakamaki, who became POW No. 1. (National Park Service photo)

Japanese sampans seized after the attack. Military authorities viewed Hawaii's fishermen of Japanese ancestry with deep suspicion and believed them to be Japanese
naval auxilliaries. Several fishing boats were strafed and crewmen killed by panicky
American pilots on December 7. (National Park Service photo)

Several hundred Japanese residents of Hawaii were arrested immediately after the attack. These prisoners line up for food at Honolulu's immigration station, where they were held until the establishment of a camp on Sand Island in Honolulu Harbor. (National Park Service photo)

Sand Island internment camp. Only the opposition, based on practical grounds, of the Hawaiian Department prevented the repetition in Hawaii of the mass internment of Japanese that took place on the West Coast. (National Park Service photo)

Admiral Chester Nimitz presents the Navy Cross to Mess Attendant Doris Miller for heroism aboard *West Virginia*. The prewar navy was rigidly segregated and blacks were restricted to roles as stewards and mess attendants. (National Park Service photo)

The USS *Arizona* Memorial at Pearl Harbor. Constructed in 1962, the memorial spans the sunken hull. Protruding above the waterline are the base of Turret III, ventilator shafts, and the truncated mainmast. At the extreme right is the mooring quay where many Arizona crewmen sought refuge after the ship exploded. (National Park Service photo)

19

STRANDED

Of all the Japanese attackers, only one suffered the ignominy of capture. Ensign Kazuo Sakamaki and his midget sub crewman, Petty Officer Second Class Kiyoshi Inagaki, underwent an uninterrupted series of frustrations after casting off from their mother ship, *I-24*. Despite a serious gyroscope malfunction, Sakamaki elected to proceed on his mission of entering Pearl Harbor and lying in wait until the attack was under way. He planned to surface amid the confusion and loose his two torpedoes at a capital ship. That plan, like the entire midget submarine effort, never came to fruition. Not one of the midgets inflicted any damage at Pearl Harbor.

Trouble for Sakamaki and Inagaki began at the moment of release. The trim mechanism malfunctioned, and they were barely able to right the craft. As they approached the channel entrance just after sunrise they were depth-charged by destroyers and knocked unconscious. Sakamaki refused to waste his torpedoes on the destroyers and made for the channel entrance. He was far behind schedule and could already see thick clouds of black smoke rising from the anchorage. Destroyers charged again and Sakamaki once more missed the narrow channel entrance. This time the midget hit the reef with a crash. One torpedo warhead was smashed and useless. Worse still, battery gas began to escape into the cramped interior, making the air almost unbearably foul.[1]

After four applications of full power in reverse the two submariners managed to back the vessel off the reef. Sakamaki passed up another shot at the destroyers milling about off the channel entrance. He was determined to seek bigger game—hopefully the fleet flagship *Pennsylvania*. On the third approach to the channel, Sakamaki hit the reef again. This time the engine's reverse thrust was of no avail. Franti-

225

cally Sakamaki and Inagaki shifted lead ballast blocks by hand, receiving electric shocks from the batteries and gasping in the increasingly polluted air. While the sub was caught on the reef its hull was almost entirely out of the water. *Helm* spotted the target and took several shots but missed. Just in time, the shift in ballast caused the craft to drop off the reef into deep water. To Sakamaki it seemed as though it must be past noon, but *Helm's* action report put the encounter at 8:20 A.M.[2]

A quick check showed Sakamaki that the torpedo firing mechanism was hopelessly jammed. Never mind, he told Inagaki, they would ram *Pennsylvania*. And if the warheads failed to explode they could board the flagship and die fighting hand to hand. Their submarine, however, was by this time too battered to even respond to the helm. They lost all power and drifted helplessly past the harbor channel. Sakamaki noticed Diamond Head as they were carried past Waikiki Beach. They then lost consciousness, exhausted by their ordeal, the battery fumes, and foul air. Sakamaki awoke near dawn on December 8. The current had carried them around Oahu's southeast point and fetched them up off Bellows Field. Thinking he was off the island of Lanai, where they were to rendezvous with *I-24*, Sakamaki shook Inagaki awake. At that moment waves tossed the luckless submarine onto the reef in full view of one of the U.S. military installations which had been attacked the day before.

Troops from Bellows and the 298th Infantry Regiment had spent a tense night guarding the beach. Colonel Leonard Weddington, Bellows' commanding officer, sent up an observation plane to inspect the object. He also took the precaution of telephoning Hawaiian Air Force headquarters requesting that artillery be alerted in case the craft proved to be a threat. Three navy utility planes arrived and peppered the reef with light bombs, all of which missed the submarine. Finally someone tied a line to the midget and it was towed onto the beach with a bulldozer.[3]

Sakamaki and Inagaki, however, after discovering their boat stuck for good on yet another reef, had decided to abandon ship and swim for shore. Sakamaki lit the fuse on a charge carried to destroy the sub in just such an emergency. The two men jumped into the rough surf and headed for the beach. As he swam Sakamaki listened in vain for the explosion that would tell him that, even though he had failed to sink *Pennsylvania*, at least the enemy could not use his submarine to glean any useful intelligence. His bad luck held; the charge was a dud. The heavy waves then pounded Sakamaki into merciful oblivion. Inagaki had disappeared in the surf and his body was recovered days later. A different fate awaited Sakamaki.

Sakamaki washed onto the beach and was taken prisoner by Sergeant David Akui of the 298th Infantry. Lieutenant Phillip Willis (the Texas pilot who had vowed to die with his boots on) took charge of the prisoner. An interpreter was summoned and Willis tried to interrogate Sakamaki. First the Americans gave him eggs, coffee, and a cigarette. Then he was handed paper and pencil, but Sakamaki folded his arms and refused to write. Willis and the other Americans then "started jamming a gun in his eye and pulling the hammer on the .45 back . . . and threatening him." Sakamaki responded by picking up the pencil and writing a request (in Japanese) that, having failed in his mission, the soldiers kill him. The standoff ended when a truck arrived to take Sakamaki to Fort Shafter.[4]

The Americans had yet to learn that for a Japanese warrior being taken prisoner meant disgrace. Once in regular custody Sakamaki was treated less harshly, but he was still morose about his fate. On December 14 he submitted a written statement expressing gratitude for the good treatment but complained that his "honor as a soldier has fallen to the ground" and requested that he be killed. Lest Sakamaki be thought eccentric on the subject, one need only note the glory showered by Japanese propaganda on the "nine" midget submariners in the Pearl Harbor attack. By allowing himself to be taken alive Sakamaki became a nonperson.[5]

Sakamaki certainly would have preferred the fate of the only other Japanese attacker to find himself stranded in Hawaii. That episode, one of the most unlikely in the entire Pearl Harbor operation, occurred on Niihau, westernmost of the major Hawaiian Islands. The Niihau incident captured popular imagination and acquired a permanent niche in modern Hawaii folklore. The principals in the story spoke mutually unintelligible languages: Hawaiian, Japanese, and English. Stories of the event, even by the principal actors, vary so wildly from one another that it is difficult to accept any account with certainty.[6]

The isolated island was and remains a ranch operated and entirely owned by the Robinson family. The population (all ranch employees except for the schoolteacher) of about 200 was composed almost entirely of native Hawaiians whose everyday language remains Hawaiian. The Robinson family strictly controlled access to Niihau, running the island in a manner not unlike a feudal fiefdom. The only transportation link to the outside world was a weekly boat operated by the Robinsons between Niihau and the nearest major island, Kauai. The Hawaii of 1941, dominated by the territory's sugar interests, was hardly a model of democracy, but even by the standards of the time the Robinsons' control of Niihau was an anachronism.

The Japanese staff officers planning the Pearl Harbor attack, possibly believing the island to be uninhabited, assigned a Sixth Fleet submarine, *I-4*, to stand off Niihau to rescue downed pilots. At least some of the attacking air units were instructed to make for the area if they were unable to return to their carriers.[7] Two crippled Japanese planes, both Zekes, made for Niihau on the morning of December 7 when it became apparent they were too badly damaged to complete the return trip. One plane crashed near the shoreline and sank, taking the pilot with it. The other pilot, Aviation Petty Officer First Class Shigenori Nishikaichi of *Hiryu*'s second wave, made a crash landing in a plowed field near Niihau's main village, Puuwai. Nishikaichi was knocked unconscious, but he survived without serious injury.

The plane came down near the home of Howard Kaleohano. Kaleohano pulled the pilot from his cockpit and also took his pistol, map, and other papers. When Nishikaichi regained consciousness, Kaleohano took him home, where his wife Mabel prepared a hearty breakfast for the aviator. Relations between the pilot and the islanders were friendly enough at first, since word of the Pearl Harbor attack was slow in reaching Niihau. Nishikaichi's English was poor and communication was difficult, but he managed to convey a request for the return of his papers. Kaleohano refused. Although he was still ignorant of the Pearl Harbor attack, he was generally aware of the strained relations between Japan and the United States. The appearance of a Japanese plane riddled with bullet holes made Kaleohano uneasy.

The need for an interpreter was obvious. There were three Japanese adults on Niihau (the only non-Hawaiian residents): Iematsu Shintani, an elderly *issei* (first-generation immigrant), and Yoshio and Irene Harada, the *nisei* (second-generation) couple who worked as beekeepers and the Robinsons' paymasters. Nishikaichi tried to recruit Shintani first, but after exchanging a few words with the pilot he declined to cooperate. The Haradas were then summoned to fill the breach. Nishikaichi told them of the Pearl Harbor attack and asked their help in retrieving his papers. The Haradas, probably afraid they would be associated with the enemy, did not share the news with their neighbors.

Naturally, word of the visitor spread quickly and islanders gathered for a peek at the unexpected arrival. The group adjourned to a neighbor's house and spent the afternoon in good-natured partying. There was plenty of food and Nishikaichi entertained the group by plucking a guitar like a samisen. The spell was broken in the late afternoon when news of the morning's events came over one of Niihau's two radios. The pilot could hardly deny the true reason for his presence and admitted his part in the attack.

The islanders decided that the best way to deal with the situation was to refer it to Aylmer Robinson, who controlled Niihau and visited the island once a week from his home and headquarters on Kauai. Robinson usually arrived on Monday, so a group escorted Nishikaichi to the landing several miles from the village. Robinson's status on Niihau carried little weight with the military authorities, however, who forbade the departure of any vessels after December 7. The group waited vainly all day before returning home. They repeated the fruitless trip the next day. The worried islanders tried to signal Kauai with lights, but there was no response from across the 20-mile-wide channel. During this period the islanders moved Nishikaichi to the Haradas' home and began to keep a regular guard over the pilot, who at this time apparently enlisted the Haradas to help him escape. Since none of the Hawaiians spoke Japanese and they had no suspicion that the Haradas and the pilot were in league, the trio were able to conceal their purpose from the guards.

On Thursday Nishikaichi, through Yoshio Harada, summoned Shintani to the house. Shintani ignored the summons until the next day. When he finally arrived the pilot dispatched him to Kaleohano's to ask once more for the papers taken from the plane. On this occasion Shintani offered a sizable bribe, but again Kaleohano refused. Shintani did not press the matter and avoided further involvement in Nishikaichi's increasingly desperate gambits.

Nishikaichi, with the help of Yoshio Harada, escaped from his loose confinement on Friday, December 12. Harada secreted a shotgun and a pistol in the honey shed near his house. Nishikaichi, accompanied by Harada and Niihau resident Hanaiki Niau, was allowed to use the outhouse. Harada invented a pretext to draw the group to the honey house, where he and Nishikaichi extracted the weapons, made a prisoner of Niau, and locked him inside. Harada was now openly and irreversibly committed.

The stranded airman and the beekeeper embarked on a frustrating effort to bend the islanders to their will. Controlling the only firearms on Niihau, the pair encountered no opposition when they took several hostages and searched Kaleohano's house (without success) for Nishikaichi's papers. Events took an ugly turn when the two men shot up the village and threatened several residents with death unless they cooperated. Most of the islanders fled into the bush. At 3:00 A.M. Saturday, Harada and Nishikaichi set fire to Kaleohano's home, reasoning that if the papers were hidden in the house they would be destroyed by the flames. At the same time they doused the plane with gasoline and set it ablaze.

While most of his neighbors fled the armed pair, Howard Kaleohano took a more purposeful course of action. He recruited five other islanders to join him in a difficult and dangerous rowboat voyage to Kauai to raise the alarm. They left about 12:30 A.M. Saturday for the 20-mile pull across the Kaulakahi Channel. These men were no strangers to hard work and the hazards of winter seas in Hawaiian waters, but to risk the voyage in an open rowboat at night was an act of great courage. After hours of backbreaking work they reached the port of Waimea. The last hours of the crossing were made in daylight, and they were fortunate not to be attacked by jittery U.S. airmen.

Saturday found Harada and Nishikaichi in a quandary. They had little hope of escaping from the island, yet they were still unable to impose their will on the population. Among the hostages they seized that day were Ella Kanahele and her husband Ben. Sensing that their captors were nearing exhaustion, the Kanaheles waited for an opportune moment to overpower the armed pair. It came as Nishikaichi handed the shotgun to Harada. The couple leaped on the pilot, who drew a pistol from his boot and shot Ben Kanahele twice. Although seriously wounded, Kanahele grasped Nishikaichi by the neck and leg and dashed his head against a stone wall. Ella struck the airman's head with a large stone, and Ben administered the coup de grace by slitting his throat with a hunting knife. Harada, probably in a state of shock, made no attempt to save Nishikaichi. Instead, he used the shotgun to kill himself. War, in its most primitive form, had come to peaceful Niihau.

As events moved to a climax on Niihau, Kaleohano reached the outside world with news that one of the Japanese attackers had been at large for nearly a week. Lieutenant Colonel Eugene Fitzgerald, the army commander on Kauai, dispatched to Niihau a force commanded by First Lieutenant Jack Mizuha. The lieutenant, a Japanese-American officer in the Hawaii National Guard, had been called to active duty the year before. His unit, the 299th Infantry Regiment, provided garrison troops for Hawaii's outer islands. Mizuha was anxious for a chance to help dispel the suspicion which had descended on Hawaii's Japanese and beseeched Fitzgerald for command of the expedition.

Mizuha's force consisted of thirteen enlisted men of the 299th, the six islanders who had made the rowboat crossing, Aylmer Robinson, and Eugene McManus, harbormaster of Port Allen, Kauai. The group left Kauai at 6:00 P.M. Saturday aboard the lighthouse tender *Kukui* and landed on Niihau at 7:30 Sunday morning. After a hasty breakfast on the beach and a 14-mile march from the landing spot, they reached the village of Puuwai in the early afternoon. They found on their arrival that Harada and Nishikaichi were already dead. At the village schoolhouse Mizuha conducted an inquiry, with Aylmer Robinson interpreting for the islanders. Shintani and Irene Harada, along with the Haradas' small daughter, were taken into custody and removed from the island. Ben Kanahele was taken to Kauai for treatment of his wounds, from which he recovered without permanent damage.

Shintani and Mrs. Harada were interned for the duration of the war. Neither faced charges in any judicial proceeding for their actions during the week of December 7 to 13. Aylmer Robinson banned Irene Harada from returning to Niihau after the war, but Shintani was allowed to resume his life on the island and became a U.S. citizen when Congress revised immigration laws to permit the naturalization of Japanese immigrants. Lieutenant Mizuha served in the famed 442nd Regimental Combat Team during the Italian campaign and after the war became a justice of Hawaii's state supreme court. Howard Kaleohano and Ben Kanahele became celebrities of a sort. The army decorated Kaleohano with the Medal of Freedom and awarded Ben Kanahele the Medal of Merit and Purple Heart. Ella Kanahele's role in overpowering Nishikaichi was overlooked in the flurry of official recognition.

The Niihau story has been treated by some as an operatic footnote to the Pearl Harbor attack. The isolated Polynesian island, a desperate fighter pilot stranded far from friendly forces, and the encounter between unsophisticated islanders and modern war combined to produce a tale quite remote from the conflagration engulfing the globe in 1941. Nonetheless, it was a serious piece of business in post-attack Hawaii. Harada's help to Nishikaichi was the only verified instance of a Japanese-American assisting the attacking force.

It could be argued that the special circumstances prevailing on isolated and feudal Niihau made it a special case. It could also be pointed out that a Japanese-American commanded the force dispatched to secure Niihau. Still, it hardly reassured those who harbored dark suspicions about the loyalties of Hawaii's Japanese community. One prominent Hawaii resident received a sympathetic hearing when he told the Roberts Commission investigating the Pearl Harbor attack in early 1942 that the Harada's conduct "is an example of their loyalty to us when they have a chance to be loyal to their Emperor."[8] Harada's actions did not, however, spur official retaliation against the community. Indeed, the most important point to be made about the Niihau incident is that, although the lot of Hawaii's Japanese was hardly a happy one, the affair did not stampede military government authorities into precipitate or vengeful policies.

20

ASSESSING LOSSES
AND DAMAGE

When the attack finally ended, the damage to the U.S. Pacific Fleet was staggering. Five battleships—*Arizona, West Virginia, Nevada, Oklahoma,* and *California*—had been sunk. *Pennsylvania, Maryland,* and *Tennessee,* although less seriously damaged, were temporarily useless. The light cruisers *Honolulu, Helena,* and *Raleigh* were also damaged. Four destroyers—*Cassin, Downes, Shaw,* and *Helm*—were put out of action. (*Helm* is usually omitted from the list of ships damaged at Pearl Harbor, but a near miss by a bomb put her in drydock for repairs.) An additional six auxiliaries were also damaged: The target ship *Utah* and minelayer *Oglala* capsized, and the repair ship *Vestal,* Floating Drydock Two, tug *Sotoyomo,* and seaplane tender *Curtiss* were badly hit. The total number of U.S. vessels sunk or damaged comes to twenty-one if one includes Floating Drydock Two and *Sotoyomo.*[1]

The principal target was the fleet, but the attackers wrought considerable damage on incidental targets as well. Figures for U.S. planes destroyed vary according to the source. Indeed, the definition of "destroyed" becomes a nearly metaphysical question. Many badly damaged aircraft were later reconstructed, and some of the planes destroyed on the ground were little more than sources of cannibalized parts even before the attack. The army informed the postwar congressional investigating committee that the Hawaiian Air Force had lost four B-17s, thirty-two P-40s, two A-20s, and twenty-five others (mostly obsolete types). The navy gave its losses as eighty-seven planes of all types (including marine aircraft). To these figures must be added the one B-17 of Major Landon's group destroyed and the eleven *Enterprise* planes downed by the Japanese in the morning and by U.S. antiaircraft fire that night. When these are included the number of U.S. planes lost on December 7 reaches 162. This figure is lower than the 188 often cited (by Walter Lord, for example), but it is based on information provided by the army and navy during the exhaustive congressional probe of 1945–1946.[2]

Damage to ground and shoreside facilities was serious but not disastrous. At Hickam Field, for example, the most important maintenance shops of the Hawaiian Air Depot suffered "light" damage, and 90 percent of the depot's vital machine tools survived. The Pearl Harbor navy yard estimated facilities damage at $42 million, but the bill of particulars accompanying the estimate suggests the figure was inflated. It includes $20 million for repair of Drydock One, for example, but the estimated time required for the repair work was ten days.[3]

Several miles east of Pearl Harbor, the city of Honolulu suffered approximately $500,000 worth of damage from the raid. An analysis of the impact sites by Hawaiian Department ordnance specialists revealed that all but one of the forty-four projectiles which fell on the city were improperly fused antiaircraft rounds. The most serious damage occurred in the McCully district. Several buildings, including Lunalilo Elementary School, were set ablaze. The Honolulu Fire Department stretched its resources to the limit and, despite its heavy commitment of men and equipment to Hickam Field, brought the McCully fires under control with the help of volunteers from the neighborhood.[4]

It was not in property damage, but in the toll of death and injury, that American losses were most grievous. U.S. casualty figures, surprisingly, are open to doubt. Navy figures for the number of *Arizona* dead, for example, have fluctuated. A postwar list prepared by the Bureau of Personnel lists 1,051 navy officers and enlisted men killed aboard the battleship, but in the early 1960s the navy provided 1,103 names of sailors (marine casualties were tallied separately) for inscription on the *Arizona* Memorial. Even then, the name of at least one *Arizona* fatality was missing and had to be inscribed after the wall was installed.[5] Army and marine casualty figures were also subject to confusion. The army, in various summaries, reported its death toll as 218, 228, 229, and 240.[6] A study prepared by the Marine Corps put the marine dead at 112 (all but four of those from ships' marine detachments), but that figure was later revised to 109.[7]

The total figures for U.S. casualties accepted by most authorities are 2,403 dead and 1,178 wounded.[8] (See Appendix D for the casualty tables.) The destruction of *Arizona* accounted for most of the navy and marine dead. More than 75 percent of the army casualties were suffered by Air Corps personnel at Hickam and Wheeler. Some of the civilian casualties resulted from hostile fire, but it appears the majority were caused by falling antiaircraft shells.[9]

The Japanese lost far fewer men. Commander Fuchida's fliers suffered losses amounting to less than 10 percent of the aircraft involved in the attack. Twenty-nine planes, most of them dive bombers, failed to return to their carriers. The first wave lost three fighters, one dive bomber, and five torpedo planes. Losses from the second wave, which found U.S. gun crews and interceptor pilots on the alert, were twice as high. Of that group six fighters and fourteen dive bombers failed to return. None of the high-flying horizontal bombers were shot down. In addition to those which never returned to their carriers, some seventy-two Japanese planes were damaged, some beyond repair. Aircrew deaths for both waves combined came to fifty-five.[10]

The Sixth Fleet submariners lost men, too. Of the ten midget submarine crewmen, nine were lost in action and one, Sakamaki, was taken prisoner. In addition, the fleet boat *I-70* was sunk on December 10. No exact figures for *I-70* are available, but submarines of that class had a normal complement of sixty-five. Assuming she carried a normal complement, the total Japanese loss of life for the Pearl Harbor attack was 129.[11]

The disparity in losses did not affect the dedication displayed by the servicemen under attack. Despite the disadvantage of being surprised, U.S. soldiers, sailors, and marines on Oahu acquitted themselves well. Although there was much confusion, there was little panic. Exceptional acts of bravery (fifteen of which were recognized by awards of the Medal of Honor) were numerous. In December 1941 the U.S. Army and Navy were already in a state of transition from the small professional prewar services to a military establishment which would number more than 12 million at the end of World War II. The army's Hawaiian Department had been augmented by draftees and activated National Guard units. Admiral Kimmel estimated that more than half the Pacific Fleet's officers were reservists. Many of his destroyers (including *Ward*) were crewed almost entirely by mobilized reservists. The fleet was expanding so rapidly that on some ships 70 percent of the crews had never heard the sound of naval gunfire.[12] Given the incomplete state of training, the tactical surprise, and the psychological unpreparedness for war, the rank and file acquitted themselves well on December 7.

The Japanese too performed with courage and ability. Nagumo's sailors and fliers were embarked on a dangerous mission and they knew it. Although their losses were far less than expected, they faced the prospect of death without complaint. Furthermore, the difficult voyage across the North Pacific and the flight discipline of the aircrews indicate superb seamanship and flying ability.

Yet despite the overwhelming tactical success of the raid, errors of judgment in the planning stage cast a long shadow on the achievements of the Japanese fleet. In concentrating the attack on the ships of the U.S. Pacific Fleet, for example, the Japanese inflicted only minor damage on the shoreside facilities at Pearl Harbor. These installations—the repair shops, supply warehouses, submarine base, and fuel storage tanks—were the *sine qua non* of Pearl Harbor's role as an advanced base for the U.S. Navy in the Pacific War. Without the use of Pearl Harbor, the Pacific Fleet would have been burdened with an additional 5,000-mile (round-trip) distance between its bases on the West Coast and the battle areas. This logistical nightmare would have made the war against Japan longer, costlier, and more difficult.

In war, moreover, even the most meticulous preparation cannot always offset the factor of luck. The aircraft carrier, not the battleship, proved to be the decisive naval weapon in the war against Japan. Admiral Yamamoto had hoped to destroy Kimmel's carrier force with one stroke, but circumstances denied the Japanese that chance. With *Enterprise* still west of Oahu, *Lexington* off Midway, and *Saratoga* on the West Coast, all the U.S. carriers escaped damage on December 7. *Lexington* and *Enterprise* were to play vital roles in the battles of the Coral Sea and Midway, which turned the tide of the Pacific War within six months of Pearl Harbor.

From a planning and operational perspective, one of the most inexplicable defects of the Japanese conduct of the operation was the failure to use their large submarine force effectively. Twenty-five submarines were committed to the attack as a separate force, but they sank not a single warship. Five of the undersea craft were wasted as mother ships for the midget submarines. Instead of remaining concentrated in Hawaiian waters, most of the force drifted off to the West Coast and other distant areas within days of the attack. The few that remained did sink some transports and cargo vessels near Hawaii, but Yamamoto declined to commit the Sixth Fleet boats to maintaining positions where their presence in the converging sea lanes around Hawaii would have made them a formidable blockade force.

Such a course of action would have posed serious supply and reinforcement problems for the continued American use of Hawaii as an advanced base. The Pacific Fleet's large numbers of surviving destroyers would have been a serious counterthreat, but Japanese naval doctrine, not an impulse to conserve the submarines, seems to have been the major factor in Yamamoto's failure to keep the boats near Hawaii. The Japanese Navy used its submarines to prowl singly in search of enemy warships. Merchant vessels, in contrast to U.S. doctrine, were considered less worthy of attention. As a final observation, it is worth noting that there was little coordination between the operations and command of Nagumo's carrier fleet and Shimizu's submarines.

In many ways the weaknesses of the Pearl Harbor attack plan, although masked by the overwhelming success of the operation, foreshadowed factors which were to contribute to later Japanese defeats in the Pacific. The unimaginative employment of submarines has been noted. The lack of coordination between the submarine and air forces suggests that Yamamoto's undeniable talents as a naval strategist and commander did not embrace a profound understanding of submarine warfare.

Further, the command structure of the attack forces was decidedly top-heavy. Two flag officers accompanied the submarine group and another seven were afloat with the First Air Fleet. Vice Admiral Nagumo commanded both the air fleet and the First Carrier Division; Rear Admirals Ryunosuke Kusaka, Tamon Yamaguchi, and Chuichi Hara served respectively as fleet chief of staff and commanders of the Second and Fifth Carrier Divisions. Vice Admiral Gunichi Mikawa commanded the heavy guns of the support force; Rear Admiral Koki Abe commanded Cruiser Division Eight; and Rear Admiral Sentaro Omori led Destroyer Squadron One.

The Pearl Harbor attack plan was complex. It made little allowance for error or unexpected developments, and it depended for success on the enemy's behaving according to the expectations of staff planners. Such conditions rarely prevail in battle, and the Japanese were to pay dearly at Midway and the Coral Sea for their inflexibility. Finally, the Pearl Harbor plan envisaged heavy losses in the attacking force. Indeed, Japanese military and naval commanders accepted rates of attrition which other nations deemed unacceptable except in the most desperate circumstances. Japanese losses at Pearl Harbor were exceptionally light. But heavy loss of life, especially among the highly trained carrier pilots, in subsequent battles was an important factor in the inability of the Japanese Navy to meet the Pacific Fleet on equal terms as the war progressed.

The most fundamental Japanese mistake in planning the Pearl Harbor attack was the failure to foresee that it would unite the American people in a furious resolve to exact vengeance and push the conflict to a decisive conclusion. The launching of the attack while negotiations were still under way enraged the American public past the point of accepting a compromise peace. Such "sneak attacks" were an accepted military practice for the Japanese, and those in decision-making positions did not anticipate the violence of the American reaction. In fact, the 1904 raid on the Russian fleet at Port Arthur, which bears many similarities to the Pearl Harbor attack, was praised as a bold initiative by authoritative Western commentators who viewed the Japanese as plucky underdogs struggling against the overbearing Czarist autocracy.[13]

America, however, was in no mood to look back. Japan was now the enemy, and President Roosevelt's address to Congress set the tone for a determined and angry nation when he characterized December 7, 1941, as "a date which will live in infamy." Public opinion, as reflected in newspaper editorials, echoed that message. The *Los Angeles Times* told its readers: "It was the act of a mad dog, a gangster's parody of every principle of international honor." The *San Francisco Chronicle,* referring to the interventionist/isolationist debate, announced: "Politics is adjourned." Even the bitterly anti-Roosevelt *Chicago Tribune* stated: "Recriminations are useless and we doubt that they will be indulged in, certainly not by us."[14]

Despite Japanese expectations, the attack did not weaken U.S. national morale to the point of accepting Japanese domination of the Western Pacific, as Yamamoto had hoped. Instead, American isolationism, if not destroyed overnight, became dormant for the duration of World War II. It is remarkable that Yamamoto, one of the most sophisticated and knowledgeable of Japan's military leaders, failed to foresee the reaction. That failure provides dramatic proof of Clausewitz's dictum that politics and morale, rather than tactics and strategy, are often decisive in the conduct of war.

VI

AMERICA REACTS

21

GIRDING

FOR INVASION

Governor Poindexter's declaration of martial law wrought radical changes in Hawaii's civil life. General Short, acting under powers delegated by Poindexter, assumed the title of military governor and took nearly complete control of the functions formerly exercised by the territory's civilian authorities. Lieutenant Colonel Thomas Green, Hawaiian Department judge advocate, was installed in Iolani Palace and exercised day-to-day control as the military governor's executive officer.

Until the battle of Midway (June 4–6, 1942) removed any substantial threat of invasion or attack Hawaii was a frontline war zone. Most people viewed military control and the maintenance of public order as military necessities, and few at first questioned the transfer of civil power to General Short and succeeding commanders. Since another attack or an invasion might be mounted at any time strict curfew and blackout hours were imposed. Sale of liquor was banned and houses of prostitution were closed for several months after December 7.[1]

Other martial law measures raised questions, however, particularly as the war moved westward after Midway. The receding threat of invasion tended to vitiate the argument of military necessity as a justification for the continuation of martial law, which remained in place until October 1944. Labor controls were more stringent than on the mainland United States. Stiff fines and even jail sentences were imposed on workers who violated military restrictions on wage and job freeze orders. The military government's labor policies, whether intentionally or not, weakened the union movement in Hawaii during the war years.[2]

Press censorship extended far beyond the realm of information which might have military value to the enemy. It included a licensing system for newspapers and the prohibition of criticism and news which would embarrass military government authorities. In 1942, for example, the military government attempted to confine Honolulu's flourishing brothels to a compact and manageable district. Prostitutes responded with a three-week "strike" complete with a picket line and placards outside police headquarters. (The Honolulu Police Department operated under military control.) The daily newspapers ignored the story.[3]

Other martial law measures, ranging from the vexatious to the merely comic, impinged more directly on the life of the average citizen. Strict control of liquor sales began with a total prohibition in the weeks after the attack. After the ban was lifted the army could (and in several instances did) close establishments guilty of selling short drinks. Colonel Frank Steer, the provost martial, assumed overall control of organized prostitution (technically illegal) and permitted the inmates of Honolulu's brothels to live, but not to ply their trade, outside the red light district.[4]

Some martial law dictates appear ludicrous, at least in retrospect. At one point, someone in authority became convinced that Hawaii's pigeon fanciers constituted a potential auxiliary for fifth columnists. Steer and his men were ordered to raid every pigeon coop in the territory and confiscate the birds. On the appointed night the order was duly executed, and the military policemen emerged from the operation suffering nothing worse than an application of pigeon droppings and the attendant loss of dignity.

For civil libertarians the most troubling aspect of martial law was the suspension of civil courts and their replacement by military provost courts. Under that system army officers dispensed a rough and ready justice for offenses ranging from murder to traffic violations. Legal formalities which protected the rights of the accused were often honored more in the breach than the observance. Prosecutorial bias is difficult to prove, but a 1942 conviction rate of more than 98 percent (all but 359 of 22,480 cases) suggests that at the very least the procedures of the provost courts tended to give an edge to the prosecution.[5]

The case of martial law in Hawaii raises still unanswered (and perhaps unanswerable) questions about how best to judge conflicting claims of constitutional principles versus the need of military commanders to discharge their responsibilities under wartime conditions. Military government was often unreasonable and sometimes unjust (particularly in its policies toward Japanese-Americans), but it fell short of any reasonable definition of tyranny. There is no doubt that Hawaii was, for the first six months after Pearl Harbor, a frontline outpost. But it is also difficult to deny that stringent military restrictions on civilian life were kept in place long after the need for those measures had passed.

General Short justified martial law by invoking fear of invasion. His fears were genuine and well founded. In the weeks after Pearl Harbor Japanese forces occupied and consolidated a vast empire in Asia and the Western Pacific. British forces in Hong Kong and the U.S. garrisons on Wake and Guam surrendered within three weeks of December 7. The Japanese made successful landings in the Philippines, Malaya, and the Dutch East Indies. On December 10 Japanese naval aircraft sank the British battleship *Prince of Wales* and battle-cruiser *Repulse* in the South China Sea. A mid-February 1942 surprise raid by aircraft from Nagumo's carriers on the Australian harbor of Port Darwin was an Allied disaster comparable to Pearl Harbor. The capitulation of the "impregnable" British bastion of Singapore that same month sent a deep and prolonged chill down the spines of Hawaii's defenders.

U.S. and British strategists had made contingency plans before December 7 to deal with the prospect of Japan and the United States entering the war as belligerents. These plans gave first priority to the war effort against Germany and Italy. Allied forces in the Pacific would have to hold the line as best they could until the demands of the Atlantic, European, and African campaigns had been satisfied. Admiral Kimmel and General Short (and their successors, Admiral Chester W. Nimitz and Lieutenant General Delos Emmons) were in the unenviable position of apparently being next on the list of major Japanese objectives while being well down on the list of Allied priorities. Although the immediacy of the threat in the Pacific resulted in a temporary and limited reversal of those priorities, it would be many months before U.S. forces in the mid-Pacific were strong enough to face the prospect of another Japanese attack with confidence.

The isolated Hawaiian Islands depended on shipping from the U.S. mainland—not only for men and supplies to strengthen and maintain armed forces in the islands, but for sustenance of the populace as well. (The islands' rich agricultural lands were devoted almost exclusively to the production of sugar and pineapple; basic food supplies were imported.) One of the first orders of business was the removal of unnecessary mouths in order to free available shipping for war purposes. First priority was given to the evacuation of military dependents, and within a short time after December 7 nearly 30,000 people had departed for the mainland.[6]

Reinforcements for the Hawaiian Department's defense garrison was obviously a high priority for ships coming from the mainland. The Twenty-seventh Division, which landed on Kauai in March 1942, was the first major reinforcement unit for the Hawaiian Department. General Emmons thought he needed more troops and invoked the example of Singapore in his appeals to Washington for additional forces.[7]

Hawaii's commanders particularly felt the shortage of long-range aircraft. The day after the attack, Kimmel begged Short to expedite the assignment of army bombers to the defense forces. On January 26, Emmons wrote General Arnold: "Our crying need is for long range bombing equipment." Additional naval units were transferred from the Atlantic to the Pacific Fleet, but February 1942 found Admiral Bellinger claiming he still had far too few aircraft to detect and attack an approaching Japanese fleet.[8]

These shortages were not due to any skepticism in Washington that the Japanese could or would invade Hawaii; there were simply not enough trained men and equipment available in the first months of the war. If anything, staff officers in the War and Navy Departments were increasingly pessimistic about the prospect of Hawaii remaining in U.S. hands. One series of army G-2 analyses made in December and January flatly predicted, "Japan will probably make an all out attack on Hawaii if and when a decision in her favor occurs at Singapore." The fall of Singapore did nothing to relieve anxiety.[9]

Facing that prospect, but with adequate reinforcements months in the future, the services had to make plans to meet an invasion with the resources on hand. Even in the wake of the December 7 disaster, however, interservice bickering continued. Overall command in Hawaii was vested in the new CincPac, Admiral Nimitz. Marshall anticipated that interservice friction and "local embarrassments" would arise. He urged General Emmons to make the best of the arrangement and refer to Washington any interservice problems on which he and Nimitz could not agree.[10]

The new Hawaiian Department commander had little choice, but he maneuvered as best he could to win for the army an expanded role in the new command structure. In commenting on a defensive plan for Hawaii drafted by the navy, Emmons lobbied for the designation of the Hawaiian Department commanding general to assume overall command in Hawaii in the absence of the commander-in-chief of the Pacific Fleet.[11]

There was bad blood between the services on other matters, too. The army, being responsible for defense on the ground, guarded many navy installations. But since soldiers were in short supply in the weeks after the attack, sailors and marines performed many functions that, strictly speaking, were within the army's purview. When Nimitz expressed anxiety over the inadequate army forces guarding Maui Airport, Emmons replied, "If you are not satisfied with the present defense of Maui Airport, it is recommended that this field be temporarily closed." Nimitz's plans officer, Captain Charles McMorris, angrily wrote the Pacific Fleet chief of staff that the letter should be returned to Emmons for "rephrasing in more dignified and courteous language; together with a *directive* to provide more suitable defenses *now.*" McMorris realized, though, that such heavy-handed tactics could backfire and recommended that Emmons be informed that if more troops were not added to the Maui garrison, "CincPac will be obliged to withdraw some of the armament and personnel now performing Army duties on Oahu and send them to Maui until the Army can assume its own responsibilities."[12]

The army partially met its shortfall in personnel by mobilizing local civilians into militia units known collectively as the Organized Defense Volunteers. These forces operated under the command of the Hawaiian Department and acted as auxiliary troops. They were employed as sentries, coastwatchers, and guides. In the event of invasion they were to deal with uprisings by Hawaii's Japanese (who were barred from bearing arms in these units), implement a scorched earth policy, and serve as last-ditch defense forces. In 1942 the army had 20,000 of these volunteers organized into nine units throughout the territory, including mounted cavalry on the islands of Maui and Hawaii.[13]

Oahu possessed an impressive system of coastal fortifications long before the Pearl Harbor attack. The prospect of invasion made the strengthening of these defenses a high priority. Pillboxes and observation posts were established around the island's perimeter and in the interior. Additionally, the navy donated obsolete naval guns which the army used for coastal defense. Eight two-gun 8-inch turrets had been removed from the carriers *Lexington* and *Saratoga* before Pearl Harbor. They were emplaced in batteries overlooking the north and south shores of the island. Later, two of *Arizona*'s three-gun 14-inch turrets were removed from the wreckage of the battleship for use in coastal defense installations.[14]

The employment of auxiliaries and the improvised use of naval guns in fortifications highlighted the serious shortages borne by Hawaii's regular military defenders. It made painfully obvious the necessity for planning for the grimmest possibilities: a successful Japanese landing and last-ditch defense of Oahu. Army planning was based on the premise that its primary mission was the defense of the Pearl Harbor operating base. Should that prove impossible, however, Emmons listed the secondary missions for his forces:

1. Deny the use of Pearl Harbor to the Japanese.
2. Protect airfields in the interior of Oahu to enable the landing of reinforcements from the U.S. mainland.
3. Assist in the recapture of Pearl Harbor should reinforcements arrive.
4. Delay hostile operations against the mainland.

For his "final defensive positions" which would be "held at all costs" Emmons selected a line overlooking Pearl Harbor running from Waiawa Stream to Puu Makakilo (the southern anchor of the Waianae Range). He admitted to Nimitz that the line "would not secure Pearl Harbor but would by artillery fire deny its use by the enemy." The general also advised Nimitz to begin planning the systematic destruction of Pearl Harbor's facilities and the blocking of the channel. Plans were made to destroy key industrial facilities and public works, and evacuation areas were designated well away from potential invasion beaches.[15]

Civilians, as well as military planners, had to adjust to the possibility that Oahu might become a desperate battleground. Paper currency was overprinted "HAWAII" to render it useless should it be captured by the invaders and smuggled to the mainland or offered in international money markets. Much of the money lying in bank vaults was simply destroyed. Norman Godbold, the territorial treasurer, oversaw the collection of the cash, and Colonel Steer provided a security force as the bills were fed into the flames of a crematorium. One of the MPs present enjoyed a memorable moment as he was permitted (under the watchful eyes of Steer and Godbold) to light his cigar with a hundred dollar bill.[16]

Individuals made their own preparations according to their personal circumstances. Dr. Otto Degener, an authority on Hawaiian flora, was informed by the commander of troops entrenched near his home on Oahu's north shore that his house would be bulldozed in the event of a landing in the area. Degener's lifework was threatened, but he rose to the challenge. With the help of his servant ("paroled from the home for feebleminded") and a thirteen-year-old neighbor boy he packed his collection of specimens, which had taken twenty years to assemble, and mailed it off to the New York Botanical Garden. Degener also took the opportunity to clear his attic of several hundred unsold copies of his books on Hawaiian plant life by mailing them at random to public libraries throughout the United States.[17]

The anxiety over a possible Japanese invasion was no manifestation of hysteria. The Imperial Japanese Navy staff officers who framed the plans for the Pearl Harbor attack briefly considered and then rejected the prospect of an invasion of Hawaii in conjunction with the raid. They judged that an invasion would be beyond Japan's capabilities. Their astounding successes in the months after Pearl Harbor, however, caused the Japanese to reconsider. The British, Dutch, and American empires in Southeast Asia and the Western Pacific had fallen with unexpected ease. Were the vaunted defenses of Hawaii really so formidable as they seemed?

Admiral Yamamoto himself began reevaluating Japanese strategy immediately upon receiving news of the extent of his fliers' success. On December 9 he directed his staff to begin serious planning for an invasion and occupation of Hawaii. Yamamoto's plan was based on the assumption that Japan would use the islands as a bargaining chip to force the United States to agree to a compromise peace. According to Combined Fleet staff officers, he envisioned a settlement which would leave Japan master of East Asia and the Western Pacific.[18]

At first the Navy General Staff and the army opposed the Hawaii invasion. Admiral Nagano and his subordinates assigned a higher priority to operations in the Southwest Pacific. The army was unenthusiastic about diverting its resources from what it viewed as Japan's principal strategic priority—the war in China. As usual, though, Yamamoto prevailed. He received help from an unexpected quarter on April 18, when U.S. bombers led by Lieutenant Colonel James Doolittle attacked Tokyo and other Japanese cities. The planes were land-based B-25 bombers flown off the deck of the carrier *Hornet* in an improvised operation designed primarily to boost American morale. The attack did little actual damage, but it demonstrated in a dramatic and undeniable fashion that the Japanese homeland was embarrassingly vulnerable to U.S. carriers operating from Pearl Harbor.

Yamamoto carried the day with the argument that the Doolittle raid proved the Japanese must seek a decisive battle which would eliminate U.S. carrier strength and neutralize Pearl Harbor as an operating base for the Pacific Fleet. The best way to accomplish that end, he argued, was to seize Midway Island, which lay 1,100 miles northwest of Oahu. The Americans could hardly allow an enemy base so close to Pearl Harbor and would have to challenge the Japanese move. Yamamoto was confident that the ensuing naval battle would leave the U.S. carriers at the bottom of the Pacific.

Midway, however, was to be only the first step of a campaign which would culminate with the invasion and capture of Oahu. The Japanese planned to take Midway in early June 1942. Johnston and Palmyra Islands, lying to the south and southwest of Hawaii, would be occupied in August. In October the Japanese would take the island of Hawaii, largest and easternmost of the Hawaiian Islands. The capture of Palmyra, Johnston, and Hawaii would leave Oahu virtually encircled and effectively cut off from reinforcement from the U.S. mainland. Furthermore, Hawaii Island's size and its 200-mile distance from Oahu would permit the construction of dispersed airfields from which Japanese aircraft could dominate the skies over Oahu. The campaign was to climax with a March 1943 amphibious assault in which at least three divisions would overrun the defenses of Oahu and Pearl Harbor.[19]

The easy victories of the first months of the Pacific War, however, made the Japanese overconfident. At Midway, brilliant codebreaking work by Commander Rochefort's team and careless execution by the First Air Fleet turned what should have been another Japanese victory into a disastrous defeat. In the course of the Midway battle (June 4–6, 1942) the heart of Nagumo's fleet—*Akagi, Kaga, Hiryu,* and *Soryu*—was sunk and a large proportion of Japan's elite carrier pilots were killed. After the U.S. victory at Midway there was no realistic prospect of a Japanese invasion of Hawaii.

22

A QUESTION

OF LOYALTY

While the threat of invasion hung over Hawaii the army's policy toward the Japanese community became the subject of searching reviews and heated discussion in Hawaii and Washington. Hawaii's Japanese had never enjoyed the confidence of U.S. military authorities, and Secretary Knox's early accusation of a massive fifth column helped create a climate of intensified, though unjustified, suspicion. In March 1942 all Japanese on the Pacific Coast, regardless of citizenship, were removed from the area and similar action in Hawaii was seriously considered at the highest levels of the U.S. government.

Surprisingly, given the army's prewar attitudes toward Hawaii's Japanese, the Hawaiian Department resisted the trend. General Short's efforts to encourage loyalty marked a new approach to the Japanese community, and Emmons continued that *démarche*. He was abetted by others in key positions: Colonel Fielder, who remained as G-2; Robert Shivers, head of the FBI's Honolulu office; and Captain John Burns, liaison officer from the Honolulu Police Department.[1]

There were practical arguments, too, against mass internment in Hawaii. The Japanese population was just too large, and the logistical problems of transportation were prohibitive. The Japanese comprised such a large proportion of the work force that internment would cripple the massive infrastructure of civilian labor which supported military requirements in Hawaii. Moreover, Japanese farmers contributed significantly to Hawaii's food supply, lessening the demand on precious shipping. Finally, the fact that the December 7 attack had been executed without local auxiliaries undoubtedly did much to assuage

Emmons's doubts about Japanese loyalty. Still, the prewar suspicion was only ameliorated; it did not disappear.

Navy officers had less confidence that Hawaii's Japanese would be loyal or even neutral. Captain Ellis Zacharias, considered one of the navy's experts on Japan and the Japanese, characterized Emmons' unwillingness to take draconian measures as "supine."[2] Nimitz expressed his own misgivings in a sharply worded memo saying the December 7 raid proved that "the security of the Fleet in the Hawaiian Area against the activities of foreign agents, spies and informers was of an unacceptably low order." He asked a series of pointed questions about the Japanese community which clearly conveyed his distrust.[3] Captain William Fechteler of navy intelligence followed up by meeting with his army counterparts on January 10. In a disturbed report on the meeting Fechteler told Nimitz:

> There is evidently a distinct difference of opinion between the Navy (ONI) and the Army (MID) with regard to the Japanese problem. The Army is inclined to regard drastic action as impossible because of the large numbers involved, and therefor [sic] to rely on the cultivation of loyalty in the second generation to control the Japanese population as a whole.[4]

The navy was dubious about the Hawaiian Department's policy, but the army was responsible for internal security in Hawaii. Nimitz theoretically could have exercised his prerogative as overall commander in Hawaii and reversed the Hawaiian Department's policy, but evidently he did not feel strongly enough to make an issue of it.

Admiral Nimitz may have been unwilling to insist on drastic measures, but there were others who were. As early as December 19 Roosevelt's cabinet decided that all Japanese aliens in Hawaii (a third of the community) should be interned on Molokai or another neighbor island. Emmons pointed out the practical difficulties. The Hawaiian Department was already critically short of the shipping, troops, and materiel which would be needed to transport, guard, and support the internees. Furthermore, he argued, those individuals identified as dangerous had already been arrested. And, finally, Japanese labor was indispensable to Hawaii's economy.[5]

As the pressure from Washington continued, the Hawaiian Department produced a steady stream of reasons why mass evacuation, either to the mainland or another island, was impractical. Secretary Knox was the most vigorous proponent of Hawaii evacuation and he had the president's ear. With his commander-in-chief calling for mass internment of Hawaii's Japanese, Emmons was in a delicate position. At least he enjoyed the backing of the Army General Staff, which lent credence and support to his strategy of stalling by raising practical objections. His radiogram to the War Department on February 4 is a good example of his response to demands for internment. He began by agreeing in principle: "It is desirable for health, supply and security reasons to evacuate as many Japanese as practicable and as soon as practicable." He then, however, pointed out the importance of Japanese labor to the local economy and the need to give evacuation priority to military dependents.[6]

Washington continued to issue plans and directives on the subject until well after Midway. The army command in Hawaii never implemented these instructions; rather, it continued to respond with practical objections and assurances that the Japanese were under control. Emmons skirted the edges of disobedience with his stand, but he prevailed. There was no mass evacuation or internment of Japanese in Hawaii, as there was on the Pacific Coast.

It is difficult at this distance to divine the motives of the army officers who opposed mass internment. Under the prevailing conditions they were not particularly concerned about constitutional rights. Even though the practical difficulties of internment were, as they maintained, formidable, it is difficult to imagine that they would have hesitated to assign first priority to evacuation had they believed Hawaii's Japanese represented a serious and immediate threat. It is testimony to their faith in the policy of winning over the Japanese— and to the readiness of Hawaii's Japanese to respond—that the army avoided mass internment in Hawaii.

Army policy emphasized the carrot but did not neglect the stick. A policy of selective detention immobilized those Japanese (mostly *issei*) judged "dangerous" and provided an example to the rest of the community. Within twenty-four hours of the attack authorities had seized some 300 to 400 Japanese on a "grab list" prepared previously by military intelligence agencies and the FBI. The detainees were held first at the immigration station on Ala Moana Boulevard; as the detention program expanded, camps were constructed at Sand Island in Honolulu Harbor and later at Honouliuli, northwest of Pearl Harbor.[7]

Of the 1,441 Japanese detained by the martial law administration for varying periods of time, few were arrested for specific manifestations of disloyalty. Rather, most came from classes of people which the military authorities believed had an actual or potential disposition to aid Japan's war effort. The consular agents, Shinto clergy, Japanese language school teachers, *kibei* (born in the United States but educated in Japan), fishermen (whose knowledge of coastal waters would be invaluable to an invasion force), and community leaders were all heavily represented among the detained.[8]

Once in custody they were examined by hearing boards composed of prominent (mostly Caucasian) local citizens and army officers. The purpose of the boards was to determine whether the detainee harbored loyalties toward Japan. Boards were less concerned with fairness than with immobilizing any person who might conceivably hinder the U.S. war effort. Most of those brought before the boards had close relatives in Japan or other incidental ties with that nation. These links, over which the arrestees had no control, were often seen as evidence of allegiance to the Japanese Empire when they responded with ambivalence to such questions as "Would you rather see America or Japan win the war?" Under the circumstances such questions were simplistic, but the martial law administration advised the boards that "any doubt should be resolved in favor of the government and internment should follow." One board member admitted that the boards used "any kind of evidence, rumor, surmise, conjecture or anything else" in judging those brought before them.[9]

The internment program served more than one purpose. In addition to neutralizing real or imaginary enemies it was meant also to deter those who might be contemplating hostile acts. It served as well to instruct Hawaii's Japanese on the norms of acceptable "American" behavior.[10] These measures of control and instruction were supplemented by an organized effort of the military government to reach into Japanese communities, neighborhoods, and even families to obtain information on pro-Japan sentiment, explain martial law policies, and control rumors.

Operating under the military government's Morale Section was the Contact Group, composed of representatives of Japanese community organizations and law enforcement and military intelligence agencies. The Morale Section and the Contact Group guided the activities of a number of committees (on Oahu the Emergency Service Committee; on Kauai the Morale Committee). These committees were composed of Japanese-Americans who were, in effect, the military government's face-to-face representatives with members of the Japanese community.[11]

These representatives were motivated by patriotism and a desire to persuade other Americans to accept Japanese-Americans into the mainstream of American life. They viewed their work as both a contribution to American victory and an effort to erase the image of the Japanese as a suspect and unassimilable presence. They encouraged the learning and use of English, an understanding of the principles of American government, and such patriotic activities as donating blood and buying war bonds.

At the same time, some who claimed to speak for the military government aroused fear and resentment by an excess of zeal. Colonel Fielder used them as "informers" (Fielder's term) to detect hidden pro-Japan sentiment. Afraid of denunciation and arrest, many families destroyed priceless heirlooms such as kimonos, family documents in Japanese, and pictures of relatives living in Japan. Most of this fear was unjustified and bordered on paranoia, but resentment against some individuals was strong enough to label them *inu* ("dog") and deep enough to arouse bitterness decades after the war's end.[12]

Morale Section representatives also found they had to work to alleviate the hostility and suspicion of people of other races who had been their neighbors and coworkers. After the fall of Bataan and Corregidor tension between Filipinos and Japanese in Hawaii became so great that military government authorities feared the outbreak of mass violence.[13] One Japanese-American remembered: "They [Filipinos] spent days working on their knives; and on many occasions told us that if there was another attack, they'd use the knives on us. It used to send shivers up and down our spines to hear them practicing throwing those knives against the walls of their houses at night, knowing that someday we might be their targets. We all had a common fear of Filipinos and it was a great fear."[14]

Like the Japanese community as a whole, the agents of the Morale Section were in a difficult and ambiguous position. They were sincere and public-spirited, but inevitably their motives were suspect to some. Their work helped significantly to convince other Americans that Hawaii's Japanese were worthy of acceptance and trust, and they played no small part in persuading other Japanese that achievement of that end was worth the effort.

For some Japanese-Americans the die was already cast, for the outbreak of war found many already in uniform. The Hawaii National Guard's 298th and 299th Infantry Regiments, called to active duty the year before, were already deployed throughout the territory. During the months of federal service the original body of guardsmen had been significantly augmented by draftees inducted in Hawaii. When war came the two regiments contained about 2,000 Japanese, more than half their strength.[15] When the National Guard was activated the Hawaii Territorial Guard was organized as a reserve military force under the command of the territorial governor. The Territorial Guard was composed primarily of ROTC cadets from the University of Hawaii and Honolulu high schools. Like the 298th and 299th, Japanese-Americans were heavily represented in its ranks.

The Territorial Guard was activated on December 7 and assigned to guard important public buildings and other installations. The *nisei* guardsmen derived a special pride and satisfaction from their service. One recalled: "We had not only the immediate emergency to spur us on, but the deeper purpose of establishing, once and for all, confidence in the actions of the Nisei in Hawaii as well."[16] It came as a shock and disappointment, then, when the Territorial Guard was dissolved by the military government on January 23. It was painfully obvious that, with a critical shortage of military manpower, distrust of the Japanese-Americans was the reason for the unit's dissolution. One member wrote:

> Never in my life did I feel so bitter, so disappointed and so hopeless as when the discharge papers were handed to us. How can one feel otherwise when he expatriates from the country of his ancestors to which he was a subject by legal formality and tries to become 100% American and further voluntarily enlists in the Army in time of war to sacrifice himself and is told "You are not wanted." What country can I now call "Mea Patria"? I am no longer a subject of Japan. I am an American citizen, but am treated as a despicable outcast.[17]

Most of the discharged *nisei* volunteered to serve the war effort in any capacity. General Emmons accepted the offer and 160 were taken to Schofield Barracks and utilized as auxiliaries by the Army Corps of Engineers. The group, known as the Varsity Victory Volunteers because most were University of Hawaii students, performed a variety of tasks from road building to tending vegetable gardens. Their work, and the spirit in which it was offered, caused some in authority to pause and reconsider their beliefs about the loyalties of Hawaii's Japanese.

If the army officers responsible for defending Oahu considered the Japanese in the Territorial Guard a problem, questions about the predominantly Japanese-American 298th and 299th Infantry Regiments loomed even larger. The 298th occupied shoreline positions in the Kaneohe–Bellows area; the 299th was scattered in isolated detachments on Kauai, Molokai, Maui, and Hawaii Island. Concern about the loyalty and reliability of the Japanese-American troops was expressed in the cabinet meeting of January 30.[18]

General Emmons and his subordinate commanders shared those doubts. Major General Maxwell Murray, as commander of the Twenty-fourth Infantry Division, was responsible for the 298th. He admitted that "its soldierly spirit, training progress, and efficiency have been outstanding. It has met in a most satisfactory manner every demand made upon it, and the attitude of its members during the attack on December 7th and in subsequent alerts has been all that could be asked."[19] Murray was uneasy, though, because most of the 298th had first donned their uniforms while Japan and the United States were at peace, and the Japanese-American soldiers had been given no opportunity to formally declare their loyalty since December 7. He warned Emmons:

If the bulk of persons of Japanese extraction in the 298th Infantry should prove disloyal to the United States, we will have a potential force in our midst completely armed and equipped for organized resistance, and already occupying an extensive portion of the Island [Oahu] which includes two important air bases and a third in the process of construction.[20]

The division commander went on to make specific recommendations:

1. The regiment's Japanese-Americans should be given the opportunity to state whether they had any reservations about fighting Japanese troops. Those who had qualms should be transferred to noncombatant units.

2. The 298th should be relieved and its positions occupied by a regiment from the mainland.

3. Upon relief the 298th should be transferred to the mainland or "some other locality where its chances of coming in close combat with the Japanese are negligible."

The Japanese-American soldiers, although not discharged en masse like the territorial guardsmen, soon felt the cold breath of suspicion in the form of army policies. On March 31 General Emmons was directed to discontinue enlisting and inducting Japanese-Americans. The Hawaiian Department began, with the help of informers, compiling lists of troops whose loyalty was suspect. Of the ten soldiers on a list prepared April 2, 1942, only one appears to have been included on the basis of clear indications of disloyalty. He condoned the Japanese attack on Pearl Harbor, looked forward to Japan "freeing" Hawaii, and stated he would fire on U.S. troops if captured by the Japanese. Two men in his company told the FBI that "the safest thing to do with L_____ in case of attack would be to shoot him."[21] Inclusion of the others on that list seems to have been prompted by the same sort of innuendo and dubious logic that characterized the internment process. One soldier was deemed of questionable loyalty because he wrote his girlfriend that he disliked army life. Another, it was noted ominously, was a "good listener, keen observer."[22]

As General Emmons considered the subject it became increasingly clear to him that the solution to his worries lay in the constitution of an all-Japanese unit. Troops for this force could be drawn from the Japanese-Americans now in uniform in Hawaii, and it should be assigned to the European theater. He broached the idea to his staff on April 5 on a routing slip. That he was more concerned about divesting his command of Japanese-American soldiers than in the European theater's manpower problems is suggested by Emmons' other comments on the same routing slip: "Are we not," he asked anxiously, "making constant searches for weapons and poisons?"[23]

The Hawaiian Department commander proposed to Washington on April 6 the formation of an all-Japanese unit composed of men currently in the 298th and 299th Regiments and others in Hawaii not yet in military service. In the proposal Emmons avoided any mention of his doubts about their loyalty. He stressed the numbers of Hawaii *nisei* "who desire to demonstrate their loyalty to the United States in a concrete manner" and explained that in North Africa or Europe "their physical characteristics will not serve to confuse our other troops."[24]

These points were true enough, but Emmons used them to mask his doubts about the *nisei* soldiers. With Hawaii braced for an invasion he could provide ample opportunity for any American infantryman to prove his loyalty. As for the possibility of confusing Japanese invaders with Japanese-American defenders, there were two sides to that coin. Japanese-American troops could (and later did) render valuable service as battlefield interpreters and translators, and on several occasions they infiltrated Japanese lines to create confusion by shouting bogus orders. The Hawaiian Department, so far as can be determined, gave no consideration to using its *nisei* troops in this fashion.

The War Department rejected Emmons' proposal. In a May 2 message Washington ordered that the Japanese-Americans in combat units be transferred to existing service units.[25] Emmons protested in a May 11 radiogram and, demonstrating increasing confidence in his Japanese-American troops, insisted that they not be transferred to the service forces. He still wanted them sent to the mainland but worried about the effect on the morale of Hawaii's Japanese community if they were rejected for use in combat units. Whatever happened, it was clear that the Japanese-Americans in uniform in Hawaii would be transferred to the mainland. In mid-May the 298th was relieved of its assignment to guard the Kaneohe sector and preparations were under way for stripping the 299th of its Japanese personnel.[26]

The effect on their morale was devastating, but the War Department reversed itself before the month ended. On May 28, as Yamamoto's fleet steamed toward Midway, Marshall wired the Hawaiian Department authorizing the formation of an overstrength infantry battalion from the Japanese-Americans of the 298th and 299th. He ordered that the unit be sent to the mainland for training, but made no mention of when and where it would be deployed subsequently.[27] The unit was designated the 100th Infantry Battalion, and its performance during the training period was so impressive that the army created a larger Japanese unit, the 442nd Regimental Combat Team. (The 442nd later absorbed the 100th.) The battle record established by these units in Italy and France has been well documented. It is sufficient to note here that the 18,143 individual decorations (including 9,486 Purple Hearts) earned by their members put to rest the doubts and suspicions which had hovered over Japanese-Americans.[28]

23
OPERATION K

While military commanders in Hawaii remained needlessly concerned with the Japanese-Americans in their midst, the Japanese Navy continued to test the islands' post-attack defenses. Air reconnaissance and token raids, although alarming to the Americans, stretched the Imperial Navy's resources to the limit. Japanese submarines prowling the Pacific, however, were a more substantial menace.

The few Japanese submarines left in the Hawaii area after the Pearl Harbor strike made random attacks on shipping in the weeks following the raid. It was not a systematic campaign, but the damage they inflicted offers a clue to the potential of submarines to isolate Hawaii. Japanese sub commanders much preferred to hunt for warships, but they were unsuccessful in that effort and turned to merchant vessels as targets of opportunity.[1]

The first submarine attack of the Pacific War occurred on December 7, even before the start of the Pearl Harbor air raid. The steam schooner *Cynthia Olsen* was halfway between Seattle and Honolulu when she radioed that she was being attacked by a surfaced submarine. The Matson liner *Lurline* picked up the signal fifty-five minutes before the first bombs fell on Pearl Harbor. No trace of the schooner was ever found, and she presumably went down with all hands.

On December 11 a surfaced submarine destroyed the Matson freighter *Lahaina* 800 miles from Hawaii. The crew of thirty-four managed to get aboard a lifeboat, but two men died during ten days afloat. Two more drowned as they tried to swim ashore when the boat reached Maui. On December 14 the Norwegian motorship *Heough* was sunk near Kauai. The crew was rescued by a U.S. warship. A few days later another Matson freighter, *Manini*, was torpedoed near Hawaii. Most of the crew were able to board her well-stocked life-

258

boats and were rescued. On December 18 a Japanese submarine torpedoed the freighter *Prusa* 120 miles south of Hawaii; again, there was little loss of life. Japan's Sixth Fleet submarines assigned to the Hawaii operation met with limited success in striking at U.S. Pacific Fleet vessels. *Saratoga* was damaged by a torpedo from *I-6* on January 12, and *I-72* sank the oiler *Neches* on January 23.

The most disastrous submarine attack in Hawaiian waters was the sinking of the army transport *Royal T. Frank*. On the morning of January 28, 1942, the 224-ton vessel, accompanied by a destroyer and the tug *Kalae,* was in the Alenuihaha Channel bound for Hawaii Island. She carried a group of twenty-six recent draftees (most from Hawaii) en route to reinforce the garrison there. A lurking Japanese submarine (probably *I-1* or *I-2*) put one torpedo into the transport, and she sank within seconds.[2]

The ship's radio operator, Private Victor Rabinowitz, was trapped by a mast cable which fell across his leg. As the ship sank he was dragged down, but at last the cable loosened and he bobbed to the surface. Chief Engineer Francis Wilson also had a narrow escape. He was pinned between a beam and an automobile being carried as cargo. Like Rabinowitz, he managed to free himself after the ship went under. The escorting destroyer and *Kalae* rescued most of the vessel's crew and passengers, but seventeen draftees and twelve crewmen went down with *Royal T. Frank*.

Japanese submarines near Hawaii did not confine their activities to attacks on shipping. They also attacked a number of Hawaii ports with gunfire. *I-1, I-2,* and *I-3,* each armed with two 12-centimeter (4.7-inch) guns, shelled neighbor island harbors during December. Termed a "reconnaissance attack" by the Japanese, the strategic objective of these operations is something of a mystery. The purpose may have been to probe the defenses of these secondary ports. Or perhaps the Japanese hoped to lower U.S. morale or prod the U.S. command to divert its resources from the defense of Oahu to the neighbor islands. In any case, the Japanese forces involved were too small to inflict much damage and the targets too unimportant for the attacks to disrupt the U.S. defense effort.[3]

The first attack occurred shortly before dark on December 15. A surfaced submarine fired about ten shots into the Kahului, Maui, harbor area. The only hits were on a pineapple cannery, where three rounds caused about $700 worth of damage. A coordinated shelling on the night of December 30–31 of Nawiliwili (Kauai), Hilo (Hawaii), and Kahului was just as ineffective. All the shots fired by *I-*

3 against Nawiliwili landed in nearby fields and inflicted no damage. *I-2* likewise failed to do any damage to Kahului. The army was prepared for the return engagement at Kahului, but return fire from field artillery pieces scored no hits on *I-2*. At Hilo *I-1* fired eight to ten shots at harbor facilities with minor damage to the docks. A navy vessel in Hilo harbor returned the fire but did not hit the submarine.[4]

Japanese submarines also sought to provide reconnaissance to the Combined Fleet. In the quest for post-attack intelligence on recovery work at Pearl Harbor the Japanese used seaplanes launched from submarines. These aircraft, Yokosuka E14Y1 (Glen), were small biplanes with folding wings carried in watertight deck hangars aboard the larger I-boats. The two-man plane had a top speed of only 133 knots and was unarmed. To venture over a heavily defended enemy base in such an aircraft was an act of courage which bordered on foolhardiness.

The first flight, from *I-7*, took place at dawn on December 17. Repair and salvage work on the Pacific Fleet was already proceeding at an energetic pace. A second flight was made on the night of January 6–7 from *I-19*. In late February another pilot scouted the Pearl Harbor area from *I-9*. Although civilian areas were blacked out the lights at Pearl Harbor illuminated the round-the-clock salvage work then under way. The lights, in fact, were so bright that the glare prevented the airmen from ascertaining which vessels were in the harbor.[5]

The flight in February was a prelude to a larger and more spectacular plan. Known to the Japanese as Operation K, it was originally conceived as a follow-up air raid on Pearl Harbor. The December and January flights gave evidence of the unexpected pace of U.S. recovery from the Pearl Harbor disaster, and the Japanese Navy high command hit upon the idea of a second air attack to slow the salvage work.[6]

The problem for the Japanese, though, was that the resources available for the project were no match for the task. Nagumo's fleet in early 1942 was fully occupied with operations in the Indian Ocean and Southeast Asian waters, so the burden of execution fell on the shoulders of the navy's Twenty-fourth Air Flotilla. The only aircraft suitable for another raid on Hawaii were the new Kawanishi H8K1 (Emily) flying boats. With their 3,000-mile full load range they could, with intermediate refueling, negotiate the 4,000-mile round trip between Hawaii and Japan's advanced bases in the Marshalls. Although there were only two of these huge craft available for Operation K, the effort had taken on a life of its own and the absurdity of trying to repeat the results of December 7 with two aircraft did not halt the operation.

The flying boats were to depart from Wotje, an advanced base in the Marshalls, each carrying four 250-kilogram (550-pound) bombs. They would fly 1,600 miles to French Frigate Shoals, an uninhabited atoll northwest of Oahu, to be refueled by the submarines *I-15* and *I-19*. The two planes would proceed to Pearl Harbor, drop their bombs, and return to Wotje without refueling. Additional submarines would be posted at various locations along the route to act as radio navigation beacons and plane guards.

With Ensign Tomano in command of one flying boat and Lieutenant Toshio Hashizumi, the flight leader, commanding the other the planes took off from Wotje as planned in the predawn hours of March 3. They landed at sunset and rendezvoused with the submarines at French Frigate Shoals. Hoses buoyed by floats were played out from the subs' gasoline tanks and fitted to the planes' fuel tanks. The water in the lagoon was rough, however, and the planes' mooring lines broke during refueling. The problem was solved by using the Emilys' engines to reduce the strain on the lines, and refueling was completed within three hours. Tomano and Hashizumi lifted off for Pearl Harbor at 9:38 P.M.

Unknown to the Japanese fliers, their arrival was not completely unanticipated. Commander Rochefort's codebreakers at Pearl Harbor had made considerable progress on the Japanese fleet's ciphers since December 7. They noticed the heavy volume of unusual traffic associating the Combined Fleet with submarine and land-based air units. Rochefort told an interviewer after the war that he had deduced the Japanese plan and warned Commander Layton, still serving as fleet intelligence officer under Nimitz. Layton's reminiscences do not confirm Rochefort's story, but the unusual radio traffic had not escaped Layton's attention.[7]

Radar stations on Kauai detected the Japanese planes on March 4 shortly after midnight as they approached from the northwest. Air controllers soon decided that the unidentified blips were not U.S. strays, and the defense apparatus was put in motion. Air defense officers thought the aircraft might have come from a carrier, so five PBYs armed with torpedoes took off at 1:15 to search for the ship. At 1:36 four P-40s were airborne to intercept the Japanese planes, now approaching Kaena Point at 15,000 feet and unaware they had been detected. They sighted the Kaena Point light and turned south for the bombing run over Pearl Harbor but clouds obscured most of

Oahu, including the target area. The two raiders overshot Pearl, and Hashizumi radioed Tomano to turn north. Hashizumi made the turn but Tomano did not receive the message.

The flight leader dropped his four bombs at 2:10 on what he thought was the U.S. naval base. When Tomano realized he had somehow become separated from the lead plane and was south of Oahu he turned north and released his bombs at 2:30. Although Hashizumi radioed, "Surprise attack successful," both bomb loads landed quite wide of the mark. Hashizumi's had fallen on the slopes of Puu Ohia, or Mount Tantalus, a good 5 miles east of Pearl Harbor. The only casualties were a few kiawe trees. No explosions were ever reported from Tomano's bombs, which probably fell into the sea.[8] The Japanese retired without ever having contact with the U.S. defenders. Tomano proceeded as planned to Wotje, where he arrived about 3:00 that afternoon. Hashizumi had damaged his flying boat on takeoff from Wotje and flew directly to the base at Jaluit, where repair facilities were better equipped.

On Oahu an acrimonious round of army-navy finger pointing followed the raid. Still not convinced that the intruders had been Japanese, U.S. officers thought the bombs had been jettisoned by a lost American pilot. Each service determined that none of *its* pilots had been responsible and each blamed the other. Layton, however, knew that Japanese aircraft had once again penetrated Oahu's defenses. He and others soon deduced the means used by the attackers, and the Pacific Fleet took action to prevent a recurrence. Patrol vessels were dispatched to French Frigate Shoals to prevent the area's future use as a sub-to-aircraft refueling point—and that action was to have wide-ranging consequences.

The Japanese had planned another K-type operation for reconnaissance in conjunction with the Midway invasion. Had it been successfully executed they might have sighted the U.S. carriers en route to ambush Nagumo's force, a sighting which could well have reversed the course of the battle. But when the refueling submarine crept into the lagoon on May 30 she discovered the presence of U.S. vessels, which made the operation impossible. The reconnaissance was scrubbed, and so the Japanese paid dearly for their second attack on Oahu.

24

SALVAGE AND REPAIR

The destruction of the battle line at Pearl Harbor eradicated the mainstay of U.S. surface forces in the Pacific. It would be months before ship construction, even under the pressure of wartime conditions, could replace the vessels lost. The need, then, was to repair the damaged ships at Pearl Harbor as quickly as possible. The shallow depth of the anchorage made it feasible to consider raising even the most badly damaged vessels.

Captain James Steele, formerly commanding officer of *Utah*, served as chief salvage officer from December 7, 1941, to January 9, 1942. He was succeeded by Captain Homer Wallin, a salvage specialist who held the position until late 1942. The bulk of the salvage and repair work was done under Wallin's superintendency, and it was in this period that the navy met the most formidable challenges to its engineering skills.

Salvage personnel were organized into teams centering on particular specialties (such as ordnance). These specialists rotated from one damaged ship to another as the salvage work on each ship moved from one phase to the next. The labor for the projects came from a variety of sources. Crews of the stricken vessels supplied some men; Destroyer Repair Units I and II (later merged to form the Pearl Harbor Repair and Salvage Unit) provided others. Pearl Harbor's civilian workers also participated in the effort as did divers and other skilled workers of the Pacific Bridge Company, a private contractor. The crews of various repair vessels which moved in and out of Pearl Harbor throughout the war also rendered valuable help. Unskilled labor came from transient sailors in Pearl Harbor's receiving barracks.[1]

Difficult, dangerous, and unpleasant conditions were the rule for the men and women (many contractor workers and navy civilian employees were women) engaged in this task. Most of the sunken battleships were flooded with tons of viscous fuel oil when torpedoes ruptured their oil tanks. Flooding seawater carried the fuel into virtually every nook and cranny of these ships and covered nearly every exposed surface with a thick coat of oil. And, of course, salvage workers encountered bodies at unexpected intervals during their work. The resulting distress was so great that Wallin established a practice, when pumping out flooded compartments, of leaving about 2 feet of standing water. Crews with body bags would then enter and collect the floating corpses before the other workers would enter.[2]

There were special hazards, as well. The salvage work required some 5,000 individual dives involving a total of 20,000 hours underwater. Unexploded ordnance heightened the danger to all the workers involved, whether above or below the surface. In addition, there was the omnipresent danger of fire and explosion from flammable gases and liquids (particularly aviation gas) on the vessels.[3]

Explosive gases figure in one persistent Pearl Harbor legend that divers were killed aboard *Arizona* when an underwater cutting torch ignited a pocket of gas. The story has been repeated over the years by "witnesses" and has found its way into print. An examination of contemporary records, however, including the daily wartime entries of the Pearl Harbor Navy Yard War Diary, reveals no mention or indirect evidence of the incident. Wallin's own book on the salvage operation states that there was only one "casualty" (of an unspecified nature) during the dives. The victim was a contractor's employee, and it occurred on *Oklahoma*.[4]

This is not to say there were no hazards from gas and explosions. Two men perished from deadly concentrations of hydrogen sulfide aboard the wreckage of *Nevada;* there was one small harmless explosion aboard the *Arizona* hulk; and gasoline vapor caused a powerful explosion on *California*. The probable origin of the *Arizona* divers story lies in the pressure-cooker atmosphere prevailing at Pearl Harbor during the war years. Strict censorship was the rule, and it applied with special force to the salvage work. Rumor is always rampant in such circumstances. The yard's 20,000 civilians and the greater number of sailors there circulated stories which were impossible for anyone to verify. Accounts of the *Nevada* deaths probably merged with stories about the *Arizona* and *California* explosions to create a legend which no doubt will survive its originators.

The legend obscures the impressive safety record compiled by the salvage workers. The two recorded deaths are not to be dismissed, but the safety program of Wallin and his subordinates is seen in a different light when these two deaths are viewed against the backdrop of the incalculable number of work hours and the magnitude, special hazards, and urgency of the task. Wallin's Salvage Division had its own medical officer, Lieutenant Commander C. M. Parker, who established special testing procedures to detect the presence of poisonous or explosive gases before workers entered ships' compartments. Special teams of workers were organized and trained in the testing techniques.[5]

These teams worked on all the damaged ships, but each vessel had its own tale. The fleet flagship, *Pennsylvania,* was undocked from Drydock One on December 12 after completion of her shaft alignment. A damaged 5-inch gun was replaced with one recovered from *West Virginia* and, after other minor repairs, she was ready for action on December 20.[6]

Tennessee was found to be wedged tightly between her mooring quays and the sunken *West Virginia*. It was necessary to dynamite part of the quays to release *Tennessee*. Damage to her stern plates caused by *Arizona*'s fires was repaired by specialists from the repair ship *Medusa*, and *Tennessee* was back in service on December 20.

Maryland's major damage was the hole caused by the bomb which entered her hull below the waterline. A small caisson was built around the hole and the flooded compartments were pumped dry. Like the work on *Pennsylvania* and *Tennessee,* repairs on *Maryland* were completed on December 20, less than two weeks after the attack.

Helena was the first ship docked in Pearl Harbor's hastily completed Drydock Two on December 10. After temporary repairs to the torpedo hole in her starboard side she was undocked on December 21. She left for Mare Island, California, on January 5 for further work.

Repairs to the destroyer *Helm*'s buckled plates were completed quickly after she was put on Pearl Harbor's marine railway on January 15, 1942.

When put into Drydock One on December 13 the cruiser *Honolulu* was found to have suffered hull buckling 5 to 6 feet deep over a length of 40 feet. She was drydocked until January 2; final touches were complete ten days later.

Raleigh took *Honolulu*'s place in drydock the day after the latter was undocked. The Pearl Harbor work force made permanent repairs to the hull and bulkhead damage, and she was taken out of drydock in early February. *Raleigh* sailed for Mare Island on February 14 for new engine parts and repairs to her electrical system.[7]

Floating Drydock Two was raised on January 9 and temporary repairs were made quickly. She received her first ship on January 26, and final repairs were made by May 15. Appropriately, *Shaw* was the first vessel to be placed in the raised Floating Drydock Two on January 26. She was fitted with a temporary bow fabricated in the Pearl Harbor shops and left for Mare Island on February 9. After further work she returned to full duty in the fall of 1942.

The repair ship *Vestal*'s own complement of artisans performed most of the work necessary to refloat and repair their vessel. She put into Drydock One on February 7 and permanent repairs were completed on February 18.

The yard work force labored on *Curtiss* from December 19 to 27. Delays in shipping vital material caused further work to be put off until April 26. Final repairs were completed on May 25.

The small tug *Sotoyomo* burned and sank at Floating Drydock Two. Because of a long wait for needed parts, repair was delayed until the late summer of 1942.

The badly damaged *Downes* remained in Drydock One until February 6. The hull was mangled by the explosions of bombs, torpedoes, and depth charges, and only her machinery could be saved. The hull was scrapped in August 1942 and her machinery sent to Mare Island where it was installed in a new hull in November 1943. Technically *Downes* was "repaired," but essentially she was a new ship incorporating salvaged parts.

Cassin was in even worse condition than *Downes*. She had toppled over in drydock, her keel warped and her hull hogged. She was righted on February 5 and removed from Drydock One on February 18. Her hull was scrapped in October 1942 and her machinery sent to Mare Island. Like *Downes,* she was "repaired" by building a new hull around the old machinery. The ship was ready for service in February 1944.

Salvage of the ancient *Oglala* was not considered a high priority, but clearing the Ten Ten Dock was an important matter. The Salvage Division briefly considered dynamiting *Oglala* and removing the remains as scrap, but the project demanded more resources than could be justified. Accordingly, it was decided to raise the ship with salvage pontoons sunk alongside the vessel and then pumped dry. The first attempt on April 11, 1942, failed when the pontoons broke loose. A second attempt on April 23 was successful. Then, on the night of June 25–26, *Oglala* sank again at dockside when one of her unwatering pumps failed. She was refloated, but bad luck dogged the project as she sank again on June 29. Refloated a second time, the minelayer nearly sank once more when a fire broke out aboard the hulk on July 2. She entered Drydock Two the next day for temporary repairs which would enable her to make the voyage to Mare Island, and after reconditioning there *Oglala* was back in service in February 1944.

Nevada, aground at Waipio Point, was almost completely flooded and badly damaged by bomb and torpedo hits. Even Admiral Nimitz, an incurable optimist, expressed his doubts to Captain Wallin about the possibilities for salvage and repair. Wallin persisted, however, and set to work.

On February 7, 1942, Lieutenant James Clarkson and Machinist Mate Peter DeVries were killed and six other men overcome by hydrogen sulfide which had accumulated in the steering engine room. The gas was formed by the interaction between seawater and decomposing organic material. In normal concentrations hydrogen sulfide has a distinctive "rotten egg" odor, but when highly concentrated, as it was in the closed compartments of the sunken ships, it is odorless. It was this tragedy which spurred the development of the gas testing program implemented on all the salvage jobs at Pearl Harbor.

Nevada was refloated on February 12 and taken to Drydock Two for hull repairs. Undocked on March 15, her machinery was overhauled by April 22, and she left for Puget Sound for further reconditioning and modernization. Before the end of 1942 she was back in service and saw action in the Aleutian, Normandy, Iwo Jima, and Okinawa campaigns.

Salvage workers constructed cofferdams around *California*'s forecastle and quarterdeck. After removal of the ship's main battery guns to lessen her weight, pumps unwatered the interior compartments and she was refloated on March 24, 1942. On April 5, before she could be taken into drydock, a powerful explosion rocked *California*. Subsequent investigation revealed that gasoline vapor from the aviation fuel storage compartment had been ignited, probably by a naked light bulb or defective wiring insulation.[8]

The explosion was powerful enough to blow off the "window frame" patch over a bomb hole and shatter a number of 12-inch timbers, but it did not slow the repair work appreciably. The battleship was taken into Drydock Two on April 9, where repair began on the hull. Navy and civilian personnel also made efforts to service *California*'s electrical machinery. Wallin drew on the expertise of engineers from General Electric and the navy's Bureau of Ships, including

Commander Hyman Rickover. Before she was undocked on June 7
Pearl Harbor personnel made permanent repairs on her structural
damage. In October 1942 she steamed to Puget Sound under her own
power for further repair work and modernization. *California* was back
in service less than one year later.

West Virginia, which had suffered exceptional hull damage from
torpedo hits, proved difficult to raise. The repair force overcame the
challenge of sealing the hull before pumping by fabricating and
installing two large wooden patches sealed at the edges with a special
underwater concrete. Each patch was composed of individual sections
measuring some 13 by 50 feet. These patches were pierced by doors to
allow divers access to the hull before unwatering. During salvage
operations some 800,000 gallons of oil was removed from *West Virginia.* About 40,000 gallons was floating free and removed with
skimmers; the remainder was pumped from her tanks. The hulk
yielded at least sixty-seven bodies. Three of the dead men had suffo-
cated after exhausting the air supply in a storeroom near the ship's
freshwater pump; empty ration containers and marks on a calendar in
the compartment indicated they had survived until December 23.[9]

West Virginia was finally refloated on May 17 and entered Drydock
One on June 9. After temporary repairs she sailed for Puget Sound
for permanent repairs and modernization. She was ready for action
again on July 4, 1944. Later that year she took part in the Surigao
Strait action during the battle of Leyte Gulf, one of the few battle-
ship-to-battleship actions of World War II, and was present in Tokyo
Bay for the signing of Japan's surrender.

The righting of *Oklahoma* was one of the most technically difficult
challenges faced by the engineers of the Salvage Division. It was
solved by the installation of twenty-one winches on Ford Island which
pulled the ship over by means of cables attached to 40-foot struts
welded to the ship's overturned hull. Before the winches were
engaged some 350,000 gallons of oil was pumped from the battleship's tanks, and more than 2,000 tons of crushed coral was dumped
onto the harbor floor to prevent the hulk from slipping on the
muddy bottom when the righting began.

The pulling began on March 8, 1943, and continued at a very slow
rate until June 16, when *Oklahoma* was nearly upright. A huge patch
was placed over the torpedo damage and, as on *West Virginia,* sealed
with underwater concrete. After the installation of pumps and cofferdams the ship was refloated on November 3. She was taken to Drydock Two on December 28 and stripped of her guns and other equip-

ment. Too badly damaged to be worth the effort and expense of rehabilitation, *Oklahoma* was decommissioned on September 1, 1944, and sold as scrap for $46,000. While being towed to the mainland she sank at sea in a storm on May 17, 1947.

The target ship *Utah*, which like *Oklahoma* had capsized, was fitted with a similar winch and strut arrangement. The navy decided in early 1942 that the ex-battleship was of limited military value and that salvage operations should be confined to the removal of useful equipment. Instead of being fully righted like *Oklahoma, Utah* was pulled over in late 1943 and early 1944 only far enough to rest on her port side. The remains of the ship still lie in Pearl Harbor off the northwest shore of Ford Island.

The salvage crews faced special challenges with *Arizona,* the most heavily damaged warship. Divers began exploring the *Arizona* wreckage within a week of her sinking. Preliminary dives revealed that the after part of the ship was relatively intact and that it would be feasible to attempt recovery of safes containing cash, valuables, and confidential documents.[10]

Initially salvage officers believed it would be possible to refloat the ship and return her to service. One of the first proposals for salvaging *Arizona* suggested the driving of sheet piling around the ship and filling the space between the ship and the piling with mud to seal the hull. If a cofferdam were built around the perimeter of the deck the ship could then be pumped dry. Further study revealed, though, that the porosity of the harbor's coral bottom would allow water to seep into the enclosed areas, and the idea was abandoned.[11]

Divers continued to examine the wreckage throughout 1942 and most of 1943 even as work progressed on salvaging scrap and reusable items from the ship. They found that the forward magazine explosion had vented through the deck forward of Turret I, separating the bow from the rest of the ship. Between frames 10 and 70—particularly between frames 10 and 33—the blast had vented through the sides of the ship. Here the diving parties found "the sides blown outward almost to a horizontal position." Much of the exterior hull inspection was done by jetting mud away from the hull with high-pressure hoses.[12]

Efforts to penetrate the interior spaces in the forward half of the ship were generally unsuccessful. Divers working on the main and second decks were blocked by wreckage at frame 76. Similar circumstances on the third deck prevailed forward of frame 78, except in two ammunition passageways where divers could move as far as frame 66, where progress was blocked by a downward slope of the second deck and a converging upward slope of the third. Access via deck hatches in this area was frustrated by twisted structural metal inside the hull. The two forward turrets, uptake, and conning tower were found to have dropped as much as 20 feet. An effort to verify survivors' statements that a bomb had gone down the ship's funnel led divers to inspect the armored uptake gratings, which were only partially accessible because of the wreckage. They found that insofar as inspection was possible the grating was "believed to be intact."[13]

In the more accessible areas of the ship, divers recovered a large collection of valuable and reusable material. A number of safes, including the post office safe, were raised. *Arizona*'s postal canceling machine was also recovered, as were large amounts of chinaware and silver from the officers' messes. Chairs from the battleship's barber shops were salvaged and reused as makeshift stands for antiaircraft guns. Two of the ship's anchors were found on the harbor bottom near the vessel.[14]

Hundreds of tons of scrap metal were cut away above and below the waterline. This material included many prominent structural features which remained above the surface after *Arizona* settled into the mud. The toppled foremast was cut away May 5, 1942, and the mainmast (which remained upright) was taken down on August 23. The stern aircraft crane kingpost was removed on December 3, 1942, and the conning tower a few weeks later on December 30. Much of this material was moved by barges to Waipio Point.[15]

The removal of 14-inch and 5-inch shells and powder, as well as aircraft bombs, from *Arizona*'s after magazines was an intricate and demanding undertaking. This work, performed under the direction of Gunner Roman Manthei, involved the unwatering of compartments by pumping and burning holes through decks and bulkheads to reach magazine storerooms blocked from normal entry by wreckage. It was during this work on April 20, 1942, that torches caused two minor explosions while cutting into the deck of the Turret III handling room. There were no casualties, and operations quickly resumed. By October 24, 1942, all ammunition had been removed from the after magazines. The amount totaled thousands of pieces of 5-inch ammunition, three hundred and fifty-nine 14-inch projectiles, more than eleven hundred 14-inch powder cans, fifty-six 100-pound bombs, plus miscellaneous explosives.[16]

The next major task was the removal of the ship's after turrets for use as army coastal defense weapons. It was a formidable and time-consuming project. Each turret was cut horizontally into three sections and removed by barges. The navy did not consent to the transfer until August 1942, and it was not until May 1943 that the removal of the turrets was completed. In addition to the turrets, eight hatches and frames from the after magazines were taken for use in the army installations. The guns from Turret II were removed in August 1943, but those from Turret I were left where they lay.[17] The army encountered many problems in transporting and assembling the massive components of Turrets III and IV. Accurate blueprints were often unavailable, and vital parts had been damaged by the cutting torches of salvage workers before any thought had been given to reusing the guns. Only one turret installation, Battery Pennsylvania at Mokapu Head, was completed before the war's end; it was test fired on the eve of Japan's surrender. Work on the other turret site, Battery Arizona on Oahu's western shore, was abandoned with the advent of peace.

The turret removal was undertaken only when it became apparent that the resources needed to raise *Arizona* were too great to justify the project. The commandant of the Pearl Harbor Navy Yard wrote to Washington in July 1942 that rehabilitation of the battleship would be "a task of great magnitude entailing the diversion of large numbers of men and equipment from other work" and suggested the abandonment of salvage work after recovering useful material and scrap metal from the vessel. He also recommended striking *Arizona* from the list of commissioned ships.[18] Admiral Nimitz concurred in a letter of endorsement, and *Arizona* was officially removed from the list of commissioned ships by order of the secretary of the navy on December 1, 1942.[19]

Salvage work on *Arizona* continued after the issuance of the strike notice, but by the fall of 1943 all useful and accessible material had been recovered. In September the Bureau of Ordnance proposed using the hulk as a target for testing a new type of torpedo warhead, but the request was turned down. In October salvage officers concluded that their work on *Arizona* was finished, and crews dismantled the platforms, pumps, and other equipment on the wreckage and moved on to other projects.[20]

25

REACTIONS

AND REFLECTIONS

"Remember Pearl Harbor" was a ubiquitous theme in American wartime propaganda. It reflected rage at what was seen as Japanese perfidy and, on a deeper level, an obsession with lingering questions about U.S. unpreparedness. It seemed inconceivable to most Americans that Japan could have delivered such a devastating blow against the mighty U.S. fleet.

The prevailing American view of Japanese, colored by attitudes of racial superiority, was that they were an imitative people. They were clever mimics but lacked the bold vision, technological mastery, and creative genius that marked Western civilization. U.S. military intelligence officers seriously underestimated the skill and training of Japanese pilots as well as the quality and capability of Japanese military equipment. Some Americans were so unshakable in these views that many, including eyewitnesses to the attack, believed that the Japanese planes at Pearl Harbor were piloted by Germans.[1]

How could they have approached the heavily defended bastion of Hawaii undetected and won such an overwhelming victory on December 7? Inevitably many Americans were convinced that the answer lay in the poor performance of U.S. commanders. American postmortems of the attack tended to be (and often still are) characterized by scapegoating and a spirit of partisanship. Generally they can be divided into positions which place the lion's share of responsibility for the disaster either on the local commanders in Hawaii or on the shoulders of the higher command echelons in Washington.

The latter school of thought, known as revisionism, focuses especially on the actions and policies of President Roosevelt. There was a natural tendency of FDR's opponents to espouse the revisionist view and a corresponding predeliction of FDR's champions to saddle General Short and Admiral Kimmel with responsibility. During and immediately after World War II there were no less than nine official inquiries into Pearl Harbor, but their varying conclusions helped to fuel the debate rather than settle the questions of responsibility for U.S. unpreparedness.

Navy Secretary Frank Knox made a flying visit to the scene immediately after the attack and spent December 11 and 12 in Hawaii. In his report to the president, Knox made a fairly accurate summary of the events of December 7 and the damage sustained by U.S. forces. He stressed the courage and coolness of U.S. personnel in responding to the surprise attack and did not delve deeply into the question of responsibility for U.S. unpreparedness. Knox did, however, inferentially raise doubts about the performance of Short and Kimmel. He noted that neither had considered an air raid on Hawaii likely and that they were more concerned, respectively, with the prospects of sabotage and submarine attack. The navy secretary concluded that the decisive factor was superior Japanese planning and execution and, by inference, not American dereliction.[2]

The situation would not rest there. Roosevelt thought it imperative to address the question of responsibility for unpreparedness. Admiral Kimmel and Generals Short and Martin were relieved in mid-December, ostensibly to ensure that the energies of the Hawaii commanders would not be diverted from vital war tasks to the upcoming inquiries. Whatever the truth of that rationale, it was inevitable that the public would interpret the action as condemnation of their performance. The impression was reinforced by the absence of similar action against their counterparts in the Philippines, Admiral Thomas Hart and Generals Douglas MacArthur and Lewis Brereton. And what of General Marshall and Admiral Stark, both of whom remained in their posts (although Stark was reassigned to Europe in March 1942)?

To answer the public demand for a full investigation and to head off calls for a congressional inquiry Roosevelt appointed a commission chaired by Supreme Court Justice Owen Roberts, whose reputation stemmed from his role as prosecutor in the Teapot Dome scandal. Other members of the Roberts Commission were Major General Frank McCoy, Brigadier General Joseph McNarney, Admiral William Standley, and Rear Admiral Joseph Reeves. They conducted their investigation by taking testimony from witnesses and principals during December and January in both Washington and Hawaii.

The commission's charge from the president specified it was "to provide bases for sound decisions whether any derelictions of duty or errors of judgment on the part of United States Army or Navy personnel contributed to such successes as were achieved by the enemy . . . and if so, what these derelictions or errors were, and who were responsible therefor."[3] The commissioners heard testimony from witnesses ranging from cabinet officers to privates and seamen, but the report had one glaring omission. Although the commission had learned about Magic, its final report made no mention of the top secret program.

The Roberts Commission concluded that "errors of judgment" by General Short and Admiral Kimmel were "the effective causes for the success of the attack." It found the secretaries of war, state, and the navy to have fulfilled their obligations by frequent consultations with one another and with the chief of staff and chief of naval operations. The commissioners judged Marshall and Stark to have fulfilled their command responsibilities. Kimmel and Short were faulted for "dereliction of duty" by failing to confer and coordinate adequately after receipt of the November 27 war warnings and by not responding to those warnings with heightened air patrols and antiaircraft readiness.

The high command in Washington (no individuals were specified) was blamed for a number of "causes contributory to the success of the Japanese":

1. Emphasis in warnings to Hawaii about the danger of sabotage and the probability of Japanese aggression in the Far East

2. Not reacting to General Short's notice that he responded to the war warning by placing the Hawaiian Department on antisabotage alert

3. Failure to dispatch General Marshall's December 7 warning by the most expeditious means available

The Roberts Commission noted the most egregious mistakes committed by the Washington command echelon, but it clearly reserved its most damning condemnation for Kimmel and Short.[4] Since the report did not consider Magic, its conclusions are shadowed by lingering doubts as to whether the blame might have been apportioned differently had it weighed the Magic issue openly. Defenders of Short and Kimmel maintain that access to the Japanese ambassadors' cable traffic gave the authorities in Washington an inside look at Japan's intentions. It can be argued just as strongly that Magic gave FDR and his advisers no indication that Pearl Harbor had been selected as a target and that the general drift of Japanese policy could be divined as accurately from the pages of the Honolulu dailies as from the Purple traffic.

The Roberts Commission report did not close the books on Pearl Harbor; instead, it added fuel to the flames. Kimmel wanted a public court martial, which he expected would clear him of the "errors of judgment" charge, but such action was clearly out of the question while the war was in progress. Congress passed and President Roosevelt signed legislation in December 1943 extending the statute of limitations in order to allow courts-martial after the war for offenses connected with the Pearl Harbor attack. There was the danger, however, that memories would fade with the passage of time or important witnesses might be killed in battle.[5]

To preserve the testimony of important witnesses the navy undertook a fact-finding investigation headed by Admiral Thomas Hart, former commander of the Asiatic Fleet. Between March and June 1944 Hart and his small staff examined witnesses in Washington and throughout the Pacific theater. Conspicuous by their absence among those questioned were Admirals Stark and Kimmel. Kimmel was invited to take part in the proceedings as an "interested party" (that is, a potential defendant), but wary of the navy's conditions he declined to participate. Hart's brief was to record the recollections of potential witnesses. It was beyond the scope of his duty to reach conclusions or apportion blame.[6]

Clearly the navy knew that the subject was far from closed. Congress validated that appreciation in June 1944, when it adopted a joint resolution calling on the army and navy to conduct their own inquiries into Pearl Harbor to assess culpability of those who had been in positions of responsibility. The army appointed a board chaired by Lieutenant General George Grunert to conduct its investigation, which ran from July to October 1944. Also on the board were Major Generals Walter Frank and Henry Russell.

The Army Pearl Harbor Board mildly censured General Short for placing the Hawaiian Department on antisabotage alert only. This judgment was softened somewhat by noting that the information supplied by Washington was "incomplete and confusing." The board thought also that Short should have pressed Kimmel for implementation of interservice agreements for defense of Hawaii, ascertained the effectiveness of the navy's long-range reconnaissance, and replaced inefficient officers on his staff.

Army officers in Washington came in for much heavier criticism. General Marshall, said the board, failed to keep his Hawaiian Department commander adequately informed and instructed as Japan and the United States drifted toward war. The chief of staff should have corrected Short's action in placing his command on anti-sabotage alert and made a greater effort to dispatch a last-minute warning to Hawaii. General Gerow, chief of the War Plans Division in 1941, was castigated for the same shortcomings. The army board also criticized Secretary of State Cordell Hull for the conduct of negotiations with Japan. The investigators thought he should have played for time as the services hastened to prepare for the conflict. Despite these conclusions Grunert and his colleagues made no recommendations for courts-martial or any other action.[7]

The navy responded to the congressional resolution of June 1944 by establishing a court of inquiry. Like the army board the navy's court of inquiry sat from July through October 1944. It was chaired by Admiral Orin Murfin and included Admiral Edward Kalbfus and Vice Admiral Adolphus Andrews. These board members seem to have been less inclined than their army counterparts to criticize the performance of their fellow officers. The court absolved Kimmel and his Pacific Fleet subordinates of any responsibility for unpreparedness. It reported that, given the information available, their judgments in keeping the battle fleet in Pearl Harbor, in maintaining the state of alert in effect on December 7, and in not ordering more extensive air patrols were sound. Admiral Stark came in for some light criticism for failing "to display the sound judgment expected" by not keeping Kimmel fully informed of the information gleaned from the Magic intercepts. The court's final judgment was that "no offenses have been committed nor serious blame incurred on the part of any person or persons in the naval service." It recommended that "no further proceedings be had in the matter."[8]

The conclusions of the court of inquiry were coolly received in the Navy Department. Although Stark had been transferred out of Washington and Frank Knox had died, the new secretary of the navy, James Forrestal, was dissatisfied with the court's conclusions absolving Kimmel. Forrestal directed Admiral H. Kent Hewitt to conduct yet another investigation of the subject. In his formal directive to Hewitt, Secretary Forrestal stated that his disagreement with the court's conclusions was not the only factor behind his desire to reopen the investigation. In an oblique reference to inadequate information about Magic and witnesses' disagreements about whether a Winds execute message had been received, Forrestal wrote: "The previous investigations have not exhausted all possible evidence."[9]

Hewitt's investigation lasted from May to July 1945. It covered much of the same ground surveyed by earlier inquiries but delved more deeply into the Magic intercepts and the Winds controversy. It concluded that a Winds execute message had *not* been intercepted. Regarding responsibility for unpreparedness, the conclusions of the Hewitt inquiry, while not as damning as those of the Roberts Commission, did not treat Kimmel quite as gently as the court of inquiry. Kimmel had, Hewitt concluded, "sufficient information in his possession to indicate that the situation was unusually serious, and that important developments with respect to the outbreak of war were imminent." At the same time the report stated that the failure to supply Kimmel with additional information—especially the 1:00 P.M. deadline—was "unfortunate."[10] On the whole the judgment of the Hewitt investigation more closely resembled the conclusions of the court of inquiry than the Roberts Commission's.

The findings of the Army Pearl Harbor Board produced repercussions similar to the reaction provoked by the navy's court of inquiry. General Marshall appointed Colonel Carter Clarke in September 1944 to reexamine the lingering questions, rumors, and conflicting testimony surrounding the handling of Magic intercepts, the Winds messages, and information which might or might not have been dispatched to the Hawaiian Department. Clarke's investigation did not encompass the formulation of judgments; he limited his conclusions to findings of fact (albeit disputed facts).

After interviewing a number of highly placed general staff officers in mid-September, Clarke concluded that neither the army nor Federal Communications Commission monitors had intercepted a Winds execute message and that if the navy made an interception it did not inform the army. Marshall ordered Clarke to reopen the investigation in July 1945 to address rumors that the chief of staff had ordered records tampered with to conceal evidence that he knew or should have known of the impending attack. Clarke concluded, after a month's investigation, that there was no foundation for the rumors.[11]

Secretary of War Henry L. Stimson was disturbed by the Army Pearl Harbor Board's criticism of General Marshall's performance. Stimson directed Lieutenant Colonel Henry C. Clausen to go over the same ground once more. The Clausen investigation ran from November 1944 to September 1945, and his conclusions tended to support Marshall's actions. Clausen thought his evidence showed that Gen-

eral Short had available more information about Japanese preparations for war than the Army Pearl Harbor Board believed. Although
he did not accuse Short of responsibility for unpreparedness, Clausen's report was, by inference, a partial refutation of the board's conclusions.[12]

The credibility of the wartime investigations was compromised by a
number of factors. Certainly the secrecy surrounding the proceedings
tended to raise serious questions about their fairness, completeness,
and objectivity. Security considerations prevented a full and comprehensive review of the Magic intercepts, for example, a vital aspect
which had to be carefully considered in any examination of Pearl Harbor. Finally, the findings of those inquiries were open to question by
virtue of the fact that the convening authorities all had a stake in the
outcomes. The reputations and careers of President Roosevelt, General Marshall, and the secretaries of war and the navy obviously would
be affected by the work of their investigators. By 1944 the question of
unpreparedness at Pearl Harbor had become such a thoroughly partisan issue that Governor Thomas Dewey, the Republican nominee for
president, seriously considered raising Magic as a public issue in the
campaign. A fervent appeal from Marshall, who argued that the
action would compromise the U.S. war effort, dissuaded Dewey.[13]

In the increasingly partisan atmosphere surrounding public discussion of Pearl Harbor, Congress wasted little time convening its own
investigation after the surrender of Japan. The composition of the
investigating committee reflected the Democratic control of both
houses. Senator Alben Barkley, the majority leader, chaired the committee. He was joined by fellow Democratic Senators Walter George
and Scott Lucas; Senators Owen Brewster and Homer Ferguson came
from the Republican side of the aisle. From the House of Representatives came Democrats Jere Cooper (vice chairman of the committee),
J. Bayard Clark, and John Murphy. Republican Representatives
Bertrand Gearhart and Frank Keefe brought the total to ten. The
committee heard testimony from November 15, 1945, to May 31,
1946; its report was submitted on July 20.

The testimony of witnesses before the committee took more than
10,000 pages. The total material considered by the lawmakers,
including direct testimony, exhibits, and the transcripts of previous
investigations, filled thirty-nine volumes. It differed from previous
investigations in that it was public and gave considerable attention to
the Magic messages. Witness testimony and other evidence inevitably
contained contradictions on some points. Commander Safford's dif-

ferences with others concerning the receipt of a Winds execute message were perhaps the most striking. Although the committee did not call every witness who might have shed light on Pearl Harbor (Kimmel felt particularly that Admiral Halsey should have been called), there is no indication of an effort to suppress evidence.[14]

This is not to say the proceedings were all sweetness and light. The postures of individual members reflected their party affiliations. Democrats strove to apportion most of the blame to the Hawaii commanders; Republicans tried to lay the onus on Washington. These divisions, with the important exceptions of Representatives Gearhart and Keefe, were reflected in the committee's final report. Admiral Kimmel was not a detached observer, but he was accurate when he noted that "in the main the views of the [Democratic] administration prevailed."[15]

The report signed by the majority of the joint committee (the Democrats and Representatives Gearhart and Keefe) put the question of responsibility in broad perspective: "The ultimate responsibility for the attack and its results rests upon Japan, an attack that was well planned and skillfully executed." It went on to absolve prewar U.S. policy or diplomacy of any blame for provoking Japan. The majority concluded that army and navy officers in positions of responsibility in both Washington and Hawaii had to share the blame for unpreparedness.[16] Specifically, Kimmel and Short were faulted for:

Not establishing closer interservice liaison and coordination after receiving the war warnings.

Not conducting more thorough reconnaissance measures.

Failing to ready their commands to repel attacks from any source.

Failing to use their personnel and material effectively once the attack was under way.

Not appreciating the significance of intelligence available to them before December 7.

The Washington high command came in for a smaller portion of the blame. It included:

Failure to convey the substance of the bomb plot messages to Hawaii.

Failure to appreciate and notify Hawaii of the significance of the 1:00 P.M. deadline.

"Not being sufficiently alerted on December 6 and 7, 1941, in view of the imminence of war."

Representative Keefe signed the majority report but felt constrained to make some additional points. He was dissatisfied with the amount of information made available to the committee (he particularly wanted more from Secretaries Hull and Stimson); he believed that the mistakes of Kimmel and Short stemmed from Washington's failure to fully alert the Hawaii commanders; and he blamed "secret diplomacy" for keeping Kimmel and Short ignorant of the imminence of war.[17]

Senators Brewster and Ferguson filed a dissenting report in which they burdened Washington with most of the blame. They held:

Washington should have explicitly alerted Kimmel and Short to the possibility of an attack on Hawaii (although Brewster and Ferguson did *not* say that Washington knew or believed the Japanese would attack Hawaii).

The war warnings sent to Hawaii were phrased ambiguously.

The intercepted Japanese messages were not handled efficiently or expeditiously.

The minority report did not, however, absolve the Hawaii commanders completely. They were cited for failing to discharge the fundamental command responsibility of assuring the security of their forces. Brewster and Ferguson also made a left-handed criticism of Kimmel and Short for "errors of judgment" and "mismanagement" by pointing to Washington's "obligation to have a care for competence in the selection of subordinates for positions of responsibility in the armed forces of the United States."[18]

The joint investigating committee, with its divisions reflected in the majority and minority reports, failed to achieve a unanimous judgment on the reasons for U.S. unpreparedness at Pearl Harbor. It did, however, consider the structural weaknesses of the command system that contributed to the disaster. The committee's majority report offered recommendations which contributed to the framing of legislation establishing the postwar U.S. defense system.

The committee recommended unity of command at all military and naval outposts and the centralization of intelligence functions. The majority report held that army/navy rivalry retarded the development of interservice cooperation which might have resulted in more effective preparations for the defense of Hawaii. The report also strongly advocated the establishment of a professional intelligence system. The committee majority advocated a personnel policy which carefully selected officers for intelligence work, assigned them to that duty for extended periods, and, above all, did not jeopardize their prospects for promotion or career advancement. These lessons learned from Pearl Harbor resulted in legislation in the late 1940s establishing the Department of Defense and the Central Intelligence Agency.[19]

The wartime and congressional investigations took place in the context of strong political and interservice partisanship. That factor, although not precluding a degree of objectivity, certainly colored their conclusions. And the spirit of advocacy often marks studies of Pearl Harbor written decades later by professional American historians.

Americans, it seems, still need to pinpoint the factors and individuals responsible (if not "guilty" in a legal or moral sense) for America's unpreparedness at Pearl Harbor. Yet the search for scapegoats fails to yield any single person or group who can be burdened with responsibility. Roosevelt and his advisers were not diabolical conspirators; nor were Kimmel and Short criminally incompetent. Responsibility lay, rather, in a complex of attitudes shared by all the major players. They failed, first of all, to recognize that the Japanese might be willing to make a desperate gamble and risk the key units of their fleet in an attack on Hawaii. That failure went hand in hand with a condescending view of Japan's ability to plan and execute an operation as bold and demanding as Pearl Harbor.

Both Washington and Hawaii were burdened with a bastion mentality which bred false assumptions about Hawaii's "invulnerability" to attack. These assumptions sprang in part from a failure (or refusal) to recognize that the aircraft carrier had replaced the battleship as the decisive weapon at sea. It is no less difficult for admirals than it is for generals to resist the temptation to prepare for the last war.

The fixation on the supposed danger posed by Hawaii's Japanese-American community played a crucial role in shifting the army's psychological focus away from the danger of overseas attack. The constellation of racial attitudes then predominant in the armed forces, the Territory of Hawaii, and American society as a whole led Hawaii's defenders to view the islands' Japanese as an ominous alien presence awaiting the signal to do the emperor's bidding. American citizenship, shared values, and overt declarations of loyalty meant nothing to those held in thrall by the fifth-column menace.

Unpreparedness also flowed from the inchoate organization of U.S. intelligence efforts. American cryptanalysts had penetrated some of the most secret Japanese codes, but their achievements were vitiated by mismanagement. In this instance Washington must bear the primary responsibility. Access to the revelations offered by the penetration of the Purple code lulled Roosevelt and others into the false belief that they had access to Japan's most important plans. Yoshikawa's bomb plot messages, meanwhile, went to Washington to wait their turn in the piles of low-priority code traffic.

None of the American principals—Roosevelt, his cabinet, or the high command—emerge with much credit. But by the same token, they were conscientious and competent. A balanced inquest would have to come to the unexciting but inescapable conclusion that responsibility for U.S. unpreparedness stemmed from institutional and cultural factors, rather than any single individual or clique.

Beyond the issue of responsibility lies the question of *why* Americans seem so obsessed with blaming someone for unreadiness at Pearl Harbor. Since the answer lies in the speculative realm of "national psychology," it is too abstruse a subject for exhaustive exposition here. Yet the question is worth asking, for it adds perspective to our understanding of the place of Pearl Harbor in the American historical imagination.

Perhaps the answer lies in Pearl Harbor's location at the intersection of two crucial planes in the national experience—the chronological and the psychic. Chronologically, the attack is a milestone in America's development as a world power: In the half century since the event the United States has held a central position on the world stage. Psychically, for some, the loss of (debatable) innocence is too deeply disturbing to have occurred without the work of a hidden hand.

The trauma also drew a response from ambivalent American attitudes toward authority. Journalists, politicians, and ordinary citizens expressed a traditional American skepticism toward the boss and the bureaucrat with an instinctive conviction that on December 7 someone in charge must have been incompetent or worse. At the same time, outraged national pride rejected the idea that those in positions of responsibility, the products of the American system, could have been caught so unprepared unless someone in a key position had let down the side.

These attitudes implicitly discount the magnitude of the Japanese success. They betray more than a hint of the denigration of Japanese capability that marked American estimates of that nation in 1941. The survival of that mental posture carries implications—not all of them pleasant—about the ways in which the United States interacts with the world today. Given the increasingly complex, interdependent, and potentially destructive nature of international relations in the late twentieth century, these attitudes are ever more self-defeating and dangerous. This is perhaps the most important lesson we can draw from Pearl Harbor.

CHRONOLOGY

SETTING THE STAGE

1853: "Opening" of Japan.

Late nineteenth century: Growth of sugar industry in Hawaii; importation of Japanese workers.

1894–1895: Sino-Japanese War.

1898: Spanish-American War; U.S. annexation of Hawaii and Philippines.

1904–1905: Russo-Japanese War.

1917: Early military suspicion of loyalty of Hawaii's Japanese.

1920: Japanese and Filipino workers strike on Hawaii sugar plantations; army sides with growers.

1921: Pearl Harbor defense plans predicated on hostile Japanese fifth-column.

1921: Lt. Col. Brooke worries Japanese voters will vote against American interests in Hawaii.

1922: Washington Naval Conference (5–5–2 ratio).

1922: Japanese language schools become an issue in Hawaii; Maj. Hoadley characterizes them as indoctrination centers.

1928: Ryunosuke Kusaka Pearl Harbor air raid study.

1931–1932: Manchurian Incident.

1932: Massie case.

1932: Japanese Army mutiny.

1932: Fleet Problem XIII—*Saratoga* and *Lexington* surprise air raid on Oahu.

1935: Lt. Col. George S. Patton, Jr., prepares Japanese-American hostage plan.

1936: Japanese Army mutinies again.

1936: FDR suggests placing suspect Japanese-Americans in "concentration camps."

1937: Marco Polo Bridge incident.

1939: War erupts in Europe.

1940: Hawaiian Department "counter-propaganda" campaign among Hawaii Japanese.

March 1940: Stark tells Richardson that Pacific Fleet may have to remain in Hawaii indefinitely.

April 2, 1940: Pacific Fleet departs for Hawaii.

June 1940: Germany defeats France, Netherlands.

Sept. 1940: Tripartite Pact.

Oct. 1940: Richardson urges FDR to return Pacific Fleet to West Coast.

Nov. 12, 1940: British air attack on Taranto.

Nov. 22, 1940: Stark suggests anti-torpedo nets for Pearl Harbor; Richardson responds: "neither necessary nor practicable."

Jan. 1941: Bloch and Richardson voice concern to Stark over adequacy of Hawaii defenses.

Jan. 7, 1941: Yamamoto proposes Pearl Harbor plan to Navy Minister Oikawa.

Jan. 27, 1941: Grew cables rumor of Pearl Harbor attack plan.

Feb. 1, 1941: Kimmel assumes command of Pacific Fleet.

Feb. 1, 1941: Chief of Naval Operations (CNO) tells CincPac of Grew rumor but expresses doubt about its reliability.

March 10, 1941: Onishi presents preliminary Pearl Harbor study to Yamamoto.

March 31, 1941: Martin/Bellinger plan foresees possibility of surprise air attack on Oahu.

April 10, 1941: First Air Fleet organized.

April 1941: Turner seizes preparations of estimates from Office of Naval Intelligence (ONI).

Late April 1941: Yamamoto sends Kuroshima to Navy General Staff to argue for Pearl Harbor plan.

April 1941: Takeo Yoshikawa posted to Japanese consulate in Honolulu.

April 1941: Magic compromised by Welles–British–German leak.

Early May 1941: Japanese naval air units begin training for Pearl Harbor attack.

May 15, 1941: Short asks for funds to guard Hawaiian Department installations against fifth-columnists and saboteurs.

June 1941: Honolulu establishes Major Disaster Council.

July 2, 1941: Japanese government makes decision to move south.

July 18, 1941: Short urges no prosecution of unregistered Japanese consular agents in Hawaii.

July 29, 1941: Yamamoto orders sixth (submarine) fleet to prepare for Hawaii operation.

July 1941: Japan occupies southern Indochina.

August 1941: Kuroshima again presents Pearl Harbor plan to Navy General Staff.

Sept. 12–16, 1941: Naval map exercises for Pearl Harbor and southern advance.

Sept. 1941: Kimmel orders Pacific Fleet planes dispersed to reduce air attack vulnerability.

Sept. 24, 1941: Bomb plot message: Yoshikawa directed to divide Pearl Harbor into five areas.

Oct. 3, 1941: Kusaka and Onishi object to Yamamoto about Pearl Harbor plan.

Oct. 1941: U.S. Army and Navy establish joint intelligence committee (no meetings until after Pearl Harbor attack).

Oct. 17, 1941: Stark tells Kimmel he expects no Japanese attack on United States.

Oct. 18, 1941: Kuroshima tells Navy General Staff that Pearl Harbor plan requires use of all six heavy carriers and that Yamamoto will resign if the plan is rejected—Navy General Staff acquiesces, accepts Yamamoto's demands.

Early Nov. 1941: First Air Fleet assembles for rehearsal.

Nov. 1, 1941: Routine change in Japanese Navy codes.

Nov. 1, 1941: *Taiyo Maru,* with Japanese Navy staff officers aboard, docks in Honolulu.

Nov. 5, 1941: Japanese Foreign Ministry sets Nov. 25 deadline for success of negotiations.

Nov. 15, 1941: Tokyo directs Yoshikawa to report at least twice weekly.

Nov. 17, 1941: First Air Fleet officer pilots briefed on Pearl Harbor plan.

Nov. 19, 1941: Winds message sets up the contingency communications.

Nov. 22, 1941: Foreign Ministry extends negotiation deadline to Nov. 29.

Nov. 23, 1941: Nagumo issues final orders for Pearl Harbor attack to First Air Fleet.

Nov. 26, 1941: First Air Fleet sails from Etorofu.

Nov. 27, 1941: Hawaiian Department warned by Washington that negotiations have ceased, hostilities imminent, be prepared for subversive activity; War Department G-2 sends Hawaiian Department G-2 a similar warning cable.

Nov. 27, 1941: CNO "war warning" to Kimmel.

Nov. 28, 1941: Arnold cables sabotage warning to Martin.

Nov. 28, 1941: Short tells War Department that Hawaiian Department is alerted against sabotage.

Nov. 28, 1941: *Enterprise* task force under Halsey departs Pearl Harbor to deliver fighters to Wake.

Nov. 29, 1941: Yoshikawa directed to report even if no ship movements occur.

Dec. 1, 1941: Unexpected change in Japanese Navy radio codes.

Dec. 1, 1941: ONI mistakenly places Japanese carriers in home waters.

Dec. 1, 1941: Kimmel jokes to Layton about Japanese carriers rounding Diamond Head.

Dec. 2, 1941: Yoshikawa ordered to report daily.

Dec. 2, 1941: "Climb Mt. Niitaka" signal to First Air Fleet to proceed with Pearl Harbor attack plan.

Dec. 4, 1941: First Air Fleet hits heavy weather.

Dec. 5, 1941: First Air Fleet encounters *Uritsky*.

Dec. 5, 1941: Gen. Miles (G-2) puzzles over Japan's strategic options.

Dec. 6, 1941: Mori call to Tokyo hints at Japanese interest in military preparedness in Hawaii.

Dec. 6, 1941: Kaneohe Naval Air Station (NAS) personnel lectured on threat of Japanese fifth-column in Hawaii.

Dec. 6, 1941: First Air Fleet final refueling before attack; *Akagi* hoists Z flag.

Dec. 6, 1941: Report from *I-72* to First Air Fleet—no U.S. naval units at Lahaina.

Dec. 6, 1941: Japanese Foreign Ministry begins transmission of fourteen-part message breaking off negotiations with United States; Nomura and Kurusu instructed to deliver the message to Hull at 1300 EST—thirty minutes before Pearl Harbor attack begins.

DECEMBER 7, 1941 (all times approximate)

0357: *Condor* notifies *Ward* of periscope sighting off Pearl Harbor.

0530 HST/1100 EST: Marshall arrives at his office.

0530: *Tone* and *Chikuma* launch scout planes.

0600: First Air Fleet launches first wave.

0615: Halsey launches eighteen dive bombers for Ford Island.

0630: First Air Fleet launches battleship and cruiser scout planes to cover approaches to the fleet.

0630: *Ward* sights and attacks submarine off Pearl Harbor.

0630 HST/1200 EST: Marshall sends warning message to Short re ultimatum time.

0700: First Air Fleet launches wave.

0700: *Cynthia Olson* sunk with all hands by Japanese sub between Seattle and Honolulu.

0700: Lockhard and Elliot spot first wave on radar.

0700: *Ward* notifies Pearl Harbor of sub sinking.

0720: Lockhard and Elliot report blip to Lt. Tyler.

0730 HST/1300 EST: Kurusu and Nomura scheduled to deliver ultimatum to Hull.

0733: Marshall's message received by RCA in Honolulu.

0735: *Chikuma* scout plane radios that Pearl Harbor contains battleships but no carriers.

0740: Fuchida crosses northern shoreline of Oahu.

0748: Attack on Kaneohe begins.

0749: Fuchida signals "To To To" for attack to begin on Pearl Harbor.

0753: Fuchida signals "Tora Tora Tora" for success in achieving surprise.

0755: Air attack on Pearl Harbor, Hickam, Ewa, Wheeler, Schofield Barracks, and Fort Kamehameha begins.

0800 HST/1330 EST: Knox, Stark, and Turner in meeting; receive news of Pearl Harbor attack.

0800: Pearl Harbor Naval Hospital releases patients in brig and locked wards.

0801: *Raleigh* antiaircraft begins firing.

0805: *Oklahoma* capsizes.

0805: Tug *Nokomis* under way for Battleship Row.

0808: Capt. Bennion wounded aboard *West Virginia*.

0810: Power goes out on *California*.

0810: *Arizona* explodes.

0813: Fort Kamehameha antiaircraft fire commences.

0815: Second group of planes attacks Kaneohe.

0815: Maj. Landon lands B-17 at Hickam during attack.

0818: *Helm* first ship to clear harbor.

0820: Taylor and Welsh airborne from Haleiwa.

0820: Large numbers of casualties begin arriving at Pearl Harbor Navy Yard dispensary.

0820: Sakamaki fouled up on Pearl Harbor reef; fired at by *Helm*.

0830: Lt. Saltzman and Sgt. Klatt down Val with BAR's.

0830 HST/1400 EST: Kurusu and Nomura arrive at Hull's office; receive scathing reception.

0830: Strafing pass at Haleiwa.

0830: Lone Japanese plane strafes Bellows.

0835: Second attack on Ewa.

0840: *Monaghan* sinks minisub in Pearl Harbor.

0842: *Neosho* finishes discharging aviation gas; backs away from Ford Island across Pearl Harbor channel.

0842: *YG 17* casts off from *Nevada*.

0850: Lts. Rogers, Brown, Dains, Sanders, Shifflet, Thacker, and Rasmussen airborne; Lt. Stirling "steals" Lt. Norris's plane.

0850: *Monaghan* rams midget sub in Pearl Harbor.

0850: *Nevada* under way.

0900: *YG 21* moors at Merry Point to pick up firefighters for Ford Island.

0900: Six *Enterprise* SBD's land at Ewa; advised to take off immediately.

0900: Air attack begins on *Pennsylvania*, *Cassin*, and *Downes*.

0900: Second strafing attack on Bellows.

0900: Third attack on Kaneohe; Lt. Iida crash-dives into the base.

0900: Taylor and Welsh take off again from Wheeler after replenishing ammunition.

0900: *Shaw* and Floating Drydock Two targeted by Japanese bombers.

0900: Fuqua orders *Arizona* abandoned.

0905: Lt. Suzuki crash-dives into *Curtiss*.

0907: *Nevada* attacked in Pearl Harbor channel narrows.

0907: *Dale* clears Pearl Harbor.

0910: *Blue* clears Pearl Harbor under command of Ens. Asher.

0910: *Nevada* ordered aground at Hospital Point.

0910: *Raleigh* attacked again; heavily damaged by bomb.

0912: *Curtiss* attacked again by dive bombers.

0915: *YG 21* departs from Merry Point for Ford Island with firefighters aboard.

0920: Yard personnel begin flooding Drydock One.

0920: Near miss on *Pyro* at West Loch.

0920: Lt. Moore airborne from Wheeler.

0925: USS *Honolulu* damaged by bomb explosion on dock.

0930: Dains and Welch sortie from Haleiwa.

0931: *St. Louis* under way.

0936: *Curtiss* fires brought under control.

0942: *YG 17* proceeds to *West Virginia* to fight fires.

0945: Second wave heads back to carriers; air attack breaks off.

0950: CincPac informs Task Force Eight: Japanese 30 miles southwest of Barbers Point.

0950: *Vestal* grounded in Aiea Bay.

1000: First wave raiders back on carriers.

1004: *St. Louis* fires at midget sub outside Pearl Harbor entrance.

1015: PBY's directed to search north of Oahu.

1018: CincPac signals units at sea there is "some indication" Japanese northwest of Oahu.

1020: *Enterprise* dispatches SBD's to search off Barbers Point.

1030: First Air Fleet breaks radio silence to signal success to Tokyo; intercepted by Americans but bearing uncertain.

1046: CincPac to Task Force Eight: Japanese carriers off Barbers Point.

1100: Charles Harkins wounded by falling antiaircraft at Pier 31A, Honolulu Harbor.

1105: Kimmel organizes Task Force One under Rear Adm. Draemel; composed of surface ships which escaped Pearl Harbor.

1115: Lt. Reeves' Seagulls launched from *Northampton*.

1127: Four A-20s dispatched from Hickam to search off Barbers Point.

1140: Reeves' Seagulls attacked by Zero.

1140: Two B-17s dispatched from Hickam to search off Barbers Point.

1200: Chart showing Japanese carrier positions recovered from Zero at Fort Kamehameha.

1200: Short visits Poindexter, confers by phone with FDR—martial law declared.

1200: *Minneapolis* directed to search south of Oahu for Japanese.

1208: CincPac signals that it has no confirmed location of Japanese positions; four SBD's dispatched to search northeast of Oahu.

1232: CincPac to all ships: Japanese transports off Barbers Point.

1300: Three A-20s dispatched to search north of Oahu.

1300: Last planes recovered aboard Japanese carriers.

1330: Two B-18s dispatched to search north of Oahu.

1315: Nagumo orders attack to break off.

1332: CincPac signals that *Akagi* and other units are south of Oahu.

1345: Nine SBD's launched to search southwest of Task Force Eight.

1435: CincPac notifies fleet units at sea Japanese ships believed to be north *and* south of Oahu.

1642: Bombers and fighters launched from *Enterprise* on false report of Japanese carriers.

2100: Four of six *Enterprise* Wildcats downed by friendly fire.

THE AFTERMATH

Dec. 8, 1941: Aldrich and ten other *Oklahoma* sailors rescued from bottom of hull.

Dec. 8, 1941: FDR addresses Congress; war declared.

Dec. 9, 1941: Yamamoto orders staff to begin planning Hawaii invasion.

Dec. 11, 1941: *Lahaina* sunk by Japanese sub.

Dec. 11, 1941: Hitler declares war on United States.

Dec. 11–12, 1941: Navy Secretary Frank Knox visits Hawaii—fifth-column remark.

Dec. 14, 1941: *Heough* sunk near Kauai.

Dec. 15, 1941: Sub shells Kahului.

Dec. 17, 1941: *I-7* Glen reconnoiters Pearl Harbor.

Dec. 18, 1941: Japanese sub sinks *Prusa*.

Dec. 19, 1941: FDR cabinet decision to intern Hawaii Japanese-Americans; Emmons disagrees.

Dec. 30–31, 1941: Subs shell Kahului, Hilo, and Nawiliwili.

Jan. 6–7, 1942: *I-19* Glen scouts Pearl Harbor.

Jan. 12, 1942: *I-6* damages *Saratoga* with torpedo.

Jan. 23, 1942: Hawaii Territorial Guard, composed mostly of Japanese-Americans, disbanded.

Jan. 23, 1942: *I-72* sinks *Neches*.

Jan. 28, 1942: *Royal T. Frank* sunk in Alenuihaha channel.

Feb. 4, 1942: Emmons argues again against internment of Japanese-Americans.

Late Feb. 1942: *I-9* Glen scouts Pearl Harbor for operation K.

March 4, 1942: Operation K—Emilies bomb Hawaii.

March 1942: Twenty-seventh Division arrives Kauai—first major reinforcement of Hawaii garrison.

April 6, 1942: Emmons proposes formation of a Japanese-American combat unit.

April 18, 1942: Doolittle raids Tokyo.

May 2, 1942: War Department orders all Japanese-Americans removed from combat units.

May 28, 1942: War Department reverses earlier order and authorizes creation of Japanese-American infantry unit.

June 4-6, 1942: Battle of Midway; victory lifts invasion threat to Hawaii.

Oct. 1944: Martial law lifted in Hawaii.

APPENDIX A

A Note on Sources and Revisionism

The work of the congressional joint committee did not definitively fix responsibility for U.S. unpreparedness, but it did provide historians with a splendid documentary base for studying the Pearl Harbor attack. The transcripts of the committee's proceedings contain some close and none too gentle probing of Kimmel, Short, and other important figures. The report contains as exhibits hundreds of critical documents, including communications between Washington and the Hawaii commanders, the Magic intercepts, intelligence estimates, and operational plans. Also appended as exhibits are the reports of Secretary Knox, the Roberts Commission, the navy court of inquiry, the Army Pearl Harbor Board, and the investigations conducted by Hart, Hewitt, Carter, and Clarke. Prospective users of these transcripts and exhibits should be warned, however, that the paucity of indexing requires a substantial investment of time and patience.

The National Archives is another rich source of material. Of particular interest here are the records of the Hawaiian Department in Record Group 338, the Pacific Fleet in Record Group 313, and the Marine Corps in Record Group 127. The records of the National Security Agency (which holds material relating to Magic) contain a large number of decrypted messages and other material important to an understanding of the codebreaking operations. These are stored in Record Group. 457.

The history offices of the individual U.S. armed services also contain valuable resources. Most important for studying the Pearl Harbor attack is the Naval Historical Center's Operational Archives. On file here are the action reports and damage reports of the Pacific Fleet,

shore bases, and individual vessels. The Operational Archives also
house a great deal of material on the salvage operations.

The principal center for air force history is located at Maxwell Air
Force Base, Alabama, but the Office of Air Force History facility at
Bolling Air Force Base in Washington, D.C., has microfilmed copies
of most air force records pertaining to the Pearl Harbor attack. These
include reports of individual squadrons and airfields. The army's
Center of Military History has some interesting in-house historical
studies, but archival material relating to the Pearl Harbor attack has
been turned over to the National Archives. The archives section of
the Marine Corps Historical Center controls access to Marine Corps
records, but they are housed at the Federal Record Center at
Suitland, Maryland.

Firsthand accounts of the Pearl Harbor attack are sometimes of
questionable reliability. The shock, stress, and chaos which prevailed
understandably caused witnesses to "see" events that never happened or to be confused about the timing. This is particularly true of
accounts written or recorded well after the event; witnesses often
incorporate as memories details they learned from other survivors or
even secondary accounts. Oral history interviews done years, even
decades, after the event are especially susceptible to this sort of distor-
tion.

Bearing in mind these caveats about the imperfection of human
memory, eyewitness accounts form an important source of information about the Pearl Harbor attack. They provide the human detail so
often missing from official reports and can often clarify points left
unclear in contemporary documentary sources. The transcript of the
Roberts Commission investigation contains the testimony of witnesses from the ranks who left accounts of their personal experiences
for posterity. Appended to ships' action reports are many survivors'
statements. Some of these statements illustrate the dangers of uncriti-
cal acceptance of eyewitness reports. More than one affiant stated that
a Japanese bomb went down *Arizona*'s stack, but inspection by salvage divers led to the conclusion that the armor grating in the uptake
was still intact.[1]

Oral history interviews can be another valuable source, provided
the interviewer has a solid grasp of the events being discussed and can
probe and question the subject on doubtful statements. The Columbia University and U.S. Naval Institute oral history programs include

1. USS *Arizona* Loss File.

transcripts of interviews with Roosevelt administration figures and senior officers which bear on the Pearl Harbor attack. The air force and Marine Corps history offices conduct oral history programs which include interviews with Pearl Harbor attack survivors. North Texas State University's oral history program has on file transcripts of interviews with more than 200 survivors of the attack. The USS *Arizona* Memorial oral history program also has survivor interviews and will ultimately include interviews with civilian witnesses bearing on December 7 and the immediate post-attack period.

One of the great handicaps in researching the Pearl Harbor attack from the Japanese perspective is a dearth of contemporary documentary sources. The destruction wrought by bombing raids in World War II destroyed many records. Others were lost or deliberately destroyed in the chaos following the surrender. Much of what remains of Japan's World War II records is held in the National Diet Library or by the National Defense College War History Office.

While most of the nearly 100,000 U.S. servicemen on Oahu on December 7, 1941, survived the war, comparatively few Japanese veterans of the attack were still alive in 1945. Of the Japanese ships which participated in the Hawaii operation, all but one destroyer, one tanker, and seven submarines were sunk by the U.S. Navy. Most of Japan's carrier pilots were killed at Midway and subsequent battles. This heavy casualty rate left few surviving Japanese witnesses to the Pearl Harbor attack.

A few of the Japanese principals did survive, however, and wrote accounts of their experiences after the war. Most notable among these are *Shinjuwan Sakusen no Shinso,* by Mitsuo Fuchida; *Shinjuwan Sakusen Kaikoroku,* by Minoru Genda; *Rengo Kantai,* by Ryunosuke Kusaka; and *Shikan: Shinjuwan Kogeki,* by Shigeru Fukudome. These works have not been translated into English, but Fuchida's book, *Midway: The Battle that Doomed Japan,* includes some material on Pearl Harbor. The experiences of Kazuo Sakamaki, the only midget submarine survivor, were published in English under the title *I Attacked Pearl Harbor.* Takeo Yoshikawa, the Japanese Navy's spy in Honolulu, recounted his work in a *U.S. Naval Institute Proceedings* article, "Top Secret Assignment."

Interrogations conducted in connection with the International Military Tribunal for the Far East contain material related to the Pearl Harbor attack. Interrogees ranged from Admiral Nagano to seamen. Japanese officers were also questioned by representatives of the U.S. Strategic Bombing Survey in wide-ranging sessions which elicited much valuable information about Pearl Harbor. The U.S. occupation forces published the Japanese Monograph series, in which former Japanese officers recorded, mostly from memory, the major Japanese operations. Monograph 102 on submarine operations and Monograph 97 on Japanese planning for Pearl Harbor are important sources. The Japanese Self-Defense Agency's War History Office has undertaken the publication of a massive series of works on Japan's World War II military history. *Hawai Sakusen,* the volume on the Pearl Harbor attack, is an invaluable source for the Japanese perspective on the operation.

Among American historians there are conflicting viewpoints on the background to Pearl Harbor. The anger and shock generated by the attack helped shape a widely accepted interpretation of the raid as an example of unprovoked aggression. As the dissenting minority report of the congressional joint committee indicates, this interpretation was not shared by all Americans. Some viewed U.S. prewar foreign policy as a goal by which Japan was driven, either deliberately or unintentionally, to attack the United States. In his *President Roosevelt and the Coming of the War, 1941,* published in 1948, historian Charles Beard challenged the prevailing view. Beard argued that the primary goal of President Roosevelt's diplomacy was to prevent the defeat of Great Britain by drawing the United States into war against the Axis powers. Herbert Feis, former U.S. diplomat and author of *The Road to Pearl Harbor,* and others weighed in with opposing views. They argued that it was the aggressive expansionist policies of Japan which brought about war in the Pacific.

The arguments over the role of U.S. policy in bringing the United States into the war broadened into the "revisionist" school of history. The revisionists not only criticized Roosevelt's diplomacy but held that the onus of responsibility for unpreparedness at Pearl Harbor lay at the Washington command level, not with Kimmel and Short. Some revisionists have gone further and maintain that Washington had advance knowledge of Japanese intentions to attack Pearl Harbor but deliberately withheld the information from the Hawaii commanders. The motive, they argue, was to engineer an incident that would plunge the United States into the war in circumstances which would sweep away domestic opposition to the Roosevelt administration's interventionist policies.

Not all revisionists accept the theory that Roosevelt and his advisers had foreknowledge of Japanese intentions and suppressed a warning to Hawaii. Most attribute the miscues in Washington to incompetence rather than malice. In discussing the mishandling of the bomb plot messages, for example, revisionist historian Bruce Bartlett believes that no one in a position to authorize or suppress a warning message to Pearl Harbor ever saw the messages.[2]

Of the revisionists who saw evidence of a conspiracy in the pattern of Washington's mishandling of information before the attack, none has offered conclusive evidence. Kimmel's defender and former subordinate, Rear Admiral Robert Theobald, wrote that the failure to provide CincPac with the means to decode the Purple messages was "a deliberate act . . . part of a definite plan" to ensure the success of a Japanese surprise attack. Harry Elmer Barnes, perhaps the most firmly convinced of the revisionists, declared: "Steps were taken to insure that the Hawaiian commanders . . . would not be forewarned" of the impending attack. Theobald offers no supporting evidence for his charge, and Barnes, for his part, admits that "there is no definitive documentary evidence which has thus far [1972] been revealed and fully *proves* that Roosevelt had been informed" of the Japanese plans.[3]

Infamy, by John Toland, is the most recent work to assert that President Roosevelt had foreknowledge of the attack and withheld warnings to Kimmel and Short. Unlike earlier writings in this vein, Toland presents evidence to support the thesis. He claims that radio messages from Nagumo's task force were intercepted as the carriers approached Hawaii. These intercepts, Toland says, were correctly interpreted by U.S. naval intelligence to track the First Air Fleet's movements across the North Pacific.

The core of Toland's evidence is a series of interviews with a former U.S. Navy radio technician (called by Toland "Seaman Z," actually James Ogg), the diary of Leslie Grogan, a *Lurline* radio operator, and the diary of and an interview with the Dutch naval attaché in Washington. The *Lurline* operator detected what he believed to be Japanese signals coming from an area north and west of Hawaii. The U.S. Navy radio technician, working in San Francisco, told Toland he plotted strange radio signals emanating from the same area. The diary of

---

2. Bruce Bartlett, *Cover-Up: The Politics of Pearl Harbor, 1941–1946* (New Rochelle, N.Y.: Arlington House, 1978), p. 55.

3. Robert Theobald, *The Final Secret of Pearl Harbor: The Washington Contribution to the Japanese Attack* (Old Greenwich, Conn.: Devin-Adair, 1954), pp. 38–39; Harry Elmer Barnes, *Pearl Harbor After a Quarter of a Century* (New York: Arno Press, 1972), pp. 20, 83.

the Dutch naval attaché, Captain Johan Ranneft, recorded a December 2 visit to the Office of Naval Intelligence. Toland says Ranneft was told there by U.S. Navy officers that a Japanese carrier force was approaching Hawaii.[4]

A number of questions arise from Toland's claims. First, the continuing insistence of the Japanese that they made no radio transmissions en route presents a major stumbling block. Even if Grogan and Ogg detected signals as they said, the Japanese claims of radio silence raise grave doubts as to whether they were signals from the First Air Fleet. Robert Haslach, a Dutch historian specializing in intelligence matters, claims that the Ranneft diary entry used by Toland "was compiled and edited at some considerable time after the events recorded." The most serious problem with Toland's work is that even if his account of the experiences of Grogan, Ogg, and Ranneft is accepted, Toland presents no supporting evidence for his statement that Roosevelt himself had foreknowledge of the attack.[5]

There remain, nonetheless, unanswered questions about America's allies. Nagumo's encounter with the Soviet freighter Uritsky, which was allowed to proceed unmolested, raises the distinct possibility that Stalin may have known of the composition, course, and likely target of the task force. And Eric Nave, a senior British cryptographer, claims in his unpublished memoirs that his group had broken the Japanese naval code, deduced the plan for the First Air Fleet, and reported it to senior government officials who presumably informed Churchill. Did Stalin and Churchill in fact know in advance of the raid? And if so, did they withhold warning from Roosevelt? Eager as they were to draw the United States into the war as a full-fledged combatant, it is conceivable that either or both would have chosen the course of realpolitik, but the question is unanswerable on the basis of the evidence now available.

Most historians reject the extreme revisionist position that Roosevelt and his advisers knew of the attack in advance and agree with Gordon Prange, who labeled the thesis a "tissue of unsupported assumptions and assertions."[6] This is not to say, however, that the entire burden of responsibility rests on the shoulders of the U.S. com-

---

4. John Toland, *Infamy: Pearl Harbor and Its Aftermath* (Garden City, N.Y.: Doubleday, 1982), pp. 278–283.

5. Letter Robert Haslach to Thomas K. Kimmel, November 18, 1983, copy in the author's files provided by Kimmel; Toland, *Infamy*, p. 318.

6. Prange, *At Dawn We Slept*, p. 850.

manders in Hawaii. It is not necessary to be of the "Roosevelt knew" school to recognize that there were serious shortcomings in the actions of the Washington echelon. Among those which come to mind are the failure to correct Short's action placing his command on sabotage alert, the negligent handling of the bomb plot messages, and the sloppy transmission of Marshall's 1:00 warning message. Kimmel and Short were judged harshly by the Roberts Commission, but that judgment was modified considerably by subsequent investigations and historical research.

APPENDIX B

Japanese Ships in the Pearl Harbor Attack

FIRST AIR FLEET

Aircraft Carriers
First Carrier Division
   Akagi (First Air Fleet flagship)
   Kaga
Second Carrier Division
   Hiryu
   Soryu
Fifth Carrier Division
   Shokaku
   Zuikaku

Battleships
Hiei
Kirishima

Heavy Cruisers
Chikuma
Tone

Light Cruiser
Abukuma

Destroyers
Akigumo
Arare
Hamakaze
Isokaze
Kagero
Kasumi
Shiranui
Tanizake
Urakaze

Submarines
I-19
I-21
I-23

Tankers
Kenyo Maru
Kokuyo Maru
Kyokuto Maru
Nihon Maru
Shinkoku Maru
Toei Maru
Toho Maru

SIXTH FLEET (SUBMARINES)

I-1	I-8	I-22*	I-72
I-2	I-9	I-24*	I-73
I-3	I-15	I-25	I-74
I-4	I-16*	I-68	I-75
I-5	I-17	I-69	
I-6	I-18*	I-70	
I-7	I-20*	I-71	

---

*Carried a midget submarine.

APPENDIX C

U.S. Navy Vessels In or Near Pearl Harbor on

December 7, 1941

Allen (DD 66)
Alwyn (DD 355)
Antares (AKS 3)
Argonne (AG 31)
Arizona (BB 39)
Ash (AN 7)
Avocet (AVP 4)
Bagley (DD 386)
Blue (DD 387)
Bobolink (AM 20)
Breese (DM 18)
Cachalot (SS 170)
California (BB 44)
Case (DD 370)
Cassin (DD 372)
Castor (AKS 1)
Chew (DD 106)
Cinchona (YN 7)
Cockatoo (AMC 8)
Condor (AMC 14)
Conyngham (DD 371)
Crossbill (AMC 9)
Cummings (DD 365)
Curtiss (AV 4)

Dale (DD 353)
Detroit (CL 8)
Dewey (DD 349)
Dobbin (AD 3)
Dolphin (SS 169)
Downes (DD 375)
Farragut (DD 348)
Gamble (DM 23)
Grebe (AM 43)
Helena (CL 50)
Helm (DD 388)
Henley (DD 391)
Honolulu (CL 48)
Hulbert (AVD 6)
Hull (DD 350)
Jarvis (DD 393)
Keosanqua (AT 38)
LG 17
MacDonough (DD 351)
Maryland (BB 46)
McFarland (DD 237)
Medusa (AR 1)
Monaghan (DD 354)
Montgomery (DM 17)

Mugford (DD 389)
Narwhal (SS 167)
Navajo (AT 64)
Neosho (AO 23)
Nevada (BB 36)
New Orleans (CA 32)
Oglala (CM 4)
Oklahoma (BB 37)
Ontario (AT 13)
Patterson (DD 392)
Pelias (AS 14)
Pennsylvania (BB 38)
Perry (DMS 17)
Phelps (DD 360)
Phoenix (CL 46)
Preble (DM 20)
Pruitt (DM 22)
Pyro (AE 1)
Rail (AM 26)
Raleigh (CL 7)
Ralph Talbot (DD 390)
Ramsey (DM 16)
Reed (DD 369)
Reedbird (AMC 30)
Rigel (AVD 11)
Sacramento (PGS 19)
San Francisco (CA 38)
Schley (DD 103)
Selfridge (DD 357)
Shaw (DD 373)
Sicard (DM 21)
Solace (AH 5)
Sotoyomo (YT 9)
St. Louis (CL 49)
Sumner (AG 32)
Sunnadin (AT 28)
Swan (AVP 7)
Tangier (AV 8)

Tautog (SS 199)
Tennessee (BB 43)
Tern (AM 31)
Thornton (AVD 11)
Tracy (DM 19)
Trever (DMS 17)
Tucker (DD 374)
Turkey (AM 13)
Utah (AG 4)
Vestal (AR 4)
Viero (AM 52)
Ward (DD 139)
Wasmuth (DMS 15)
West Virginia (BB 48)
Whitney (AD 4)
Widgeon (ARS 1)
Worden (DD 352)
YC 417
YDD 68
YFD 2
YG 15
YMT 15
YN 47
YN 53
YNG 17
YO 30
YO 43
YR 20
YR 22
YT 119
YT 129
YT 130
YT 146
YT 152
YT 153
YTT 3
Zane (DMS 14)

APPENDIX D

Losses in the Pearl Harbor Attack

PERSONNEL

United States

Service	Dead	Wounded
Navy	2,008	710
Marine	109	69
Army	218	364
Civilian	68	35
Total	2,403	1,178

Japan

Service	Dead	Prisoner
Airmen	55	0
I-70 (approx.)	65	0
Midget sub crewmen	9	1
Total (approx.)	129	1

Note: There are no reliable figures for Japanese wounded.

SHIPS

United States
Total loss: *Arizona, Oklahoma, Utah*

Serious damage: *California, Nevada, West Virginia, Helena, Raleigh, Cassin, Downes, Shaw, Curtiss, Vestal, Oglala, Sotoyomo, YFD 2*

Moderate or light damage: *Maryland, Tennessee, Pennsylvania, Honolulu, Helm*

Japan
Lost: *I-70* and five midget submarines

AIRCRAFT DESTROYED

United States
Army: 64 (including one B-17 arriving from California during attack)

Navy: 98 (including 11 *Enterprise* planes)

Total: 162

Source: Figures given by army and navy to congressional committee investigating Pearl Harbor attack.

Japan	
Torpedo bombers	5
Dive bombers	15
Fighters	9
Total	29

APPENDIX E

Navy War Warning on November 27, 1941

November 27, 1941
From: Chief of Naval Operations
Action: CINCAF, CINCPAC
Info: CINCLANT, SPENAVO

This dispatch is to be considered a war warning. Negotiations with Japan looking toward stabilization of conditions in the Pacific have ceased and an aggressive move by Japan is expected within the next few days. The number and equipment of Japanese troops and the organization of naval task forces indicates an amphibious expedition against either the Philippines Thai or Kra Peninsula or possibly Borneo. Execute an appropriate defensive deployment preparatory to carrying out the tasks assigned in WPL46. Inform district and army authorities. A similar warning is being sent by War Department. Spenavo inform British. Continental districts Guam Samoa directed to take appropriate measures against sabotage.
Copy to WPD, War Dept.[1]

---

1. *PHA* 14:1406.

APPENDIX F

Army War Warnings on November 27 and December 7, 1941, and Short's Reply

November 27, 1941

Commanding General,
Hawaiian Department, Fort Shafter, T.H.
NO. 472

Negotiations with Japan appear to be terminated to all practical purposes with only the barest possibilities that the Japanese Government might come back and offer to continue. Japanese future action unpredictable but hostile action possible at any moment. If hostilities cannot, repeat cannot, be avoided the United States desires that Japan commit the first overt act. This policy should not, repeat not, be construed as restricting you to a course of action that might jeopardize your defense. Prior to hostile Japanese action you are directed to undertake such reconnaissance and other measures as you deem necessary but these measures should be carried out so as not, repeat not, to alarm civil population or disclose intent. Report measures taken. Should hostilities occur you will carry out the tasks assigned in Rainbow Five so far as they pertain to Japan. Limit dissemination of this highly secret information to minimum essential officers.
Marshall

Headquarters Hawaiian Department
Fort Shafter, T.H.

November 27, 1941

War Department
Washington DC

Reurad four seven two twentyseventh report department alerted to prevent sabotage. Liaison with navy.
Short

Hawn Dept Ft. Shafter, T.H.

529 7th Japanese are presenting at one pm Eastern Standard Time today what amounts to an ultimatum also they are under orders to destroy their code machine immediately. Just what significance the hour set may have we do not know but be on alert accordingly. Inform naval authorities of this communication.
Marshall[1]

---

1. *PHA* 14:1334, 18:3174–3175, 3177.

APPENDIX G

President Roosevelt's Address to Congress
on December 8, 1941

Yesterday, December 7, 1941—a date which will live in infamy—the United States of America was suddenly and deliberately attacked by naval and air forces of the Empire of Japan.

The United States was at peace with that Nation and, at the solicitation of Japan, was still in conversation with its Government and its Emperor looking toward the maintenance of peace in the Pacific. Indeed, one hour after Japanese air squadrons had commenced bombing in Oahu, the Japanese Ambassador to the United States and his colleague delivered to the Secretary of State a formal reply to a recent American message. While this reply stated that it seemed useless to continue the existing diplomatic negotiations, it contained no threat or hint of war or armed attack.

It will be recorded that the distance of Hawaii from Japan makes it obvious that the attack was deliberately planned many days or even weeks ago. During the intervening time the Japanese Government has deliberately sought to deceive the United States by false statements and expressions of hope for continued peace.

The attack yesterday on the Hawaiian Islands has caused severe damage to American naval and military forces. Very many American lives have been lost. In addition American ships have been reported torpedoed on the high seas between San Francisco and Honolulu.

Yesterday the Japanese Government also launched an attack against Malaya.

Last night Japanese forces attacked Hong Kong.

Last night Japanese forces attacked Guam.

Last night Japanese forces attacked Wake Island.

This morning the Japanese attacked Midway Island.

Japan has, therefore, undertaken a surprise offensive extending throughout the Pacific area. The facts of yesterday speak for themselves. The people of the United States have already formed their opinions and well understand the implications to the very life and safety of our Nation.

As Commander-in-Chief of the Army and Navy I have directed that all measures be taken for our defense.

Always will we remember the character of the onslaught against us.

No matter how long it may take us to overcome this premeditated invasion, the American people in their righteous might will win through to absolute victory.

I believe I interpret the will of the Congress and of the people when I assert that we will not only defend ourselves to the uttermost but will make very certain that this form of treachery shall never endanger us again.

Hostilities exist. There is no blinking at the fact that our people, our territory, and our interests are in grave danger.

With confidence in our armed forces—with the unbounded determination of our people—we will gain the inevitable triumph—so help us God.

I ask that Congress declare that since the unprovoked and dastardly attack by Japan on Sunday, December seventh, a state of war has existed between the United States and the Japanese Empire.[1]

---

1. *Congressional Record* 87:95045 (December 8, 1941).

NOTES

CHAPTER 1. CHALLENGE AND RESPONSE

1. Paul S. Dull, *A Battle History of the Imperial Japanese Navy (1941-1945)* (Annapolis: U.S. Naval Institute Press, 1978), p. 5.

2. Hiroyuki Agawa, *The Reluctant Admiral: Yamamoto and the Imperial Navy* (Tokyo: Kodansha International, 1983), p. 226; Gordon W. Prange, with Donald M. Goldstein and Katherine V. Dillon, *At Dawn We Slept: The Untold Story of Pearl Harbor* (New York: McGraw-Hill, 1981), p. 169.

3. John Costello, *The Pacific War* (New York: Rawson, Wade, 1981), p. 652.

4. James O. Richardson, as told to George C. Dyer, *On the Treadmill to Pearl Harbor: The Memoirs of Admiral James O. Richardson, USN (Retired)* (Washington: Department of the Navy, Naval History Division, 1973), p. 307.

5. U.S. Congress, *Hearings Before the Joint Committee on the Investigation of the Pearl Harbor Attack*, 39 parts, 79th Cong., 1st sess., 1946 (hereafter *PHA*), 1:259–261, 2:463, 616–618.

6. *PHA* 1:263–265.

7. *PHA* 14:973–975.

8. Omar Titus Pfeiffer interview, Marine Corps Oral History Collection, U.S. Marine Corps Historical Center, Washington.

9. Sadao Asada, "The Japanese Navy and the United States," in *Pearl Harbor as History: Japanese-American Relations, 1931–1941*, ed. Dorothy Borg, Shumpei Okamoto, and Dale K. A. Finlayson (New York: Columbia University Press, 1973), pp. 235–236.

10. Shigeru Fukudome, "Hawaii Operation," *U.S. Naval Institute Proceedings* 81 (December 1955), p. 1317.

11. Prange, *At Dawn We Slept*, p. 21; Dull, *Battle History*, p. 7.

12. John Dean Potter, *Yamamoto: The Man Who Menaced America* (New York: Viking, 1968), p. 43.

13. "Remarks by Rear Admiral Harris Laning, U.S. Navy," February 19, 1932, Records of the Fourteenth Naval District, Commandant's Classified Correspondence, 1912–1941, National Archives, Pacific-Sierra Region.

14. Agawa, *Reluctant Admiral*, p. 193.

15. Prange, *At Dawn We Slept*, p. 16; Agawa, *Reluctant Admiral*, p. 219.

16. Yamamoto's often quoted statement that Japan had "awakened a sleeping tiger" with the attack was made *after* the event, when the consequences were obvious

to all. See Fukudome, "Hawaii Operation," p. 1318; *PHA* 1:178; Prange, *At Dawn We Slept*, pp. 18–19; Agawa, *Reluctant Admiral*, pp. 221, 229.

17. Prange, *At Dawn We Slept*, pp. 25–26.

18. The senior staff officer, a position for which there is no exact equivalent in American military staffs, was a sort of assistant chief of staff.

19. Hitoshi Tsunoda et al., *Hawai Sakusen* (Tokyo: Boeicho. Boei Kenshujo Senshishitsu, 1967), p. 93; John J. Stephan, *Hawaii Under the Rising Sun: Japan's Plans for Conquest After Pearl Harbor* (Honolulu: University of Hawaii Press, 1984), pp. 81–83.

20. Fukudome, "Hawaii Operation," pp. 1319–1320.

21. Prange, *At Dawn We Slept*, p. 184.

22. Heita Matsumura interview with the author, Honolulu, December 9, 1983.

23. Prange, *At Dawn We Slept*, pp. 161–162.

24. In Japanese military usage, the designation "Type Zero" indicated only that the model was introduced in 1940; this label was therefore applied to a number of types of aircraft.

25. Prange, *At Dawn We Slept*, pp. 161–162.

CHAPTER 2. YAMAMOTO'S MASTER PLAN

1. Prange, *At Dawn We Slept*, pp. 202–203.

2. U.S. Army Forces, Far East, Military History Section, "Submarine Operations, December 1941–April 1942" (Japanese Monograph 102), in *War in Asia and the Pacific, 1937-1949* (New York: Garland, 1980), ed. Donald S. Detweiler and Charles B. Burdick, 4:9–11.

3. Kazuo Sakamaki, *I Attacked Pearl Harbor* (New York: Association Press, 1949), p. 33.

4. Japanese Monograph 102, pp. 13–14.

5. Sakamaki, *I Attacked Pearl Harbor*, p. 30.

6. Tsunoda, *Hawai Sakusen*, pp. 97–98.

7. Ibid., p. 101.

8. Ibid., p. 104; Agawa, *Reluctant Admiral*, p. 228.

9. Genda, *Shinjuwan Sakusen Kaikoroku*, p. 115.

10. Agawa, *Reluctant Admiral*, p. 229; Prange, *At Dawn We Slept*, p. 223.

11. Prange, *At Dawn We Slept*, pp. 261–262.

12. Agawa, *Reluctant Admiral*, p. 230.

13. Ibid., p. 231; Prange, *At Dawn We Slept*, p. 297.

14. International Military Tribunal for the Far East, Court Proceedings, Exhibit 1197-A, p. 10317, Record Group 238, National Archives.

15. Sources conflict on the exact date of Nagano's capitulation. See Agawa, *Reluctant Admiral*, p. 231; Prange, *At Dawn We Slept*, p. 299, n. 22; *PHA* 1:236.

16. *PHA* 1:239; Prange, *At Dawn We Slept*, p. 285.

17. International Military Tribunal for the Far East, Court Proceedings, Exhibit 1201-A, pp. 10480–10481.

18. *PHA* 1:237–238; Prange, *At Dawn We Slept*, pp. 269, 340.

19. Tsunoda, *Hawai Sakusen*, p. 203; *PHA* 1:178.

20. For Nagumo's operation orders see U.S. Army Forces, Far East, Military His-

tory Section, "Pearl Harbor Operations: General Outline of Orders and Plans" (Japanese Monograph 97), in Detweiler and Burdick, *War in Asia*, 4:7–20.

21. *PHA* 1:238–242.

22. U.S. Strategic Bombing Survey, Interrogation of Mitsuo Fuchida, Tokyo, November 28, 1945 (Interrogation no. 603), U.S. Strategic Bombing Survey Interrogation Reports, Record Group 243, National Archives.

CHAPTER 3. "NO CREDENCE IN THESE RUMORS"

1. Oscar W. Koch with Robert G. Hayes, *G-2: Intelligence for Patton* (Philadelphia: Whitmore, 1971), p. xv.

2. Walter C. W. Ansel interview, U.S. Naval Institute Oral History Collection (hereafter USNIOH), Operational Archives, Naval Historical Center; *PHA* 2:209.

3. Pfeiffer interview; *PHA* 4:1925–1926.

4. *PHA* 14:1042.

5. *PHA* 2:819; 14:1044.

6. Technically codes are characters or words signifying ideas, whereas ciphers are systems in which one letter is substituted for another. Purple and other systems discussed here are actually ciphers, but for simplicity they will be called codes.

7. Roberta Wohlstetter, *Pearl Harbor: Warning and Decision* (Stanford: Stanford University Press, 1962), pp. 168–186; *PHA* 4:1734, 8:3558–3559, 8:3899, 9:4594–4595, 29:2454, 35:96, 36:23.

8. *PHA* 2:808.

9. Ruth Harris, "The 'Magic' Leak of 1941 and Japanese-American Relations," *Pacific Historical Review* (February 1981): pp. 77–96.

10. *PHA* 1:237; 5:2175.

11. *PHA* 12:100.

12. *PHA* 12:165.

13. A. A. Hoehling, *The Week Before Pearl Harbor* (New York: Norton, 1963), p. 156; Ronald Lewin, *American Magic: Codes, Ciphers and the Defeat of Japan* (New York: Farrar, Straus and Giroux, 1982), p. 129.

14. *PHA* 14:1377.

15. *PHA* 14:1402; 15:2171, 2176, 2214.

16. *PHA* 12:154.

17. *PHA* 8:3579; LEWIN, *American Magic*, p. 73; U.S. Naval Security Group, "Interview with Mr. Ralph T. Briggs," Records of the National Security Agency (NSA), Record Group 457, National Archives. Briggs claimed he intercepted the execute message but said that records were altered to obliterate the evidence.

18. *PHA* 8:3411.

19. U.S. Army Forces Pacific to Military Intelligence Service, November 13, 21, and 30, 1945, "Interrogation of Japanese Concerning Possible Broadcast of the 'Winds Execute' Messages" (SRH 177), Records of the NSA.

20. Ellis Zacharias, *Secret Missions* (New York: Putnam's, 1956), p. 247.

21. Takeo Yoshikawa, with Norman Stanford, "Top Secret Assignment," *U.S. Naval Institute Proceedings* 86 (December 1960): 30–34.

22. *PHA* 9:4375.

23. *PHA* 12:261–263, 266.

24. *PHA* 2:7974; 6:2610.

25. *PHA* 6:2543.

26. Joseph J. Rochefort interview, USNIOH.

27. "A Version of the Japanese Problem in the Signal Intelligence Service" (SRH 252), Records of the NSA.

28. *PHA* 36:16.

29. *PHA* 10:4674, 4682, 4687.

30. *PHA* 15:1889, 1895–1898; 26:230; 28:886; 36:126–128.

31. Rochefort denied that the Japanese made deceptive transmissions, but *Soryu's* communications officer contradicted him. See Prange, *At Dawn We Slept,* p. 338; Rochefort interview, pp. 156–157.

32. Wohlstetter, *Warning and Decision,* p. 387.

CHAPTER 4. THE ORANGE RACE

1. Memo Lt. C. C. Windsor to Commandant Fourteenth Naval District, July 20, 1917, Records of the Fourteenth Naval District, Hq., Commandant's Classified Correspondence, 1912–1941, Record Group 181, National Archives, Pacific-Sierra Region.

2. "Estimate of the Japanese Situation As It Affects the Territory of Hawaii, from the Military Point of View," Records of the War Department General and Special Staffs, Military Intelligence Division (MID 1766-S-87), Record Group 165, National Archives.

3. Memo Hoadley to C.O. Marine Barracks Pearl Harbor, August 29, 1922, Box 10, Records of the Marine Corps, Record Group 127, National Archives.

4. Edward D. Beechert, *Working in Hawaii: A Labor History* (Honolulu: University of Hawaii Press, 1985), pp. 205–208, 257.

5. "Estimate of the Japanese Situation."

6. Ibid.

7. Report Hawaiian Department G-2 to Army Assistant Chief of Staff, G-2, November 30, 1929, Records of the War Department General and Special Staffs, Military Intelligence Division (MID 1766-D-132/4).

8. "The Organization of the 14th Naval District, Co-ordination of Naval Activities Therein and Operation and Defense of the District in War," June 3, 1921, Records of the Fourteenth Naval District, Commandant's Classified Correspondence, 1912–1941.

9. For a treatment of the Massie case see Peter Van Singerland, *Something Terrible Has Happened* (New York: Harper & Row, 1966).

10. *PHA* 2:868.

11. Memo FDR to CNO, August 10, 1936, Joint Board Records 304 (Serial 593), Activities of Japanese Naval and Civil Personnel in Hawaii, Records of Joint Army and Navy Boards and Committees, Record Group 225, National Archives.

12. "A General Staff Study. Plan: Initial Seizure of Orange Nationals," n.d., Records of the Hawaiian Department, Adjutant General's Office, Emergency Defense and Mobilization Plans, 1940–1941, Record Group 338, National Archives.

13. Quoted in Martin Blumenson, ed., *The Patton Papers,* vol. 1: *1885–1940* (Boston: Houghton Mifflin, 1972), p. 899.

14. "Department Maneuvers, 1940," Adjutant General's Office, Emergency Defense and Mobilization Plans, 1940, Records of the Hawaiian Department.

15. Operations Orders, Hawaiian Division, Adjutant General's Office, Emergency Defense and Mobilization Plans, 1940, Records of the Hawaiian Department.

16. Memo Short to Adjutant General, May 15, 1941, Adjutant General's Office, Emergency Defense and Mobilization Plans, 1940–1941, Records of the Hawaiian Department.

17. Radiogram Short to War Department, July 22, 1941, Records Relating to the Attack on Pearl Harbor and to Sabotage Activities, ca. 1937–1947, Records of the Army Staff, Office of the Assistant Chief of Staff, G-2, Record Group 319, National Archives.

18. "General Japanese Intelligence Survey in the Honolulu Field Division" (Island of Maui), December 16, 1941, Records of the War Department General and Special Staffs, Military Intelligence Division (MID 2327-H-60/4).

19. Radiogram Short to War Department, July 22, 1941, Records Relating to the Attack on Pearl Harbor and to Sabotage Activities, ca. 1937–1947, Records of the Army Staff, Office of the Assistant Chief of Staff, G-2.

20. *PHA* 23:650, 738.

21. Roland N. Smoot interview, USNIOH.

22. *PHA* 14:1329.

23. *PHA* 14:1330.

24. *PHA* 35:507.

25. *PHA* 12:267–268, 35:327–332.

26. Confidential Memorandum, Military Intelligence Division, March 10, 1942, Records of the Army Staff, Office of the Assistant Chief of Staff, G-2, Records Relating to the Attack on Pearl Harbor and Sabotage Activities, ca. 1937–1947.

27. *PHA* 35:274.

28. *PHA* 28:875.

29. Prange, *At Dawn We Slept,* pp. 478–479.

30. Ibid., pp. 315–316.

31. Ibid.; Yoshikawa, "Top Secret Assignment," pp. 36–38; *PHA* 12:262, 35:342, 517, 596. Yoshikawa mistakenly places delivery of the questionnaire "about ten days before the attack."

CHAPTER 5. A CLASSIC MISUNDERSTANDING

1. For the full text of the joint defense plan see *PHA* 33:1153.

2. *PHA* 22:146.

3. Ibid.

4. Interview with Robert J. Fleming, Walter C. Short Collection (hereafter Short Collection), Hoover Institution of War, Revolution, and Peace, Stanford University.

5. Memos Bloch to CNO, December 30, 1940, and Richardson to CNO, January 7, 1941, Husband E. Kimmel Collection (hereafter Kimmel Collection), Archives of the American Heritage Center, University of Wyoming.

6. *PHA* 7:3007.

7. Moreel to Kimmel, October 20, 1941; Kimmel to Moreel, November 6, 1941, "1941. Admiral Kimmel's personal file," Record Group 313, National Archives.

8. *PHA* 6:2788.

9. *PHA* 6:2786.

10. Letter Stark to Kimmel, September 23, 1941, Kimmel Collection.

11. *PHA* 1:310; 6:2602; 32:234.

12. *PHA* 22:568.

13. *PHA* 1:379; 33:1182.

14. *PHA* 1:275, 278–279.

15. *PHA* 1:385.

16. *PHA* 6:2577; 22:325.

17. *PHA* 3:1069; 22:211–218.

18. *PHA* 22:468.

19. *PHA* 33:1176.

20. *PHA* 6:2756–2757.

21. *PHA* 23:608.

22. *PHA* 2:828.

23. *PHA* 14:1329; 22:198.

24. *PHA* 14:1330.

25. *PHA* 10:4662; Robert E. Sherwood, *Roosevelt and Hopkins: An Intimate History* (New York: Harper & Brothers, 1948), pp. 427–428.

26. *PHA* 12:245.

27. *PHA* 12:248.

28. *PHA* 14:1335.

29. *PHA* 27:105–115.

30. *PHA* 8:3828–3829; 24:1370; Sherwood, *Roosevelt and Hopkins*, pp. 430–431.

31. Cordell Hull, *The Memoirs of Cordell Hull* (New York: Macmillan, 1948), II:1096–1907.

32. *PHA* 6:2730.

33. *PHA* 7:3078; 27:157.

34. *PHA* 7:2922.

35. *PHA* 7:3081; 22:485.

36. John W. Dower, *War Without Mercy: Race and Power in the Pacific War* (New York: Pantheon Books, 1986), p. 102–105; William A. Leary, "Assessing the Japanese Threat: Air Intelligence Prior to Pearl Harbor," *Aerospace Historian* (December 1987):273–277.

37. *PHA* 26:148.

38. *PHA* 2:877.

39. Wohlstetter, *Warning and Decision*, p. 354.

40. *PHA* 12:345–349; *PHA* 21: Item 23 ("Disposition of U.S. Pacific Fleet, 7 Dec. 1941").

41. *PHA* 6:2569.

42. *PHA* 6:2498–2499; "Pearl Harbor" reference card file, Office of the Chief of Military History, Washington.

43. Commander-in-Chief, Pacific Fleet, to Secretary of the Navy, February 15, 1942, "Report of the Japanese Raid on Pearl Harbor 7 December 1941," CincPac Reports, World War II Action Reports, Operational Archives, Naval Historical Center, Washington.

44. *PHA* 1:149–150; 7:2963; 12:319–320.

45. *PHA* 12:323–324.

46. Memo Hawaiian Air Force to Roberts Commission, December 26, 1941, appended to "Operational History of the Seventh Air Force, 7 December 1941 to 6

November 1943" (AAF Historical Study No. 41), 1945, typescript in Office of Air Force History, Bolling AFB, Washington, D.C. (hereafter AF History).

47. *PHA* 12:351–352; 32:232.

CHAPTER 6. THE APPROACH

1. *PHA* 1:185.

2. Tsunoda, *Hawai Sakusen,* p. 266; Prange, *At Dawn We Slept,* pp. 415–417, 453.

3. Prange, *At Dawn We Slept,* pp. 391, 431–432, 460; International Military Tribunal for the Far East, Exhibit 1265 (SCAP Research Report 132).

4. Prange, *At Dawn We Slept,* pp. 376–379.

5. Prange, *At Dawn We Slept,* pp. 376–377; "Japanese Challenge New Book on Pearl," *Honolulu Advertiser,* March 6, 1982; Heijiro Abe, Iyozo Fujita, Junichi Goto, Hideo Maki, Heita Matsumura, and Sadao Yamamoto interview with the author, Honolulu, December 9, 1983.

6. Edwin T. Layton, Roger Pineau, and John Costello, *"And I Was There:" Pearl Harbor and Midway—Breaking the Secrets* (New York: Morrow, 1985), pp. 260–263; Agawa, *Reluctant Admiral,* p. 251.

7. Prange, *At Dawn We Slept,* pp. 427, 445, 468, 477, 483–484.

8. IMTFE, Exhibit 1265 (SCAP Research Report 132).

9. Prange, *At Dawn We Slept,* pp. 479, 487; *PHA* 18:3015. The *I-72* message, transmitted much later than signals which revisionists claim were intercepted by U.S. intelligence, is the only verifiable instance of radio transmission by *any* Japanese ship in the Hawaii operation before December 7.

10. Not to be confused with the Nakajima A6M2-N, the floatplane version of the Zero fighter.

11. Prange, *At Dawn We Slept,* pp. 490–492; U.S. Strategic Bombing Survey, Interrogation of Mitsuo Fuchida, Tokyo, November 28, 1945 (Interrogation No. 603), Interrogation Reports, Record Group 243, National Archives.

12. Prange, *At Dawn We Slept,* pp. 376, 492; Walter Lord, *Day of Infamy* (New York: Bantam Books, 1958), p. 30. Lord says there were 170 planes in the second wave, but because Prange's figures are from Japanese sources, they seem more reliable.

13. William F. Halsey and J. Bryan III, *Admiral Halsey's Story* (New York: Da Capo Press, 1976), p. 76.

14. Scouting Squadron Six, "Report of Action with Japanese at Oahu on December 7, 1941," undated (probably on or about December 15, 1941), CincPac Reports.

15. *Enterprise* Air Group, "Report of Action with Japanese Air Force at Oahu, T.H., December 7, 1941," December 15, 1941, CincPac Reports.

16. George Raynor Thompson, Dixie R. Harris, Pauline M. Oakes, and Dulany Terrett, *The Signal Corps: The Test (December 1941 to July 1943)* (Washington: Department of the Army, 1957), p. 4.

17. *PHA* 27:517–536.

18. *PHA* 27:517–536, 566–572.

19. *PHA* 37:1298–1299.

20. PHA 36:55–58; report of USS *Ward,* December 13, 1941, Fourteenth Naval

District Reports of Pearl Harbor Attack, World War II Action Reports, Operational Archives (hereafter Fourteenth Naval District Reports).

21. *PHA* 37:704.

22. Lord, *Day of Infamy*, pp. 36, 38; report of Patrol Wing Two, CincPac Reports; *PHA* 22:567.

CHAPTER 7. AN UNOBSTRUCTED RUN

1. *PHA* 26:210; Prange, *At Dawn We Slept*, pp. 449, 501.

2. Mitsuo Fuchida and Masatake Okumiya, *Midway: The Battle That Doomed Japan* (Annapolis: U.S. Naval Institute Press, 1955), pp. 27–28; Prange, *At Dawn We Slept*, pp. 502–503.

3. *PHA* 7:3359; various ships' reports, CincPac Reports.

4. Carl Lee interview, North Texas State University Oral History Collection, North Texas State University, Denton, Texas (hereafter NTSU).

5. Karl Johnson interview, NTSU.

6. Robert Johnson interview, USS *Arizona* Memorial Oral History Project (hereafter USAMOH)

7. U.S. Senate Committee on Veterans' Affairs, *Medal of Honor Recipients, 1863-1978* (Washington: Government Printing Office, 1979), p. 693.

8. John Vaessen interview, NTSU.

9. *PHA* 23:748–751; report of USS *Raleigh*, December 13, 1941, and supplementary report of USS *Raleigh*, June 10, 1943, CincPac Reports.

10. Robert Hudson interview with the author, February 28, 1983, Honolulu.

11. *PHA* 22:595–602.

12. Warren Thompson interview, NTSU; report of USS *Helena*, December 14, 1941, CincPac Reports.

13. Felix Balodis interview, USAMOH.

14. Report of USS *Helena;* statement of Arthur F. Trimbur, December 12, 1941, Fourteenth Naval District Reports.

15. Reports of USS *Oglala*, December 11 and December 31, 1941, CincPac Reports.

16. Ibid.; George Nakamoto interview with the author, October 4, 1983, Honolulu.

17. *PHA* 22:596–597; report of Rear Adm. William R. Furlong to Chief of Bureau of Personnel, February 13, 1944, copy in the author's files.

CHAPTER 8. THE TORPEDO ATTACK

1. Goto interview.

2. Reports of USS *Oklahoma*, December 16 and December 18, 1941, CincPac Reports; "Summary of War Damage to U.S. Battleships, Carriers, Cruisers, and Destroyers, 17 Oct 41 to 7 Dec 1942" (undated), Wallin Papers, Operational Archives (hereafter "Summary of War Damage").

3. Leon Kolb interview, USAMOH.

4. *PHA* 23:723–726.

5. Russell Davenport interview, USAMOH; USS *Oklahoma* Rescue and Salvage Report, CincPac Reports.

6. Chester Kelly interview, USAMOH; *Medal of Honor Recipients*, pp. 551, 705.

7. Matsumura interview; "Summary of War Damage."

8. Steven Woznick interview, USAMOH.

9. Report of USS *West Virginia,* December 11, 1941, CincPac Reports.

10. Statement of Lt. Comdr. John S. Harper, December 11, 1941, CincPac Reports.

11. Statement of Lt. C. V. Ricketts, undated (probably December 11, 1941), Cinc-Pac Reports.

12. Reports of USS *California,* December 13 and December 22, 1941, CincPac Reports; "Summary of War Damage."

13. Warren Harding interview, NTSU.

14. R. D. Nicholas interview, NTSU.

15. *Medal of Honor Recipients,* p. 655.

16. John Kuzma interview, USAMOH.

17. Statement of Vernon Oliver Jensen, December 24, 1941, Wallin Papers.

18. USS *California* Report, December 13, 1941, CincPac Files; *Medal of Honor Recipients,* pp. 586, 655, 664, 676.

19. Report of USS *Vestal,* December 11, 1941; report of USS *Nevada,* December 15, 1941, CincPac Reports; USS *Arizona,* "Material Damage Sustained in Attack on December 7, 1941," January 28, 1942, Wallin Papers; "Summary of War Damage."

CHAPTER 9. THE BOMB ATTACK

1. Fuchida and Okumiya, *Midway,* pp. 28–29.

2. "Summary of War Damage."

3. Wilford Autry interview, NTSU.

4. Werner Land interview, NTSU.

5. Merle Newbauer interview, NTSU.

6. Abe interview; "Summary of War Damage."

7. Report of USS *Tennessee,* December 11, 1941, CincPac Reports.

8. Statement of Lt. Comdr. T. T. Beattie, undated (probably December 1941); statement of Lt. (jg) F. H. White, December 11, 1941, CincPac Reports.

9. Statements of Lt. Claude Ricketts and Lt. Comdr. D. C. Johnson, undated (December 1941), CincPac Reports.

10. White and Ricketts statements; report of USS *West Virginia,* December 11, 1941, CincPac Reports.

11. Statement of Lt. Comdr. John S. Harper, undated (December 1941), CincPac Reports.

CHAPTER 10. THE END OF *ARIZONA*

1. USS *Arizona* Material Damage Report, January 28, 1942, Wallin Papers; "Summary of War Damage."

2. Alan Shapley interview, Marine Corps Oral History Collection.

3. Statement of John M. Baker, December 15, 1941, USS *Arizona* Loss File, Operational Archives.

4. James Cory interview, NTSU; statement of Earl C. Nightengale, December 15, 1941.

5. Memo Commandant Navy Yard, Pearl Harbor, to Chief, Bureau of Ships, October 7, 1943, Records of the Bureau of Ships, General Correspondence, Record Group 19, National Archives.

6. Film No. 428 NPC 1730, Motion Picture, Sound, and Video Branch, National Archives.

7. See statements of John M. Baker, William Parker, and Samuel Fuqua, USS *Arizona* Loss File.

8. Artis Teer and James Cory interviews, NTSU; USS *Arizona* War Damage Report, October 7, 1943, General Correspondence, Records of the Bureau of Ships, Record Group 19, National Archives; Russell Lott interview, USAMOH; statement of J. A. Doherty, undated (December 1941), USS *Arizona* Loss File.

9. Cory interview; Nightengale statement; Shapley interview.

10. Nightengale statement; Cory interview.

11. Statement of D. Hein, undated (December 1941), Wallin Papers.

12. USS *Arizona* Damage Control Report, January 28, 1942, General Correspondence, Records of the Bureau of Ships, Record Group 19, National Archives.

13. John Anderson interview; James Forbis interview, USAMOH.

14. Statements of George Campbell, Earl Pecotte, and William Peil, USS *Arizona* Loss File.

15. Statement of Guy S. Flannigan, undated (December 1941), Wallin Papers.

16. Forbis interview; statement of Jim Miller, undated (December 1941), Wallin Papers.

17. Statement of H. D. Davison, undated (December 1941), Wallin Papers.

18. Statements of Donald A. Graham, December 15, 1941; Milton Thomas Hurst, January 2, 1942; E. L. Wentzlaff, December 15, 1941; S. G. Fuqua, undated (probably December 1941); G. H. Lane, undated (probably December 1941), Wallin Papers.

19. Fuqua and Miller statements; statement of T. A. White, undated (December 1941), USS *Arizona* Loss File.

20. Forbis interview; Fuqua statement.

21. Lane and Wentzlaff statements.

22. Cory interview.

23. Nightengale statement.

24. John Anderson interview.

25. Fuqua statement.

26. Baker, Graham, Pecotte, Peil, Wentzlaff statements.

27. Report of USS *Vestal*, December 11, 1941, CincPac Reports.

28. Ibid.; Prange, *At Dawn We Slept*, p. 514.

29. Forbis and John Anderson interviews; Campbell and Graham statements.

CHAPTER 11. MACHINE GUNS ON WORKBENCHES

1. *PHA* 12:351–352, 357–358.

2. Ernest Cochran interview, NTSU.

3. Carl Hatcher interview, NTSU.

4. Merion Croft interview, USAMOH.

5. Robert Johnson interview, USAMOH.

6. *PHA* 12:357–358, 23:729–738; report of Naval Air Station, Pearl Harbor, December 21, 1941, Fourteenth Naval District Reports.

7. Ibid.; report of USS *Neosho*, December 11, 1941, CincPac Reports. *Neosho* was sunk at the battle of the Coral Sea less than six months later.

8. Report of Naval Air Station, Pearl Harbor.

9. Gordon A. Blake oral history interview, AF History.

10. U.S. Army Air Force Historical Office, *Operational History of the Seventh Air Force, 7 December 1941 to 6 November 1943* (typescript, 1945), p. 89, AF History.

11. Fiftieth Reconnaissance Squadron War Diary (Microfilm Roll A0911), AF History.

12. Seventy-second Bomb Squadron Reports (Microfilm Roll A0563), AF History.

13. James Latham interview, USAMOH.

14. Harold Fishencord interview, USAMOH.

15. Report of 1st Lt. James Dyson to Col. Raley, December 12, 1941, in "Seventh Air Force Interviews and Reports Concerning the Japanese Attack on Pearl Harbor on 7 Dec 1941" (Microfilm Roll 740.674-2), AF History (hereafter Interviews and Reports).

16. Eleventh Bomb Group, Headquarters Squadron Reports (Microfilm Roll B0067), AF History; James Duncan interview, USAMOH.

17. Leon Webster interview, USAMOH.

18. *PHA* 22:284.

19. "Summary of Enemy Action at Hickam Field, 7 Dec 41," December 20, 1941, in "Seventh Air Force Messages, Correspondence and Reports Concerning the Japanese Attack on Pearl Harbor and Hickam Field on 7 Dec . . ." (Microfilm Roll 740.162), AF History.

20. Memo Lt. Col. Clyde Rich to Hawaiian Air Force G-2, December 12, 1941, in "Seventh Air Force Reports of Japanese Attack on Bellows Field . . ." (Microfilm Roll 740.674-1A); report of Maj. R. L. Tscharer, undated, in "History, Air Depot, APC #953 . . ." (Microfilm Roll A7374), AF History.

21. Max Itoga interview, USAMOH; John E. Bowen, "December 7, 1941—The Day the Honolulu Fire Department Went to War," *Hawaiian Journal of History* 13 (1979): 126–135.

22. Hawaiian Air Depot Engineering Department, "Journal of Events and Production Report," December 1941 (Microfilm Roll A7380); memo from Orville C. Fuhr to Engineering Officer, Hawaiian Air Depot, May 11, 1943, in "History, Air Depot, APC #953 . . .," AF History.

23. Untitled and undated report in "History, Air Depot, APC #953."

24. Memo Capt. Charles Brombach to Commanding Officer, Hawaiian Air Depot, September 25, 1942; report of C. H. Van Arsdale, undated, in "History, Air Depot, APC #953."

25. Harold Lenburg, Ray Dudly, and James Duncan interviews, USAMOH.

26. Report of Maj. R. L. Tscharner, undated, in "History, Air Depot, APC #953"; Hawaiian Air Depot Engineering Department, "Journal of Events and Production Report," December 1941.

27. *PHA* 22:262–271.

28. Ibid.

CHAPTER 12. AGAINST THE ODDS

1. U.S. Army Air Force Historical Office, *Operational History of the Seventh Air Force, 7 December 1941 to 6 November 1943* (typescript, 1945), AF History, p. 87; *PHA* 22:110.

2. "Wheeler Field Report on Enemy Action, 7 December 1941" (undated), in "Reports of Japanese Attack on Wheeler Field, Hawaii, on 7 December 1941" (Microfilm Roll A7581), AF History.

3. Howard C. Davidson oral history interview, AF History.

4. Edmund H. Russell interview, USAMOH.

5. Commanding General, Hawaiian Interceptor Command, to Commanding General, Hawaiian Air Force, December 18, 1941, copy in the author's files; John W. Lambert, *The Long Campaign: The History of the 15th Fighter Group in World War II* (Manhattan, Kans.: Sunflower University Press, 1982), p. 19.

6. "Report of Ground Defense Activities," December 20, 1941, in "Seventh Fighter Command History, 1 November 1940–7 December 1941: Report of the Japanese Attack Against Wheeler Field on 7 December 1941 and the Reaction of the 14th Pursuit Wing" (Microfilm Roll 741.01), AF History.

7. Lambert, *Long Campaign*, pp. 17–18; "Seventh Fighter Command History, 7 Dec 1941–Jul 1944" (Microfilm Roll A7587), AF History.

8. Kenneth B. Bergquist oral history, AF History.

9. *PHA* 22:160.

10. Elzer N. Coates, Jr., interview, USAMOH.

11. James Jones, *WW II, A Chronicle of Soldiering* (New York: Ballantine, 1975), p. 16.

12. *PHA* 22:272–280.

13. "History of the 47th Fighter Squadron" (Microfilm Roll A0740), AF History.

14. Reports of aerial combat over Oahu, even those of participants, are confusing and inconsistent. This account is distilled from several sources: various reports in Microfilm Rolls AO740 and AO741, AF History; Fujita interview; Lambert, *Long Campaign*, pp. 18–23; *PHA* 22:249–256.

15. Lambert, *Long Campaign*, p. 21.

16. *PHA* 22:299–301.

17. *PHA* 22:301–304; Ernest Haynes interview, USAMOH.

18. Memo Capt. Lester A. Milz to Navy Department, December 9, 1941, Records of the Fourteenth Naval District Headquarters, Commandant's Office, Classified Correspondence, 1912–1941.

19. Eugene Camp interview, NTSU.

20. *PHA* 23:738–741.

21. Ibid.; Charles H. Roberts interview, NTSU.

22. Report of U.S. Naval Air Station, Kaneohe Bay, December 8, 1941, Fourteenth Naval District Reports; *Medal of Honor Recipients,* pp. 549–550; *PHA* 23:738–741.

23. Report of Patrol Wing One, January 1, 1942, CincPac Reports; Fujita interview.

24. Ibid.; report of U.S. Naval Air Station, Kaneohe Bay.

CHAPTER 13. A "PRACTICALLY PERFECT" ATTACK

1. Report of Executive Officer, Bellows Field, December 20, 1941, in "Reports of Japanese Attack on Bellows Field, Hawaii, on 7 Dec 1941" (Microfilm Roll 740.674-1A), AF History.

2. *PHA* 22:293–296; 23:741–745.

3. Fujita interview.

4. Phillip Willis interview, NTSU.

5. Report of Executive Officer, Bellows Field, December 20, 1941.

6. *PHA* 22:294.

7. Report of Marine Aircraft Group Twenty-one, December 30, 1941, Personal Papers of Maj. Gen. Claude A. Larkin, U.S. Marine Corps Historical Center, Washington (hereafter Larkin Papers).

8. Ibid.

9. Letter Charles S. Barker, Jr., to James G. Daniels III, undated (probably August 1, 1986), copy in the author's files; Marine Aircraft Group Twenty-one, "Operations and Training Office, "Record of Events, Sunday, 7 December 1941," copy in the author's files.

10. Report of Marine Aircraft Group Twenty-one.

11. Report of USS *Enterprise* Air Group, December 15, 1941, CincPac Reports.

12. *PHA* 23:611–612.

13. Report of Scouting Squadron Six, undated, CincPac Reports.

14. Report of USS *Enterprise* Air Group, December 15, 1941, CincPac Reports.

15. Irwin Cihak interview with the author, December 4, 1983, Honolulu.

16. Ibid.

17. *PHA* 22:124–127.

18. *PHA* 1:38.

CHAPTER 14. "CAPTAIN, THEY'RE HERE!"

1. Report of USS *Tangier,* January 1, 1942; report of USS *Curtiss,* December 16, 1941; report of USS *Monaghan,* December 30, 1941, CincPac Reports.

2. Ibid; *PHA* 32:309; *Tangier's* claim to have hit the conning tower was confirmed when the sunken sub was later raised. The conning tower was found to have been holed by a 5-inch projectile.

3. Report of USS *Monaghan;* G. J. Bennett interview, NTSU.

4. Ibid.

5. G. J. Bennett interview.

6. Report of USS *Monaghan.*

7. Albert Fickel interview, USAMOH; report of USS *Pennsylvania,* December 16, 1941; report of USS *Cassin,* December 13, 1941; report of USS *Downes,* undated, CincPac Reports.

8. Report of USS *Downes;* report of USS *Cassin.*

9. Ibid.; report of USS *Pennsylvania.*

10. Report of USS *Downes.*

11. Lord, *Day of Infamy,* pp. 139–140; report of USS *Pennsylvania,* December 16, 1941, CincPac Reports.

12. Report of USS *Downes;* report of USS *Cassin.*

13. Ibid.

14. Ibid.; report of USS *Pennsylvania.*

15. Ibid.

16. Report of USS *Pennsylvania;* memo Comdr. H. A. Turner to Manager, Pearl Harbor Navy Yard, December 13, 1941, Fourteenth Naval District Reports.

17. Memo Lt. W. R. Spear to Captain of the Yard, Pearl Harbor Navy Yard, December 20, 1941, Fourteenth Naval District Reports.

18. Statement of Tai Sing Loo, Hawaii War Records Depository, University of Hawaii Library, Honolulu (hereafter HWRD).

19. Statement of Ponciano Bernardino, HWRD.

20. Report of USS *Downes;* report of USS *Cassin;* report of USS *Pennsylvania.*

21. Lord, *Day of Infamy,* p. 142.

22. Report of Public Works Officer, Pearl Harbor Navy Yard, December 15, 1941, Fourteenth Naval District Reports.

23. Log of USS *Honolulu,* December 7, 1941, Operational Archives.

24. Ibid.

25. Report of USS *Raleigh,* December 13, 1941; supplementary report of Capt. R. B. Simons, June 10, 1943, CincPac Reports.

26. Report of USS *Curtiss.*

27. Ibid.; Lord, *Day of Infamy,* pp. 142–143.

28. Report of USS *Nevada,* December 15, 1941, CincPac Reports; Lord, *Day of Infamy,* pp. 135–136.

29. Dan Wentrcek interview, NTSU.

30. Statements of CSM W. Pryor and SM3 A. J. Houghton, undated, Fourteenth Naval District Reports.

31. Ibid.; report of USS *Nevada;* Prange, *At Dawn We Slept,* p. 536.

32. Report of USS *Nevada; PHA* 23:704–705; Lord, *Day of Infamy,* p. 137.

33. Report of USS *Nevada;* James Clark interview, USAMOH; Artis Teer interview, NTSU.

34. *PHA* 23:719–720; *Medal of Honor Recipients,* p. 668.

35. Charles Merdinger interview, USNIOH.

36. Report of USS *Nevada;* Lord, *Day of Infamy,* pp. 138–139; statements of various signal tower personnel and reports of various yardcraft, Fourteenth Naval District Reports.

CHAPTER 15. A BATTLESHIP ADMIRAL'S NOTICE

1. Statement of BM1 J. D. Shepard, undated; memo Yard Craft Repair Officer to Captain of the Yard, Navy Yard, Pearl Harbor, December 13, 1941, Fourteenth Naval District Reports.

2. Log of *YT 129,* Fourteenth Naval District Reports.

3. Report of USS *Rigel,* December 9, 1941, CincPac Reports.

4. Log of *YT 153,* Fourteenth Naval District Reports.

5. Log of *YT 142 (Nokomis),* Fourteenth Naval District Reports.

6. Statement of CQM J. J. Reams, December 16, 1941, Fourteenth Naval District Reports.

7. Log of *YG 17;* memo Commander Battleships, Battle Force, Pacific Fleet, to Commandant Fourteenth Naval District, Fourteenth Naval District Reports.

8. Report of USS *Pyro,* December 10, 1941, CincPac Reports.

9. Ben Cummings interview, NTSU.

10. *PHA* 23:637–640.

11. Norwood McGill interview, USAMOH.

12. Report of Motor Torpedo Boat Squadron One, December 12, 1941, CincPac Reports.

13. Report of USS *Helm,* December 11, 1941, CincPac Reports.

14. Report of USS *Dale*, December 28, 1941, CincPac Reports.

15. Nathan Asher interview with the author, Honolulu, May 17, 1982.

16. Ibid.; report of USS *Blue*, December 11, 1941, CincPac Reports; *PHA* 23:692–698.

17. Report of USS *Henley*, December 15, 1941, CincPac Reports.

18. Report of USS *Alwyn*, January 4, 1942, CincPac Reports.

19. Report of USS *Phelps*, December 30, 1941, CincPac Reports.

20. Report of USS *Bagley*, December 11, 1941, CincPac Reports.

21. Reports of USS *St. Louis*, December 10 and December 25, 1941, CincPac Reports; Lord, *Day of Infamy*, p. 146–147; Prange, *At Dawn We Slept*, p. 538.

22. Ibid.; Asher interview.

23. Report of USS *Keosanqua*, December 14, 1941; report of Assistant Port Director, N.T.S. Aloha Tower, December 15, 1941, Fourteenth Naval District Reports; Lord, *Day of Infamy*, p. 159.

24. Alexander Beck interview, USAMOH.

25. Statement of Charles Harkins, HWRD.

CHAPTER 16. TENDING THE WOUNDED

1. Floyd Jenkins and Leo Hovde interview, USAMOH.

2. Report of U.S. Naval Hospital, Pearl Harbor, December 19, 1941, Fourteenth Naval District Reports; Russell Jensen interview, USAMOH.

3. Report of U.S. Naval Hospital, Pearl Harbor, December 19, 1941; Clay Musick interview, NTSU; Charles Brewer interview, USAMOH.

4. Russell Jensen interview; reports of U.S. Naval Hospital, Pearl Harbor, December 19 and December 29, 1941, Fourteenth Naval District Reports.

5. Ibid.

6. Report of Medical Officer, Pearl Harbor Navy Yard, January 2, 1942, Fourteenth Naval District Reports.

7. Herbert Boyd and Shikumi Yoshida interviews, USAMOH.

8. Kathy Cooper interview, USAMOH.

9. Report of Public Works Officer, Pearl Harbor Navy Yard, December 15, 1941, Fourteenth Naval District Reports.

10. Reports of E. I. Adolphson and Comdr. Harold Pilgrim, undated, Fourteenth Naval District Reports.

11. Statement of Mary Helen Stevens, HWRD.

12. John Cowden interview, NTSU.

13. James Anderson interview, USAMOH.

14. Ibid.; report of Commander-in-Chief, U.S. Pacific Fleet, February 15, 1942, CincPac Reports.

15. Report of USS *Solace*, December 12, 1941, CincPac Reports.

16. James Anderson interview, USAMOH; Steven Woznick interview, USAMOH; Albert Olson interview with John Martini, Honolulu, November 3, 1983.

17. James Anderson interview, USAMOH; USS *Dobbin* material damage report, January 10, 1942, Wallin Papers.

18. Statement of Ruth Winne, HWRD.

19. The 1941 Tripler Hospital should not be confused with the present-day Tripler Army Medical Center, constructed after World War II at a different location.

20. Elizabeth Elmer Murphy and Florence Washburn interviews, USAMOH.

21. Statements of Frederick F. Alsup and Ethel Hensley Brown, HWRD.

22. Lord, *Day of Infamy,* pp. 192–194; Gwenfread Allen, *Hawaii's War Years, 1941-1945* (Honolulu: University of Hawaii Press, 1950), p. 31.

23. Allen, *Hawaii's War Years,* pp. 29–30; Alexander Holcomb interview, U.S. Marine Corps Oral History Collection.

24. Allen, *Hawaii's War Years,* pp. 29–30; Patricia Morgan Swenson interview, USAMOH.

25. Report of U.S. Naval Hospital, Pearl Harbor, December 19, 1941.

26. Nick Kouretas interview, NTSU.

27. Report of Naval Hospital, Pearl Harbor, December 19, 1941; Karl Johnson interview, NTSU; Charles Brewer interview, USAMOH.

28. Robert Johnson interview, USAMOH.

29. Report of Kaneohe Naval Air Station, December 8, 1941; report of Naval Hospital, Pearl Harbor, December 19, 1941; Allen, *Hawaii's War Years,* p. 32.

CHAPTER 17. RETURN FLIGHT

1. Lord, *Day of Infamy,* pp. 179, 181; *PHA* 1:241.

2. Fuchida and Okumiya, *Midway,* p. 31; Fujita interview.

3. Prange, *At Dawn We Slept,* pp. 543–544; Fuchida and Okumiya, *Midway,* p. 32.

4. Prange, *At Dawn We Slept,* p. 542.

5. Fuchida and Okumiya, *Midway,* p. 33; Prange, *At Dawn We Slept,* pp. 541–543, 546.

6. Ibid.

7. Prange, *At Dawn We Slept,* p. 543.

8. *PHA* 22:205; Thompson et al., *The Signal Corps,* p. 7.

9. *PHA* 23:1162; transcript of interview with Comdr. E. B. Mott, March 22, 1944, World War II Command Files, Operational Archives.

10. *PHA* 24:1372.

11. *PHA* 23:699–703; Asher interview.

12. *PHA* 22:194, 204; Prange, *At Dawn We Slept,* p. 564; Patrick Bellinger, unpublished autobiography (typescript), pp. 323, 325, Operational Archives.

13. *PHA* 22:204–205; Prange, *At Dawn We Slept,* p. 564; memo Maj. A. M. Meehan to Roberts Commission, December 26, 1941, appended to *Operational History of the Seventh Air Force, 7 December 1941 to 6 November 1943* (typescript, 1946), AF History (hereafter Meehan memo).

14. *PHA* 22:195, 32:427; Meehan memo; Prange, *At Dawn We Slept,* p. 566.

15. *PHA* 22:529.

16. *PHA* 24:1371–1372, 32:426; Lord, *Day of Infamy,* p. 176.

17. Report of Task Force Nine, CincPac Reports; Bellinger manuscript, p. 322.

18. *PHA* 23:683–685.

19. *PHA* 7:3357–3358, 23:683–685, 24:1372; Lord, *Day of Infamy,* p. 176; Prange, *At Dawn We Slept,* p. 548.

20. Brooke Allen oral history transcript, AF History; *PHA* 32:426–427.

21. Hawaiian Department Intelligence Summary No. 3, December 8, 1941, Seventh Air Force Messages, Correspondence, and Reports, AF History; Lord, *Day of Infamy,* p. 204; Allen transcript, pp. 40–41; statement of Matsue Kida, HWRD.

CHAPTER 18. WHAT NEXT?

1. Halsey, *Halsey's Story,* p. 80.
2. Report of Task Force Eight, December 18, 1941, World War II Action Reports, Operational Archives.
3. Ibid.; *PHA* 23:611.
4. Ibid.; memo to *Enterprise* Air Officer, December 17, 1941, in "War Record of Fighting Squadron Six," World War II Command Files, Operational Archives.
5. Report of USS *Northampton,* December 17, 1941, World War II Action Reports, Operational Archives.
6. Ibid.; Rear Adm. Malcom Reeves (ret.), letter to the author, June 22, 1984.
7. Halsey, *Halsey's Story,* p. 80.
8. James Daniels, interview with the author, Kailua, Oahu, Hawaii, July 5, 1984; diary of James Daniels, December 7, 1941.
9. Merion Croft interview, USAMOH; report of *Enterprise* Air Group, December 15, 1941, CincPac Reports; *PHA* 23:611–612; Bellinger manuscript, pp. 327–328.
10. Daniels interview; diary of James Daniels, December 7, 1941.
11. Norman Godbold interview, USAMOH.
12. Diary of Charles Hite, secretary of the Territory of Hawaii, December 7, 1941, HWRD; Grew Pallette, *Martial Law in Hawaii: The First Eight Months* (typescript, 1942), pp. 3–4, Military Government of Hawaii, Office of Internal Security, Record Group 338, National Archives.
13. "Saboteurs Land Here," *Honolulu Advertiser,* December 8, 1941, p. 1.
14. Report of Kaneohe Naval Air Station, December 8, 1941; report of Barbers Point Light Station, December 10, 1941, Fourteenth Naval District Reports.
15. "File Record of Important Telephone Communication," December 8, 1941, in Seventh Air Force Messages, Correspondence, and Reports.
16. Statement of Mrs. Robert Thompson, HWRD.
17. Stephen and Flora Bell Koran interview, NTSU; "G-2 Information Bulletin No. 2," December 8, 1941, in Seventh Air Force Messages, Correspondence, and Reports.
18. Wymo Takaki interview, USAMOH.
19. Shikumi Yoshida interview, USAMOH.
20. Letter (holograph) Kimmel to Short, December 8, 1941, Short Collection; letter Kimmel to Stark, December 12, 1941, Kimmel Collection.
21. "Knox Reports One Battleship Sunk at Hawaii," *New York Times,* December 16, 1941, p. 1.
22. U.S. Naval Intelligence Service Investigation Report, February 18, 1942, Records of the Army Staff, Records of the Assistant Chief of Staff, G-2.
23. Memo Maj. F. M. McAllister to Commanding General, Department of the Pacific, June 1, 1942, Records of the Marine Corps (1J, Oahu TH NAD Reports).
24. Albert Fickel interview, USAMOH.
25. Elzer Coates interview, USAMOH.

CHAPTER 19. STRANDED

1. Sakamaki, *I Attacked Pearl Harbor,* pp. 37–46.
2. Report of USS *Helm,* December 11, 1941, CincPac Reports.
3. Telephone message slip, Lt. Col. Weddington to Hawaiian Air Force G-3

(December 8, 1941), Seventh Air Force Messages, Correspondence, and Reports; *PHA* 16:2019.

4. Phillip Willis interview, NTSU.

5. *PHA* 16:2020–2021.

6. This account is drawn from the report of the Fourteenth Naval District intelligence office; the report of the first U.S. officer to reach the scene (both reports in *PHA* 24:1448–1453); and Allan Beekman, *The Niihau Incident* (Honolulu: Heritage Press of the Pacific, 1982).

7. Japanese Monograph 102, p. 10.

8. *PHA* 23:908.

CHAPTER 20. ASSESSING LOSSES AND DAMAGE

1. "Summary of War Damage."

2. *PHA* 1:38, 12:323, 12:357–358, 23:611–612; Lord, *Day of Infamy*, p. 220.

3. Hawaiian Air Depot Engineering Department, "Journal of Events and Production Report," December (14?), 1941, AF History; report of Public Works Officer, Pearl Harbor Navy Yard, December 15, 1941, Fourteenth Naval District Reports.

4. Bowen, "Fire Department Went to War," pp. 132–133; *PHA* 18:3351, 21:item 37, 28:1059, 28:1372.

5. Casualty List, Book 1, Pearl Harbor–Midway, 7 December 1941 to May 1942 (Microfilm Roll No. 1980-1), Operational Archives.

6. Stetson Conn, Rose C. Engleman, and Byron Fairchild, *Guarding the United States and Its Outposts* (Washington: Chief of Military History, 1964), pp. 193–194

7. Frank O. Hough, Verle E. Ludwig, and Henry I. Shaw, Jr., *History of U.S. Marine Corps Operations in World War II* (Washington: U.S. Marine Corps Historical Branch, n.d.), pp. 74–75.

8. Lord, *Day of Infamy*, p. 220; Prange, *At Dawn We Slept*, p. 539.

9. Casualty Report of Hawaiian Air Force, December 16, 1941, in Seventh Air Force Messages, Correspondence, and Reports.

10. *PHA* 1:243; Prange, *At Dawn We Slept*, p. 545.

11. Japanese Monograph 102, pp. 20, 55.

12. *PHA* 6:2499–2500.

13. B. H. Liddell Hart, *History of the Second World War* (New York: Putnam's, 1971), pp. 217–218.

14. *Congressional Record*, 87:9504–9505 (December 8, 1941).

CHAPTER 21. GIRDING FOR INVASION

1. Brian Nicol, interview with Col. Frank Steer, *Honolulu* (November 1981), pp. 69–84.

2. Territory of Hawaii, Office of the Military Governor, General Orders Nos. 38 (December 20, 1941) and 91 (March 31, 1942), HWRD.

3. Territory of Hawaii, Office of the Military Governor, General Orders No. 14 (December 10, 1941), HWRD; J. Garner Anthony, *Hawaii Under Army Rule* (Honolulu: The University Press of Hawaii, 1975), p. 40.

4. Frank Steer interview, USAMOH.

5. Territory of Hawaii, Office of the Military Governor, General Orders No. 4 (December 7, 1941), HWRD; Anthony, *Under Army Rule*, p. 50.

6. Allen, *Hawaii's War Years,* p. 107; radiogram Emmons to Adjutant General, War Department, February 4, 1942, "War Operations–General" file, Records of the Pacific Fleet, Record Group 313, National Archives.

7. Radiogram Emmons to Adjutant General, War Department, February 18, 1942, "War Operations–General" file, Records of the Pacific Fleet.

8. Letter Kimmel to Short, December 8, 1941, Kimmel Collection; letter Emmons to Arnold, January 26, 1942, Emmons Collection; memo Bellinger to CincPac, February 16, 1942, "War Operations–General" file, Records of the Pacific Fleet.

9. Memos Maj. John W. Coulter to Asst. Chief of Staff, G-2, December 23, 1941, and January 16, 1942, Records Relating to the Attack on Pearl Harbor and Sabotage Activities, ca. 1937–1947.

10. Letter George C. Marshall to Delos Emmons, December 20, 1941, Delos Emmons Collection, Hoover Institution of War, Peace, and Revolution.

11. Memo Lt. Gen. Delos C. Emmons to Adm. C. W. Nimitz, February 3, 1942, "War Operations–General" file, Records of the Pacific Fleet.

12. Memo Lt. Gen. Delos C. Emmons to CincPac, January 19, 1942; memo C. H. McMorris to chief of staff, January 21, 1942, "War Operations–General" file, Records of the Pacific Fleet.

13. Allen, *Hawaii's War Years,* pp. 95–98.

14. Robert N. S. Clark, "Coast Defenses of Hawaii," Council on Abandoned Military Posts–U.S.A., *Periodical* 5:(2) (Summer 1973):23.

15. Allen, *Hawaii's War Years,* pp. 92–93; memos Lt. Gen. Delos C. Emmons to CincPac, February 12 and February 22, 1942, "Readiness for War Reports" file, Records of the Pacific Fleet.

16. Norman Godbold and Frank Steer interviews, USAMOH.

17. Otto Degener statement, HWRD.

18. Stephan, *Hawaii Under the Rising Sun,* pp. 92–93.

19. Ibid., pp. 110–111.

CHAPTER 22. A QUESTION OF LOYALTY

1. Testimony from Japanese community leaders confirms the roles of Fielder, Shivers, and Burns. See Y. Baron Goto, Masaji Marumoto, and Shigeo Yoshida interviews, USAMOH.

2. Memo Zacharias to CincPac, January 2, 1942, Kimmel Collection.

3. Memo CincPac to Commandant Fourteenth Naval District, January 9, 1942, Records of the Fourteenth Naval District, Series 58-3402.

4. Memo Capt. W. M. Fechteler to CincPac, January 11, 1942, "Subversive Activities, Espionage" file, Records of the Pacific Fleet.

5. Conn, Engleman, and Fairchild, *Guarding the United States,* pp. 207–208.

6. Ibid., p. 209; radiogram Emmons to War Department, February 4, 1942, "War Operations–General" file, Records of the Pacific Fleet.

7. About 200 Caucasians with suspected Axis ties were also arrested; Allen, *Hawaii's War Years,* p. 134.

8. Andrew Lind, *Hawaii's Japanese: An Experiment in Democracy* (Princeton: Princeton University Press, 1946), pp. 74–75.

9. Quoted in Michael John Gordon, "Suspects in Paradise: Looking for Japanese 'Subversives' in the Territory of Hawaii, 1939–1945" (M.A. thesis, University of Iowa, 1983), pp. 73–74.

10. Ibid., pp. 83–84.

11. For a detailed description of the organization and functioning of these agencies see Lind, *Hawaii's Japanese*, pp. 132–142.

12. *PHA* 23:1008; Lind, *Hawaii's Japanese*, pp. 103–104.

13. Memo Fielder to Military Intelligence Division, April 6, 1942, Records of the Army Staff, Office of the Assistant Chief of Staff, G-2, Records Relating to the Attack on Pearl Harbor and Sabotage Activities, ca. 1937–1947.

14. Quoted in Lind, *Hawaii's Japanese*, p. 107.

15. Memo Maj. Gen. Maxwell Murray to Hawaiian Department, March 23, 1942, Records of the Hawaiian Department, Adjutant General's Office, Reports, Correspondence, and Revision Sheets, 1932, 1937–1943, Record Group 338, National Archives (hereafter Hawaiian Department AG).

16. Quoted in Lind, *Hawaii's Japanese*, p. 145.

17. Ibid., p. 148.

18. Conn, Engleman, and Fairchild, *Guarding the United States*, p. 208.

19. Memo Maj. Gen. Maxwell Murray to Hawaiian Department, March 23, 1942, Hawaiian Department AG.

20. Ibid.

21. Name omitted by the author.

22. Memo Col. Thomas C. Burgess to Commanding General, Hawaiian Department, April 2, 1942, Hawaiian Department AG.

23. Although I found this routing slip attached to the April 2, 1942, loyalty report in the National Archives, internal evidence suggests it was originally attached to another document.

24. Memo Emmons to War Department, April 6, 1942, Hawaiian Department AG.

25. Memo War Department to Hawaiian Department, May 2, 1942, Hawaiian Department AG.

26. Radiograms Emmons to War Department, May 11 and May 26, 1942, Hawaiian Department AG.

27. Radiogram Marshall to Hawaiian Department, May 28, 1942, Hawaiian Department AG.

28. Chester Tanaka, *Go for Broke: A Pictorial History of the Japanese-American 100th Infantry Battalion and the 442nd Regimental Combat Team* (Richmond, Calif.: Go for Broke, Inc., 1982), p. 146.

CHAPTER 23. OPERATION K

1. For a summary of sinkings in Hawaiian waters see Allen, *Hawaii's War Years*, p. 58.

2. Lawrence Nakatsuka, "The Last Thirty Seconds," *Pacific Features and Sports* 5:6 (September 1947):8.

3. Radio Submarine Force 1 to Submarine Force 2, December 27, 1941 (SRN 130312), Translations of Japanese Navy Messages, 5 Dec 41–25 Mar 42, Records of the NSA.

4. Conn, Engleman, and Fairchild, *Guarding the United States*, p. 206; statement of Col. V. S. Burton, HWRD.

5. *PHA* 13:650–651; Sixth Fleet to Combined Fleet, December 30, 1941

(SRN130393); Subron One to Sixth Fleet, February 26, 1942 (SRN132928), Translations of Japanese Navy Messages, 5 Dec 41–25 Mar 42, Records of the NSA.

6. John J. Stephan, "The Night They Bombed Tantalus," *Honolulu*, November 1980, pp. 74–77, 130–131; Edwin T. Layton, "Rendezvous in Reverse," *U.S. Naval Institute Proceedings* (May 1953):478–485.

7. Layton and Rochefort interviews, USNIOH; Operation K messages in Translations of Japanese Navy Messages, 5 Dec 1941–1926 Mar 1942, Records of the NSA, confirm the large volume of radio intercepts.

8. Hashizumi radio message, March 4, 1942 (SRN133043), Translations of Japanese Navy Messages, 5 Dec 41–26 Mar 42, Records of the NSA.

CHAPTER 24. SALVAGE AND REPAIR

1. Homer Wallin, *Pearl Harbor: Why, How, Fleet Salvage and Final Appraisal* (Washington: Naval History Division, 1968), p. 181.

2. Wallin to Commandant, Pearl Harbor Navy Yard, "Report of the Repair and Salvage of Naval Vessels Damaged at Pearl Harbor, T.H., on December 7, 1941" (typescript, July 13, 1942), Wallin Papers (hereafter Repair and Salvage Report).

3. Wallin, *Fleet Salvage*, p. 277; Repair and Salvage Report.

4. Tom Yoneyama, "Sunday, Dec. 7—A 90-Hour Workday," *Waikiki Beach Press*, December 7–10, 1981, p. A-21; Wallin, *Fleet Salvage*, pp. 261, 277.

5. Wallin, *Fleet Salvage*, p. 230; George Sheridan interview with the author, Kailua, Oahu, Hawaii, March 23, 1982.

6. Unless otherwise noted, information on the repair and salvage of individual vessels is from the Repair and Salvage Report and Wallin, *Fleet Salvage*, pp. 189–267.

7. Wallin gives two different dates for *Raleigh's* undocking: February 14 in *Fleet Salvage*, p. 197; February 6 in Repair and Salvage Report.

8. Memo Salvage Officer to Commandant Pearl Harbor Navy Yard, April 15, 1942, Wallin Papers.

9. Wallin says sixty-six bodies were recovered, but the Pearl Harbor War Diary records the higher figure. See Wallin, *Fleet Salvage*, pp. 237–238; War Diary, Pearl Harbor Navy Yard (hereafter PH War Diary), May 27, 1942, entry, Operational Archives.

10. Memo C.O. USS *Arizona* to Commander, Battleships, Battle Force, December 15, 1941, USS *Arizona* Loss File.

11. Memo Lt. Comdr. J. A. McNally to Wallin, March 10, 1942, Wallin Papers.

12. Memo Commandant Navy Yard, Pearl Harbor, to Chief, Bureau of Ships, October 7, 1943, Records of the Bureau of Ships, General Correspondence, Record Group 19, National Archives; PH War Diary, July 13, 1942.

13. Memo Commandant Navy Yard, Pearl Harbor, to Chief, Bureau of Ships, October 7, 1943, Records of the Bureau of Ships, General Correspondence.

14. PH War Diary, March 14 and April 13, 1942, April 13, May 6, May 27, July 18, and October 1, 1943.

15. Ibid., May 6, August 24, December 3, and December 31, 1942.

16. Ibid., April 21 and October 25, 1942; memo Comdr. F. H. Whitaker to Commandant, Pearl Harbor Navy Yard, October 17, 1942, Whitaker Collection, Photographic Section, Naval Historical Center.

17. PH War Diary, April 20, April 26, May 7, May 10, July 26, August 6, August

12, September 24, 1943; memo Comdr. F. H. Whitaker to Commandant, Pearl Harbor Navy Yard, October 26, 1942, USS *Arizona* Loss File.

18. Memo Commandant Pearl Harbor Navy Yard to Vice Chief of Naval Operations, July 24, 1942, USS *Arizona* Loss File.

19. Memo Secretary of the Navy to Navy Bureaus and Offices, December 1, 1942, General Correspondence, Secretary of the Navy, Record Group 80, National Archives.

20. Memo Chief, Bureau of Ordnance to CincPac Fleet, September 21, 1943, Records of the Bureau of Ships, General Correspondence; PH War Diary, October 11 and 13, 1943.

CHAPTER 25. REACTIONS AND REFLECTIONS

1. Statement of Harold Kay, HWRD; Wohlstetter, *Warning and Decision*, p. 268.

2. *PHA* 24:1749–1756.

3. *PHA* 23:1247–1248.

4. *PHA* 39:19–21.

5. Prange, *At Dawn We Slept,* pp. 616–617; Martin Melosi, *The Shadow of Pearl Harbor: Political Controversy Over the Surprise Attack, 1941–1946* (College Station: Texas A&M University Press, 1977), pp. 61–62.

6. James Leutze, *A Different Kind of Victory: A Biography of Admiral Thomas C. Hart* (Annapolis: Naval Institute Press, 1981), pp. 293–299; *PHA* 26:474–475.

7. *PHA* 39:175–179.

8. *PHA* 39:297–321.

9. *PHA* 36:359–360.

10. *PHA* 39:523–527.

11. *PHA* 34:74–76.

12. *PHA* 35:117–121, 127–130.

13. Melosi, *Shadow,* pp. 83–88.

14. *PHA* 8:3555–3813, 8:3842–3927; Husband E. Kimmel, *Admiral Kimmel's Story* (Chicago: Regnery, 1955), pp. 167–168.

15. Kimmel, *Story,* p. 169.

16. U.S. Congress, Joint Committee on the Investigation of the Pearl Harbor Attack, *Report,* 79th Cong., 2nd sess., July 20, 1946, pp. 251–252.

17. Ibid., pp. 266S–266U.

18. Ibid., pp. 503–506.

19. Ibid., pp. 252–266.

SELECTED BIBLIOGRAPHY

OFFICIAL DOCUMENTS

U.S. Army. Army Forces, Far East, Military History Section. "Submarine Operations, December 1941–April 1942." Japanese Monograph 102. Library of Congress.

———. "Pearl Harbor Operations: General Outline of Orders and Plans." Japanese Monograph 97. Library of Congress.

U.S. Congress. *Hearings Before the Joint Committee on the Investigation of the Pearl Harbor Attack. (PHA)* 39 parts, 79th Cong., 1st sess., 1946.

———. *Report of the Joint Committee on the Investigation of the Pearl Harbor Attack.* 79th Cong., 1st sess., 1946.

U.S. Department of Defense. *The "Magic" Background of Pearl Harbor.* 8 vols. Washington: Government Printing Office, 1980.

U.S. Department of State. *Papers Relating to the Foreign Relations of the United States: Japan, 1931–1941.* 2 vols. Washington: Government Printing Office, 1943.

U.S. Navy. Bureau of Personnel. "Casualty List, Book #1, Pearl Harbor–Midway, 7 December 1941 to May 1942." (microfilm). Operational Archives, Naval Historical Center, Washington.

———. Commander-in-Chief, Pacific Fleet. "Report of the Japanese Raid on Pearl Harbor 7 December 1941," with unit action reports attached (microfilm, 1942). Operational Archives, Naval Historical Center, Washington.

———. Fourteenth Naval District. Fourteenth Naval District Reports on Pearl Harbor Attack (microfilm). Operational Archives, Naval Historical Center, Washington.

———. Naval Facilities Engineering Command, Pacific Division. *Historic Preservation Plan: U.S. Naval Base, Pearl Harbor National Historic Landmark,* 1978.

———. Navy Yard, Pearl Harbor. "War Diaries," 1942–1943. Operational Archives, Naval Historical Center, Washington.

———. "Reports of the Repair and Salvage of Naval Vessels Damaged at Pearl Harbor, T.H., on December 7, 1941." Operational Archives, Naval Historical Center, Washington.

U.S. Strategic Bombing Survey. *Interrogations of Japanese Officials.* 2 vols. Washington: Government Printing Office, 1946.

ARCHIVES

National Archives (Washington D.C., San Bruno, Calif., and Suitland, Md.)
Record Group 19, Bureau of Ships
Record Group 80, Department of the Navy General Records
Record Group 127, U.S. Marine Corps
Record Group 181, Fourteenth Naval District
Record Group 238, International Military Tribunal for the Far East
Record Group 243, U.S. Strategic Bombing Survey
Record Group 313, Pacific Fleet
Record Group 319, Attack on Pearl Harbor and Sabotage Activities, ca. 1937–1947.
Record Group 338, Hawaiian Department
Record Group 457, National Security Agency (Magic records)

Operational Archives, Naval Historical Center
World War II Command Files
World War II Action Reports
Papers of Vice Admiral Homer Wallin

Marine Corps Historical Center
Papers of Major General Claude Larkin

Office of Air Force History (Bolling AFB, Washington D.C.)
Microfilmed reports of Army Air Corps units and stations

Hawaii War Records Depository (University of Hawaii) (HWRD)
Office of the Military Governor, General Orders series
Personal statements series

Hawaii State Archives (Honolulu)
Pacific War Memorial Commission records

American Heritage Center (University of Wyoming)
Husband E. Kimmel Collection

Hoover Institution on War, Revolution, and Peace (Stanford University)
Delos C. Emmons Collection
Walter C. Short Collection

INTERVIEWS

With the Author
Heijiro Abe, December 9, 1983
Comdr. Nathan Asher, May 17, 1982
Irwin Cihak, December 4, 1983
Capt. James Daniels, July 5, 1984
Iyozo Fujita, December 9, 1983
Junichi Goto, December 9, 1983

Robert Hudson, February 28, 1983
Hideo Maki, December 9, 1983
Shirata Matsumura, December 9, 1983
George Sheridan, March 23, 1982
Sadao Yamamoto, December 9, 1983

North Texas State University Oral History Program (NTSU)

Wilford Autry
G. J. Bennett
Eugene Camp
Ernest Cochran
James Corey
John Cowden
Ben Cummings
Warren Harding
Carl Hatcher
Karl Johnson
Stephen/Flora Bell Koran
Nick Kouretas

Werner Land
Carl Lee
Elizabeth Elmer Murphy
Clay Musick
Merle Newbauer
R. D. Nicholas
Charles H. Roberts
Artis Teer
Warren Thompson
John Vaessen
Dan Wentrcek
Phillip Willis

USS *Arizona* Memorial Oral History Program (USAMOH)

James Anderson
John Anderson
Felix Balodis
Alexander Beck
Herbert Boyd
Charles Brewer
Emigdio Cabico
James Clark
Elzer N. Coates
Frank Cook
Kathy Cooper
Merion Croft
James Daniels III
Russell Davenport
James Duncan
Albert Fickel
Harold Fishencord
James Forbis
Douglas Frias
Norman Godbold
Y. Baron Goto
Myron E. Haynes
Leo Hovde

Benjamin F. Heal
Max Itoga
Floyd Jenkins
Dr. and Mrs. Russell Jensen
Robert Johnson
Chester Kelly
Leon Kolb
John Kuzma
James Latham
Harold Lenberg
Norwood McGill
Elizabeth Elmer Murphy
George Nakamoto
Alfred Preis
Edmund H. Russell
Frank Solomon
William Frank Steer
Patricia Morgan Swenson
Wymo Takaki
Florence Washburn
Steven Wozniak
Shikumi Yoshida

Office of Air Force History Transcripts

Maj. Gen. Brooke E. Allen
Maj. Gen. Kenneth B. Bergquist
Lt. Gen. Gordon A. Blake
Maj. Gen. Howard C. Davidson

Marine Corps Oral History Collection

Brig. Gen. Alexander Holcomb
Brig. Gen. Omar T. Pfeiffer
Lt. Gen. Alan Shapley

U.S. Naval Institute Oral History Program (USNIOH)

Vice Adm. Walter C. W. Ansel
Rear Adm. Edward T. Layton
Capt. Charles Merdinger
Capt. Joseph J. Rochefort

Miscellaneous

Makoto Bando (with Gary Cummins)
Ralph T. Briggs (Record Group 457, National Archives)
Comdr. E. B. Mott (WW II Command Files, Operational Archives)
Robert D. Ogg (Record Group 457, National Archives)
Albert Olsen (with John Martini)

BOOKS AND ARTICLES

Agawa, Hiroyuki. *The Reluctant Admiral: Yamamoto and the Imperial Navy.* Tokyo: Kodansha International, 1983.

Allen, Gwenfread. *Hawaii's War Years, 1941–1945.* Honolulu: University of Hawaii Press, 1950.

Anthony, J. Garner. *Hawaii Under Army Rule.* Honolulu: The University Press of Hawaii, 1975.

Baker, Leonard. *Roosevelt and Pearl Harbor.* New York: Macmillan, 1970.

Barker, A. J. *Pearl Harbor.* New York: Ballantine, 1969.

Barnes, Harry Elmer. *Pearl Harbor After a Quarter of a Century.* New York: Arno Press, 1972.

Bartlett, Bruce R. *Cover-Up: The Politics of Pearl Harbor, 1941–1946.* New Rochelle, N.Y.: Arlington House, 1978.

Beard, Charles A. *President Roosevelt and the Coming of the War, 1941: A Study in Appearances and Realities.* New Haven: Yale University Press, 1948.

Beekman, Allan. *The Niihau Incident.* Honolulu: Heritage Press of the Pacific, 1982.

Bellinger, Patrick. "The Gooney Birds." Manuscript autobiography. Operational Archives, Naval Historical Center, Washington.

Bergamini, David. *Japan's Imperial Conspiracy.* New York: William Morrow, 1971.

Borg, Dorothy, Shumpei Okamoto, and Dale K. A. Finlayson, eds. *Pearl Harbor as History: Japanese-American Relations, 1931–1941.* New York: Columbia University Press, 1973.

Bowen, John E. "December 7, 1941—The Day the Honolulu Fire Department Went to War." *Hawaiian Journal of History* 13 (1979):126–135.

Bratzell, John F., and Leslie B. Rout, Jr. "Pearl Harbor, Microdots and J. Edgar Hoover." *American Historical Review* 87 (5) (December 1982):1342–1351.

Britten, Burdick S. "We Four Ensigns." *U.S. Naval Institute Proceedings* 92 (12) (December 1966):106–109.

Brownlow, Donald Grey. *The Accused: The Ordeal of Rear Admiral Husband E. Kimmel, U.S.N.* New York: Vantage Press, 1968.

Burtness, Paul S., and Warren U. Ober. "Research Methodology: Problem of Pearl Harbor Intelligence Reports." *Military Affairs* 25 (3) (Fall 1961):132–146.

Butow, Robert J. C. *Tojo and the Coming of the War.* Princeton: Princeton University Press, 1961.

Caiden, Martin. *The Ragged, Rugged Warriors.* New York: Bantam Books, 1979.

Choshobo Company. *The Maru Special—Japanese Naval Operations in W.W. II: Hawai Sakusen,* No. 92. Tokyo: Choshobo Company.

Clark, Blake. *Remember Pearl Harbor!* New York: Modern Age Books, 1942.

Clark, Robert N. S. "Coast Defenses of Hawaii." *Council on Abandoned Military Posts-U.S.A. Periodical* 5 (2) (Summer 1973):15-25.

Conn, Stetson, Rose C. Engleman, and Byron Fairchild. *Guarding the United States and Its Outposts.* Washington: Chief of Military History, 1964.

Correspondents of *Time, Life,* and *Fortune. December 7: The First Thirty Hours.* New York: Knopf, 1942.

Costello, John. *The Pacific War.* New York: Rawson, Wade, 1981.

Craven, Wesley Frank, and James Lea Cate, eds. *The Army Air Forces in World War II.* Vol. 1. Chicago: University of Chicago Press, 1948.

Dallek, Robert. *Franklin D. Roosevelt and American Foreign Policy, 1932-1945.* New York: Oxford University Press, 1979.

Daniels, Roger. *Concentration Camps USA: Japanese Americans and World War II.* New York: Holt, Rinehart and Winston, 1972.

Detweiler, Donald S., and Charles B. Burdick, eds. *War in Asia and the Pacific, 1937-1949.* Vol. 4. New York: Garland, 1980.

Dower, John W. *War Without Mercy: Race and Power in the Pacific War.* New York: Pantheon Books, 1986.

Dull, Paul S. *A Battle History of the Imperial Japanese Navy (1941-1945).* Annapolis: U.S. Naval Institute Press, 1978.

Dupuy, T. N. "Pearl Harbor: Who Blundered?" *American Heritage,* February 1962, pp. 64-81.

Esthus, Raymond A. "President Roosevelt's Commitment to Britain to Intervene in a Pacific War." *Mississippi Valley Historical Review* 50 (1) (June 1963):28-38.

"Eye-Witness to the Pearl Harbor Attack." *East-West Photo Journal* (Fall 1980):4-12.

Feis, Herbert. *The Road to Pearl Harbor.* Princeton: Princeton University Press, 1950.

Friedman, Norman, Arthur D. Baker III, Arnold S. Lott, and Robert F. Sumrall. *USS Arizona (BB 39).* Ship's Data 3. Annapolis: Leeward Publications, 1978.

Fuchida, Mitsuo. *Shinjuwan Sakusen no Shinso: Watakushi wa Shinjuwan Joku ni Ita.* Nara: Yamato Taimusu Sha, 1949.

———. "I Led the Air Attack Against Pearl Harbor." *U.S. Naval Institute Proceedings* 78 (9) (September 1952):939-952.

———, and Okumiya, Masatake. *Midway: The Battle that Doomed Japan.* Annapolis: U.S. Naval Institute Press, 1955.

Fukudome, Shigeru. *Shikan: Shinjuwan Kogeki.* Tokyo: Jiyu-Ajiya Sha, 1955.

———. "Hawaii Operation." *U.S. Naval Institute Proceedings* 81 (12) (December 1955):1315-1331.

Genda, Minoru. *Shinjuwan Sakusen Kaikoroku.* Tokyo: Yomiuri Shinbum, 1972.

Gordon, Michael John. "Suspects in Paradise: Looking for Japanese 'Subversives' in the Territory of Hawaii, 1939-1945." Master's thesis, University of Iowa, 1983.

Grew, Joseph C. *Ten Years in Japan.* New York: Simon & Schuster, 1944.

Habbe, Edwin Donals. "Pearl Harbor: A Case Study in Administration." Ph.D. dissertation, University of Wisconsin, 1957.

Halsey, William F., and J. Bryan III. *Admiral Halsey's Story*. New York: Da Capo Press, 1976.

Hoehling, A. A. *The Week Before Pearl Harbor.* New York: Norton, 1963.

Hollingshead, Billie. "The Japanese Attack of 7 December 1941 on the Marine Corps Air Station at Ewa, Oahu, Territory of Hawaii." Operational Archives, Naval Historical Center, Washington.

Hone, Thomas C. "The Destruction of the Battle Line at Pearl Harbor." *U.S. Naval Institute Proceedings* 103 (12) (December 1977):49–59.

Hough, Frank O., Verle E. Ludwig, and Henry I. Shaw, Jr. *History of U.S. Marine Corps Operations in World War II*. Washington: U.S. Marine Corps Historical Branch, n.d.

Hull, Cordell. *The Memoirs of Cordell Hull*. 2 vols. New York: Macmillan, 1948.

Ike, Nobutake, ed. *Japan's Decision for War: Records of the 1941 Policy Conferences*. Stanford: Stanford University Press, 1967.

Jackson, Charles L. *On to Pearl Harbor—and Beyond*. Dixon, Calif., Pacific Ship and Shore, 1982.

Kahn, David. *The Code Breakers: The Story of Secret Writing*. New York: Macmillan, 1967.

———. "Did FDR Invite the Pearl Harbor Attack?" *New York Review of Books*, May 27, 1982, pp. 36–40.

Karig, Walter, and Wellbourn Kelley. *Battle Report: Pearl Harbor to Coral Sea*. New York: Farrar and Rinehart, 1944.

Kase, Toshikazu. *Journey to the Missouri*. New Haven: Yale University Press, 1950.

Kimmel, Husband E. *Admiral Kimmel's Story*. Chicago: Regnery, 1955.

Kirchner, D. P., and E. R. Lewis. "The Oahu Turrets." *Military Engineer* 392 (November–December 1967):430–433.

Kusaka, Ryunosuke. *Rengo Kantai*. Tokyo: Mainichi Shinbun, 1952.

Lambert, John W. *The Long Campaign: The History of the 15th Fighter Group in World War II*. Manhattan, Kans.: Sunflower University Press, 1982.

Layton, Edwin T. "Rendezvous in Reverse." *U.S. Naval Institute Proceedings* 79 (5) (May 1953):478–485.

Layton, Edwin T., with Roger Pineau and John Costello. *"And I Was There:" Pearl Harbor and Midway—Breaking the Secrets*. New York: Morrow, 1985.

Lewin, Ronald. *American Magic: Codes, Ciphers and the Defeat of Japan*. New York: Farrar, Straus & Giroux, 1982.

Lewis, Emmanuel Raymond. *Seacoast Fortifications of the United States: An Introductory History*. Annapolis: Leeward Publications, 1979.

Lind, Andrew. *Hawaii's Japanese: An Experiment in Democracy*. Princeton: Princeton University Press, 1946.

Lord, Walter. *Day of Infamy*. New York: Bantam Books, 1958.

Lott, Arnold S., and Robert F. Sumrall. *Pearl Harbor Attack (An Abbreviated History)*. Annapolis: Leeward Publications, 1977.

Lowman, David M. " 'Rendezvous in Reverse'." *U.S. Naval Institute Proceedings* 109 (12) (December 1983):132–133.

Mason, Theodore. *Battleship Sailor*. Annapolis: U.S. Naval Institute Press, 1982.

Melosi, Martin V. *The Shadow of Pearl Harbor: Political Controversy Over the Surprise Attack, 1941-1946*. College Station: Texas A&M University Press, 1977.

———. "The Triumph of Revisionism: The Pearl Harbor Controversy, 1941–1982." *Public Historian* 5 (2) (Spring 1983):85–103.

Millis, Walter. *This is Pearl! The United States and Japan—1941*. New York: William Morrow, 1947.

Morgenstern, George. *Pearl Harbor: The Story of the Secret War*. Old Greenwich, Conn.: Devin-Adair, 1947.

Morison, Samuel Eliot. *The Rising Sun in the Pacific, 1931–April, 1942*. Boston: Little, Brown, 1958.

Morton, Louis. "Pearl Harbor in Perspective: A Bibliographical Survey." *U.S. Naval Institute Proceedings* 107 (4) (April 1981):461–468.

Nakatsuka, Lawrence. "The Last Thirty Seconds." *Pacific Features and Sports*, September 1947, p. 8.

Nicol, Brian. "Interview" (with Col. Frank Steer). *Honolulu*, November 1981, pp. 69–84.

Pantzer, Eric. "Debacle at Pearl Harbor: A Failure in American Logistics; An Accounting for Deficiencies." Library of Congress, n.d.

Pogue, Forrest C. *George C. Marshall: Ordeal and Hope, 1939–1942*. New York: Viking, 1966.

Popov, Dusko. *Spy, Counter Spy*. New York: Grosset & Dunlap, 1974.

Potter, John Dean. *Yamamoto: The Man Who Menaced America*. New York: Viking, 1968.

Prange, Gordon W., with Donald M. Goldstein and Katherine V. Dillon. *At Dawn We Slept: The Untold Story of Pearl Harbor*. New York: McGraw-Hill, 1981.

———. *Pearl Harbor: The Verdict of History*. New York: McGraw-Hill, 1986.

Richardson, James O., as told to George C. Dyer. *On the Treadmill to Pearl Harbor: The Memoirs of Admiral James O. Richardson, USN (Retired)*. Washington: Naval History Division, 1973.

Riley, J. F., and B. L. Delanoy. "The Last of the Midgets." *U.S. Naval Institute Proceedings* 87 (12) (December 1961):127–128.

Sakamaki, Kazuo. *I Attacked Pearl Harbor*. New York: Association Press, 1949.

Schroeder, Paul W. *The Axis Alliance and Japanese-American Relations, 1941*. Ithaca: Cornell University Press, 1958.

Sheehan, Ed. *One Sunday Morning*. Norfolk Island, Australia: Island Heritage Press, 1961.

Sherwood, Robert E. *Roosevelt and Hopkins: An Intimate History*. New York: Harper & Brothers, 1948.

Slackman, Michael. *Remembering Pearl Harbor: The Story of the USS Arizona Memorial*. Honolulu: Arizona Memorial Museum Association, 1984.

Stephan, John J. *Hawaii Under the Rising Sun: Japan's Plans for Conquest After Pearl Harbor*. Honolulu: University of Hawaii Press, 1984.

———. "The Night They Bombed Tantalus." *Honolulu*, November 1980, pp. 74–77.

Stillwell, Paul, ed. *Air Raid! Pearl Harbor: Recollections of a Day of Infamy*. Annapolis: U.S. Naval Institute Press, 1981.

Stimson, Henry L., and McGeorge Bundy. *On Active Service in Peace and War*. New York: Harper & Brothers, 1947.

Tanaka, Chester. *Go for Broke: A Pictorial History of the Japanese-American 100th*

Infantry Battalion and the 442nd Regimental Combat Team. Richmond, Calif.: Go for Broke, Inc., 1982.

Theobald, Robert A. *The Final Secret of Pearl Harbor: The Washington Contribution to the Japanese Attack.* Old Greenwich, Conn.: Devin-Adair, 1954.

Thompson, George Raynor, Dixie R. Harris, Pauline M. Oakes, and Dulany Terrett. *The Signal Corps: The Test (December 1941 to July 1943).* Washington: Department of the Army, 1957.

Thorpe, Elliot R. *East Wind Rain.* Boston: Gambit, 1969.

Togo, Shigenori. *The Cause of Japan.* New York: Simon & Schuster, 1956.

Toland, John. *Infamy: Pearl Harbor and Its Aftermath.* Garden City, N.Y.: Doubleday, 1982.

Tolley, Kemp. *Cruise of the Lanikai: Incitement to War.* Annapolis: Naval Institute Press, 1973.

———. "The Strange Assignment of the USS Lanikai." *U.S. Naval Institute Proceedings* 88 (9) (September 1962):70–83.

Trefousse, Hans L. *Pearl Harbor: The Continuing Controversy.* Malabar, Fla.: Robert E. Kreiger, 1982.

Tsunoda, Hitoshi, et al. *Hawai Sakusen.* Tokyo: Boeicho. Boei Kenshujo Senshishitsu, 1967.

U.S. Army Air Forces. "Operational History of the Seventh Air Force, 7 December 1941 to 6 November 1943." AAF Historical Study No. 41. Washington: Office of Air Force History, Bolling AFB, n.d.

U.S. Army Forces, Middle Pacific. Office of Internal Security. "Wartime Security Controls in Hawaii, 1941–1945: A General Historical Survey." Washington: Office of the Chief of Military History, 1945.

Waller, George M., ed. *Pearl Harbor: Roosevelt and the Coming of the War.* Rev. ed. Boston: D. C. Heath, 1965.

Wallin, Homer. *Pearl Harbor: Why, How, Fleet Salvage and Final Appraisal.* Washington: Naval History Division, 1968.

Watson, Mark Skinner. *Chief of Staff: Prewar Plans and Preparations.* Washington: Office of the Chief of Military History, 1950.

Willmont, H. P. *Pearl Harbor.* Englewood Cliffs, N.J.: Prentice-Hall, 1983.

Wohlstetter, Roberta. *Pearl Harbor: Warning and Decision.* Stanford: Stanford University Press, 1962.

Yoneyama, Tom. "Sunday, Dec. 7—A 90-Hour Workday." *Waikiki Beach Press,* December 7–10, 1981, p. A-21.

Yoshikawa, Takeo, with Norman Stanford. "Top Secret Assignment." *U.S. Naval Institute Proceedings* 86 (12) (December 1960):27–39.

Zacharias, Ellis. *Secret Missions.* New York: Putnam's, 1956.

FILM AND VIDEO

Film No. 428 NPC 1730 (16 mm). Motion Picture, Sound, and Video Branch, National Archives. (Taken early in the attack from *Solace;* Japanese planes; bombs exploding in water; *Nevada* at moorings; *Arizona* exploding; antiaircraft fire.)

Film No. 428 NPC 20565 (16 mm). Motion Picture, Sound, and Video Branch, National Archives. (Taken from attacking Japanese plane; aircraft in flight; approach to Oahu; bombing of Pearl Harbor and Kaneohe.)

Film No. 428 NPC 21950 (16 mm). Motion Picture, Sound, and Video Branch, National Archives. (Destruction on Ten Ten Dock and Battleship Row; *California* burning; *Oklahoma* capsized; *Oglala* being moved by tugs, listing, and capsizing; small craft under way; handling of wounded; warship sortying; antiaircraft fire.)

U.S. National Park Service. "USS *Arizona* Memorial/War in the Pacific National Historical Park Submerged Cultural Resources Report" (videotape). 1984.

INDEX